CASES IN ELECTRONIC COMMERCE

Sid L. Huff

Michael Wade

Michael Parent

Scott Schneberger

Peter Newson

All of the Ivey School of Business Administration
University of Western Ontario; Sid L. Huff is also
Chair, Information Systems, Victoria
University of Wellington

 **Irwin
McGraw-Hill**

Boston   Burr Ridge, IL   Dubuque, IA   Madison, WI   New York   San Francisco   St. Louis
Bangkok   Bogotá   Caracas   Lisbon   London   Madrid
Mexico City   Milan   New Delhi   Seoul   Singapore   Sydney   Taipei   Toronto

McGraw-Hill Higher Education

A Division of The **McGraw-Hill** *Companies*

CASES IN ELECTRONIC COMMERCE

This book is printed on acid-free paper.

domestic   2 3 4 5 6 7 8 9 0 DOC/DOC 9 0 9 8 7 6 5 4 3 2 1 0
international   1 2 3 4 5 6 7 8 9 0 DOC/DOC 9 0 9 8 7 6 5 4 3 2 1 0 9

ISBN 0-07-237516-7

Vice president/Editor-in-chief: *Michael W. Junior*
Publisher: *David Kendric Brake*
Senior sponsoring editor: *Rick Williamson*
Developmental editor: *Christine Wright*
Senior marketing manager: *Jeffrey Parr*
Project manager: *Christine A. Vaughan*
Manager, new book production: *Melonie Salvati*
Senior designer: *Kiera Cunningham*
Cover illustration: © *Guy Crittenden / SIS*
Senior photo research coordinator: *Keri Johnson*
Supplement coordinator: *Jason Greve*
Compositor: *Carlisle Communications, Ltd.*
Typeface: *10/12 New Century Schoolbook*
Printer: *R. R. Donnelley & Sons Company*

Library of Congress Cataloging-in-Publication Data

Cases in electronic commerce/ Sid L. Huff ... [et al.]
     p.   cm.
   ISBN   0-07-237516-7 (softcover)
   Includes index.
    1. Electronic commerce — Case studies. I. Huff, Sidney
Laurence.
HF5548.32.C365 2000
658.8'00285dc—21   99040843

INTERNATIONAL EDITION ISBN 0-07-116835-4
Copyright © 2000. Exclusive rights by The McGraw-Hill Companies, Inc. for manufacture and export.
This book cannot be re-exported from the country to which it is consigned by McGraw-Hill. The International Edition is not available in North America.

http://www.mhhe.com

Preface

In just a few years, the term *electronic commerce* (e-commerce) has entered the world's lexicon in a huge way. While the concept is not at all new, the astoundingly rapid emergence of the Internet after 1994 has poured buckets of gasoline on what was until then a minor brush fire.

Today, companies of all sizes—from the world's largest to tiny start-ups—are scrambling to figure out what electronic commerce means for them now and in the future. While there is still a great deal of jockeying for position, out of the dust and turmoil there are emerging many new businesses, some of them based on entirely new, never-seen-before business models. Examples abound of companies trying new things. Peapod, Homegrocer (described in depth in Chapter 6), Netgrocer, and Streamline, for example, represent four new, different, Internet-based approaches to the good old grocery store.

The purpose of this book is to provide a collection of case studies of companies operating in the broad domain termed electronic commerce. The cases are targeted for use in teaching programs such as business schools or commercial business programs. They also provide interesting and instructive reading for anyone seeking a deeper understanding of the Internet commerce phenomenon. Each case study provides a rich description of a real company and specifically focuses on the actual decisions faced by the manager or managers in the companies at that time.

This book was written for three audiences: first for students, second for e-commerce practitioners, and third for general managers. The 24 cases describe in substantial detail a set of organizations "doing" e-commerce in a variety of different ways. The cases were written as *teaching* cases, as opposed to purely *descriptive* cases often found in books aimed principally toward managers. (The nature and purpose of a teaching case is discussed further below.) For this reason, the cases in this book are ideally suited for use in university or college courses on electronic commerce—whether offered by faculty in information systems, marketing, business strategy, or elsewhere. As well, these cases will be of interest to people working in e-commerce–related businesses. Studying these 24 cases will provide e-commerce practitioners with a multifaceted look at "how the other guys are doing it," and in so doing, perhaps provide new ideas, approaches, or principles to apply in their own firms. Finally, general managers will also benefit from studying the cases in this book. Many managers in traditional companies have not yet truly absorbed the import of e-commerce, for themselves or for the companies for which they now work. An examination of the cases will help these managers to learn by example and extension what the future may hold for them.

WHY A CASEBOOK?

The Socratic method, upon which the case method of learning is based, has been understood and employed in some teaching/learning arenas—for example, philosophy—since antiquity. However, it has only been since the Harvard Business School introduced case teaching to its curriculum in the first decades of the twentieth century that the case method has been accepted as a tool for management education. Since that time, the case method has spread across North America and, more recently, to other parts of the world. Today, most management education programs use cases, either as the preferred approach to learning or as a supplement to traditional learning methods.

A case is a description of an actual situation, commonly involving a decision, a challenge, an opportunity, a problem, or an issue faced by a manager or managers in an organization. It is a kind of unbiased, textual snapshot of a company, with a decision/issue focus. In effect, a case challenges the reader: What would you do here? Teaching with cases really amounts to guiding students in answering that question and justifying their answers. This teaching/learning approach is termed the case method.

The cases in this book are not hypothetical; rather, they are based on real situations faced by real managers in real businesses, making decisions about real electronic commerce problems. Due to the sensitive nature of the material, the names of individuals in a few cases (and in one instance the name of the company) have been disguised. However, other than that, each case in this book reflects accurately the reality in that organization at that time.

Cases give students an opportunity to practice management in real-life situations without any of the real-life corporate or personal risk. It has been said that cases are to management students what cadavers are to medical students: the opportunity to practice on the real thing, but harmlessly. Cases are also an effective tool to test the understanding of theory, to connect theory with application, and to develop stronger theoretical insights. Best of all, cases frequently make learning more interesting and more fun.

This is the first book of true teaching cases in the field of electronic commerce. There is a rapidly growing number of books being published about various aspects of electronic commerce, ranging from traditional textbooks (e.g., Choi, Stahl & Whinston, *The Economics of Electronic Commerce*), to "how to" books (e.g., Minoli & Minoli, *Web Commerce Technology Handbook*), to books for general readers wishing to understand the phenomenon better (e.g., Hagel & Armstrong, *Net Gain*). A few of the general business books in this area include a limited number of case studies. However, these case studies are not particularly useful as teaching cases; they are usually written from third-party sources as simple descriptions of what some company has done. They generally lack the richness, first-person credibility, and decision/issue focus of good teaching cases.

Because electronic commerce is changing so rapidly (it is widely joked that a year in the electronic commerce world is like a dog year: it's equivalent to roughly seven normal human years) it is critical that cases be current. To maintain currency, it is our intention to revise the material in this book, introducing new cases frequently, and in some cases extending existing cases (by writing B or C cases that carry the story of the particular organization through its next stage).

ORGANIZATION

This book is organized into 11 chapters. The first and last chapters do not include cases. The introduction provides a brief overview of electronic commerce, sets the stage for the remainder of the book, and provides a detailed look ahead. The final chapter summarizes a set of critical success factors we have distilled from our research on electronic commerce. The nine critical success factors are illustrated with examples drawn mainly from the cases in the book.

Chapters 2 through 4 examine the history and underpinnings of e-commerce. Chapter 2 concerns the roots of electronic commerce, Chapter 3 the infrastructure issues that impact e-commerce, and Chapter 4 the Internet service provider (ISP) business. Chapters 5 and 6 constitute the core of the book, focusing on Internet-based commercial transactions. Chapter 5 involves selling *services* (intangibles) over the Internet, and Chapter 6 addresses selling physical goods. Chapters 7 through 9 address specific e-commerce niche issues: Internet-based payment mechanisms, financial services, and e-commerce marketing. Finally, Chapter 10 concerns business-to-business e-commerce and the emergence of virtual organizations.

Because the primary audience for this book is comprised of students studying electronic commerce, we have prepared a set of teaching notes to accompany the cases. These notes—which provide such things as suggested assignment questions, suggested class discussion questions, analyses of each case, and suggested detailed case teaching plans—are available as an Instructor's Manual from the publisher to instructors who adopt this book for their e-commerce courses.

ACKNOWLEDGMENTS

A number of individuals have assisted us in creating this book. Most, though not all, of the cases were drawn from field research conducted by the Ivey School of Business. We thank Dean Lawrence Tapp for making the time and resources available for this work. We also thank Associate Dean Ken Hardy for his support, and Frank Kearney and the Ivey Publishing group for their assistance in the preparation of both the original cases and this book. Financial support for researching and writing most of the Ivey cases was provided through the Ivey Business School's Plan for Excellence.

Many of the cases were co-authored with others. We are grateful for the efforts of Rob Attwell, David Beckow, Stewart Ellman, Harvey Enns, Jane Farley, David Keane, Paul Kedrosky, David Koltermann, Murray McCaig, Tracey Priest, Sandy Staples, and Lisa Surmon. Ivey Business School colleagues David Shaw and Duncan Copeland also contributed to cases included herein.

Cases prepared by individuals outside the Ivey Business School include "America Online Inc.," written by Edward Stohr, Sivakumar Viswanathan, and Larry White (Stern School of Business, NYU); "Dominion Trust," by Paula Bund and James McKeen (Queen's School of Business); "Dell Online," by V. Kasturi Rangan and Marie Bell (Harvard Business School); "Celebrity Sightings," by Arnoud De Merey, Soumitra Dutta, and Lieven Demeester (INSEAD); and "The French Videotex System, Minitel," by W. Cats-Baril, T. Jelassi, and J. Teboul (INSEAD). We appreciate the kindness of these individuals for allowing us to include their cases in this book.

We would also like to express our appreciation to Judith McCrea, Camilla Lindsay, Pat Avery, and Cheryl Lojzer, of the Ivey Business School, and also Christine Wright, Rick Williamson, and Christine Vaughan at Irwin/McGraw-Hill Publishers, all of whom provided invaluable support through the writing of the cases and the development of this book.

Finally, we thank the numerous managers who invited us into their companies, allowed us to ask dozens of pertinent as well as impertinent questions, and shared their time and resources with us so that we might create the case studies of their organizations. Without their cooperation and assistance this book would not have been possible.

Sid Huff
Michael Wade
Michael Parent
Scott Schneberger
Peter Newson
June 1999

Brief Contents

Contents

Chapter 1

Introduction

Computers and communications networks have been a part of business for decades. Something new—and big—is happening today, however. No longer just a support mechanism (for "data processing" or "information systems"), information technology is now becoming the very *medium* of business. How many managers used electronic mail to communicate with business associates in other companies on a regular basis five years ago? Who had ever even *heard* of a "web page" as little as three or four years ago? And, in some ways most significantly of all, how many people had ever conducted commerce—including looking for information about goods or services as well as ordering them, paying for them, and obtaining after-sales support for them—using their personal computers prior to 1995? The answer to all these questions is, of course, almost nobody.

We are seeing the beginning of a true paradigm shift. Today, few informed observers disagree that something new and big is happening, though many still disagree on just *how* big it is going to be. Recent forecasts of the impact on Internet commerce on business range wildly. In estimating the increase of business-to-consumer electronic commerce from 1997 to 2000, forecasters varied from a "low" estimate of a sevenfold increase, to a high estimate of 180-fold increase. In short, nobody really knows how big Internet commerce is going to be, but everyone agrees it is going to be *big*.

And this paradigm shift is occurring with incredible speed, largely due to the emergence of the Internet, and specifically the World Wide Web (WWW), during the last half-decade. The growth of awareness of and use of the Internet may well be seen by future historians as the most incredible technology story of all time.

SOME BACKGROUND

The roots of electronic commerce developed over two decades ago, with what was then called "electronic data interchange," or EDI. EDI was driven primarily by the recognition that firms in transactional economic relationships were wasting time and money by printing, transferring, then having to re-key interorganizational transaction data from one firm's computer to the other's. To avoid this cumbersome process, a few firms worked together to agree on common formats and structures for exchanging computer-based data. For example, a company might write its payroll data onto a reel of magnetic tape, which would then be taken to the company's bank, read by the bank's computers, and checks printed out and mailed. Exchanging reels of computer tape was eventually replaced by the use of telecommunication networks, but the principle was the same: computer-to-computer electronic data interchange.

A problem with early EDI efforts was the lack of broad-based standards for exactly how different transaction data types should be represented. If the sending company and receiving company did not agree exactly—down to the last bit—on their data structures and formats, EDI wouldn't work. Early EDI relationships between organizations led to the development of a variety of proprietary coding schemes and layouts for exchanging data, which soon threatened to become so difficult to manage that the benefits of EDI might have been lost. Fortunately, standards bodies—ANSI in North America and the United Nations in Europe, Asia, and elsewhere—came forward to create sets of data interchange standards, used by most organizations doing EDI today.

Originally, EDI was limited to nonfinancial transactions: for example, order placements and acknowledgments. Payments were still handled the old-fashioned way, usually by printing and mailing paper checks. Initially, there was sufficient uncertainty about the security and reliability of EDI that most managers could not stomach the idea of actually sending (or receiving) *money* electronically. Over time, however, it became clear that unless the financial side of a firm's business transactions was included in its EDI processes, it would only be reaping a portion of the potential benefit that EDI promised.

Hence in recent years, more and more organizations have undertaken to combine their financial and nonfinancial business transactions together into complete electronic relationships with their business partners. Frequently this included employing electronic mail for unstructured communications, as well as EDI for structured transactions, and EFT—or electronic funds transfer—for financial payments. This larger concept—the complete business-to-business electronic relationship—became known as *electronic commerce*. Only one thing was missing: consumers!

THE RISE OF THE INTERNET

The rise of the Internet as a business mechanism during the past few years has changed yet again the meaning of electronic commerce. Today the concept of electronic commerce is often equated with "doing business over the Internet." Interestingly, the Internet—which has existed in one form or another since 1969—has been used as a business medium for decades. But the scale of business was so small, and the participants so few and so specialized in their technical interests, that very few people noticed or cared. Two recent events changed this: one was the abolition of the so-called Acceptable Use Policy (AUP); the other was the invention of the World Wide Web.

The Acceptable Use Policy was established in the late 1980s, when the U.S.-based National Science Foundation (NSF) assumed the responsibility for partially funding the Internet backbone. Essentially, the AUP forbade anything but research and educational traffic on the backbone. In effect that meant that the Internet could not be used for commercial purposes. The NSF relinquished its funding role in the mid-1990s, and at that time the AUP was dropped. This opened the Internet floodgates to the world of business.

However, the Internet as a medium for business would not have progressed very far if it had continued to be as user-unfriendly as it was in the 1980s or early 1990s. Using the Internet in those days was not for the technologically fainthearted. The world needed a new, friendly Internet interface that was intuitive, graphical, and above all, simple to use. Tim Berners-Lee, a computer scientist working at CERN high-energy physics lab in Geneva, thought so also. In 1991, he and a few of his colleagues invented what we now call the World Wide Web (WWW). Along with the basic architecture of the WWW, they also invented a new type of software, the web *browser*. They introduced the first web browser, which they called Mosaic, in 1993. This led to the creation of the new company, Netscape Communications Corp., and the development of the groundbreaking Netscape Navigator web browser, followed some time later by its chief competitor, Microsoft's Internet Explorer browser.

The WWW and Mosaic had been developed initially to make it easier for physicists and other researchers to more easily share technical information. As bright as they were, those pioneers at CERN had no idea that their brainchild would soon change the world of business. In fact they probably would have been aghast at the very thought. Nonetheless, during the past four years, their brainchild—the World Wide Web—has become *the* backbone for global electronic commerce.

People are sometimes confused as to the difference between the Internet and the Web. Imagine a highway network as an infrastructure, on which numerous services operate—such as shipping of goods (trucks), personal transportation (automobiles), exercise (bicycles), and so forth. The Internet may be compared to the highway network (an "information highway," to borrow an overused phrase) while the World Wide Web is a *service* that operates *on* the highway network. Numerous other services also operate on the Internet, including electronic mail, newsgroups (Usenet), file transfer (FTP), remote login (Telnet), and so forth. The service termed the World Wide Web, however, is becoming so dominant—in part because the other popular Internet services can be executed within the confines of a web browser—that many people today equate the Internet with the World Wide Web.

The WWW and associated software, mainly the well-known web browsers, have made the Internet broadly accessible, enjoyable, and useful. Furthermore, the creation and growth of thousands of Internet service provider companies, or ISPs, has brought access to the Internet within local-phone-call reach of most people in developed countries; developing nations are also moving quickly to provide their citizenry with access to the Internet as well. For example, anyone with a PC and a telephone in Ulan Bator, the capital of Mongolia, can today acquire an Internet account through Datacom Mongolia, that country's first ISP. Worldwide, spending on Internet and related technologies will reach almost $100 billion (US) in the year 2000, five times higher than the $19 billion spent in 1996, according to the International Data Corporation.

ELECTRONIC COMMERCE

These two streams—business-to-business EDI-centered electronic commerce, and individual use of the Internet and the WWW—came together in the mid-1990s. 1995 is usually cited as the first year in which the Internet first began to be taken seriously as a basis for commerce. Today, the roots of electronic commerce in business-to-business EDI transactions are largely ignored by the business press; the web-based, business-to-consumer side of electronic commerce garners almost all of the attention.

The growth of electronic commerce has given rise to a plethora of new terminology. Figure 1 illustrates the relationship among a number of the new terms.

The largest oval is labeled "electronic business." Simply put, this includes everything having to do with the application of information and communication technologies (ICT) to the conduct of business between organizations or from company to consumer. Within the electronic business oval is a smaller oval labeled "electronic commerce." This highlights the fact that there are numerous forms of business-related ICT-based interactions that can occur between businesses, or between a business and an end consumer, which do not directly concern buying and selling (i.e., "commerce"). Only those forms of interaction having to do with commerce are included in the electronic commerce oval. This includes advertising of

FIGURE 1   New Terminology of Electronic Commerce

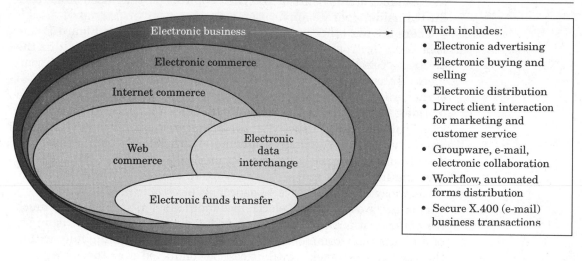

Electronic business

Electronic commerce

Internet commerce

Web commerce

Electronic data interchange

Electronic funds transfer

Which includes:
- Electronic advertising
- Electronic buying and selling
- Electronic distribution
- Direct client interaction for marketing and customer service
- Groupware, e-mail, electronic collaboration
- Workflow, automated forms distribution
- Secure X.400 (e-mail) business transactions

Source: Orion Group.

products or services, electronic shopping, and direct after-sales support. It would not include such things as interorganizational collaboration, using ICT-based collaboration systems, for the development of a new product.

Within the electronic commerce oval is a smaller oval labeled "Internet commerce." This reflects the fact that electronic commerce need not be conducted only over the Internet. In fact a great deal of business-to-business electronic commerce is still today conducted over private networks, using primarily traditional EDI channels and value-added network (VAN) service providers. This is changing, as more and more companies adopt the Internet for some or all of their business-to-business electronic commerce, but it will be many years before the Internet largely displaces the VANs.

Within the Internet commerce domain lies an even smaller subset, termed "web commerce." This is the component of electronic commerce conducted strictly over the World Wide Web. The WWW is not the only way of using the Internet for commercial interactions. Electronic mail, for example, serves well for certain forms of electronic commerce. Software may be conveniently sold over the Internet using the file transfer protocol (FTP) for product distribution. Nevertheless, the Web is clearly the dominant medium for the large majority of Internet commerce today. Furthermore, since modern web browsers incorporate other Internet applications, including electronic mail and file transfer via FTP, all under one hood, users today have the perception that they are relying solely on the Web even as they send and receive e-mail, transfer files, and conduct other forms of Internet application that used to be conducted using separate application programs.

There are two other important domains represented in Figure 1. One is labeled "electronic data interchange." It is shown to lie fully within the electronic commerce realm, but it overlaps the other domains of web commerce, Internet commerce and electronic funds transfer. As discussed earlier, EDI precedes modern-day electronic commerce by almost two decades. It is clearly a type of electronic commerce, since EDI comprises standard formats for a variety of business commercial transactions such as orders, invoices, shipping documents, and the like. But EDI can be conducted either over private networks or over the Internet. If conducted over the Internet, it may or may not make use of the World Wide Web. Also, it may or may not involve aspects of electronic funds transfer.

Finally, the oval labeled "electronic funds transfer," or EFT, bears much the same relationship with the other domains as does EDI. It is an aspect of electronic commerce, hence is represented as falling fully within the electronic commerce oval. It can be conducted over the Internet or over private networks, and if over the Internet, it may or may not be conducted over the Web. Also, EFT may be executed using EDI standards or alternately may be done in non-EDI fashion (see the case Mondex Canada (A) in Chapter 7 for an example of a non-EDI form of EFT).

With that as background, let us turn to the cases that comprise the main part of this book.

OVERVIEW OF THE CASES

The cases in this book have been grouped into nine chapters:

- The Roots of Electronic Commerce
- Electronic Commerce Infrastructure
- The ISP Business—Internet Service Providers
- Electronic Commerce—Services
- Electronic Commerce—Products
- Internet Payment Mechanisms
- Financial Services and Electronic Commerce
- Electronic Commerce Marketing
- Business-to-Business Electronic Commerce and Virtual Organizations

The Roots of Electronic Commerce

Chapter 2 of the book addresses antecedents to electronic commerce. Perhaps the key antecedent is electronic data interchange, or EDI, the focus of the Hong Kong Tradelink case. The Minitel system in France is also an important precursor of modern electronic commerce (and in fact is one of the reasons France lags behind in the adoption of Internet-based electronic commerce methods today).

Hong Kong's Tradelink: An EDI Vision The city-state of Hong Kong, in part to be able to compete more effectively with its sister city-state, Singapore, decided it had to introduce wide-scale EDI in order to make trade more efficient. This is a huge project, with many false starts and errors along the way.

Establishing a National Information Technology Infrastructure: The Case of the French Videotex System, Minitel This case describes the development of the French national videotex system, Minitel. It explores the political and sociological context in which Minitel was established, and examines the critical factors that have contributed to its success.

Electronic Commerce Infrastructure

Chapter 3 addresses infrastructure issues pertaining to the Internet and electronic commerce. The cases in this chapter have to do with putting in place the basic facilities upon which electronic commerce programs and applications can be constructed. Both cases address networking in one form or another, although numerous other infrastructure issues arise as well.

Wired Wellington: The Info City Project and the City Link Network This is the story of how Wellington, New Zealand, sought to turn itself into an "info city," positioned to address the requirements of the twenty-first century.

CERNET: Managing Internet Growth in China CERNET—the China Education and Research Network—was a nonprofit, central government–controlled body formed to oversee the development and implementation of a university-based, nationwide Internet backbone. With over half of China's population yet to make their first telephone call, this was no easy task.

The ISP Business—Internet Service Providers

The cases in Chapter 4 address the Internet service provider business. The Internet never would have grown to such prominence if there had not been a large number of mostly smaller companies willing and able to hook up individuals and other companies to the Internet. CanNet illustrates a typical smaller ISP struggling to survive and grow. AOL, in contrast, is the quintessential large ISP, well known to just about everyone today. Both face challenges of providing appropriate customer service, keeping ahead of the technology growth curve, and trying to make a profit.

CanNet Info Communications Inc.   CanNet was a small company whose main business was the provision of Internet services. Two entrepreneurs, David and Lisa Sampson, were considering whether to invest a substantial portion of their personal resources in this company. The recent very rapid growth of the World Wide Web made CanNet appear to be an interesting venture for them.

America Online Inc.: The Portal Era   AOL established itself as the world's largest Internet service provider. Starting out as a smaller competitor to the better-known CompuServe and Prodigy services, AOL's success has been a mirror image of the success of the Internet generally. This case describes AOL's background, business strategies, and potential future directions.

Electronic Commerce—Services

Perhaps the most fascinating aspect of electronic commerce is the selling, or buying, of physical products, as well as services, over the Internet. Chapter 5 includes cases focused on services; Chapter 6 focuses on products.

Open Text Preferred Listings (A)   Open Text Corporation's main product was the Open Text Index, one of the first search engines on the Internet. The company experimented with an alternative revenue generation model—"bought" words—and challenged the culture of the Internet in doing so.

Jobnet: Finding a Job through the Internet   Jobnet focused on providing job matching and placement using the Internet. The case explores the advantages and shortcomings of the Internet as a medium for job placement and the challenges facing Internet startup companies generally.

Stockgroup Interactive Media   Stockgroup Interactive Media (SRG) is an information broker, or "infomediary." Its primary business was serving as a collection point for information useful to investors seeking to invest in small-cap stocks. SRG illustrates the creation of a very successful virtual community and the challenges faced by the company's managers in deciding how best to exploit it.

Celebrity Sightings   Celebrity Sightings provides entertainment on the World Wide Web: information about popular teenage celebrities, chat rooms, and other celebrity-related features. Financing growth through sponsorship was just one of many challenges facing the firm.

Electronic Commerce—Products

Chapter 6 parallels Chapter 5, with the focus here being on products, as opposed to services, being sold via the Internet.

Dell Online   Dell Computer is perhaps the best-known firm in the business-to-consumer electronic commerce arena. Dell has pioneered the art of selling physical products over the Internet, direct to end users (and, increasingly, to businesses). Today Dell sells over 10 million dollars' worth of computer and related equipment through its web sites, every day. Indeed, these words are being typed using a Dell computer ordered over the Internet!

Homegrocer.com   Homegrocer is a new Internet-based grocery store. The company sells its products only over the World Wide Web; it does not provide walk-in shopping. While the economics of the business are quite favorable, the biggest challenge Homegrocer faces is building adoption by customers, which entails convincing individuals to fundamentally change their grocery shopping behavior.

Good Night Ben   Good Night Ben is a high-end baby furniture store. Robert Brown, the store's proprietor, was an early adopter of the World Wide Web as a way to get the word out about his store and products. Brown serves as his own webmaster, and through his own experimentation, he has discovered numerous tricks and techniques for using the WWW to better develop the reputation of his company.

Internet Liquidators: www.internetliquidators.com   Internetliquidators began life as a Canadian-based Dutch auction web site. The Dutch auction idea, with the price of an item declining over time, was thought to generate excitement and fun, making the auction a kind of computer game. More recently, Internet Liquidators, operating under its new name Bid.com, has partaken of the roller-coaster ride experienced by other Internet auction sites, such as Onsale and eBay.

Internet Payment Mechanisms

Payment mechanisms are an area of hot innovation. A host of different digital payment mechanisms has been developed recently. None yet has taken the world by storm, although some have experienced more success than others. Most observers believe that it is just a matter of time until one or more of the digital payment schemes becomes widely accepted. The cases in Chapter 7 describe two different mechanisms: First Virtual's "virtual pin" approach, and Mondex International's smart card–based stored-value approach.

First Virtual Holdings Inc. (A)   First Virtual Holdings was an Internet payments pioneer. The company developed a system whereby buyers and sellers could complete transactions on the Internet securely and efficiently. The case outlines the First Virtual system as well as competing payments systems such as smart cards, electronic cash systems, and encryption-based systems. The key question is whether the system will gain widespread acceptance among the Internet commerce community. The case also provides a good segue into a discussion of Internet payment systems.

Mondex Canada (A)   Mondex is an electronic cash application that resides on a smart card. Value can be loaded onto Mondex cards from ATM machines, through modified pay phones, or through specially designed home phones. Smart cards also have the capability to hold multiple applications on a single card. The director of marketing is responsible for organizing the roll-out of Mondex in Canada. The students must evaluate the many roll-out options as well as decide which applications apart from Mondex, if any, should be placed on the smart cards.

Mondex Canada (B)   The Mondex (B) case is set a few months after the (A) case. Unexpectedly, one of the main sponsoring financial institutions pulled out of further active cooperation with Mondex, and the pilot test program already underway had to be canceled. Usage of the Mondex cards in the pilot site were below expected levels. Now, the director must decide what steps to take next.

Financial Services and Electronic Commerce

Financial services represent one special category of services that can be provided via electronic commerce. Many financial services are provided via networks and in digital form already, so the Internet/electronic commerce in effect represents just one more, new distribution channel for these services. Nonetheless, the challenges of effectively utilizing this new channel are substantial, as the two cases in Chapter 8 illustrate.

Metropolitan Life Insurance: E-Commerce   Metropolitan Life's first vice president of interactive commerce faced a plethora of opportunities, challenges, and decisions in charting MetLife's strategy for e-commerce. He wanted to move quickly into conducting web-based commerce, but he had to consider executive support, infrastructure requirements, disenfranchisement of the sales force, fast-moving competitors, and the frenzied rate of technology change. The case addresses many e-commerce start-up issues, but from the perspective of a large, established bricks-and-mortar business.

Dominion Trust: Distribution Channel Development   Dominion Trust, one of the five largest, full-service financial institutions in Canada, wanted to be a strong player in virtual banking with a nationwide, full-service, Internet banking web site—even though there were many doubts about the Web's profitability. Dominion Trust senior management needed to determine how to price the service to bank customers, how to counter growing virtual banking services from competitors, whether to partner with other vendors or service providers, and how to add value to virtual banking.

Electronic Commerce Marketing

The Internet and electronic commerce pose new, complex challenges for the marketing of goods and services, whether sold via electronic commerce or not. What is the best way of advertising over the Web? How does one get noticed? Are there issues in Internet culture that should be respected in planning advertising over the Internet? How much should one pay for advertising-type services? The cases in Chapter 9 address these types of Internet-based marketing and advertising challenges.

First Virtual Holdings Inc. (B)   First Virtual Holdings Incorporated has just switched its strategy to focus on interactive messaging solutions. The company developed interactive banner ad software that functioned as its own mini-web page within a web page. The company intended to market this product to Internet retailers and direct marketing firms. The case addresses effectiveness issues of online marketing and the acceptability of various marketing techniques.

Creating a Web Site for Medisys Health Group Inc.   Medisys is a holding company for a consortium of corporate health care program providers. Sheldon Elman, Medisys' founder, president, and CEO, believes the company needs to create a web site. France Moilhot, the vice president of operations, is left to ponder on exactly what this means. What should be the purpose of a Medisys web site? Where would a site fit into the company's overall marketing strategy? This case illustrates the decision-making process a company goes through as it establishes a presence on the World Wide Web.

Business-to-Business Electronic Commerce and Virtual Organizations

Electronic commerce can be subdivided into the business-to-consumer segment and the business-to-business segment. While the former receives much more press, in fact the business-to-business segment is considerably larger than the business-to-consumer segment today. The three cases in Chapter 10 address business-to-business electronic commerce, in particular the role of the "virtual organization" in the world of electronic commerce.

The National Library of New Zealand   The National Library of New Zealand launched a large project to redevelop the computer systems it used for interfacing with its customers. Because of the expense involved, it decided to undertake the project jointly with the Australian National Library. Among other challenges, the system designers had to determine how to best utilize the newly emergent World Wide Web in their ambitious plans. This case draws the reader's attention to the emergence of "digital libraries" and the many challenges real libraries face as they try to embrace the electronic future.

Euro-Arab Management School   The Euro-Arab Management School is an academic institution established in 1995 by the European Union and the Arab League. The school is a virtual organization: it does not operate bricks-and-mortar classrooms. Instead, programs are offered in an innovative manner that combines web-based learning with local tutoring. The case focuses on the management of a virtual organization and addresses issues of the future of education in the age of the Internet.

Scantran   Scandinavia Translations, or Scantran, offers translation services between English and the languages of Scandinavia and Finland. The company operates the business on a completely virtual basis. While it is doing well to date, the question of expansion is ever present. What are the limits of the virtual work model developed by the firm? The case illustrates the power of the Internet to facilitate the creation of new forms of business.

The final chapter of the book contains no cases. Chapter 11 provides a list of critical success factors for companies operating, or wishing to operate, an online business. The list is based on research conducted by the authors on electronic commerce companies. Each of the critical success factors discussed in the chapter is illustrated with examples drawn from cases in the book, or from other well-known electronic commerce ventures.

There is endless talk these days about how electronic commerce will affect business. In most areas, however, more questions are raised than answers. For example, what exactly is electronic commerce? How are companies incorporating electronic commerce into their businesses? What does it require to run a successful online business? This book provides 24 examples of real-world companies 'doing' electronic commerce in one form or another. From studying these cases, it is possible to gain a firm understanding of what electronic commerce is, and how it is being used in practice.

Chapter 2

The Roots of Electronic Commerce

A person could be forgiven for assuming that electronic commerce began shortly after the emergence of the World Wide Web, in late 1994. The two today are so inextricably linked that we often think of them as one and the same.

In fact, the roots of electronic commerce extend back to the 1970s, when a few large organizations first began experimenting with rudimentary electronic data interchange. The Internet in those days was a bare shadow of its present self, with just a few thousand computers interconnected—mostly large mainframe systems in universities and research labs. Furthermore, it would be many years before the Internet saw its first commercial use. The Acceptable Use Policy imposed by the National Science Foundation in the United States during much of the 1980s, together with the culture of the Internet itself, ruled out any usage that smacked of commercial activity until the early 1990s.

The earliest EDI applications were created by large, resourceful companies that had to design their own private formats for data interchange, since no standards existed then. While this represented a major undertaking for those early pioneering companies, the anticipated benefits of EDI were significant enough to warrant the investments. It soon became clear that it didn't make a lot of sense for every company to reinvent EDI standards for itself and its trading partners. Standards bodies eventually assumed the role of defining a set of EDI standards that everyone could use. Two such groups assumed leadership in EDI standards development: ANSI (the American National Standards Institute) in North America, and EDIFACT (EDI for Accounting, Commerce and Trade—a United Nations effort) in most of the rest of the world.

EDI standards provided a basis for any organization to be able to interchange trade data with any other. EDI is in widespread use today and is implemented largely using private networks. Today it is much more common for companies to implement their EDI using special service provider "middlemen" called VANs—value-added network providers—than it is to connect directly to other trading partners. VANs play the role of an EDI buffer: one company sends its EDI transactions to its VAN, which in turn forwards them on to the intended trading partner companies. Most major VANs are interconnected as well, so a firm's trading partners do not necessarily all have to be connected to the same VAN for EDI to work.

The first case in this section, "Hong Kong's Tradelink: An EDI Vision," tells the story of one of the world's largest EDI development and implementation projects: the entire country of Hong Kong. The government and private industry in Hong Kong recognized the centrality of trade to their prosperity. Trade, in turn, is greatly facilitated by a smooth, efficient flow of information, which accompanies all goods being shipped internationally. Hong Kong's great rival, Singapore, had implemented a massive networking and EDI effort a few years earlier and consequently had gained a major competitive advantage as a trade-friendly port city. The case describes Hong Kong's effort to catch up to, and hopefully surpass, Singapore by implementing a huge, nationwide EDI project.

Of course, standards-based EDI is not the only possible way of sharing information widely by means of networked computers. Another precursor technology, called videotex, was first introduced in the late 1970s. Videotex was originally envisioned as a means for widely distributing information—both text and graphics—in a one-to-many fashion, using the predominant technology of the day: dumb terminals. Special videotex terminals sprouted up in hotels and similar places in trials in North America. While videotex generally experienced a short life in North America, passing out of fashion almost as quickly as it came in, this was not the case everywhere.

In France, the Minitel project, begun in the late 1970s and first implemented in 1982, aimed to place a videotex terminal in every French home. The purpose of the Minitel system was to provide a wide variety of information services to essentially all telephone users throughout the country. The project was quite successful and continues in France to this day. The second case in this section describes the Minitel project, and particularly its use as a retailing information channel. Interestingly, what was once seen as a sophisticated, leading-edge national infrastructure project is today often cited as a key reason for France's lagging status with respect to the Internet, the World Wide Web, and Internet-based electronic commerce.

Hong Kong's Tradelink: An EDI Vision

By Professors Sid L. Huff and Duncan Copeland and Lisa Surmon

The sun shimmered on the eastern horizon over Hong Kong in the hazy heat of the early morning as the crowd jostled to get the best seats on the 7:00 A.M. high-speed ferry to Hong Kong's central business district. A competitive atmosphere really did permeate all aspects of life in Hong Kong, Juletta Broomfield thought as she slipped into her favourite seat at the front of the ferry. Sitting quietly, gazing out over Hong Kong's productive harbour, the 25-minute ferry ride to Central gave Juletta, General Manager of Tradelink, a chance to think ahead to the Board of Directors meeting scheduled to take place later that day.

It was early September 1992 and the Tradelink Board would once again be faced with a thorny decision: whether to delay the planned issue of an open Request for Proposals (RFP) for the provision of hardware, software and services required to implement the Community Electronic Trading Service (CETS). The Hong Kong Government's formal approval to grant Tradelink the exclusive franchise to operate CETS and to take a minority shareholding in Tradelink had recently been delayed and was now expected within a few months. By issuing the RFP as planned, Tradelink would be forging ahead without these formal assurances. As she watched a loaded container ship head out to sea, Juletta was thinking that after all the delays already experienced on Hong Kong's trade-related Electronic Data Interchange (EDI) project, perhaps a few more months were inconsequential. On the other hand, Juletta had recently heard claims that Singapore was now at least five years ahead of Hong Kong in its EDI programme. Perhaps making commitments now, albeit in an environment of greater uncertainty for all, would be the better decision.

HONG KONG

Economic and Political Situation

The name Hong Kong, which means "fragrant harbour," was appropriate in some ways, as the sweet smell of success seemed to fill the air. On the other hand, anyone actually visiting the harbour itself would find that it was anything but fragrant.

Historically, the island of Hong Kong and the Kowloon peninsula were ceded to the British Government by the Chinese in 1842, following the British-Chinese Opium Wars. In 1898, a 99-year lease to the British for the land now called the New Territories was established with the Chinese, bringing the total land area of Hong Kong to 1,074 square kilometers. See Exhibit 1 for maps of South East Asia and Hong Kong.

In 1984, after extensive negotiations between the British and Chinese, it was agreed that Hong Kong would be transferred back to China as of June 30, 1997. A key aspect of the transfer was that Hong Kong would be governed by the Chinese as a Special Administrative Region (SAR), retaining its own economic and administrative systems for a minimum of 50 years. A quasi-constitutional document, the Basic Law, was created as a blueprint for governing the territory following the transfer, and a special diplomatic committee called the Joint Liaison Group (JLG) was set up to oversee the transfer, including decision-making on all issues straddling the 1997 transfer date.

With no natural resources other than its location, deep-water harbour and industrious people, Hong Kong had become an economic success story. For the fiscal year ended December 1992, per capita Gross Domestic Product (GDP) was expected to exceed $16,000 (US[1]), fourth highest in the world. Trade had always been a key factor in the economic success of the territory. Hong Kong was among the top 20 trading nations in the world, despite its small size and population of only 5.9 million people. Annual growth in total trade was increasing more than 10 per cent each year.

The Government of Hong Kong was headed by an appointed Governor who reported to the British Foreign Office. Reporting to the Governor were three Secretaries, who together had responsibility for managing the Administration: the Chief Secretary, the Financial Secretary and the Attorney General. Branch Secretaries, Department Heads and other Government agencies in turn reported to these three senior positions.

The Governor was assisted in his decision-making by the Executive Council (EXCO), an influential advisory body, and the Legislative Council (LEGCO), a legislative and budgetary approval body. Historically both the Executive Council and Legislative Council consisted of appointed members; however, this changed in 1991 with the election of 18 out of LEGCO's 60 members.

The Government had always adopted a very pro-business, non-interventionist policy. Examples of this policy included: the free port status of most goods traded in Hong Kong; low personal and corporate taxes; a virtually non-existent social safety net; encouragement of the

---

[1]All monetary units in the case are US dollars unless otherwise noted.

EXHIBIT 1   Maps of Hong Kong and South East Asia

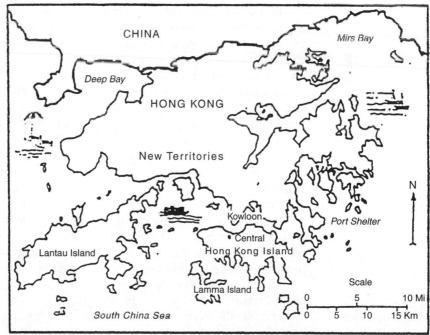

private sector to provide the territory's infrastructure, including port and airport facilities, utilities and cross harbour tunnels; and encouragement of industry to self-regulate itself in order to minimize Government regulation and involvement.

Despite Hong Kong's impressive performance, there were some economic and political concerns as the 1997 transfer date approached. A labour shortage was affecting the territory in the early 1990s due to low labour force growth and high levels of emigration. (Some 62,000 residents, many of them highly educated professionals, emigrated in 1990.) Partially due to the labour situation, inflation was also an ongoing concern as it continued to drift upward over 10 per cent. Hong Kong's high costs were beginning to earn it a reputation of being one of the world's most expensive cities. On the political front, many of the newly elected members of LEGCO were advocating the further democratization of Hong Kong as well as greater spending on social programmes. The Governor, Mr. Chris Patten, was somewhat sympathetic to these views. However, the Chinese were highly critical of Mr. Patten, certain elected members of LEGCO (some of whom they labelled as "subversive"), and plans for extending democracy in Hong Kong before 1997. In this political environment, Government administrators were finding decision-making more and more difficult.

The Trading Community

In Hong Kong, as elsewhere in the world, the international trading of goods involved many parties across diverse industries, including manufacturers of traded goods, exporters and importers, freight forwarders, couriers, land/rail/sea/air carriers, port operators, cargo terminals, banks, insurance companies, warehouse providers, sworn measurers and Government departments and agencies.

All trade transactions started and finished with the buyer (importer) and seller (exporter or manufacturer). All costs associated with a trade transaction, including the costs of documentation, were absorbed between the buyer and seller at the end of the day.

Most other participants in the trade cycle were called "trade service providers." Without the traders, they wouldn't be in business. Some trade service providers, such as the banks, major freight forwarders and couriers, deep sea and air cargo carriers and cargo terminals, were large and sophisticated organizations operating in advanced and competitive industries. At the other end of the scale, some small freight forwarders, road carriers and sworn measurers operated as one-person proprietorships with little or no automation.

In 1991 there were approximately 110,000 importers, exporters and manufacturers operating in Hong Kong. Of these, approximately 82 per cent or 90,000 were considered "small" (fewer than 10 employees if an importer or exporter; fewer than 20 employees if a manufacturer). The computerization rate (at a minimum, a personal computer with word processing capability) in these small organizations was estimated at 38 per cent. It was estimated that there were between 5,000–10,000 trade service providers operating in the territory during the same time period.

Occupying a special place in Hong Kong's trade sector was the Government and its appointed agencies. While Government functioned as a trade service provider in some respects, it was also required to carry out tasks to meet its own statutory requirements. Traders were usually charged fees for services provided by the Government and its agencies.

There were three Government departments involved in the international trade process: Trade Department, Customs and Excise Department, and Census and Statistics Department. Trade Department was responsible for managing all quota and trade restrictions as negotiated under bilateral/multilateral trade agreements. Census and Statistics Department was responsible for collecting and compiling trade statistics. Customs and Excise Department was responsible for customs clearance and the enforcement of trade regulations.

In addition to the above Government departments, there were five Government Authorized Certification Organizations (GACOS) which were authorized to issue Certificates of Origin (COS). All were non-profit, local trade associations or chambers of commerce. Over the years, all of the GACOS had proven themselves to be more efficient than Government in the issuing of COS.

Exhibit 2 provides an overview of the key participants in Hong Kong's trading sector.

Trade Documentation

The documentation involved in international trade transactions was staggering. Estimates varied, but for a single shipment of goods as many as 40 multi-copy documents were exchanged among up to 28 different organizations. The cost of preparing, processing and storing this information was also staggering, with estimates ranging from five to eight per cent of the value of the goods being traded. Much of the same information was used on all trade documents, with most data originating from the buyer and the seller. The trade documents and associated procedures that existed in 1992 were the result of practices which evolved over hundreds of years of international commerce. The documents and procedures had become an ingrained way of doing business.

There were four main categories of documents: commercial, transport, finance, and official. Commercial documents included the purchase order, order confirmation and invoice, among others. Transport documents included the bill of lading, air waybill, shipping order, dock receipt, manifest, sworn measurer's certificate, freight invoice, etc.

EXHIBIT 2   Key Participants in Hong Kong's Trading Sector

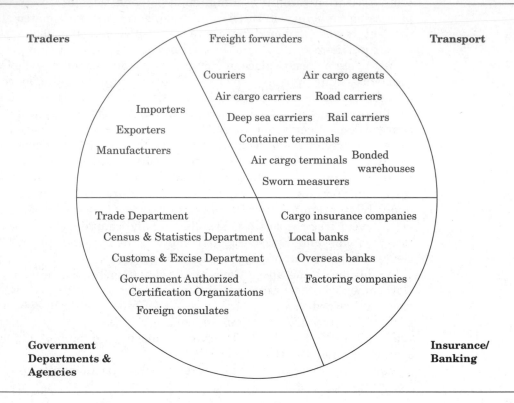

Traders   **Transport**

Freight forwarders

Couriers   Air cargo agents

Air cargo carriers   Road carriers

Importers   Deep sea carriers   Rail carriers

Exporters   Container terminals

Manufacturers   Air cargo terminals   Bonded warehouses

Sworn measurers

Trade Department   Cargo insurance companies

Census & Statistics Department   Local banks

Customs & Excise Department   Overseas banks

Government Authorized   Factoring companies
Certification Organizations

Foreign consulates

Government   **Insurance/**
Departments &   **Banking**
Agencies

Banking documents included letters of credit, bills of exchange, cargo insurance certificates, payment instructions and so on. The main documents collected and processed by the Hong Kong Government were Export and Import Licences for quota-controlled goods, Trade Declarations, Certificates of Origin, Dutiable Commodities Certificates and Cargo Manifests. Exhibit 3 provides a brief explanation of the main trade documents in each category.

The volume of Hong Kong Government documents provides an indication of the magnitude of paper being processed. Figure 1 summarizes the 1991 volumes and projected growth rates for the six main Government trade documents.

Finally, the completion and processing of trade documents could be quite complex, often involving multi-copy forms being exchanged among four or more different organizations. A summary of the procedures related to the completion and processing of a Restrained Textiles Export Licence (RTEL) is provided in Exhibit 4, as an example.

EXHIBIT 3 Commonly Used Trade Documents

Document Type	Purpose	Typical Copy Distribution
Commercial		
1. Quote	An offer to an importer from an exporter to provide certain goods at a specific price & terms	Exporter, importer
2. Purchase order	An authorized order from an importer to purchase certain goods from an exporter	Exporter, importer, bank
3. Order confirmation	An authorized response from an exporter to an importer that a purchase order will be filled	Exporter, importer, bank
4. Invoice	A description of goods sold, terms & request for payment, issued by an exporter to an importer	Exporter, importer, bank, insurance company
Transport		
1. Bill of lading	A contract between an exporter & sea carrier for the transport of goods, which also serves as a receipt & document of title for the goods	Exporter, sea carrier, importer, bank
2. Air waybill	A contract between an exporter & an air carrier for the transportation of goods by air.	Exporter, air carrier, importer, bank
3. Packing list	A list detailing how exported goods have been packaged for shipment & the contents/dimensions of the packages	Exporter, carrier, importer, freight forwarder, government, bank, insurance company
4. Dock receipt	A document used to transport account-ability for cargo between different carriers at a cargo terminal	Road/rail carrier, sea/air carrier, exporter, freight forwarder, insurance company
Banking/ Insurance		
1. Letter of credit	A financial document issued by a buyer's bank authorizing a seller to receive payment for goods subject to certain terms and conditions	Importer, exporter, bank
2. Bill of exchange	A written instruction for a certain sum of money to be transferred at a certain date from the importer to the exporter	Exporter, importer, bank
3. Debit advice/credit advice	Documents notifying the buyer that payment has been debited (debit advice) or the seller that payment has been credited (credit advice) from/to their bank account	Exporter, importer, bank
4. Insurance certificate	A document providing proof of insurance against loss or damage for goods shipped	Exporter, insurance company, bank
Official (HK)		
1. Trade declaration	A declaration and description of goods exported or imported by an organization, primarily for statistical purposes	Exporter, importer, government
2. Export licence	An official document issued by the Government authorizing the export of goods subject to trade control	Exporter, importer, manufacturer, government, carrier, bank
3. Certificate of origin	A document evidencing the origin of goods being exported	Exporter, manufacturer, government, GACOs, importer, bank
4. Cargo manifest	A document describing the cargo being transported by a carrier on a particular voyage	Carrier, government, cargo terminal, insurance company

---

FIGURE 1   Volumes and Projected Growth Rates for Government Trade Documents (1991)

Document	Volumes	Proj. Growth Rate
Trade Declaration	10,900,000	10.0%
Restrained Textiles Export Licence	747,000	3.8%
Non-Restrained Textiles Export Licence	610,000	9.5%
Dutiable Commodities Certificate	256,000	8.0%
Certificate of HK Origin	729,000	−4.5%
Cargo Manifest	6,896,000	22.5%

EXHIBIT 4   Summary of Processing Procedures for Restrained Textiles Export Licence (RTEL)

The purpose of the RTEL is the management and enforcement of textile quota controls imposed by other countries under bilateral and multilateral trade agreements. The RTEL application is a one-page form consisting of two main sections: the exporter's Application for an Export Licence; and the manufacturer's Declaration as to the category and quantity of goods being shipped. It has four copies for distribution.

An exporter who is planning on shipping quota-controlled textiles to an overseas buyer will purchase the blank forms from the Trade Department. The exporter completes and signs the Application section of the form and then takes the document to the manufacturer for completion of the Declaration section. The exporter then delivers the document to a Trade Department counter.

At the counter, a fee is paid to the Government clerk, who does a quick check on its contents for obvious mistakes before the exporter leaves. The RTEL application is then passed to the Trade Department back office where more detailed checking is carried out and the contents are entered into the Government's quota management computer system. If there is any suspicion of quota fraud, Customs Department is notified and a surprise inspection is carried out. Provided no problems are found, Government stamps and authorises the document, meaning the Export Licence has been granted. One copy is retained by Government and three copies are picked up by the Exporter, usually three to four days after the Application was originally submitted.

The exporter must then arrange for one copy of the approved RTEL to be delivered to the carrier transporting the goods overseas. Carriers are under an obligation to not ship any textiles consignments unless they have been provided with an approved Licence.

The third copy of the RTEL is sent by the exporter to his overseas buyer who will require the document to secure release of the shipment by his country's Customs service and may also require it for Letter of Credit documentary requirements. The fourth copy is retained by the exporter.

Finally, the carrier of the shipment is subsequently required to submit its copy of the Licence to Trade Department together with their vessel's manifest (list of cargo) as a double check that quota-controlled goods were not shipped without a Licence.

ELECTRONIC DATA INTERCHANGE (EDI): A WAY OUT OF THE QUAGMIRE

A More Efficient Communications System

EDI developed out of the need of businesses to communicate more efficiently with each other. Business communications occurred in two forms: unstructured (e.g., letters, memos, telephone conversations) and structured (e.g., invoices, packing slips, payment advices). Information technology revolutionized both unstructured and structured communication. Electronic mail, facsimile, and more recently, video conferencing, greatly changed the nature of unstructured communication. By 1992, EDI had begun to revolutionize structured business-to-business communication as well.

EDI was the transfer of structured business data from one computer to another in such a format that the receiving computer could understand and act upon the information received. Traditionally, structured business communications took place using paper documents, with organizations having to produce, check, transfer, receive, key, process and file massive quantities of paper. Such information exchange was slow, error-prone and costly. Using EDI, companies could significantly streamline and speed up the transfer and processing of business information, as well as reduce errors and delays associated with paper documents. Meaningful savings were often realized in the areas of purchasing, accounting, shipping, inventory and production planning. Beyond this, EDI was said to result in strategic benefits due to the closer business relationships which developed between trading partners.

EDI was not EDI without an agreed standard for formatting the data being exchanged. Without a standard, the receiving computer would be unable to understand and act on information being sent to it by its trading partner. When EDI started in the 1960s, formats were agreed upon between individual companies. However, as the number of trading partners using different formats increased, organizations found this ad hoc approach to be increasingly problematic and expensive. This situation led to the development of industry standards (e.g., auto, chemical, retail) to meet the needs of wider communities of interest, then national standards and finally, with the explosion of global commerce, an international standard for EDI, UN/EDIFACT.

The UN/EDIFACT standard (EDI for Administration, Commerce and Transport), developed under the auspices of the United Nations, was recognized by the International Standards Organization (ISO) as the international standard for EDI messages. While many organizations in North America and Europe were still using their respective national or industry EDI standards in 1992, the use of EDIFACT for international transactions was becoming widely accepted.

The EDIFACT standard consisted of a set of rules and procedures which were then applied to specific documents (e.g., invoices, purchase orders, customs declarations, etc.) For each document type, the agreed standard set out what information was to be included, and precisely how it was to be represented (e.g., text, numeric, based on a code, etc.)

For an organization wishing to begin using EDI, the first requirement was to find at least one trading partner also willing to introduce EDI and then, to agree on the transaction(s) which would be electronically exchanged. A next important, although often overlooked, step was for the trading partners to agree on revised operational procedures and legal arrangements related to the EDI messages to be exchanged.

Each organization had to have a computer (PC, mini or mainframe) and to acquire EDI software. Such software, which translated an organization's data to the appropriate standard (and vice versa) could range from being very simple, operating on a stand-alone PC with manual data entry, to very sophisticated, being fully integrated with the company's in-house computer systems. The integrated EDI approach was really what EDI was all about, eliminating the need for human intervention. However, as it involved more time, skill and expense to set up, some organizations found a stand-alone solution more justifiable, at least initially.

The next step was deciding how the EDI messages would be communicated between trading partners. There were two principal ways: via a direct (point-to-point) connection; or via a value-added network (VAN)—sometimes referred to as an EDI service provider. A direct connection was often used when there were large volumes of messages among only a few organizations or when there was one large organization with many smaller trading partners. A VAN, an electronic post office for EDI traffic, allowed an organization to access many different trading partners for many different transactions. A VAN provided a measure of independence between trading partners, allowed asynchronous communication (i.e., the VAN would hold a sending company's EDI messages until the receiving company's computer called in to collect them) and provided added security and service features. For these services, of course, usage charges had to be paid.

The Global EDI Revolution

In North America and Europe, companies had been using EDI since the 1970s. EDI really took off in these regions in the mid-1980s with the development of industry, national, and subsequently, international standards. In the broad and sophisticated economies of these regions, EDI had tended to develop by major industry. There was also a tendency for EDI to be adopted first by larger organizations, and for these larger organizations to "promote" the use of EDI with their smaller trading partners in order to reach a critical mass of users. Such "promotions" ranged from providing help and advice, to providing free turn-key solutions, to mandating the use of EDI as a condition of business.

The retail and automotive sectors provided two examples of industries which were at the forefront of EDI usage in North America and Europe. Quick Response, which combined EDI with bar coding and other information technologies, was becoming the standard for the retail industry as it strove to meet consumer demand more accurately and efficiently than ever before. In the auto industry, General Motors reported that it had saved as much as $250 per car produced as a result of EDI.

Government administrations were also adopting EDI rapidly. Computer-aided Acquisition and Logistics Support (also known as CALS), an EDI system developed by the U.S. Government Department of Defense, was being implemented worldwide. The U.S. Customs Service currently operated one of the most advanced EDI systems for Customs clearance and management in the world, with over 90 per cent of all incoming Customs data being received electronically. In Canada, Revenue Canada allowed businesses to use EDI over regular telephone lines to file T4 (employee income tax) information. Meanwhile in Europe, a pan-European EDI project called TEDIS, designed to automate and streamline international trade procedures, was well underway.

EDI in the Asian Region

The Asian region, a later entrant into the EDI world, had been making up for lost time in the early 1990s. In Singapore a number of EDI services, including TradeNet, MediNet and LawNet, had been launched successfully by Singapore Network Services (SNS), leading to claims that Singapore operated one of the most advanced EDI systems in the world. SNS was created as part of the city-state's long-range Information Technology (IT) strategy and operated as the sole provider of value-added network services within Singapore. The company was owned by four quasi-government agencies: the Singapore Trade Development Board (55%); the Civil Aviation Authority of Singapore (15%); the Port of Singapore Authority (15%); and Singapore Telecoms (15%).

TradeNet, an EDI service for exchanging trade documentation electronically between participants in Singapore's trade sector, became operational in January 1989, and by mid-1991 had captured over 1,800 users exchanging 95 per cent of certain Government-related trade documents. By 1993 SNS operated EDI and other network services in over 14 business sectors in Singapore, with a goal of making electronic communication the accepted way of doing business throughout the territory.

SNS also hoped its advanced stage of EDI development would put the company in a strong position to capitalize on EDI opportunities throughout the Asia Pacific region.

In Japan, a proliferation of over 700 EDI "standards" was used by narrow bands of trading partners throughout the country in the early 1990s. To speed the implementation of EDI and rationalize its provision, a national standard was being developed and adopted by major organizations. For international transactions, UN/EDIFACT was being promoted and used. The Japanese Government was strongly behind the country's EDI efforts.

Major trade-related EDI systems were also in advanced stages of implementation in Korea and Taiwan. Both were heavily supported (funding and top level commitment) by their respective local Governments. As well, a number of small-scale EDI programmes were also underway in the People's Republic of China (PRC). The Chinese Government had openly pledged its commitment to EDI for the future.

EDI in Hong Kong: More Evolution than Revolution

The concept of a trade-related EDI service for Hong Kong was first discussed in 1984 by the Trade Facilitation Council (TFC), a non-profit organization consisting of traders, trade service providers and Government departments and agencies. The TFC underwrote a project called Hotline, which proposed that a centralized data base of all trade information be created to streamline the exchange of such data.

Hotline was never implemented because of an impasse between the Hong Kong Government and private sector members of TFC. From the Government's perspective, the Hotline proposal was still too new a concept to warrant backing. At the time, no similar implementations existed elsewhere. The Government thought that the private sector stood to benefit most from such a system and therefore should fund and implement the project. The private sector companies behind Hotline countered that Government involvement was essential—it was the only entity that all participants could be comfortable with having control over their highly sensitive and competitive trade information.

In 1987 two key events occurred which opened the EDI debate in Hong Kong once more. The first was the announcement by the United Nations that an international standard for EDI, UN/EDIFACT, had been developed and accepted. Prior to this, the lack of a common global format had been a key stumbling block to the use of EDI for trade. The second event was the announcement by Singapore of its plans to implement a national EDI service for its trading community, with a goal of having a live service by 1 January 1989. Hong Kong and Singapore had traditionally been rivals in many areas, including international trade, and it was believed that if Hong Kong did not react quickly, Singapore would develop an important competitive advantage.

COMMUNITY-WIDE TRADE-LINKED EDI

Tradelink

By early 1988, seven of the original private sector organizations behind the Hotline project established Tradelink Electronic Document Services Limited for the purposes of funding a major study into the viability of a community-wide trade-related EDI service for Hong Kong. Shortly thereafter, four more organizations joined the ranks of Tradelink. See Exhibit 5 for a list of Tradelink's original 11 shareholders. Although not a Tradelink shareholder, the Hong Kong Government agreed to participate in the study, and contributed 10 per cent of its funding.

Coopers & Lybrand Consultancy

Shortly after Tradelink's incorporation, Juletta Broomfield was seconded to Tradelink from Hong Kong Bank (one of the shareholders) as Project Manager. Subsequently, Coopers & Lybrand (C&L) was chosen in November 1988 to undertake the consultancy study into territory-wide EDI. C&L's final report was presented to Tradelink and Government in August 1989. The consultancy report recommended that the

EXHIBIT 5   Original Tradelink Shareholders

Shareholder	*Explanation*	*% Shareholding*
China Resources (Holdings) Ltd.	Major trading company; Chinese *state* owned	10.8%
Hong Kong Air Cargo Terminals Ltd.	Hong Kong's only air cargo terminal	10.8%
Hong Kong Association of Freight Forwarding Agents	Trade association for freight forwarders	1.5%
Hong Kong International Terminals Ltd.	Hong Kong's largest container terminal	10.8%
Hong Kong Telecommunications Ltd.	Monopoly provider of basic telecommunication services	10.8%
Maersk Hong Kong Ltd.	Major deep sea shipping line	6.1%
Modern Terminals Ltd.	Major container terminal	10.8%
Standard Chartered Bank	One of two note-issuing banks in Hong Kong	10.8%
Swire Pacific Ltd.	Major trading company; owns Cathay Pacific	10.8%
The Hong Kong General Chamber of Commerce	Local chamber of commerce	6.1%
The Hong Kong & Shanghai Banking Corporation	Hong Kong's main note-issuing bank	10.8%

provision of EDI (VAN) services in the territory be left to market forces, with Tradelink entering the market as one of the participants. It was further proposed that Tradelink only focus on providing EDI services to large sophisticated organizations which were already highly automated. To overcome the problem of users having to subscribe to many different VANs in order to communicate with all their different trading partners, C&L recommended that the Hong Kong Government enforce and regulate the interconnection of all service providers.

The Tradelink shareholders did not agree with the recommendations and action plan set out in the consultancy report. First of all, it was pointed out that the real internal rate of return to the shareholders of 7.7 per cent over the 10-year life of the project was not sufficient, especially when the risks of operating in an open competitive market were considered. Secondly, Tradelink argued that the proposal of Government mandating and controlling the interconnection of networks and providers was unworkable. Thirdly and most importantly, Tradelink determined that under the consultant's proposal no one would benefit because small traders, the backbone of the economy, would be left without any solutions and the large users would need to retain expensive and unjustifiable dual systems. Overall, C&L's recommendation that Tradelink operate as a typical EDI VAN did not meet the shareholders' original objective—to encourage and catalyse the use of EDI throughout the trading community.

Tradelink's Counter-Proposal

Shortly after the submission of the consultancy report, Tradelink presented a counter-proposal to Government, which was widely publicized throughout the territory. Tradelink recommended that in a public sector–private sector partnership with Government it be granted an exclusive franchise as the sole EDI provider for Government trade documents. In return for this monopoly, Tradelink would undertake to provide a solution for Hong Kong's small traders as well as help in the development of a Chinese-language EDI standard, two major obstacles facing the development of EDI in the territory. Beyond the exclusive interface with Government, Tradelink advocated all other EDI services be left open to market forces.

Especially in light of the C&L report, Tradelink's proposal stirred up a great deal of debate in the territory. Such an arrangement seemed counter-intuitive to Hong Kong's entrepreneurial spirit and non-interventionist government. Among the most vocal participants in the debate were potential vendors of EDI products and services. The Government found itself under growing pressure to decide on the next step forward; however, Tradelink's counter-proposal was lacking sufficient business and technical detail for decision-making. Even more importantly, the Government thought it would be failing in its public duty if it didn't investigate alternatives to the Tradelink option.

THE SHARED PROJECT FOR EDI (SPEDI)

Developing a Community EDI Service

In response to this dilemma, the idea for the Shared Project for EDI (SPEDI) was conceived. Announced in March 1990, funding for the $1.1 million venture was to be provided on a 50-50 basis between Tradelink and Government. The objective of SPEDI was to develop a business plan and technical specification for a community EDI service for Hong Kong's trading community—providing sufficient information, it was hoped, so that the way forward for EDI in Hong Kong could be decided.

A seven person project team was set up which consisted primarily of secondees from Government and Tradelink shareholders. Managing this team, Juletta Broomfield of Tradelink and Patrick Chung, the Government's EDI Coordinator, were appointed as joint Project Managers and reported to a Steering Committee consisting of Tradelink Board Members and senior civil servants. It was thought that such a governing structure was needed to minimize any bias (real or perceived) that SPEDI might have towards either Tradelink or Government. Although paid for by Tradelink and Government, SPEDI was not to make its recommendations from either party's perspective; the Steering Committee charged the SPEDI team with taking the perspective of "Hong Kong Inc."

Deciding Where to Start

Tradelink had always argued that EDI should be implemented across the entire trading sector of Hong Kong. Others thought that EDI should be left to develop along industry lines as it had in other countries, a method which would be much simpler than trying to tackle the complex, multi-industry trade sector. It would also be much more likely to succeed, providing an impetus for larger more complex projects to proceed.

Tradelink recognized that trading was the backbone of the Hong Kong economy. Hong Kong's small size and population did not support huge industries like those in the large developed countries. For the most part, the large industrial companies that operated in Hong Kong were branch offices of multi-national organizations. Furthermore,

Hong Kong's trading sector was considered to be susceptible to outside competitive pressures from other countries in the region, and Hong Kong traders could fall behind if they were unable to keep up with international trading practices.

SPEDI agreed with these sentiments, but argued that a coordinated approach across the trading sector was essential. If individual companies and/or sectors such as the container terminals or deep sea carriers or banks developed their own EDI systems in isolation, then the importers and exporters (the ones eventually paying all trade processing costs) would have to use and manage a jumble of incompatible systems. For the benefit of the entire trading community, SPEDI argued the large players needed to buy into a coordinated approach to the implementation of trade-related EDI.

Accepting that it would not be possible to introduce all the EDI services required by the trading community on day one, SPEDI recommended that the initial focus should be on Government trade transactions. Government represented the focal point in the entire trading community. All traders were required to submit, at a minimum, a Trade Declaration document to the Government for every trade transaction. Government Departments, including those involved in trade, were experiencing budgetary pressures, which should be added incentive to introduce EDI. Government also had the ability more than any other organization in Hong Kong to make policy decisions which would encourage fast migration to EDI.

Two transactions were recommended by SPEDI for the initial phases of the EDI service: the Restrained Textiles Export Licence (RTEL) and the Trade Declaration (TD). The RTEL was chosen because of its strategic importance and complexity. The Trade Declaration was chosen because of its high volumes across the entire trading community and the potential for cost reductions for Government.

There were drawbacks to focusing on the Government trade transactions, however. Such a service would require difficult decision-making across a broad range of Government policy Secretaries, Branches and Departments. Focusing on Government transactions would also introduce additional complications. For instance, legal ordinances would need to be amended to allow for the electronic submission of Government documents. There were also some outside critics who felt that Government did not need a third-party EDI service to interface with the rest of the trading community; if EDI was needed, then Government should provide the interface itself.

Meeting the Trading Community's Requirements

The business environment in Hong Kong had always been strongly profit driven. More recently, and likely as a result of the political uncertainties facing the territory, a much shorter term orientation had taken hold. In spite of the political uncertainties, Hong Kong's economy was booming in the early 1990s, largely fuelled by the economic reforms underway in mainland China. Many business enterprises were earning extraordinary returns. A two-year payback on a major investment was not uncommon. Business opportunities were plentiful.

In this business environment, a fundamental requirement of potential users of EDI services was that there must be obvious and realizable benefits before they would consider investing in EDI for their trade transactions.

For the largest organizations, which included Government, trade service providers and major trading companies, it would be necessary to make a significant investment (in some cases, millions of dollars) in their back-office systems in order to become EDI-capable. All of these organizations were faced with a difficult problem: only if most of the trading partners of these large organizations switched to EDI would there be any benefits from investing the required large sums in their own in-house systems. Otherwise, they would be required to maintain expensive dual systems of paper and EDI for an indefinite period of time.

For small organizations, it was equally difficult to demonstrate the benefits of EDI. The minimum investment for a small organization with no previous computerisation would be about $2,000 for the required hardware, software and communication services. Ongoing usage fees would also be levied. The direct benefits from EDI to a small organization included reduced costs for things such as: local transportation (usually on inexpensive public transport); clerical time in the preparation, processing, amendment of documents; and messengers' charges for the physical delivery of documents to various local parties. An overall faster turnaround in document processing time would also be achieved. While these benefits could be quantified to some degree, it was recognized that in many small organizations the same person (often a principal in the company) who booked an order also completed the documentation and delivered it to the required parties. In other words, EDI would not necessarily result in saving the wages of a staff member.

As well, many of the small organizations were run in the traditional manner and there was a resistance to change. The paper procedures were ingrained, known and safe. The inconveniences and costs of paper were not appreciated. Computers were an unknown and to trust a computer with vital trade information would be, to some, unthinkable.

In response to these broad requirements, SPEDI proposed that EDI for Hong Kong's trading sector would only work if a sufficient number of smaller businesses could be convinced to take part. This would require providing low-cost, easy-to-use "entry level" access to EDI for small traders. Some of the more important requirements of small traders for such a system included: no or minimal purchase of new equipment; the ability to handle Chinese characters on documents (see

Exhibit 6 for a further description of this issue); improved convenience over the current paper system; and at least the same level of security as the current paper system.

Assessing Business Viability

Given the business environment, it was probable that the private sector would only be willing to provide a trade-related EDI service for Hong Kong's trading community if a reasonable return could be

---

EXHIBIT 6   A Special Requirement: The Use of Handwritten Chinese Characters on Documents

---

SPEDI proposed that the Trade Declaration (TD) should be one of the two Government trade documents implemented in the first phase of the project. However, a major issue to be overcome was the fact that some 35 per cent of all TDs submitted were completed partially or wholly in Chinese, usually handwritten. Many of the TDs with Chinese characters related to cross-border trade with mainland China. In some cases, there was no direct English translation.

The first option considered was "Chinese EDI." While a universal Chinese EDI standard based on UN/EDIFACT was under development, it was estimated that it would not be available for at least five years. The building blocks to achieving this standard included: a universally accepted and coded character set (Japan, Korea, China, Hong Kong and Taiwan all used slightly different character sets); an efficient and cost-effective data-entry method; and finally, a Chinese language EDI standard based on UN/EDIFACT. As well, computing with Chinese characters required 16-bit processing whereas English character computing and EDI, including the UN/EDIFACT standard, was based on 8-bit processing.

Another option would be for Hong Kong to create its own proprietary Chinese EDI format for use until a universal standard was agreed upon. However, with a universal EDI standard already under development, such a move might be difficult to justify.

Other options were considered. One approach could be to mandate the use of English on trade documents. However, this decision might not be politically acceptable. Focusing only on those documents completed in English was also considered. However, this would mean Government would need to retain expensive dual systems to handle those Trade Declarations completed in Chinese. As well, it might actually cause an increase in the use of Chinese on TDs by those companies wishing to continue using paper methods.

In studying the problem closer, SPEDI found that only about 85 characters of an average total of 500 were required by Government for compiling statistics (the primary purpose of the form). This information was always in alpha-numeric form. Therefore, another option for those Trade Declarations containing Chinese characters was to capture only the key alpha-numeric information for onward electronic routing to Government. However, as Government still required the remaining information for checking the accuracy of statistical data and follow-up purposes (such as when there was an error), the uncaptured information would still need to be made available to Government in some form (paper, or possibly, image). This option meant there would be one system for English-only TDs and a different system (consisting of a mix of paper/image and EDI) for those containing Chinese characters.

---

earned. However, this was not a simple task. First of all, a potential provider of an EDI service was required to make a significant upfront investment in hardware and software, with a large proportion of this amount usually required before a service was even operational. Annual operating costs were also substantial and often included large amounts for education and marketing, user support, system operation, maintenance and software licence fees. With such economics, large volumes of users and transactions would be required just to break even.

There was also a concern about the length of time required to build up enough users and transactions to make a service profitable. Singapore Network Services, considered an EDI success story, had taken four years to build up a user base of a few thousand customers based on a mandated use policy (i.e., counter services for the paper processing of Import Declarations were withdrawn). General Electric Information Services, one of the earliest EDI providers in the world, had about 11,000 users in 1992, after many years of operation.

Thirdly, the provision of EDI services was a relatively new area of business; therefore, it was difficult to make business projections with any accuracy. While the competition among the various service providers was fierce enough, all providers faced competition from a common enemy—the established way of doing things: paper forms.

An additional factor was the overwhelming size of the potential market: over 100,000 trading establishments. Using similar tactics employed by other EDI service providers around the world would mean it would take years, if not decades, to reach such a market.

The future provider of Hong Kong's trade EDI service also faced some additional risks. The first was the general political situation in Hong Kong. What business and political environment would exist after 1997? As well, what sort of relationship with the future Government could be expected? The second was an implementation risk. Given SPEDI's proposed focus on Government trade documents, the EDI service could not commence operations until the Government had its systems ready and EDI-capable.

In response to these factors, SPEDI proposed that, in addition to an exclusive franchise for Government trade documents being granted, 100 per cent of selected Government trade documents would need to be routed through the service by the beginning of the fourth year of operation. With a market of over 100,000 trading companies submitting the selected forms to Government, this would be a huge undertaking not attempted by any EDI service elsewhere. Nonetheless, it was considered essential if the trading community's requirements were to be met *and* a commercial return was to be earned. The implication to Government was that it would need to agree to close all of its paper processing operations over the same time period.

Selecting an Operator

SPEDI advocated that Hong Kong's trade-related EDI service should be a cooperative venture between the private sector and the public sector. Tradelink, with Government as a shareholder, was a prime contender to own and operate the service. Tradelink shareholders were all major players in the trading sector. As well, no one shareholder dominated the organization. They were all willing to work together cooperatively towards the goal of community-wide EDI.

However, there were some critics who charged that Tradelink wasn't necessarily the only or the best party for addressing the EDI needs of the trading sector. Some claimed that Tradelink wasn't even necessary, that Government alone could provide the required services. Others (often vendors) proposed that existing EDI service providers were capable and, in fact, might even be preferable given their experience. It was suggested that, at the very least, the provision of the service be put to public tender by the Government. Of course, this latter option would mean many further months of delays in order for Government to produce and issue a tender document, for potential vendors to prepare and submit their proposals, for the proposals to be evaluated and an operator to be chosen. There was also the issue of joint ownership by Tradelink and Government of the intellectual property arising from SPEDI which would have to be resolved before a tender exercise proceeded. In the meantime, Singapore appeared to be getting further and further ahead of Hong Kong in its EDI programme, and other Asian countries were also in advanced stages of planning their trade EDI systems.

SPEDI Recommendations

In November 1990, the SPEDI Report was completed and proposed that a Community Electronic Trading Service (CETS) be implemented as soon as possible. CETS should have three critical components: a Community Gateway, Shared EDI Facilities, and the Community Access Service (CAS).

The first of these, the Community Gateway, would serve as an electronic post office, collecting and delivering EDI messages among all trading establishments in the community, including an exclusive link to Government. SPEDI argued that this central routing facility was necessary given the complex, multi-party/multi-transaction nature of international trade. Without such a central gateway, users would be required to maintain and manage multiple connections to VANs and/or other users in order to electronically exchange data with their trading partners. The Community Gateway, which would actively use and promote international EDI and communication standards, would be a neutral interface—a level playing field for all users no matter what size or influence they might have in the community. All VANs would be welcome to interconnect with the Community Gateway, giving users the choice to connect either directly to the Community Gateway or via a third-party service.

The second critical element, the Shared EDI Facilities, would add value on top of the base routing functions of the Community Gateway, providing a range of services to facilitate the management of electronic trading. Such services would include message content validation, the matching and collation of associated messages, establishment of information data bases, and the collection of charges on behalf of users. SPEDI proposed that such processing functions would help to overcome and/or streamline some of the operational difficulties arising from the implementation of EDI, and at the same time reduce the up-front investment that would otherwise be required by users to develop such facilities themselves.

The third element was the Community Access Service, also known as CAS. CAS provided Fax-In and Walk-In access for the large segment of the trading community which was unable or unwilling to justify "pure" EDI. Trading documents would be sent via fax or delivered to special service centres where they would subsequently be converted to an EDI format for onward delivery to major trading partners such as Government. CAS would also allow small users to pick up or receive by fax (or dispatch service) hard copy documents converted from EDI messages sent by their EDI-capable trading partners. Thus CAS could provide large users with 100 per cent of chosen transactions in EDI format while still allowing smaller companies to continue using paper if they so wished. SPEDI envisioned that, over many years, these CAS users would be migrated to the "pure" EDI service.

CETS's initial focus would be on Government trade documents. The proposed exclusive link to Government via the Community Gateway meant that all Government trade transactions in electronic format would be routed through CETS. SPEDI proposed that Tradelink, including Government as a shareholder, was the best organization to own and operate the service. The total estimated cost to bring the project to fruition was in the range of $100 million. Exhibit 7 provides a diagrammatic overview of the proposed Community Electronic Trading Service.

EXHIBIT 7   Proposed Community Electronic Trading Service

Key components of CETS:	Community gateway
	Shared EDI facilities
	Community access service
Initial focus:	Routing and processing of Government trade documents
Long-range vision:	EDI for trade documents among all participants

Source: Shared Project for EDI—Executive Summary.

Beyond SPEDI

Just before Christmas 1990, the SPEDI proposals were presented in summary form to the Hong Kong Government's influential Executive Council. It was decided that the Government should undertake further discussions with Tradelink with a view to determining the next steps forward. Some members of the SPEDI project team were retained as support, but the debate on trade-related EDI for Hong Kong once again shifted back to Tradelink and Government. While the Government agreed in principle with most of the recommendations made in the SPEDI report, no commitment was made to Tradelink that the recommendations would be adopted.

The next 20 months, from January 1991 to September 1992, were a difficult time for Tradelink and its shareholders as it held extensive, detailed discussions with the Government addressing business, technical, regulatory and financial issues raised by the SPEDI recommendations. Many of the issues discussed were interrelated (e.g., the financial issues could not be resolved until the regulatory environment was known, which depended on the business viability, which in turn depended on solutions to certain technical issues, etc.), making it very difficult for the project to move forward. In order to break this cycle, Tradelink proposed that the regulatory environment should be resolved first. At the same time, all parties agreed that Government needed to decide on CETS ownership and operation. Tradelink continued to assert to Government that it, with Government as a shareholder, was the best organization to operate the service, of course subject to a satisfactory regulatory environment.

After months of discussion, analysis and negotiation, an ownership/regulatory framework was proposed whereby Tradelink would own and operate CETS with an exclusive franchise over Government trade-related documents for a seven-year period, starting when the service entered its commercial (i.e., revenue-earning) phase. Prices to users for the service would be set over the period of the franchise so that Tradelink would be able to earn an acceptable rate of return over the same time period. It was also proposed that the Hong Kong Government should immediately acquire a shareholding in Tradelink of not less than 10 per cent nor more than 49 per cent.

By September 1992, Government was in the final stages of seeking formal approval for the proposals. Tradelink had previously anticipated that all the necessary approvals would be concluded by then, but uncontrollable circumstances as well as the Government's annual summer recess had delayed the process. A final agreement was now expected sometime in November 1992.

Tradelink, anticipating an earlier formal decision from Government, had already announced that the Request for Proposals (RFP) was going to be issued later that month. Many vendors were gearing up and had already assembled their teams. Tradelink itself had recently recruited a number of technical people and moved to larger premises in anticipation of moving forward on community EDI with the issue of the RFP. The question of whether to go ahead with issuing the RFP to vendors, or to delay things once again until formal Government approval was received, needed to be resolved by the Tradelink Board.

THE DECISION

Juletta stepped off the air-conditioned boat onto the crowded pier. It was 7:25 A.M. and already the temperature was 27 degrees Celsius. Some passengers raced ahead to flag the few taxicabs that were waiting for the crowd. It was going to be another hot day in Hong Kong. As Juletta walked the one kilometer route to the Tradelink office, she pondered the advantages and the risks of issuing the RFP proposal right away, and what position she herself should take when she presented the RFP decision to the Board.

Establishing a National Information Technology Infrastructure: The Case of the French Videotex System, Minitel

By Professor J. Téboul, Associate Professor T. Jelassi and W. Cats-Baril

In the late 1970s, videotex[1] was an important fixture of the telecommunications landscape of most industrialized countries. Many national Post, Telephone and Telegraph (PTT) companies and commercial ventures

---

[1]Videotex is a generic term for an easy-to-use, computer-based, interactive system to access and selectively view text and graphics on a terminal screen. The content is usually organized into tree structures of pages that are selected from a series of hierarchical menus. Videotex systems typically offer a wide range of information retrieval, interactive, and transactional services such as directory and reservations systems, financial reports, home banking and shopping. Videotex was developed in Europe in the mid 1970s for consumer applications. Because of its consumer origins, videotex excels at delivering information to untrained or casual users. The user may use a dedicated videotex terminal or other access deliveries (e.g., personal computer). The primary objective of commercial videotex systems is the efficient delivery of value-added information and services to a maximum number of users profitably for both the system operator and the service provider.

Source: This case was written by W. Cats-Baril, T. Jelassi, Associate Professor at INSEAD, and J. Téboul, Professor at INSEAD. It is intended to be used as a basis for class discussion rather than to illustrate either effective or ineffective handling of an administrative situation. Copyright © 1993 INSEAD-CEDEP, Fontainebleau, France.

started pilot videotex projects. Some social commentators and re-searchers began discussing videotex as one of the driving forces in the movement toward an information society.

A decade later most of the enthusiasm has evaporated. France's famous Télétel[2] (over 6 million subscribers and 17,000 services, as of December 1991) is the only commercially viable national videotex system so far. The limited success of videotex ventures is surprising since there were at least 50 videotex projects in 16 countries of Western Europe, Japan and North America in 1982.

Indeed, Britain's Prestel (150,000 subscribers and 1,300 services) and Germany's Bildschirmtext (250,000 subscribers and 3,500 services) which rank second and third in the world are considered commercial failures and their prospects for growth are not very good.

What made Télétel such a success?

INFORMATION TECHNOLOGY AND FRENCH INDUSTRIAL POLICY

In the mid 1960s, particularly after the American Congress had denied a permit to export a large IBM mainframe computer to the French government, French political commentators started to voice concerns that France was falling behind the United States in information technology and that it would soon be in an intolerable situation of technological and cultural dependence. For example, President Valéry Giscard d'Estaing, in gathering support for moving France into the information age, stated that "For France, the American domination of telecommunications and computers is a threat to its independence in the crucially significant if not overriding area of technology and in the field of culture, where the American presence, through television and satellite, becomes an omnipresence." This line of thought continued to be voiced during the 1970s and became a central piece of the industrial policy of the country.[3]

In 1975, President Giscard d'Estaing asked two researchers—Simon Nora and Alain Minc—to suggest a strategy to computerize French society. The Nora-Minc report delivered in 1978 and published in 1979 went on to be a best-seller (a first for this type of report). Nora and Minc coined a new word, "Télématique" (from telecommunication and informatique), and proposed it as the cornerstone of that strategy. Télématique was the merger of computers and communication technologies to create information processing applications with broad societal impact.

---

[2]The system is popularly known as Minitel. In strict terms, however, Minitel refers only to the dedicated terminal itself. Throughout this case we use *Télétel* when we refer to the whole system and *Minitel* when we allude to the device.

[3]Although the "enemy" has changed and the main villain is now Japan, the policy is still very much in place today as illustrated by the French government's decision in 1991 to save the consumer electronics companies Bull and Thomson from insolvency.

Indeed, Nora and Minc predicted that eventually Télématique would affect all aspects of society—education, business, media, leisure, and routine day-to-day activities. The way they saw it, Télématique would, by increasing access to information, lead to decentralization of government and business decision-making and therefore to an increase in national productivity and competitiveness and an improvement in the ability to respond to an increasingly fast changing environment (Nora and Minc 1979). Nora and Minc's view, however, implied that a new national communication infrastructure was necessary for France to remain among the leading countries of the industrialized world. Their report also underlined that such a transformation would require a long-term strategy and cooperation between the government and business sectors.

One of the recommendations of the report was for the Direction Générale des Télécommunications (DGT), as France Télécom was then named, to encourage cooperation among computer services companies and hardware manufacturers to produce the technical components of the required infrastructure. Another recommendation was for the DGT to implement a research program to develop applications which would leverage and take advantage of that infrastructure (Nora and Minc 1979).

These recommendations are typical of French industrial policy. The strategy of having the government orchestrate and subsidize large technological projects by creating alliances among companies and "rationalizing" an industrial sector by encouraging mergers—the computer and electronics sector being a prime example—had been used before (e.g., Ariane, Airbus, Concorde, TGV). As a senior official of the French government put it, "This type of large industrial projects, or, as we (the French) call them, 'les grandes aventures,' have always captured the imagination of French politicians."

THE FRENCH TELEPHONE SYSTEM IN THE 1970s

In 1974, when Giscard d'Estaing became President of France, the French telecommunication system was very weak. There were fewer than 7 million telephone lines for a population of 47 million (one of the lowest penetration rates in the industrialized world, equivalent to that of Czechoslovakia), a four-year wait to get a new line, and manual switches still in use in most rural areas in the country (Chamoux 1990; Mayer 1988).

President Giscard d'Estaing decided to make the reform of the telecommunication infrastructure a top priority. In April 1975, the Conseil des Ministres (a cabinet-level meeting of the Secretaries of all agencies) approved the President's program under the banner "Le téléphone pour tous" (a telephone for everyone).

Also in 1974, Gérard Théry took over as director of the DGT. At that time, the strategic direction of telecommunication technology was set by the Centre National d'Etudes des Télécommunications (CNET). The

CNET was, and continues to be, the research and development arm of the DGT. The CNET was dominated by engineers whose responsibility and vocation was the design of new products. They focused on technical prowess and innovation.

Once the design of a product was complete, the CNET negotiated the development and commercialization of the product directly with the telecommunication industry. Housel (1990) notes that because the CNET engineers were constantly trying new technologies without a clear technological migration plan, manufacturers were forced into short production runs, making manufacturing economies of scale impossible, driving prices up, and making network compatibility difficult to achieve.

Théry changed the orientation of the CNET. From an attitude of technological change for the sake of technological change the CNET moved to a more pragmatic and commercial stance. The change in culture was difficult at first: most of the engineers went on a long and bitter strike. Eventually, Théry's vision prevailed. Not only did the internal focus of the CNET change, but a new relationship between the DGT and French telecommunication manufacturers was established (Housel 1990; Marchand 1987).

Théry's strategy to establish a more commercial orientation at the CNET was implemented creating the Direction des Affaires Industrielles et Internationales (DAII) and bringing in an outsider—Jean-Pierre Souviron—as its director. One of the principal functions of the DAII was to insure standardization of equipment. The DAII invited bids not only from the traditional suppliers of the DGT (e.g., CIT-Alcatel, Thomson) but from others as well (e.g., Matra and Philips). In order to drive equipment prices down, the DAII announced that from then on an important criterion in choosing suppliers would be their ability to export and thus acquire larger markets.

The government push toward standardization and export was partially responsible for lowering subscription charges and more than doubling the number of telephone lines between 1974 and 1979. By the late 1980s, the penetration rate was at 95 percent, one of the highest telephone penetration rates among the industrialized nations (Chamoux 1990; Housel 1990).

The transformation of the French telephone network from the "joke of Europe" to Europe's most modern ("from the ugly toad to the handsome prince," in the words of a government official) took some 10 years and very substantial resources. Indeed, from 1976 to 1980, the DGT was the largest investor in France, averaging around 4 percent of the total national investment in the country (Hutin 1981). The cost of the transformation has been estimated at around FF120 billion. The magnitude of the investment raised questions as to how to maintain expansion of the telephone network and how to leverage the modernization costs. In early 1978, with the telephone penetration rate growing very quickly, Théry realized that telephone traffic alone would not be enough to leverage the telephone network and the public packet-switched network (Transpac).

Théry asked the CNET to generate ideas for new services and established a list of requirements they would be required to fulfill. The services would have to: (1) provide greater access to government and commercial information for all citizens, (2) benefit as many elements of society as possible, (3) demonstrate the value of merging computing and telecommunications, (4) be flexible enough to avoid quick technological obsolescence, and (5) be profitable (Housel 1990).

In November 1978, Théry prepared a report for the Conseil des Ministres detailing six projects: the electronic telephone directory, the videotex, the videophone, the wide distribution of telefax machines, the launching of a satellite for data transmission, and the voice-activated telephone. The background for his presentation was the Nora and Minc report and the need to counter the threat of IBM capturing critical strategic markets if left unchallenged, as perceived by Théry. "Let us be the Japanese of Europe," was his battle cry (Marchand 1987). The Conseil des Ministres gave a green light only to the electronic telephone directory and the videotex. Three years after the successful launch of the "Le téléphone pour tous" campaign, "la grande aventure du Télétel" was about to begin.

TÉLÉTEL: A BRIEF HISTORY

Work on Télétel began in the mid 1970s. The first Télétel prototype was shown at the 1977 Berlin Trade Fair. At that show the British demonstrated a very impressive operational system (CEEFAX, the precursor of Prestel). Théry realized he had to move fast. He persuaded the government to allow the DGT to pursue the videotex project (during the interministerial meeting of November 1978). It was agreed to test Télétel in 1979. Initially, there were plans for two applications: the development of an electronic telephone directory and classified ads.

With the installation of 7 million telephone lines from 1974 to 1979, the French telephone directory was obsolete as soon as it was printed (even printed twice a year). Also, the cost of printing the directory had gone up so rapidly that in 1979 the paper telephone directory lost FF120 million. Between 1979 and 1984, 7 million additional lines were to be installed. The cost of printing the directory alone was expected to double in the next five years and the quantity of paper needed to quintuple from 20,000 tons in 1979 to a projected 100,000 tons by 1985. Directory assistance was hopelessly overloaded. It required 4,500 operators to provide a barely acceptable level of service. The number of operators needed in 1985 was forecasted to be 9,000 (Dondoux 1978; Marchand 1987).

Directory automation was proposed both to address the directory assistance problem, which was becoming a serious public relations issue, and to bring about savings by avoiding the costs of printing telephone directories. The success of the electronic telephone directory assumed that a great majority of the subscribers would be able to use it. This notion in turn implied that subscribers would need to have access to an easy-to-use, inexpensive terminal.

At the DAII, planners developed the scenario of distributing terminals free of charge to subscribers. They reasoned that as long as a dedicated terminal could be produced for FF500, the cost of the terminal could be recovered in less than five years (the cost of each paper telephone book was FF100 and it was increasing). The government agreed to try out the electronic telephone directory concept during the Conseil des Ministres of November 1978. The first test was carried out in Saint-Malo (Brittany) in July 1980.

Another application that was discussed in order to help launch Télétel was offering classified ads. But after a vicious attack from the press and its powerful lobby, which saw their main source of income threatened, the DGT capitulated. On December 12, 1980, Pierre Ribes, Secretary of the PTT, stated unequivocally that there would be no classified ads offered through Télétel in the videotex experiment to be started in Vélizy, a suburb of Paris, in June 1981. The press has consequently dropped its resistance to the Télétel project (Marchand 1987).

The initial testing of the electronic directory began on July 15, 1980, in Saint-Malo.[4] The actual videotex experiment started in Vélizy (under the name Télétel 3V) in June 1981 with a sample of 2,500 homes and 100 different services. After two years, the Vélizy test showed that 25 percent of the users were responsible for 60 percent of all traffic, one-third of the sample *never* used the device (this proportion of non-users has remained constant throughout the dissemination of minitels), and, overall, households had had a positive experience with Télétel. The experiment was considered a success in both technical and sociological terms (Chamoux 1990; Marchand 1987).

On February 4, 1983, a full-scale implementation of the electronic directory was started in the area of Ille-et-Vilaine. In the opening ceremony, Louis Mexandeau, the new Secretary of the PTT, exulted: "We are here today to celebrate the beginning of a 'grande aventure,' an experience which will mark our future." François Mitterrand had replaced

---

[4]By comparison, the British television-based system Prestel had a field trial with 1,400 participants in 1978 and started commercial service in the fall of 1979. Full nationwide operation was established in March 1980. At the end of 1981, Prestel had only one-tenth of the users predicted for that time (Thomas and Miles 1989). This failure has been attributed to the late delivery and high prices of television monitors (Prestel needed a connection between the telephone and the television set), uncoordinated marketing, and bad quality of the databases (Schneider et al. 1990).

Valéry Giscard d'Estaing as President of France, the "left" was now in power, but the rhetoric on the importance of Télématique to the future of the country and the underlying industrial policy remained the same.

Soon after the successes of Vélizy and Ille-et-Vilaine, the free, public distribution of minitel terminals was implemented: there were 120,000 minitels in France by the end of 1983, over 3 million by December 1987, and more than 6 million by December 1991 (see Exhibit 1). Videotex services went from 145 in January of 1984 to 5,000 at the end of 1987 to more than 17,000 by December 1991 (see Exhibit 2). Traffic on the Télétel system and on the electronic telephone directory has steadily increased over the last several years (see Exhibits 3 and 4). Moreover, these two systems have been continuously expanded and improved (see Exhibit 10). In 1989, France Télécom created new organizational entities (e.g., Intelmatique) to export Télétel and the accompanying know-how.

EXHIBIT 1   Rate of Minitel Distribution (1983–1991)

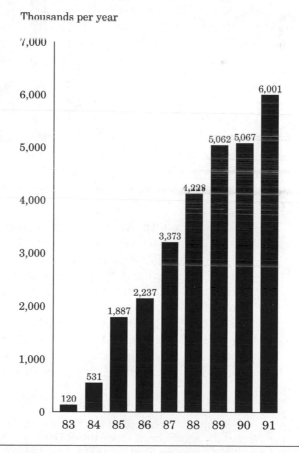

Thousands per year

Source: France Télécom.

EXHIBIT 2   Growth of Télétel Services (1985–1991)

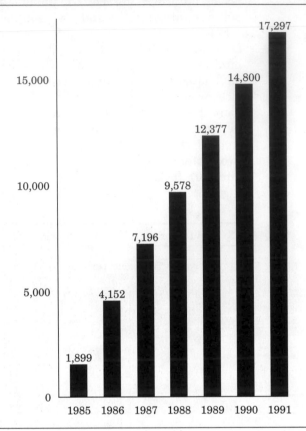

Source: France Télécom.

Télétel had to overcome four serious challenges in the early years. First, there were vicious attacks by the newspaper owners, in particular François-Régis Hutin, owner of *Ouest-France,* who found among many philosophical reasons to stop videotex one very pragmatic one (Hutin 1981).[5] Videotex was a serious threat to their main source of revenue: advertising. After a long fight, a political compromise was reached giving newspaper owners a say in the development of Télétel services, subsidies and technical help from the DGT to develop their own services, and a virtual monopoly on services for the first couple of years in exchange for dropping their resistance to the videotex concept.

---

[5]Typical of the attacks is the "call to arms" by the political commentator George Suffert. He argued, in an article titled "The fight of the century: Teletex versus paper," that it was dangerous to let the DGT have a monopoly on the videotex system. He wrote "He who owns the wire is powerful. He who owns the wire and the screen is very powerful. He who owns the wire, the screen, and the computer has the power of God."

EXHIBIT 3   Total Télétel Usage (including ETD) (1985–1991)

Millions of connect hours/year

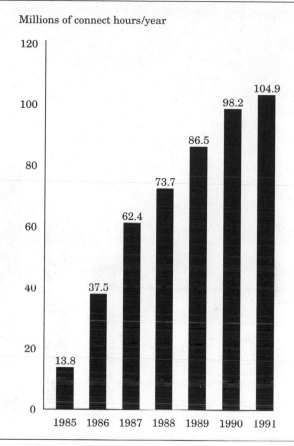

Source: France Télécom.

A second challenge was some politicians' feeling that the system could be abused by the state. These politicians declared publicly that this new mode of information dissemination was a potential threat to the liberty of the citizenry and that Télétel was the latest attempt of the state to manipulate information (the Big Brother syndrome). Later, the rapid proliferation of "chat" services (messageries), some of which were considered pornographic (messageries roses), brought criticism from both government and private groups who were concerned that the state was billing and indirectly subsidizing immorality.

A third challenge was the early battle to establish an international videotex standard. The most advanced videotex system in the 1970s was the British Prestel. Prestel was based on the CEEFAX standard, whereas the French were using XXX. The DGT realized that they were at a disadvantage and tried to have their own videotex standard recognized at several international forums. In a decision typical of the

EXHIBIT 4   Usage of the Electronic Telephone Directory (1987–1991)

Millions of connect hours/year

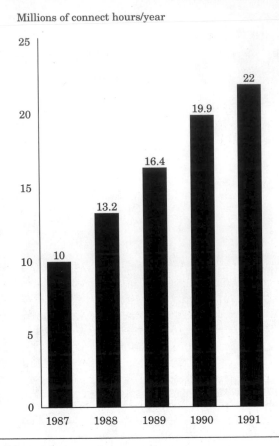

Source: France Télécom.

byzantine regulatory politics in Europe, the Conférence Européenne des Postes et Télécommunications (CEPT) established a European videotex "standard" in 1980 with 10 variations! One of these variations was the French standard. Although this decision led to the incompatibility of the European Videotex Systems during the 1980s, it allowed the DGT to continue developing Télétel as planned.

The fourth challenge that Télétel had to meet was the negative publicity that surrounded the "crash of 85," the only system failure since its inception. The crash was the result of very heavy traffic of the "messageries" services. This heavy traffic caused an overload of the Transpac switching system and the network went down. The technical problem was easy to solve: the switching system was changed to handle higher volumes and there has not been another crash since. The perception that Télétel was mostly about "sex" lingered much longer, slowed down Télétel's development, and, paradoxically, increased its international visibility.

EXHIBIT 5   Number of Calls and Connect Time on Télétel per Type of Application (1991)

Per Hour

- ■ Recruitment/training
- ☐ Banks/stock market/insurance
- ▨ Leisure/tourism/mail order
- ■ Transport/automotive
- ▧ "Chat" services (messageries)
- ■ Games/tests/astrology
- ☐ Business applications
- ■ Electronic telephone directory

In Calls

Per Hour values: 8.30%, 11.30%, 7.40%, 6%, 15%, 9%, 22%, 21%

In Calls values: 4.80%, 15%, 6%, 4%, 6%, 5%, 17%, 43.50%

Source: France Télécom.

Overcoming these public controversies made Télétel stronger in the long run. Indeed, the political fury that Télétel generated in 1978–80 and later in 1985 led to a full and rich discussion on the issues of privacy rights, authority of the telecommunication agency, regulation of computer services, and the need to prevent the creation of a second class of citizens shut out of the information age. This discussion involved the President of France and the most notable political commentators and intellectuals in the country and eventually created a broad national consensus on the use and limitations of the technology.

Today, Télétel is an integral part of the French society life style. A survey conducted by France Télécom in October 1989 indicated that some 40 percent of the population had access to minitels at home or at work. Another survey, conducted in 1991, showed that the system was used regularly by a broad cross section of the population in a variety of ways (see Exhibits 5, 11 and 12).

The success of Télétel as a sociological development and its positive impact on the technological literacy of the population are unquestionable. The primary concern about Télétel now is whether it is a profitable operation or not. But before exploring this issue, let us describe some of the technical choices and characteristics that have made Télétel the only successful commercial videotex system in the world so far.

GENERAL CHARACTERISTICS OF TÉLÉTEL

A comparison of the technical characteristics and policies that were used in implementing Télétel with those of the other commercial videotex systems (e.g., American, British and German) explains to a certain degree the great success of Télétel and the rather tepid development of the others. The comparison of videotex systems can be made on the basis of four characteristics: (1) terminal design and strategy of terminal distribution, (2) system architecture and other aspects of service provision, (3) billing system, and (4) regulatory environment (see Schneider et al. 1990).

Given the British experience, where the high price of the TV-based videotex setup chosen became a barrier to implementation, and the DGT argument that the Télétel investment would be paid back through increased telephone traffic and savings in the production of the telephone directory, it was clear that Télétel's success was critically dependent on the development of an easy-to-use, dedicated, and inexpensive terminal for mass distribution. The Vélizy experience also established the need for a user-friendly terminal with an easy-to-use interface. The motto for Télétel became "make it simple"—simple to manufacture, simple to install, simple to use.

In an approach typical of French industrial policy, the government (rather than the consumer electronics industry) decided on the specifications of the videotex terminals. The DAII opened the procurement of terminals to multiple vendors and the promise of a production run of some 20 million terminals encouraged low bids. The total cost of the original basic minitel terminal to the DGT was approximately FF1,000.

The key decision on whether or not to distribute minitel terminals free of charge generated intense controversy within the DGT. On the one hand, distributing minitels on a free and voluntary basis gave the system an aura of democracy: those who wished to have a minitel would not be impeded by cost. This also made it easier for the mass public to try out the device and the services it offered.

On the other hand, some senior officers at the DGT thought that a nominal fee on a per-month basis was not only sound policy from a financial point of view, but would also send an appropriate message to the users to counteract the "if-it's-free-it-can't-be-very-good" syndrome. They reasoned that once the system was distributed for free, it would be practically impossible to charge for it later on without generating intense public resistance. In what turned out to be a critical decision for the success of Télétel, it was decided that minitel terminals would be distributed free of charge.

Another critical success factor of Minitel was the decision to implement the Télétel concept by interfacing the public switched telephone network with the Transpac packet switching data network. The subscriber was linked to the electronic directory or any other database via his telephone through a gateway—called a videotex access point or VAP—giving access to the Transpac network to which the servers and host computers were to be connected.

This design approach had three basic advantages. First, Transpac charges are based on traffic (i.e., minutes of connect-time) and not on distance, which means that any provider, independent of its geographical location, has equal access and equal costs in gaining a national audience. Second, it established a common standard protocol (i.e., the CCITT X.29), making connections to the system straightforward and relatively cheap (FF100,000), a crucial point in attracting service providers. Third, the networks were already in place, included the latest technology and could support a rapid expansion in the number of subscribers and providers.

More importantly, the decision to use the Transpac network kept the DGT from becoming an information provider. With the exception of the electronic directory, the DGT acted as a common carrier and was responsible only for the transmission of information and administration of the network.[6] This is in contrast to the centralized solution offered by the British and German systems where British Telecom and the BundesPost provided the design and storage of the databases. In Télétel, the storage and manipulation of information was left to the information providers.

The decision to build Télétel on a decentralized network and with an open architecture went a long way in: (1) alleviating the "Big Brother" concerns of the press and politicians, and (2) encouraging innovation in information services since clear telocommunications standards were used and the entry barrier to the information provider market was very low.

Another critical element in the success of Télétel is the billing system introduced by France Télécom in March 1984 and named the "kiosk." The billing is done by France Télécom and not by the service providers. The system was named after the newsstands where a variety of publications can be bought without leaving a record of what was bought or who bought it. The Télétel charges appear on the regular telephone bill as "minitel use" with no reference whatsoever as to what specific service was used.

The kiosk works as follows: when the connection to the desired service has been set up through the VAP, the VAP sends charging pulses to the subscriber's meter at a faster-than-usual rate to cover the cost of using the Transpac network and the cost of the service. The Transpac network keeps track of the connection time and pays each provider as a function of that time. The kiosk is a very clever idea because it protects the anonymity of the users (important on both financial and philosophical levels), because it does not require passwords or payments in advance, because service providers do not have to worry about billing and its associated administrative costs, and because it allows differently priced services to be offered easily through a series of different numbers.

---

[6]That has now changed. France Télécom decided in 1990 to enter the information provision business by offering what are called added-value services. Most of these services are offered through joint ventures with privately owned companies.

France Télécom's monopoly position in basic telecommunication services and the fact that it did not have the return-on-investment pressures of a commercial firm provided Télétel with the necessary time to mature.[7] Infrastructure-based services like Télétel require a longer time horizon to assess and determine profitability. There is no doubt that the regulatory umbrella shielding Télétel in the early years is one of the critical factors in its success.

Another aspect of the French regulatory environment important to the development of Télétel was the ability of France Télécom to subsidize ventures out of its subscribers' revenue. Such subsidies are forbidden by American and British regulations. The subsidies allowed France Télécom to take a long and patient view on Télétel and helped amortize the free distribution of minitel terminals, which amounted to a cost of FF6 billion over 10 years.

Yet another specific benefit of this protective regulatory environment is described by Housel (1990). He notes that the ability to implement changes of tariffs quickly without going through a lengthy political process to justify them allowed France Télécom to respond quickly to changing market conditions. For example, there were many services that Télétel users could access and use without staying connected for very long. The user paid no fee because the tariff allowed free access. Because of the revenue sharing arrangements with the service providers, however, France Télécom had to pay for each connection. France Télécom asked the regulatory bodies to charge subscribers a small access fee for every connection regardless of its duration. The request was barely scrutinized and the charge was approved without debate.

The regulatory environment in France also enabled France Télécom to run the kiosk billing system. The arrangement has come under fire on two fronts. First, the fact that the billing system results in the state (in the form of France Télécom) collecting fees for the distribution of services which may be deemed pornographic, has been argued to be against the law. Second, it has been suggested that, even if it is not illegal, billing, which could be a very profitable stand-alone operation, should be a service offered by a third party and not by France Télécom. These criticisms have not stopped France Télécom from performing the billing.

The regulatory environment in Europe, with its myriad of standards and protocols, was also beneficial for Télétel initially because it served to protect the fledgling service from being battered by competition from abroad. However, that same environment has now become a barrier to

---

[7]France Télécom is directly accountable to the French government for all its ventures and is required to justify its fee structures. More than other state agencies, France Télécom is asked to demonstrate the viability of its investments and therefore is under some profitability pressures, mild as they may be.

Télétel's penetration of other European markets. Finally, one must note that it is to France Télécom's credit that in such a heavily regulated environment it pursued an open network architecture and stayed out of the information services business with the exception of the electronic telephone directory.[8]

This policy of decentralization and liberalization of services, contrary to the centralization policies in Britain and Germany, led to an explosion of services. Indeed, while in France the number of providers has grown steadily and the number of services today surpasses 17,000, in Britain the number has stagnated at 1,300 or so, and in Germany the number has not only stagnated but has actually declined to around less than 3,000 (Schneider et al. 1990). A comparison of the videotex systems in France, Britain, and West Germany is shown in Exhibits 6 and 13.

TÉLÉTEL: A SOCIOLOGICAL SUCCESS

It would be a mistake to analyze Télétel exclusively on return on investment without taking into consideration its sociological impact. Though measuring the nonfinancial benefits (i.e., social, educational, and political) brought by Télétel is difficult, the increase in technological awareness and literacy of society has to be factored in any cost-benefit analysis of the system.

Through its 17,000 services the Télétel system offers information about entertainment events, train schedules, television and radio programs, jobs and classified ads, interactive games, banking services, grocery and home shopping, home banking, comparative pricing, and many other consumer services (Housel 1990; Marchand 1987; Mayer, 1988; Sentilhes et al. 1989). Most services follow the same rules and command structures, and the same multicriteria search process (e.g., a subscriber deciding on whether to go to the movies or not can search what films are showing in a given area, on a given topic, or starring a particular actor or actress), making it very easy for users to move from one application to another.

It is hard to assess the impact of Télétel on business since this impact varies by company size and industry sector. France Télécom estimated in 1990 that the overall penetration of the business sector is at least 30 percent and growing and that the penetration for large companies (more than 500 employees) is 95 percent. Indeed, some industries have been profoundly affected by Télétel applications. For example, transportation companies using the Telerouting system have minimized the

---

[8]Whether France Télécom would have taken such an enlightened position without the ferocious criticism of the press lobbies and consumer watchdog groups is debatable. Still, when it comes to Télétel, the executives of the DGT and France Télécom have consistently exhibited excellent judgment.

EXHIBIT 6 Technical Configuration of Videotex Systems in Britain, France and Germany

	Terminal configuration	Modem	Telephone network	Central data bases and special networks	Information pages	Packet switching network	Remote data bases
BRITAIN	TV-based				Since 1983		Since 1982
GERMANY	Since 1981						
FRANCE	Free (Till 1990) Dedicated Terminal			DO NOT EXIST			ETD

Legend: ☐ Private market   ▩ Public monopoly   ETD = Electronic Telephone Directory

Source: Schneider et al.

number of empty return trips for their trucks and moving vans by post-ing the schedules of return trips on minitel and matching them to re-quests from customers (Marchand 1987; Sentilhes et al. 1989).

Almost every French bank has developed its own minitel-based home-banking system allowing customers to check the status of their accounts, order checks, pay utility bills and trade stocks.[9] Most re-tailers have also developed an electronic catalogue business and, al-though volumes are moderate at present, they are expected to ex-plode as soon as payment can be done directly with the minitel

[9]For more information, see case study "Home Banking: An I.T.-Based Business Philos-ophy or a Complementary Distribution Channel—CORTAL versus Crédit Commercial de France" by Tawfik Jelassi, INSEAD, 1992.

EXHIBIT 7   Professional Traffic as a Percentage of All Télétel Traffic (1986–1989)

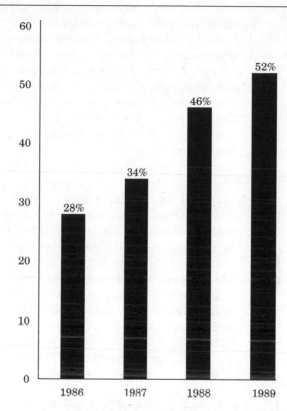

Source: France Télécom.

terminal.[10] Television stations run minitel-based surveys every night. Travel agencies, insurance companies, and consumer products companies have developed Télétel services.

Whether the aim is to be in greater touch with the client, increase efficiency in distribution, gain market share, or develop videotex products and services, minitel has become an important component of the business strategy of companies operating in France.

Exhibit 7 shows the increase in business-related volume over the years, and Exhibit 14 shows the main applications for business users in 1991.

From a social point of view, Télétel has had an impact in a wide variety of ways. For example, the success stories of the various Télétel chat

---

[10]For more information, see case study "Minitel, A Home Retailing Application" by Tawfik Jelassi, INSEAD, 1992.

services (messageries) range from relatives separated by World War II finding each other to faster matching of organ donors and people in need of a transplant. Although the chat services have been in steady decline since the mid-80s and represented only 6 percent of all the calls to Télétel in 1989, they are still one of the most popular services available (representing 15 percent of the total connect time; see Exhibit 5).[11]

The anonymity that the chat services provide has encouraged the sick (e.g., cancer, aids) and the troubled (e.g., drug addicts, divorced, abused) to discuss their more intimate problems with others. Télétel has also played a role in helping individuals who have difficulty getting out and around (e.g., the disabled, the elderly) to shop, bank, and make reservations. Universities now use Télétel to coordinate student registration, course schedules, and examination results. Other services give students access to help from teachers at all times.

Télétel services have been used in the political arena in innovative ways. During the last presidential election, a service allowed minitel users to exchange letters with the candidates. Any voter accessing the service could view the open letters and the politicians' replies. Another example is the service, sponsored by the newspaper Libération, which in December 1986 broadcasted information on the students' arrest as well as specific messages sent by the organizers of this unrest. These examples illustrate how broadly Télétel has been used as a decentralized, grass-roots vehicle for the discussion of a variety of societal issues. This utilization is very much in keeping with the original vision of Télématique proposed by Messrs. Nora and Minc back in 1978.

TÉLÉTEL: IS IT A FINANCIAL SUCCESS?

With a project of the magnitude of Télétel, it is very difficult to generate precise estimates of costs and revenues. There is a public perception, in part based on the free distribution of minitel terminals, that Télétel is another Concorde: a high-technology, money-losing proposition. A recent report from the state auditor general has stated that Télétel revenues have not covered its operating, depreciation, and capital costs. The Secretary of the PTT, Mr. Quilès, disagrees with that assessment.

On the one hand, the total investment in Télétel consists of the cost of the minitel terminals plus the cost of the gateways to the Transpac network (VAPs) plus the cost of ports to the electronic directory network. The minitel terminals cost approximately FF1,000 per terminal including R&D. The typical VAP has costs of around FF5 million.

---

[11]The chat services are very lucrative since both individuals "talking" pay for the "conversation," unlike a telephone conversation where only one party gets charged for it.

On the electronic directory network one port costs approximately FF50,000. The following are approximate figures describing the investment of France Télécom in Télétel:

Minitel terminals	FF 5.4 bn
Electronic directory	FF 1.0 bn
R&D directory	FF 0.2 bn
VAPs	FF 0.6 bn
R&D (Télétel)	FF 0.3 bn
Transpac	FF 0.3 bn
Total	FF 7.8 bn

On the other hand, the sources of revenues from Télétel include: (1) fees from revenue sharing with information providers (France Télécom takes an average of 30 percent of the revenue generated by information providers), (2) advertising (of the Minitel offerings of some service providers); (3) electronic directory usage above and beyond the free allocation; and (4) rental of minitels (Housel 1990).[12] Gross revenues from Télétel were approximately FF2 billion in 1989. Payments made by France Télécom to service providers for their share of Teletel revenues increased from FF278 million in 1985 to FF1.3 billion in 1987 and FF1.8 billion in 1989. By December 1991 they had reached over FF2.2 billion.

For purposes of cost-effectiveness analyses, however, the savings from printing fewer telephone books and having fewer directory assistance operators must be taken into consideration. Also, the additional revenues based on value-added tax from products, services, and increased employment spawned by Télétel should be included but are difficult to calculate. Finally, the Transpac revenue generated by Télétel, almost 50 percent of all Transpac revenue (close to FF1 billion), needs to be considered. Quilès estimated that the total value-added of Télétel amounted to approximately FF6 billion in 1988.

France Télécom's official version is that Télétel revenues and expenses were in balance at the end of 1989 and the system is expected to start showing a significant return on investment in 1992. Unofficial estimates give a return on investment for Télétel during the 1980–90 period between 8 and 12 percent (Housel 1990). Moreover, in 1991 France Télécom started to charge a monthly fee for the new minitel terminals.

The view of senior officials of France Télécom is that this type of accounting may be a bit premature and potentially misleading since Télétel is a major infrastructure project for which profitability needs to be

---

[12]Second- and third-generation Minitel terminals are not distributed free any longer; as of 1990 they must be paid for or leased.

measured on a long-term basis. Nevertheless, officials have been on record all along saying that the break-even point for Télétel would be 10 years. Given France Télécom's numbers, those predictions seem to be right on target.

RECENT DEVELOPMENTS

From a hardware point of view, the line of minitel terminals has been expanded to include eight models with varying levels of intelligence and functionality (e.g., color screen, extended keyboards, compatibility with ASCII standards, service number memory). More than 600,000 terminals offering these capabilities had been installed as of 1990.

The new generation of minitel terminals allows the user to prepare a message before placing a call, monitor call setup, and switch between voice and text transmission during a call. They also serve as an automatic answering device with protected access, and a portable minitel that can be used over the cellular telephone network is available. ISDN[13] terminals have already been tested for the Télétel system.

From a software point of view, the kiosk now allows eight levels of pricing. A new routing capability allows information providers to use several host computers under a single minitel access code. This new routing capability also allows the caller to access another service within Télétel without making a new phone call.

France Télécom is also experimenting with natural language interfaces for Télétel services. The Minitel Service Guide came on line in 1989 with an interface which allows users to access the guide to minitel services using French without the need for special commands or the correct spelling.

With the internal market becoming progressively saturated and growth slowing down, France Télécom has made the international market a high priority. France Télécom has created Intelmatique—a division to sell videotex infrastructure and know-how. Recent clients include the Italian and Irish telephone companies.

Intelmatique markets the Minitelnet service which provides foreign users with access to the Télétel network. The new service utilizes a multitariff billing scheme corresponding to the same tariffs on Télétel and greets foreign users with a personalized welcome in their native language. The service generated 248,000 hours of traffic in 1991, an in-

---

[13]ISDN (integrated services digital network) is capable of handling simultaneously data, voice, text, and image transmission over a digital network.

EXHIBIT 8 Growth of Télétel International Usage via MinitelNet
(1988–1991)

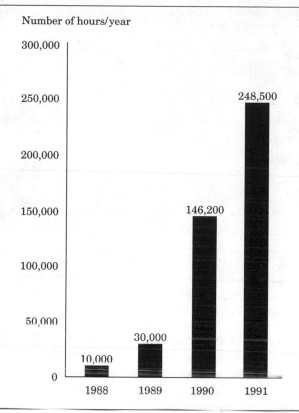

Number of hours/year

Source: Intelmatique.

crease of almost 200 percent over 1990 (see Exhibit 8). Italy (52 percent of the traffic) and Belgium (15.5 percent of the traffic) were the two major markets (see Exhibit 9).

Major efforts are currently being made to export minitel services to the U.S. market. A number of companies (e.g., US West) have established gateways with the minitel system. The Minitel Service Company, another entity of Intelmatique, was set up for the sole purpose of selling videotex know-how in the United States.

Télétel is an example of a product spawned by government industrial policy. The Télétel story is about a successful government-directed technological push sustained by political will and technical vision. However, it is also a story about how, even within an enlightened industrial policy framework, good people are needed to make decisions on the fly to adapt to changing social, political and technological environments.

EXHIBIT 9 Télétel Usage Abroad per Country (year 1991)

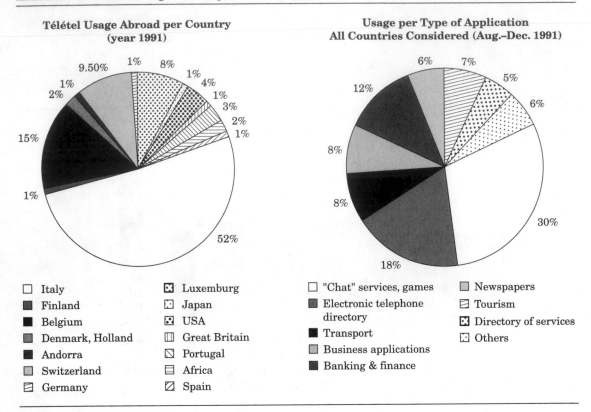

Télétel Usage Abroad per Country (year 1991)

☐ Italy	⊠ Luxemburg
■ Finland	⊡ Japan
■ Belgium	⊡ USA
■ Denmark, Holland	▥ Great Britain
■ Andorra	◩ Portugal
■ Switzerland	⊟ Africa
▤ Germany	▨ Spain

Usage per Type of Application All Countries Considered (Aug.–Dec. 1991)

☐ "Chat" services, games	▨ Newspapers
■ Electronic telephone directory	▤ Tourism
■ Transport	⊠ Directory of services
▨ Business applications	⊡ Others
■ Banking & finance	

Source: Intelmatique.

REFERENCES

Chamoux, J. P., "The French Télématique Experience," paper presented at the Conference on IT/Telecommunications, Budapest, Hungary, November 5–6, 1990.

Dondoux, J., "Problèmes Posés par la Présentation de l'Annuaire Télé-phonique," Inspection Générale des PTT, Paris, 1978.

France Télécom Annual Reports and Special Documents on Minitel, 1985–92.

Housel, T. J., "Videotex in France," manuscript, 1990.

Hutin, F. R., "Télématique et Démocratie," *Etudes,* February 1981: 179–190.

Marchand, M., *La Grande Aventure du Minitel,* Paris: Larousse, 1987.

——— *Les Paradis Informationnels,* Paris: Masson, 1987.

Mayer, R. N., "The Growth of the French Videotex System and Its Implications for Consumers," *Journal of Consumer Policy,* 11 (1988): 55–83.

Nora, S. and A. Minc, *L'Informatisation de la Société,* Paris: Documentation Française, 1978.

Prévot, H., "Report on the Future of the PTT," September 1989.

Schneider, V. et al., "The Dynamics of Videotex Development in Britain, France and Germany," paper presented at the 8th Conference of the International Telecommunication Society, Venice, Italy, March 18–21, 1990.

Sentilhes, G. et al., *La Minitel Stratégie,* Paris: Businessman/First, 1989.

Thomas, G. and I. Miles, *Telematics in Transition,* London: Longman, 1989.

EXHIBIT 10   Evolution of the Electronic Telephone Directory (ETD) and Videotex Networks

	Dec. 1987	Dec. 1988	Dec. 1989	Dec. 1990	Dec. 1991
Number of access points to the ETD	58	72	78	82	86
Number of ports to the ETD	14,220	17,280	19,020	19,020	20,640
Number of information centers	31	40	42	44	47
Number of documentation centers	15	18	22	23	25
Number of videotex access points (VAPs)	43,160	49,611	50,500	53,000	57,000

Source: France Télécom.

EXHIBIT 11   Demographic Statistics of Minitel Users

	Minitel Users Population (in %)	French Population (in %)
Sex		
Male	50.5	47.2
Female	49.5	52.7
Age		
15–24 years	17.6	19.3
25–34 years	28.2	20.6
35–49 years	31.9	22.4
50–64 years	16.9	20.6
More than 64 years	5.5	17.1
Job category		
Agriculture	4.6	6.0
Small business, handicraft, trade	12.1	7.7
Professions, executives	19.1	8.6
Office and skilled workers	36.2	24.7
Non-skilled workers	17.8	26.1
Non-working	9.8	26.8

Source: Adapted from "La Lettre de Télétel," France Télécom, June 1992.

EXHIBIT 12   Minitel Traffic Statistics

Télétel Traffic (including ETD)	*1986*	*1987*	*1988*	*1989*	*1990*	*1991*
Total number of calls (in millions)	466	807	1,010	1,242	1,482	1,656
Number of connect hours (in millions)	37.5	62.4	73.7	86.5	98.2	104.9
Average usage per minitel per month (in minutes)	105.9	111.3	97.0	93.2	92.4	90.16
Average number of calls per minitel per month	21.9	24.0	22.2	22.3	23.2	23.77
Average length of a call to Télétel, including ETD (in minutes)	4.8	4.6	4.4	4.2	4.0	3.79
Average length of a call to Télétel, excluding ETD (in minutes)	6.3	6.1	5.8	6.5	5.5	5.3

Source: Adapted from "La Lettre de Télétel," France Télécom, April 1992.

EXHIBIT 13   Implementation Strategies and Structures of the Videotex Systems in Britain, France and Germany

	Britain	*France*	*Germany*
Terminal configuration	Adapted TV set provided by TV industry and to be bought by subscriber	Simple dedicated compact terminal (Minitel); free distribution (until 1990)	Adapted TV set provided by TV industry and to be bought by subscribers (change in 1986: multitels)
Network architecture	Several central databases; one update center, closed system	Primarily privately owned databases, service computers connected to Transpac	Hierarchical network: one central database with regional subbases; interconnection to private computers
Information provision	Only by private IP (common carrier) (change in 1983: BT becomes IP)	Trigger service "electronic phone book" by PTT; other services by private IPs	Only by private (common carrier)
Billing system	Subscription fees, page-based charges, phone call charges	No subscription fees, time-based charges	Subscription fees, page-based charges, phone call charges
Regulation political control	No specific regulations, less politicized	Specific regulations liberal regime politicized; promoted by industrial policy	Specific regulations very restrictive regime politicized

Source: Schneider, V. et al.

EXHIBIT 14   Minitel Main Applications for Business Users

Electronic telephone directory	43%
Banking services, financial information and stock market	19%
Tourism/transport/hotels (timetables, reservations)	18%
Company-specific applications (including e-mail)	16%
Professional data banks	14%
General information (general data banks, newspapers, weather forecast)	32%

Source: Adapted from "La Lettre de Télétel," France Télécom, June 1992.

Chapter 3

Electronic Commerce Infrastructure

The remarkable growth of electronic commerce in the 1990s has occurred in large part due to a rapid improvement in underlying technologies. No single technology can take all the credit, rather the growth in electronic commerce has come as the result of a number of important pieces falling into place. First and foremost, the telecommunications infrastructure has evolved to allow for the high volumes of Internet traffic. The development of the World Wide Web and common languages like Java and hypertext markup language (HTML) have eased application development. Business infrastructures like electronic data interchange and various security protocols have been developed to facilitate electronically mediated exchanges. As a result, electronic commerce has exploded and, according to IBM, is expected to reach US$1 trillion by 2010.

This chapter addresses infrastructure issues pertaining to the Internet and electronic commerce. This is a logical progression from the previous chapter, which concerned the evolution of electronic commerce. Much of the subject matter pertaining to electronic commerce infrastructure is technical in nature. The cases in this chapter contain technical information, yet focus primarily on management and public policy issues. These issues include understanding the role and responsibilities of the public and private sectors in driving and sustaining infrastructure development, as well as being able to address the managerial challenges associated with developing and evolving an electronic commerce infrastructure.

The first case in the chapter is "Wired Wellington." The City of Wellington, New Zealand—the country's capital—developed Vision 2020, a vision for the city to become a "wired city." The city council approved a preliminary plan for developing various projects that will enhance the city's adoption and use of information technologies. One of the key projects is called City Link. The idea behind City Link is to string fiber-optic cable throughout the city's core business section—to wire up all the downtown buildings—then to let the various businesses use the cable for whatever purpose they wish. What's not clear is exactly who will make use of the network, and for what purpose. The Vision 2020 also encompasses numerous other initiatives, many of which involve using the Internet for the purpose of developing Wellington's status as a premier wired city. The central issue in the case concerns the extent to which the public sector can realistically attempt to lead in the social development of a city's, or country's, digital infrastructure.

The second case, "CERNET," deals with the development of a telecommunications infrastructure to support the Internet in China, circa 1997. CERNET—the China Education and Research Network—is a nonprofit, central-government-controlled body formed to oversee the development and implementation of a university-based, nationwide Internet backbone. The case deals with managing the growth of both a domestic and an internationally connected network. The issues in the case are viewed from the perspective of the director of the Technical Board and Network Center. With over half of China's population yet to make their first telephone call, and with continuous government involvement, the director's task contains numerous challenges.

Wired Wellington: The Info City Project and the City Link Network

By Professor Sid L. Huff

Wellington City Council is planning now for the year 2020. We're talking about creating a smart "info city" with an innovative and responsive economy . . .

from "2020 Vision: Wellington in the Next Century"

In just the next five years the communication bandwidth available in urban business areas will grow by a factor of 100, as network providers compete to connect concentrations of high-use customers. Businesses will be the first users of these high-speed networks.

Bill Gates, *The Road Ahead*

What we're trying to do here is to get people to look beyond their own paradigm, look outside the box. . . . Digital technology opens up new opportunities for everyone, and we want Wellington to be at the forefront of making those things happen.

Richard Naylor, in reference to Wellington's Info City project

In his open office in Wellington's Department of Economic Commissioning, surrounded by various computer screens and keyboards, Richard Naylor reflected on the status of the Info City project. Info City was a key part of Wellington's 2020 Vision strategy. Info City actually consisted of a collection of sub-projects, each focusing on a different way in which the city could promote and foster the use of information technology to help move toward the "2020 Vision." One of the sub-projects was called City Link. The objective of City Link was to create a high-speed digital communications infrastructure for the downtown business district. Fibre optic cable was to be used to "wire up," simply and inexpensively, the city's downtown businesses, to provide a backbone network that businesses could utilize, however they wished, to make themselves more competitive. A company had recently been formed, bringing together a number of parties interested in advancing the project.

A telecommunications architecture was being developed, and plans for stringing cable were under way. While Naylor wasn't sure exactly what the city's businesses would use the cable for, he was confident that once the infrastructure was in place, ideas for its utilization would readily emerge.

BACKGROUND—THE CITY OF WELLINGTON

Wellington, a city of approximately 300,000 people[1], was the capital city of New Zealand. It was situated at the south end of the North Island, on the Cook Strait, which separated the two islands comprising the country (see Exhibits 1a, b, and c). Wellington was named after the British Duke of Wellington, who was a supporter of the New Zealand Company, the group that organized the initial British settlements in New Zealand in the mid-1800s.

Wellington, a harbor city, enjoyed a spectacular setting nestled at the base and on the sides of the hills surrounding the harbor. The overall commercial ocean traffic in and out of Wellington harbor had declined in recent years. Large ocean-going ferries transporting people, automo-

---

[1]Wellington City proper's population was about 150,000, Greater Wellington (which included adjacent towns and cities such as Lower Hutt and Porirua) included 300,000 people, while the Wellington Region, an even larger area, was home to 400,000 people.

EXHIBIT 1a　Map of New Zealand and South Pacific Region

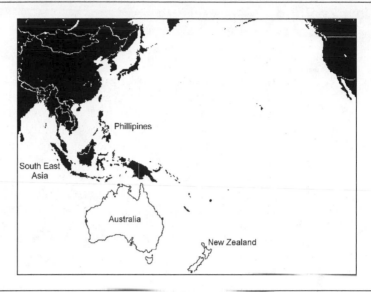

biles, and rail cars between the two islands constituted the bulk of the port's traffic, although commercial transports and other ships still visited the city's harbor on occasion.

Physically, Wellington was compact and centrally focused. The hilly nature of the surrounding countryside had served to limit the development of large suburbs, so common in North American cities. The hills, which formed a kind of bowl around the harbor, also helped to focus attention into the core of the city. Most downtown services and points of attraction were within comfortable walking distance of each other. Downtown Wellington remained vibrant, relatively crime-free, with little sign of the urban decay often seen in cities elsewhere.

As the country's capital city, Wellington was strongly influenced by the national government's presence. Approximately 20 percent of the jobs in Wellington were government-related. Wellington also enjoyed over twice the national proportion of jobs in business and financial services. In contrast, Wellington had substantially fewer jobs in the manufacturing arena: only about 7 percent of Wellington's jobs were in manufacturing, compared to 20 percent in some other centers such as Auckland and Christchurch. See Exhibit 3 for comparative employment by sector, and within the business sector, in Wellington and New Zealand as a whole.

A "functional analysis" of Wellington's local industry base, developed by Richard Naylor, is shown in Exhibit 4. It highlights some of the information-intensive activities common to Wellington-based companies.

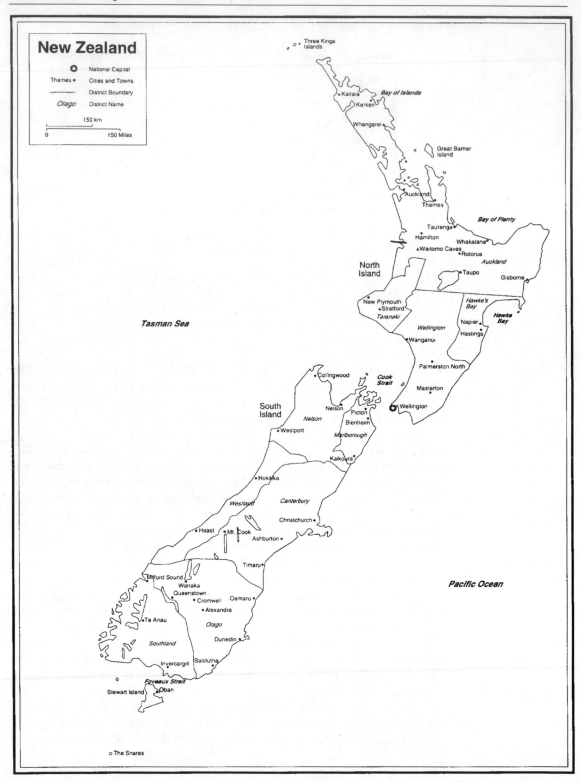

EXHIBIT 1c   Map of Wellington City and Surrounding Area

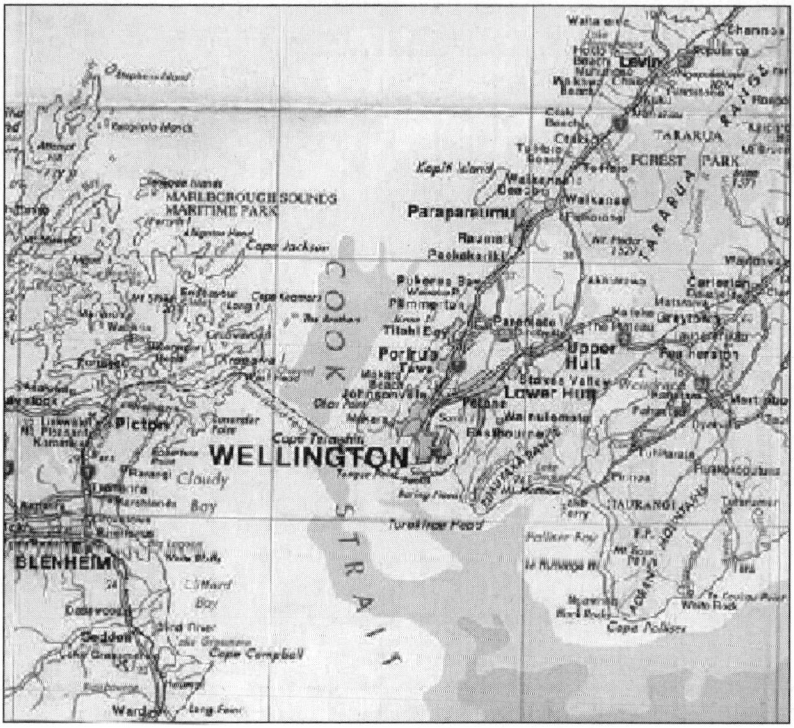

With the high proportion of knowledge and information-intensive businesses in Wellington, there was considerable scope for the infusion of computers and communications technologies. In Naylor's view, Wellington firms would prosper if inhibitors to business were removed, and business functions and processes were made to work better. These were the key principles underlying the Info City strategy.

WELLINGTON CITY COUNCIL

The government of Wellington City was headed by a mayor and an 18-member city council. One of New Zealand's largest local authorities, it managed a budget of about $200 million (including council-owned companies). The council placed special emphasis on the future growth and development of the city. An organization chart for the city government is shown in Exhibit 5. Corporate services included strategic planning function, financial, human resources and other such services. The Commissioning Department included Economic Commissioning, Social & Cultural Commissioning, and Physical, Urban and Natural

EXHIBIT 3a   Wellington Employment Patterns by Industry

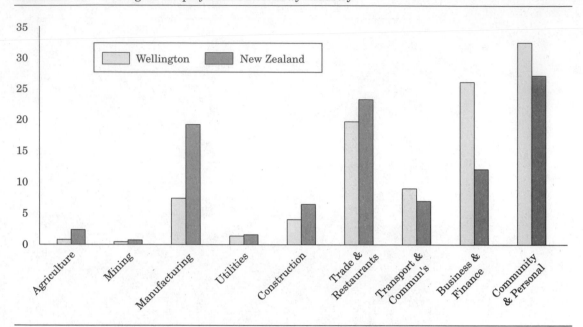

EXHIBIT 3b   Wellington Employment Patterns by Business Sector

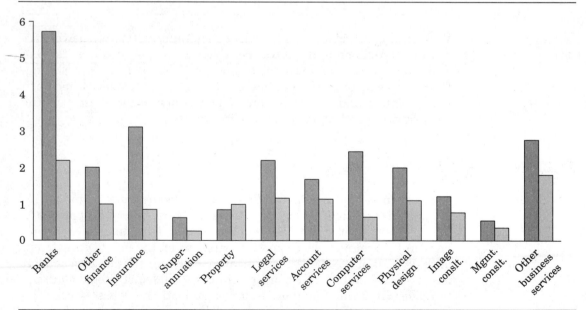

EXHIBIT 4   Functional Analysis of Wellington-Based Companies

A Brief Industry Functional Analysis

Banks and Financial Institutions

Processing of transactions between customers
Lending of money (investment)
Borrowing of money
Researching risks for investment
Communicating with customers

Insurance

Research of investment risk
Managing investments
Communicating with customers

Legal Services

Researching legal framework
Communicating with customers
Conducting legal transactions (cases, registry functions, conveyancing, etc.)

Computer Services

Production of products
Production of services
Communicating with customers

Physical Design Organizations

Conducting design process (computer aided design)
Communicating with customers

EXHIBIT 5   Wellington City Council Organization Chart

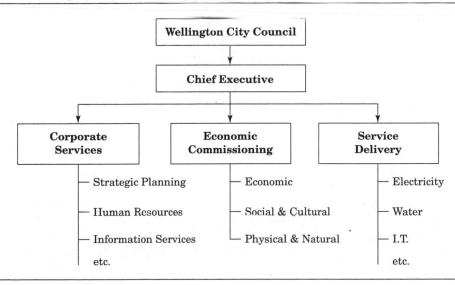

Commissioning. These groups focused on idea generation and policy development, asset management, and contracting for the implementation of policy. The third department was Service Delivery, with subgroups responsible for information technology, public works, and other such public services. A special department within Service Delivery was the Capital Development Agency, which existed to implement various projects designed to advance the growth of Wellington's economy. In effect, the Commissioning groups were the planners and promoters, whereas the Service Delivery groups were the "do-ers."

THE NEW ZEALAND ECONOMY

In years past, New Zealand followed an interventionist government model in which the state played a prominent role—much like the United Kingdom, Canada and other countries. Government grew and grew, taking on progressively more roles. To finance the growing government, taxes were raised and funds were borrowed, both at home and abroad. In the mid-1980s, New Zealand "hit the wall." At one point the flood of money out of the country, as foreign investors withdrew their funds, was so great that the country came very close to bankruptcy.

Since that time, the government had largely reversed its previous strategy. Privatization became the order of the day. Numerous government operations were sold off altogether, and most of the others were "corporatized," becoming "State-Owned Enterprises" (SOEs), charged with providing a positive financial return to the taxpayer. Deregulation occurred throughout the economy. Ironically, the move to deregulation and downsizing of government was led by the Labour party, which earlier had been the party most committed to government intervention in the economy. When the centrist National Party took over running the country in 1990, they continued the push toward deregulation and privatization. By and large the changes worked. Currently, the economy was vibrant, taxes were lower, the annual deficit had been turned into a surplus, total overseas debt was reduced, inflation was close to zero, and the signs of growth and prosperity were seen everywhere.

These improvements did not come without a price. For example, during the economic restructuring of the late 1980s, major changes were made to the structure of the country's health-care providers. Regional Health Authorities (RHAs) were established to manage funding, while many of the providers such as most of the country's hospitals were "corporatized" into Crown Health Enterprises, or CHEs. In recent years, in the urban centres, long waiting times for surgery and other hospital services had become common. At the same time, smaller outlying facilities were losing their specialists because of inadequate demand for their services. A two-tiered health-care insurance system existed, so that people with private coverage were more likely to receive prompt and effective treatment than were those with only public coverage.

One of the businesses that was privatized during the restructuring was New Zealand Telecom, the country's main provider of telephone and telecommunication services. Whereas Telecom had been a government department, and had enjoyed an effective monopoly position in the past, after deregulation it had to compete for business. As Richard Naylor pointed out, "New Zealand telecommunications is deregulated to the degree that almost anyone can establish a communications company and carry any traffic—telephone, television, and beyond."

This resulted in the establishment of new competitors for the traditional suppliers Telecom and TVNZ (the television supplier, also a monopoly prior to deregulation). Two major rivals to Telecom had recently emerged: Clear Communications and Bell South (the New Zealand arm of the U.S.-based company). In principle, these new firms were able, under deregulation, to provide any of the services Telecom provided—including local telephone connections, long distance services, cellular phone services, Internet services, and so forth. In fact, however, Telecom still owned the large majority of local connections to homes and businesses, putting competing companies at a major disadvantage.

Until very recently, New Zealand had almost no installed television cable. All TV signals were provided through the air. However, that too was changing. Kiwi Cable, another growing Telecom competitor, was busily laying communication cable for television, starting in the Kapiti Coast region about 30 kilometers north of Wellington. Kiwi Cable also had its eye on the lucrative telephony market. Once it had its cable in place, it could be used to provide both telephone and cable TV services to subscribers.

While trends toward deregulation were occurring elsewhere as well, New Zealand was well ahead of much of the rest of the world in this regard.

New Zealand was quite advanced in certain aspects of telecommunications. For example, cellular phone usage in New Zealand was among the highest in the world; only Hong Kong had a higher level of usage of this technology. New Zealand's computerized banking services were also quite advanced. For example, the banks cooperated to provide a very well developed debit-card network. A debit card was a simple mechanism for electronically paying for a good or service, by directing an immediate transfer of funds from the purchaser's account to that of the vendor. Whereas many other countries such as the U.S. and Canada were still in the late prototyping stage of debit card adoption, in New Zealand one could, and usually did, purchase everything from chocolate bars to automobiles using debit cards. Even the smallest one-person corner stores (called "dairies" in New Zealand) provided EFT-POS[2] access. And plans were in place to convert the New Zealand EFT-POS cards to "smart cards" soon.

Other factors were also at play, influencing the economy of the country and, in particular, the City of Wellington. Richard Naylor summarized these as follows:

- movement towards a "learning society," where an individual's skills require frequent updating and refreshing;
- the emergence of rough and unruly forces in the global marketplace;
- a period of positioning by telecommunications suppliers internationally, waiting for technology and regulatory frameworks to settle;
- convergence of several technologies into a common digital format;
- removal of regulatory barriers between telecommunication technologies.

RICHARD NAYLOR

Richard Naylor was born and raised in Wellington. He studied engineering at Canterbury University in Christchurch, and after graduating with a degree in electrical engineering in 1976, moved to the UK to work for London Electricity, the electrical public utility. There he learned a great deal about designing and installing power cabling within a city environment.

After returning to Wellington, Naylor continued working in the electrical utility area. However, he found that he was frequently seconded to work on the utility's computer systems, which was how he first learned about computers and information technology. Various operations within the City of Wellington were becoming more computerized, and even though Naylor didn't work directly for the City in those days (rather, for the city-owned electric utility company), he found himself being called on by the City Council for his expertise. This eventually led to his taking the position of Director of Information Systems for the City in 1986.

When Naylor assumed the position of IS Director, the City had 15 systems staff altogether, to build, operate and maintain the city's computer systems. At that time the city only had 15 terminals, and a few transaction and information systems operating. By 1990, staff had grown to nearly 70 people, and the city had about 1,000 terminals in use. Naylor commented:

That was about the end of the "acceleration" phase. At that time, the "control" stage kicked in, people started accusing me of having too big a budget.

---

[2]EFT-POS, short for "Electronic Funds Transfer at Point of Sale," was the New Zealand label for a debit card.

Downsizing was happening all throughout the public service, and we were no exception.

Naylor described an incident that occurred prior to his joining the city's IS group:

Back when I worked for the electricity board, I would see people—lawyers, real estate people—come in to our office and stand in line, to request various bits of information that were stored on our computers. So we'd call up the data they needed, print it off on a simple teletype printer, tear off the paper and hand it to them, and out they'd go. I thought at the time, it's dumb for them to come in here when we could have set things up so that someone like that could just dial in and get the same information on their own. Then, a short time after I started working for the city, I had an opportunity to buy some modems. I really only needed eight modems for my own IT staff, but instead I bought 24: eight for my staff, eight for city councillors, and eight for the general public. Of course, neither the councillors nor the public knew they needed them yet, but I figured they would soon enough.

CITY NET

It didn't take long for some technically knowledgeable people in the city to discover that Naylor had created a rudimentary public dial-in capability for connecting to its computers. These people would want to know whether they could get connected, and if so, what could they do?

It was out of this initial low level of activity that the concept of providing general network access to various parties—IT staff, city councillors, and the general public—emerged. Naylor pointed out that they were originally going to name the facility Council Net, but then he felt that that might be too narrow a name, implying that it would be restricted to the Council. Instead Naylor decided to name the fledgling network City Net.

Naylor viewed the role a city government could play in fostering the use of IT in terms of two different models: a "community pull" model and a "community push" model. The community pull model, often seen in the U.S.,

is based on the development of a network from the community itself. Typically a number of community activists will group together, and form an organizing committee. This committee will then seek funding from sponsors and start a network for the citizens of a particular area. . . . The committee will seek to involve its local city or town council, in order to get funding and information resources (content such as bylaws) made available. They will also try to get the council to use the network for communicating with its community (e.g., letters to the mayor).

In contrast, Naylor viewed a "community push" model as more typical of Australasian countries.

In Australia and New Zealand, the impetus to develop community networks has largely come from city councils. Often a council gets involved in a community network for reasons of economic development. Rarely is it developed to make council information available to the citizens. Rather, the primary motive is usually to help local businesses communicate or gain access to resources faster, and so become more efficient or effective. The second reason is to help create a new marketplace for local businesses—typically, an electronic marketplace.

Initially, City Net's primary purpose was to facilitate the work of the City Council in its day-to-day operations, and was available only to City Council members and certain city employees. In order to create the physical network, it was necessary to wire together the various buildings used by city government employees. Fortunately, many of these buildings were located near each other in the downtown area. Drawing on his experience in the electric utility business, Naylor oversaw the stringing of fibre-optic cable—a relatively new communications technology at the time—between buildings. The cable was hung over the street, suspended above the trolley bus cables. Fibre was eventually used to link seven different buildings in an extended local area network, owned and operated by WCC.

In the first few years, the network provided just a few simple capabilities for a limited number of dial-in users, mostly city employees, including basic electronic mail and an electronic bulletin board system. Some Usenet news groups were added in 1989. More news groups and other Internet services began to be made available in 1990. In 1992, with the support of Victoria University, Wellington City Council (WCC) decided to provide open public access to their network. A manual was prepared by a student volunteer, and distributed around the numerous bulletin board systems in the city. Together with word of mouth and a small newspaper article, City Net was officially launched in the community.

In 1992, City Net provided five types of facilities for its users:

- electronic mail
- file transfer over the Internet via the FTP protocol
- telnet service (allowing direct log-in connections to remote computers through the Internet)
- usenet news (the Internet-based bulletin board system)
- Internet relay chat (which allowed real-time typed "conversations" over the Internet)

The initial services were well received, in fact too well: FTP and telnet services had to be withdrawn after 12 months because of excessive network traffic. However, other services were also added, including Archie (a file locator facility) and gopher (an Internet navigational and browsing system). The number of users registered to use City Net grew by approximately 100 per month, based solely on word of mouth.

In addition to providing a gopher client through City Net, WCC also established, at the end of 1992, a gopher server.[3] As Naylor pointed out,

> Gopher is an ideal system for a government organization which is typically rich in textual information such as legislation, policies, etc. WCC found gopher, together with WAIS indexing, to be an ideal system for both internal and external distribution of information.

Initially, the City's basic bylaws were put on the gopher server. Later, as time and staff resources permitted, other documents—such as minutes of committee and council meetings, district plans, standing orders, and councillors' profiles—were added.

City Net began with only eight modems available for the public to use. That number grew somewhat over time, but there were never enough modems. Frequently, public users would get a busy signal when trying to connect into the network during peak usage times. As City Net grew, users from other walks of life discovered and started using it. The second wave of users included teachers, librarians, and parents. Commercial organizations also began discovering that they could use City Net for developing their businesses. By 1995, City Net had over 3,000 registered users (although the actual number of users at any one time was quite limited because of the limited number of modems available).

The advent of the gopher server in late 1992 began to make clear the important difference between access and content in a public network such as City Net. The dial-in modems and community-based computers constituted the technology that provided citizens *access* to the network. The actual information, most of which was stored on the city's gopher server initially, constituted the primary *content*. By 1995, the World Wide Web was becoming the information access vehicle of choice on the Internet. City Net, therefore, changed its access mechanism by establishing a World Wide Web (WWW) server to replace the older gopher server.

With the increased level of usage have come certain "behavior" problems, for example, incidents of abusive language. A policy of barring such users for a cool-down period was implemented to try to deal with the problem. However, that approach was thwarted by the self-registration procedure that had been put in place to speed the process of registering new users. It was difficult to enforce the cool-down

---

[3]In a networked computer environment it is common to distinguish between "clients" and "servers." A client is a program that a user of a computing service employs to access the service—for example, to access the information stored on a computer database somewhere. A server is a program that an organization may use to provide data or information to users—to set up and manage the database. Clients and servers work together to constitute a complete networked information system.

period when a user could re-register under an assumed name in a matter of minutes. However, the self-registration policy itself turned out to be problematic, when it was discovered that 90 percent of new registrations were being received from people in Canada! As Naylor put it,

> Clearly, work is needed to identify the target user base of City Net, and the role of external users.

2020 VISION AND THE INFO CITY PROJECT

In 1994, Wellington City Council engaged in a strategic planning process for the first time. This process led to the creation of 2020 Vision, a long-term vision for the city's development. The 2020 Vision was an attempt by the WCC to sketch out what they would like Wellington to be like 25 years in the future—i.e., the year 2020:

> We're talking about creating a smart "info city" with an innovative and re- sponsive economy. A city of opportunities for all people to achieve their po- tential, and contribute to the community. A city where today's actions take account of tomorrow's consequences. Creative partnerships between busi- ness and community.

A central component of the 2020 Vision was the Info City project. Info City, an outgrowth of the original City Net effort, was really a basket of separate projects and initiatives, developed under the auspices of the Wellington City Council, with substantial community input and in- volvement. The underlying driver for the Info City project was the recog- nition that Wellington should embrace the concept of an "information- rich society." The Info City mission was:

> to create an infrastructure that encourages the development of a wide range of advanced telecommunications products and services that can be delivered to, accessed by, and used by all Wellington residents, businesses, and the global community.

Info City objectives included:

- to accelerate the normal processes for economic development
- to create a new "frontier" for business and community development
- to enhance the achievement of social and community development principles in the adoption of emerging technologies
- to ensure environmentally responsible deployment of new technologies.

In striving to achieve these objectives, the City Council's 2020 Vision established certain principles to be followed. Access should be provided to all potential customers and service providers; access should be fully open: the technology should conform to developing international standards rather than a closed proprietary system; the cost of the access should be kept low, for both customers and service providers; the technical designs should allow future developments; and the facilities developed under Info City should not be capturable by any one company or monopolistic group.

Richard Naylor stepped down from his position as IS Director for WCC in 1993. Soon thereafter he moved over to the Economic Commissioning group, to direct all his energies to the Info City project. Naylor teamed up with Charles Bagnall, who also worked for the Economic Commissioning group, and who had been named the Project Coordinator for Info City.

Naylor:

> What are we trying to do here with Info City? Basically, our role is to use information technology as a kind of common ground for bringing interested parties together. If you can get the infrastructure in place, get the conditions right, and get the right people together, someone soon says, "Hey, we could work together to do such-and-such." Volcano-cam is a good example. I've already had a number of commercial enquiries about how we did that. . . .

Volcano-cam was a small project undertaken by Naylor and some staff members at nearby Victoria University. When the Ruapehu volcano in central New Zealand erupted in September 1995, it was big news for vulcanologists and interested observers around the world. Volcano-cam was an effort to bring Ruapehu onto the computer screens of anyone with access to the World Wide Web (WWW). A camera was set up in a building on the mountainside, with a clear view of the volcano cone. The "feed" from the camera was channelled to a computer at the university, digitized and used to update, once a minute, the image shown on the Ruapehu WWW page maintained by the university (see Exhibit 6). That way, anyone anywhere with access to the WWW could literally watch Ruapehu in near-real-time, waiting for its next eruption. In Naylor's mind, volcano-cam was a perfect example of how the emerging world of information digitization could prompt new, interesting projects that people would want to access and use.

> The hype about the information highway and 500 "channels" is really misplaced . . . it's not 500, it's more like five million, but they're not channels in the television sense. Rather, they're "things," new ways of getting at and using information. Storing files to be able to access them at the time you want, or global events that you want to see happening in real time. Why couldn't we use the technique of volcano-cam, but simply set up cameras aiming at certain busy highways, so people could check the state of the highway through the Internet before they leave for work? Virtual holidays are another example. New Zealand might be able to increase its tourism trade by creating on-line holiday sights and sounds to show off the best of what the country has to offer.

EXHIBIT 6 Volcano-Cam Image

SPECIFIC INFO CITY INITIATIVES

Operationally, the Info City project was structured as a set of specific sub-projects, i.e., delineated areas of activity. In late 1995, there were eight such sub-projects:

1. **Strategy Development** Continue the development of the Info City strategy, with the long-term goal of encouraging economic development in the City.
2. **Community Net** Lead the development of a community-based network in Wellington (i.e., City Net).
3. **Capital Directory** Develop an electronic directory of businesses and services in Wellington, together with a platform for the development of new marketplaces and services.

EXHIBIT 7   Info City Initiatives

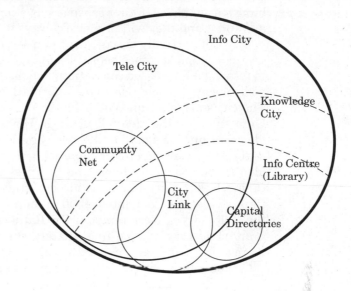

4. **Tele City**[4]   Assess the viability of providing broadband telecom-munications access to every household in Wellington.
5. **Info Centre**   Educate the public in the use of information and communication technologies by applying appropriate technologies to allow access to the Public Library network.
6. **Knowledge City**   Investigate the deployment of information technologies to support the Wellington-area schools and educational institutions.
7. **City Link**   Create a broadband city-area network in the downtown area.
8. **Corporate Response**   Promote the Info City vision within City Council, and encourage city departments to utilize the ideas and approaches of Info City.

Naylor envisioned the various Info City initiatives as a collection of overlapping activities, as shown in Exhibit 7.

THE CITY LINK INITIATIVE

City Link was one of the initiatives comprising the Info City strategy. The idea underlying City Link was simple: connect all the businesses in downtown Wellington with broadband fibre-optic cable. In effect,

---

[4]Just recently, the Tele City initiative had been merged with the City Link project.

"wire up the businesses in the City of Wellington." This initiative did not specify exactly what the different businesses might do once the cabling was in place. In that sense it was akin to the "Field of Dreams"— a "build it and they will find useful ways to use it" strategy.

City Link actually emerged out of a larger concept, called Tele City, begun a couple of years before. Bagnall, Naylor, and some others tried to interest a U.S.-based consortium in using Wellington as a kind of test bed for one of their "National Information Infrastructure"[5] projects. The city's mayor, Fran Wilde, flew to Washington to promote the idea. Unfortunately, the idea fell through. However, work on the Tele City idea continued. Bagnall and Naylor brought together a few companies in the computing and telecommunications industries to investigate the idea of "wiring" every home and business in the city with fibre cable themselves. A consultant was hired, a study commissioned, and an estimated cost was calculated: $300 million! That was enough to sideline the Tele City project temporarily. Rather than actively pursue the grand Tele City scheme immediately, the focus shifted to a smaller, more manageable (and much less expensive) idea: City Link.

Once in place, City Link would comprise a "city area network." Such networks were mid-way in scale between more localized local-area networks (typically within a single building) and the wide-area networks that often span multiple cities or entire countries. The concept of a city-area network was not new. Other cities, e.g., Boulder, Colorado, in the U.S., had experimented with such networks in recent years as well.

It quickly became clear to some members of the City Council that the City Link initiative would probably not go very far without significant involvement from the private sector. With little fanfare, a number of interested organizations were approached, and late in 1995 a company, Capital Network Holdings Limited (CNH), was formed with 16 member firms (one more was added a short time later). The initial CNH member companies included Trust Bank New Zealand, whose representative, Alan Dempster, served as the Chairman of the CNH Board of Directors—in part because Trust Bank was one of the few relatively neutral member companies. Many of the others were major players in industries such as telecommunications; the City Link network, once in place, could be a market opportunity for their products or services.

Dempster viewed the Info City project in terms of "community empowerment." He had seen the idea work, in his home town:

> I was born and raised in Glasgow, Scotland. When I left in 1972, Glasgow was a downtrodden, bleak place. It had lost its main industries, seemed to have no future. Everyone was negative. Then a few years later the city began working on a scheme to try to change people's self-esteem, city-wide. They

---

[5]The National Information Infrastructure, or NII, was the outgrowth of Vice President Al Gore's active sponsorship of the concept of an "information superhighway" in the United States.

mounted a campaign, by taking the city's old slogan "Glasgow's Miles Better," and turning it into "Glasgow Smiles Better." From then on, everything was targeted toward improving the self-esteem and empowering the community to improve itself. For example, the city provided incentives to clean the faces of the buildings. When the grime of centuries was sandblasted away, many of the buildings emerged with a beautiful deep sandstone colour. Lots of little things like that. Today Glasgow is thriving again, with a modern industrial base, excellent shopping, arts, theatre. . . . When I went back in 1990 I couldn't believe the changes.

In Dempster's view, the same sort of thing was taking place in Wellington.

A lot of things have come together in Wellington recently to make the city a much better place. "Absolutely Positively Wellington"[6] is Wellington's version of Glasgow Smiles Better. The change in the political scene in New Zealand has helped, by forcing people to stop depending on government for everything. Also, other less obvious things such as changes in earthquake regulations. In the early '80s, the city's mayor, Michael Fowler, tightened the building regulations regarding ability to withstand earthquakes. This led to a large number of old, poorly maintained buildings being torn down in a short time. This, in turn, has given rise to tremendous architectural renewal.

When I first heard about the City Link idea, I felt that it was very consistent with my own personal values, and with those of the bank. I'm not very keen on handouts, but I do believe in providing information and tools for people, then letting them do the job. That is the essence of community empowerment. Also, Trust Bank has a long history of strong community involvement. Last year the bank returned over $40 million to the communities it services, through involvement with such things as the arts, sporting activities, education, and the like. I see the Info City concept as a very positive form of community empowerment. I believe in it, and have seen it work wonders.

Dempster also saw a potential future business role for Trust Bank on the City Net network:

As well as empowering the community, I see City Link as being a way of getting electronic banking services out to the people of Wellington. Getting people to accept new ways of doing things, such as banking electronically, is a major challenge for us all. It requires cultural change on a large scale. I think City Link can play an important role in that.

Dempster pointed out that the Board of Directors of Capital Network Holdings Ltd. was a "working board." Board members themselves were called upon to perform specific tasks for the new company: administrative work, legal work, obtaining agreements, and so forth. Getting agreements to install the cable was one area of concern for the company. They would need access to such items as power poles, owned by

---

[6]"Absolutely Positively Wellington" is the promotional icon adopted by the City Council to promote the city. It is used on everything from T-shirts to billboards to brochures and maps provided through the WCC.

Capital Power, the city electricity company.[7] Naylor recognized that they might also be able to use the city's trolley bus poles and wires as a way of stringing the fibre cable. However, the trolley buses were scheduled to be phased out in the future, and the manager of the company that operated the trolley buses was reluctant to cooperate with CNH by allowing them to string their cable on his poles. Naylor knew he would have to secure an agreement with the trolley bus company manager somehow, but wasn't sure how.

CHALLENGES AHEAD

Naylor and Bagnall commented on some of the other challenges they saw ahead as they attempted to move the overall Info City—including City Link—project along. One question they frequently faced was, wasn't the idea of stringing fibre throughout the city too technically difficult for the City Council to undertake? Wasn't a great deal of special technical expertise required? John Heard, an executive with SolNet, a New Zealand–based provider of Sun Microsystems computers and services and a member of the City Link group, commented:

> There's a lot of scaremongering in the industry from some of the vendors . . . "you have to do this, you have to buy all these bits before you can do that." If you cut through all the rubbish, you find that you can do some things *very* cost effectively, very elegantly.

Naylor agreed with Alan Dempster about the difficulty of getting people to think differently about doing their work. Naylor said,

> Take the library, for example. We need to change how they think. They still think in terms of paper books. We arranged for them to put up an information kiosk, but it didn't last long. They had a strategic review and decided to use their resources to acquire more books. Or take the banks. Why do they still mail me my bank statement? Why can't they send it to me by email? How do we get the bank teller, or manager, to understand that? Our role here is to facilitate that sort of change in thinking. These sorts of steps can develop great momentum, create whole new markets. We can see a whole refurbishing of the city, based around information technology. However, it's not hard to construct future scenarios; the hard part is getting people to buy in, and to get companies to come together and pay for it themselves.

In Naylor's view, key success factors of the overall Info City strategy included the need for recognition of a basic "paradigm shift," for leadership, for infrastructure, and for partners.

The paradigm shift, moving from old to new ways of doing things, could be supported in many ways. Education would clearly be impor-

---

[7]Capital Power was 51% owned by the WCC, although the Council had been actively exploring the idea of selling some or all of its shares.

tant. Fostering a sense of pride and commitment in new accomplishments would also be important. Experiencing the benefits of the new approaches would also be critical to making the shift. But Naylor felt they couldn't wait forever for the paradigm shift to take hold in people's minds. The world was changing quickly, and Wellington had to keep up—or, even better, stay at the leading edge.

In terms of leadership, he felt that this could be best demonstrated by the visible and active promotion and use of information technologies by the city government as a whole, and especially by City Council. "Product champions" for various IT efforts were required. Much of this was dependent on the quality of the individuals involved, and their willingness to embrace new ways of doing things. "How many CEOs have their email addresses on their business cards—or their WWW home pages? If they haven't made the paradigm shift in their own lives, how can they tell you how to do so in yours?"

Development of the Info City infrastructure would necessitate various technical as well as human decisions. Naylor felt that critical factors included ease of access (e.g., via PCS in libraries, coffee shops, municipal offices, as well as homes), human interface (how easy is it to use on the screen?), content (what is really "in there"?), applications (what can you actually do with it?), and overall management (reliability, quality support, etc.).

Finally, partners would be required for Wellington to see the fruition of the Info City concept: world-class technology providers, user organizations willing to work with the city, and generally, partners who would share in the common purpose of developing the city.

Alan Dempster's view of the challenges was somewhat more pragmatic. He felt the City Link project was badly underfunded. The initial capitalization for the project was about $100,000—peanuts when compared to the estimate of $300 million needed to wire up the entire city. As Dempster said, "if you were a telecommunications company, you'd be planning on putting millions of dollars into something like this."

Dempster also saw the need for a careful balancing act between the commercial interests of many of the CNH partner companies and the guiding philosophy of City Link itself.

> CNH is not really profit-driven. We have to make a modest profit of course, but that's not the overriding objective. But the partner companies are mostly bottom-line oriented. Also, all CNH wants to do is sell access to the wire—i.e., provide cheap, high bandwidth basic access to anyone who wants to connect. We're not in the business of providing services on top of the basic access. But most of our member companies *are* in that business. So it's a balancing act.

In Dempster's mind, City Link presented a "classic chicken and egg" problem. "How do we get started doing the cabling until we have some subscribers willing to pay? But nobody wants to subscribe until the infrastructure is in place."

Finally, everyone knew that time was passing quickly, and the possibility was growing of a private sector firm beating CNH to the punch. One such firm was known to be installing cable in parts of the city already.

Due to its location just to the west of the international date line, Wellington was literally "the first capital city to see the light." As he thought about the progress they had made on Info City to date, and dreamed about where they would go next, Richard Naylor smiled at the double entendre.

CERNET: *Managing Internet Growth in China*

By Professor Michael Parent and Harvey Enns

In late April 1997, Dr. Wu Jianping, a Full Professor at Tsinghua University in Beijing, China, and also director of the Technical Board and director of the Network Centre for the China Education and Research Network (CERNET), reflected on the recent announcement that CERNET had expanded. It had been connected to the Hong Kong Academic and Research Network (HARNET) since November 1996 through a dedicated 64Kbps leased line. While this milestone brought CERNET even closer to its long-term vision of "[becoming] the world's largest national education and research computer network,"[1] many challenges lay ahead. First, there was the ongoing expansion of the network. CERNET had been linked to the United States since July 1995 through Sprint Corporation's 128Kbps SprintLink®. The Technical Committee was considering either expanding its capacity, or adding a second connection. Wu was also considering expanding the network to Germany, to connect with that country's Deutsche Foundation Network. Finally, Wu was faced with continuing to grow domestic reach, capacity, and speed. Of equal importance was management of this growing network. Wu faced the challenge of optimizing network performance, preventing abuses and security breaches, and managing resources in a way that minimized waste.

---

[1]CERNET internal document.

COUNTRY BACKGROUND[2]

China was physically the world's third largest country, after Russia and Canada. Its population of over 1.17 billion (July 1993 estimate), growing at a rate of 1.1 per cent annually, made it the largest in terms of population size.

Prior to economic reforms that began in the late 1970s, China's economy followed a Communist, Soviet-style, centrally planned model. Slow economic growth in part prompted the country's leadership to move to a more productive and flexible economy with market elements, but still within the framework of Communist control. To this end, in 1978, the government switched to a system of household responsibility in agriculture in place of the old collectivization, and increased the authority of local industry officials, permitting small-scale enterprise. Authorities also opened the country to increased foreign trade and joint ventures. As a result, there were strong growth spurts in production, particularly in agriculture, in the early 1980s. Industry also posted major gains, especially in coastal areas near Hong Kong and Taiwan.

Aggregate output had more than doubled since 1978, and China's foreign trade had outperformed the world average by a factor of more than two. China's imports grew from about US$12 billion in 1978 to more than US$132 billion by the end of 1995. In the same time frame, its exports grew from under US$10 billion to US$149 billion.

The central government in Beijing exercised a dominant role in economic leadership and in setting priorities. For example, China still remained a highly protected market, with a number of non-tariff and administrative barriers in place. However, with its 23 provinces, five autonomous regions, three municipalities, and the 1997 reacquisition of Hong Kong as a special administrative region, China should also be viewed as a collection of distinct regional markets differentiated by geography, culture and dialects, economic structure, level of development and growth prospects.

Exhibit 1 shows a map of China and its provinces.

The Canadian Government's Department of Foreign Affairs and International Trade divided the country into six distinct regions:[3]

- **Northeast China** (Heilongjiang, Jilin, and Liaoning provinces)
- **Greater Beijing** (Hebei, Beijing, Tianjin and Shandong)

---

[2]Sources: CIA World Factbook Online and *CanadExport: Focus on China,* March 17, 1997, Ottawa: Government of Canada, Department of Foreign Affairs and International Trade.

[3]Ibid., p. II.

EXHIBIT 1 Map of China

1. Beijing	12. Jiangxi	23. Guizhou
2. Tianjin	13. Shandong	24. Yunnan
3. Hebei	14. Henan	25. Xizang
4. Shanxi	15. Neimenggu	26. Shaanxi
5. Liaoning	16. Heilongjiang	27. Gansu
6. Jilin	17. Hubei	28. Qinghai
7. Shanghai	18. Hunan	29. Ningxia
8. Jiangsu	19. Guangdong	30. Xinjiang
9. Zhejiang	20. Guangxi	31. Taiwan
10. Anhui	21. Hainan	32. Chongqing
11. Fujian	22. Sichuan	33. Hong Kong

Source: http://www.edu.cn/china/index.html, June 1997.

- **Central Provinces** (Shaanxi, Henan, Hubei, Anhui, Hunan, and Jiangxi)
- **Southwest China** (Sichuan)
- **Greater Shanghai** (Shanghai, Jiangsu, and Zhejiang)
- **South China** (Guangdong, Fujian, and Hainan)

On the flip side of moving the country to a part-market economy, the leadership often experienced in its hybrid system the worst results of socialism (bureaucracy, lassitude, corruption) and of capitalism (windfall gains and stepped-up inflation). The high rates of economic growth led to problems with inflation. Real GDP growth fell from 11 per cent in 1994 to 10.3 per cent in the first half of 1995. As a result, Beijing had periodically backtracked, retightening central controls at intervals.

TELECOMMUNICATIONS IN ASIA[4]

Since the mid-to-late 1980s, there had been a growing trend towards privatization[5] of telecommunications in Asia. Economies that in the past considered themselves self-reliant, like India and China, were forced by the rapid pace of global telecommunications growth to become more open in their trade and investment policies and to forge joint ventures in order to compete in a global market. The many socialist oriented five-year plans which formed the bases of economic policies had to be abandoned under the driving forces of technology and growing consumer demand.

Exhibit 2 shows the extent to which Asian-Pacific countries have privatized their telecommunications.

Though Asian countries needed foreign direct investment in order to expand their public networks, this need for capital versus the need to develop an indigent capacity in telecommunications created a tension between the governments, labor unions, and telecommunications equipment providers.

Table 1, below, illustrates this tension in terms of four key drivers for PSTN privatization.[6] A fiscal crisis (stagflation, devaluation), as in Malaysia, can prompt the government of the day to seek either foreign aid or investment, albeit sometimes reluctantly. Alternatively, private capital, as in Hong Kong, might be available for network upgrades. Lastly, high teledensity, or the number of network telephone lines per 100 inhabitants, might precipitate a crisis which can only be resolved through network expansion.

---

[4]Sources: *Telecommunications in Asia: Transition* newsletter, The World Bank, v. 7, no. 11–12, Nov.–Dec. 1996; TeleGeography® 1996/97, Washington, DC: TeleGeography Inc.

[5]In this case, privatization refers to private, mostly foreign capital brought into the Public Switched Telephone Network (PSTN), and likely to lead to an extension of private control over part or all of the PSTN, including private networks which bypass the PSTN.

[6]Source:*Telecommunications in Asia.*

EXHIBIT 2   Telecommunications Sector Reform and Privatization in Asia-Pacific

Japan	Privatization of PSTN in the 1980s; domestic market liberalized; three international carriers.

Four Dragons

Hong Kong	Four private PSTN operators since 1995; four cellular operators and seven licences; international nonvoice traffic liberalized.
Singapore	Partial privatization 1993; two cellular licences awarded.
South Korea	VANS liberalized from 1985; two international carriers since 1990; cellular competition since 1996; partial privatization of PSTN planned.
Taiwan	Liberalization reform agreed 1996; cellular licenses to be awarded; partial privatization of PSTN planned.

Southeast Asia

Indonesia	Partial privatization 1994, 1995; liberalization on a joint-operating basis 1996.
Malaysia	Partial privatization of PSTN 1990; liberalization of VANS.
Philippines	Liberalization of private PSTN and VANS 1994.
Thailand	Privatization under policy review.

South Asia

India	Partial privatization of international traffic, liberalization of cellular in 1995 and of local PSTN 1996.
Pakistan	Partial privatization 1994.
Bangladesh	Partial liberalization of rural PSTN.
Sri Lanka	Partial privatization 1992.

China and Indochina

China	State-controlled local competition since 1994. Public offering planned for PSTN.
Vietnam	Business cooperation contracts with foreign companies.
Burma	No reform to date.
Cambodia	State joint-venture concessions to foreign companies.
Laos	State joint-venture concessions to foreign companies.

Pacific Islands

Fiji	Public offering planned for PSTN. International traffic state joint venture.
Solomon Islands	Cable and wireless traffic state joint venture.
Vanuatu	Cable and radio state joint venture.
Australia	Liberalization in 1992.
New Zealand	Liberalization in 1990.

Source: *Telecommunications in Asia.*

TABLE 1   Matrix of PSTN Privatization Drivers

Driver	Govt.	Unions	Manufacturers
Fiscal crisis	−/+	−	+
Private capital	+	−	+
Teledensity	−/+	−	−/+

TELECOMMUNICATIONS IN CHINA

Telecommunication in China was a state-owned enterprise, with the Ministry for Posts and Telecommunications (MPT) retaining responsibility.

Before economic reform and privatization, China's telecommunications revenues did not come from products or services, but from government subsidies. As a result, any budget shortfalls left the telecommunications sector starved for funds for expansion. Under the new economic policy, the central and provincial governments were free to negotiate joint ventures for technology transfer and production. Under the Ninth Five-Year Plan, ratified in 1996, investments in the telecommunications sector were to amount to US$100 billion.

During 1994, the Chinese telecommunications sector made three major breakthroughs. The first saw an investment of US$8.5 billion in equipment infrastructure. Secondly, as a result of this investment, 17 million new lines were added on the PSTN. In addition, 4.3 million new pagers, and 900,000 new cellular phones were added, making China the largest market in the world for pagers, with a total of 11 million pagers in use and 1.5 million cellular subscribers. This boosted China Telecom's world revenue ranking to 34th, with long distance revenues of US$382 million.[7]

Since 1993, the telephone sector of China's economy had been growing at a rate of 41.6 per cent annually. In 1990, China had 3.0 telephone lines for every 100 people, or a total of 6.9 million main lines. In 1995, this had grown to a teledensity of 6.9 telephone lines for every 100 people, or a total of 40.7 million main lines. MPT pledged a further US$100 billion to 2000, and intended to increase teledensity to 10 lines for every 100 people, or a total of 100 million main lines.

In 1997, MPT was planning for a global initial public offering of 2.6 billion shares of China Telecom at a value of US$1.49 per share, for a total value of over US$3.8 billion.[8] Of this global issue, 144 million

---

[7]*Communications Week International,* Nov. 27, 1995, p. 17.
[8]*South China Morning Post,* Oct. 16, 1997, B1; *China Daily,* v. 17, no. 5322, Oct. 17, 1997, 1.

shares were floated in Hong Kong, 278 million shares were offered in the United States and Canada in the form of American Deposit Certificates, and 1.8 billion shares were sold in Asian stock markets.

In China, the switching market had always been difficult to enter due to high regulatory and administrative barriers. The government's State Council gave a directive in 1990 to equipment purchasers that only Alcatel of France, NEC of Japan, and Siemens of Germany were to be considered for foreign collaboration. In 1992, this policy was changed to include all suppliers of Stored Program Controlled Switches (SPCs), without mentioning specific vendors. AT&T entered the Chinese market at this point, with a proposal to start a joint venture for the manufacture of switching equipment. Northern Telecom soon followed suit, investing US$150 million.

Despite this entry, the primary domestic supplier of Central Office Switches (COSs) remained a joint venture between MPT and Alcatel. The largest market share of 30 per cent for SPC switches in 1995 was enjoyed by Alcatel, followed by Ericsson. The major domestic competitor was Shanghai Bell (in collaboration with ITT Belgium).

The government's goal was, by 2000, to increase foreign direct investment in the telecommunications sector to US$7 billion, from US$4.7 billion in 1993.

CERNET: THE CHINA EDUCATION AND RESEARCH NETWORK

Background

At the end of 1993 and the beginning of 1994, the Chinese government was interested, along with other developing nations, in creating a country-wide academic information network that would also connect China to other parts of the world via the Internet. As Professor Wu, CERNET's eventual director of the Network Centre, stated, "China needed a nation-wide network backbone and there was country-wide demand to connect to the Internet." At the time, there was only one access point to the Internet in China.

A number of competing proposals were presented for the establishment of this national academic network and infrastructure. One of these proposals, called CSTNet (China Science and Technology Network), was backed by the MPT. A competing proposal, the Chinese Education & Research Network (CERNET), was backed by the State Education Commission (SEC). The SEC was a much larger organization than MPT, since it was responsible for overseeing all the universities, high schools, junior high schools, and elementary schools in China. Effectively, the SEC represented approximately one-quarter of China's population.

Negotiations between CERNET and the government's State Planning Commission (SPC) began in January 1994. The SPC managed all government budgets. A formal proposal was submitted in March 1994, and accepted in early July 1994 for two main reasons. First, CERNET, through its affiliation with the SEC, represented a much larger group within the Chinese academic community. Second, there was also representation from every Chinese province. Thus, it was more natural for the SEC-backed CERNET proposal to be accepted by the government because regional network sites could more easily be established.

MPT's CSTNet was eventually established, but only provided one link to the United States, had a few thousand users, and utilized a 64Kbps connection.

After formal approval of CERNET's proposal, the SPC required submission of a report which specified a detailed network design. This detailed network design report was created by Professor Wu and his colleagues at CERNET and was submitted to the SPC in July 1994, shortly after approval.

This technical report was examined and eventually validated by a sub-committee organized by the SPC. The committee consisted of representatives from different areas within the Chinese academic community. The technical report was recommended for approval by this sub-committee, and formally approved for implementation by the SPC on November 14, 1994—CERNET's "anniversary" date, according to Wu.

Given his experience, and his work in putting together the background studies and network design, Wu was appointed the Director of CERNET's Technical Board and Director of CERNET's National Network Center, located in the Main Building at Tsinghua University (see Exhibit 3 for a partial CERNET organizational chart). Professor Wu maintained dual responsibilities as both the Director of Tsinghua's Network Research Center and as a Professor of Computer Science at Tsinghua University.

The CERNET group, headed by Professor Wu, started experimenting with the network's configuration in late 1994. Utilizing the x.25 protocol, eight regional network sites, all located at universities in China, were established and connected to each other and the Internet through a national backbone which communicated at speeds of 64Kbps to 2.048Mbps. These eight regional nodes represented all 30 of China's provinces, with each regional network node representing several provinces. Exhibit 4 outlines the regional networks and which provinces/areas they represented. Four criteria were used to select regional network sites: (1) the number of universities that could be connected to the site, (2) the number of students represented, (3) the economic condition of the university, and (4) the sophistication of the telecommunications infrastructure.

EXHIBIT 3   CERNET Organization Chart

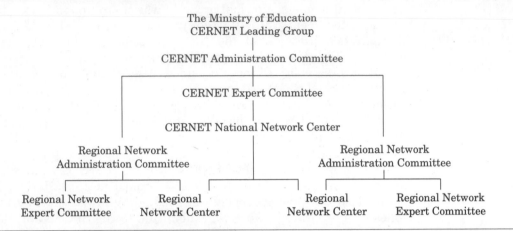

- State Education Commission CERNET Leading Group—CERNET's leading policy-making body at the highest level, consisting of State Education Commission officials concerned.
- CERNET Administration Committee—Made up of State Education Commission officials concerned and vice presidents in charge from the 10 universities, who are responsible for leading the construction of CERNET and making policies for important problems.
- CERNET Expert Committee—Made up of specialists concerned from the 10 universities, who take up full responsibility for such technical tasks as that of general planning and design.
- CERNET National Network Center—Located at Tsinghua, it is responsible for the operation and management of the national backbone and provides users with a variety of services including information resources services and high-performance computing services

---

Source: http://www.edu.cn/cernet/structure/index.html, June 1997.

A web site was created (www.cernet.org), and filled with information about the network, its sites, and connected schools.

By December 1994, CERNET was connected to 108 of China's 1,035 universities and 2,000 continuing education colleges. In December 1996, this number had grown to 198. In October 1997, CERNET connected to 280 campuses.

In July 1995, CERNET implemented its first foreign link, to the United States, using Sprint's 128Kbps SprintLink service.

In November 1996, CERNET linked with the Hong Kong Academic and Research Network (HARNET) through a dedicated 64Kbps leased-line. Plans at the time also included a 64Kbps link to DFN in Germany.

EXHIBIT 4   CERNET Nodes—1994

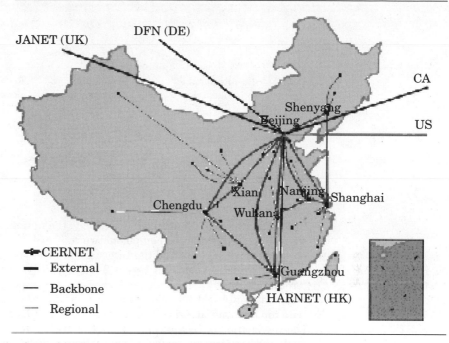

Source: http://www.edu.cn/cernet/structure/index.html, June 1997.

In September 1997, the national backbone was upgraded to 512Kbps service. Because of service upgrades by MPT, part of the network also used satellite links instead of DDNs. Exhibit 5 shows a network diagram. The network was based on a three-level hierarchy, with the national backbone at the top, regional networks in the middle, and campus networks on the bottom. The national backbone was operated and maintained by the National Network Center at Tsinghua University in Beijing. Each regional network was responsible for management of the network center as well as network planning and construction in its specific region. Finally, each university campus connected to the network provided its own administration and services.

EXHIBIT 5   CERNET Network Diagram

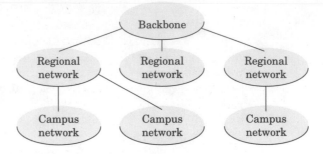

3-Level hierarchy

- CERNET's 3-level Management Hierarchy: the national backbone, the regional networks and the campus network.
- The National Backbone and the International Networking
  - the national backbone topology: a 3-ring topology structure centered round Beijing.
  - the national backbone telecommunication line: the DDN leased line, with its top transmission rate reaching as high as 64 Kbps to 2.048Mbps.
- The International Networking—From the international exit in Beijing, CERNET has already opened up the international telecommunication channel leading to the Internet in the United States, with a transmission rate of 128Kbps to 2Mbps/. It will soon build another two international telecommunication channels leading respectively to HARNET in Hongkong and DFN in Germany.

Source: http://www.edu.cn/cernet/structure/index.html, June 1997.

MANAGING GROWTH

Join the Internet club; meet today's successful people; experience the spirit of the age.

Buy Internet, use Internet. Get on board the ark to the next century.

Internet, the passport of the modern, civilized man.

> Promotional slogans for Chinese modems and Internet access software as quoted by Geremie R. Barmé in "The Great Firewall of China," *Wired*, June 1997, p. 178.

The Chinese government proclaimed 1996 as the "Year of the Internet." Despite the attendant publicity, *Wired* magazine estimated that only 150,000 Chinese, barely one in 10,000, were actually wired. According to a recent survey by the Yangshi Survey and Consulting Service Center, a Beijing marketing firm, 86 per cent of China's citizens had never touched a computer. Furthermore, only 1.6 per cent of Chinese families owned a computer, and just 4.1 per cent planned to buy. Nonetheless, in 1997, 32 Internet Service Providers (ISPs) were conducting business in Beijing. CERNET aimed to increase both access and bandwidth significantly in 1997, and to separate access from computer ownership through public sites at its participating universities.

As director of both CERNET's Technical Board and Network Center, Professor Wu had to deal mostly with managing and expanding the national backbone. He nevertheless had to be cognizant of the Regional Network's plans, capabilities, and constraints. Of special concern were three interrelated performance measures—the network's speed, capacity, and reliability.

The national backbone operated on Dedicated Dialled Network (DDN) lines and satellite links, with transmission rates from 512Kbps to 2.048Mbps (E1 standard). Given the proliferation of applications, sites, and programs available on the Internet, these transmission rates were proving to be slow. As more users logged on simultaneously, not only would transfer rates worsen, but the network would become vulnerable to breaks, noise, interruptions and crashes. Professor Wu had heard that other countries, like Canada, for example, had adopted a T3 standard. Wu wondered if expanded bandwidth might solve capacity and reliability problems, or if this might not just invite more users to do more browsing and work on the Internet, using up excess bandwidth capacity.

Wu was also concerned about abuses of the network. The Chinese for "Hacker" was "Heike," literally "dark stranger." Though Wu was not aware of any attempted hacks on the CERNET network, he had no way of really knowing. Wu wondered what precautions were necessary, and their implications for both those managing and using the network.

Network abuse, however, included more than just hacking. It included overuse, improper use by subscribers, as well as network inefficiencies (e.g., too much storage, too many applications). With nominally three jobs to do (University Professor, two CERNET Directorships), Wu had to determine how much time he would devote to planning for the network versus its ongoing daily administration.

More generally, Wu believed there were a number of major impediments to the development of the Internet in China. He was concerned, inasmuch as one of CERNET's main strategic goals was to promote global connectivity and networking in China in the pursuit of better education. If the Internet did not succeed in China, neither would CERNET.

First, Wu believed that MPT, for all its aggressive development, still needed to do more to develop the Chinese telecommunications infrastructure. Moreover, Wu felt that MPT, by virtue of its monopoly, was lax in offering good quality and service on its connections.

Most important, he felt, was for MPT to price its international circuits, DDN links, and data lines more competitively. For international circuits, MPT charged over three times the fee that other international carriers charged. For example, for an E1 link, most foreign carriers charged about US$25,000 per month. In China, MPT charged over US$80,000 per month.

Within China, MPT's pricing policies precluded quantity discounts. Like most other carriers, MPT counted a single 64Kbps circuit as one unit. MPT differed from its international competitors in that groupings of these circuits were not discounted when it came to high-speed links. For example, in North America, a T1 link of 24 units cost significantly less than the 24 single 64Kbps circuits that would be charged in China.

Thirdly, MPT also charged more for data lines than did most nations. Erroneously calling these lines "trunks," the cost would be nearly three times that of an ordinary telephone line, even though no physical differences existed. Thus, a consumer wanting to connect from home was facing a "trunk" line cost of about US$75 per month, toll charges for each telephone call made, plus monthly Internet Service Provider (ISP) charges. Wu felt that these exorbitant costs significantly impeded the diffusion of the Internet.

Wu realized that he could not resolve all these problems—maybe no one could! He knew, though, that for CERNET to succeed, the Internet needed to grow in China. To a certain extent, the establishment of CERNET had created an awareness among Chinese scholars and students, and fuelled demand for even greater access. CERNET was now in the awkward position of having to respond to the demand it had created. Many unconnected universities and colleges wanted access. Those already on the network wanted greater functionality and speed. Given scarce economic resources, Wu also realized that CERNET could not tolerate waste and inefficiency as it grew. With his many commitments, Wu needed to prioritize, and plan carefully if the success CERNET had enjoyed over the past three years was to continue.

Chapter 4

The ISP Business—Internet Service Providers

Internet service providers are the gatekeepers through which most Internet users access the Internet. This access may be provided through telephone lines, coaxial cable, local or wide area networks, or wireless media. The extent to which ISPs offer services in addition to Internet access varies considerably. Many ISPs provide and manage e-mail accounts, offer space for private web sites, and offer some local content. Some ISPs contract with third-party content providers to offer enhanced content such as news, local weather, stock quotes, and the like. Others still, offer nothing more than a connection to the Internet. Thus, some IPSs are predominantly access providers, while others are predominantly content providers. The first case in this chapter, CanNet is an example of the former; the second case, AOL, is an example of the latter.

It is important that business managers understand ISP business to thoroughly understand the opportunities of Internet electronic commerce. By providing the link between Internet users and the Internet itself, ISPs are placed in an important position as a conduit for Internet commerce. As high bandwidth becomes increasingly easier and cheaper to procure, access to customers may become the battleground for gaining and servicing online customers. The previous chapter addressed the infrastructure through which electronic commerce flows. This chapter examines two cases on the use of Internet technology by ISPs to provide users commercial access to the Internet.

The first case concerns CanNet, a nascent ISP. Two entrepreneurs are considering whether to invest a substantial portion of their personal resources in this company. The recent very rapid growth of the World Wide Web made CanNet an appealing venture for them. CanNet had a number of potential growth opportunities, but they all required an investment of funds, and a significant amount of risk. CanNet had no long range plan at the time the entrepreneurs were examining it. The case deals with the attractiveness of the ISP business as an entrepreneurial venture. Different ISP models are discussed and considered.

By mid-1996, America Online Inc. (AOL) was the world's largest and most successful ISP. The case traces the history leading up to AOL's decision in December 1996 to charge a $19.95 flat-rate, monthly fee for unlimited use of its services. The first set of case issues has to do with AOL's management of online demand and IT supply capacity. The second set concerns the future of the industry and the effectiveness of AOL's strategy to provide value-added content in addition to access services.

CanNet Info Communications Inc.

By Sandy Staples and Lisa Surmon

It was a snowy night in early December 1994, as David Sampson sat at his desk thinking about the meeting he had just come from with CanNet Info Communications Inc. (CanNet), an Internet and electronic bulletin board access provider based in Calgary, Alberta. David and his wife, Lisa, had been searching for a good investment opportunity since their return to Canada from Hong Kong 18 months ago. Their accountant had suggested to them a few weeks previously that CanNet was looking for an investor. Discussions with the company's founder and 50 per cent owner, Bruce Whidden, had confirmed this. David now had to assess the information Bruce had given him, along with information he had gathered himself about CanNet's industry. David and Lisa wanted to decide whether or not to proceed with the deal before Christmas.

COMPANY BACKGROUND

In 1993, Bruce Whidden had established CanNet, a concept which had evolved from some of his previous business ideas. A few years before, he had tried to establish an electronic yellow pages for businesses to advertise to customers using an electronic bulletin board. This didn't work; companies apparently were unwilling to pay for advertising on a bulletin board that did not already have a large, established base of users. At the same time, it was difficult to develop a large user base without having a large number of advertisers represented on the bulletin board. The customers had little incentive to use the electronic yellow pages if few businesses were present. Bruce then opened a retail computer store. About one year ago, he folded up that operation to devote his full attention to CanNet.

CanNet had originally started as a business-oriented bulletin board service (BBS) several years previously. Approximately a year ago, Bruce expanded its services by offering electronic mail (e-mail) access to the Internet for his BBS clients. This was further expanded nine months ago when customers were offered a gateway to the Internet. CanNet currently offered these two basic services to its customers: a local bulletin board service and Internet access.

CANNET SERVICES

Bulletin Board Service

CanNet's bulletin board system contained several gigabytes of programs (freeware or shareware), electronic books, and demos that had been gathered from various sources around the Internet. BDS users were able to access this information and download any programs or files they desired to try out. BBS users were also able to access and contribute to over 5,000 USENET newsgroups. USENET consisted of several thousand topic areas, called newsgroups, with topics ranging from locksmithing to pyrotechnics to religion to C++ computer programming. Users of the newsgroups could choose to subscribe to any of the USENET groups that interested them. Once subscribed, users then received messages and could post messages to the newsgroup for others to read. The last major feature of CanNet's BBS was access to several e-mail systems.

Internet Access

The Internet refers to a global network of computer networks. Access to the Internet can occur at several levels:

1. indirect, electronic-mail-only connection. This gives users an Internet e-mail address without access to any other Internet services.
2. an indirect, e-mail and USENET only connection. This gives users an Internet e-mail address and the ability to participate in USENET newsgroups, but no access to other Internet services.
3. an indirect connection through a "shell" account. This gives users Internet e-mail, access to USENET newsgroups, and character-mode access to Internet services such as Telnet, FTP, Gopher, and Archie.

EXHIBIT 1   Membership and Pricing Structure

Memberships include:
- unlimited e-mail services including e-mail links to the Internet, USENET, City2City, Intelec, Nanet, Ilink, ADAnet, & Ablelink;
- access to CanNet's file Library which held over 12,000 programs, electronic books, demos, program updates, games, drivers, and journals;
- use of the Online Doors and features, like inter-node CHAT, mail doors, USAToday, and online games; and
- free e-mail support and limited voice support.

Annual Membership	*Restrictions*
Basic membership, $80.00	1 hr/2 meg/day
Regular membership, $120.00	2 hr/4 meg/day
Each additional 1 hr/2 meg/day for a year = $40	

Charges for Internet Services

10 hours:	$ 20
25 hours:	$ 40
50 hours:	$ 75
100 hours:	$150
300 hours:	$300

Source: Company brochure.

4. a temporary TCP/IP connection via a modem, using SLIP/PPP. This gives users full Internet access on a temporary, dial-up basis, including access to the World Wide Web (WWW) using graphical Web browsers such as Netscape.
5. a permanent TCP/IP connection. This gives users a permanent, full-access connection to the Internet via a dedicated link to another Internet node.

For more information on the terms used above, see the Internet glossary in Appendix A.

CanNet offered level 2 Internet access to all its subscribers. Level 3 access, giving users Telnet, FTP, Gopher, WHOIS and Finger capabilities, was available to subscribers on an hourly fee basis. Exhibit 1 describes CanNet's memberships and pricing. Exhibit 2 illustrates CanNet's equipment layout.

Customers of CanNet used modems from their own personal computers to communicate over local phone lines to CanNet's Server #1, a 486 DX66 PC with 64 MB RAM and 10.5 gigabytes of hard disk storage. CanNet had a total of 31 modems connected to its system, which meant that, at most, 31 customers could dial in at the same time. Twenty-nine of its modems operated at 14.4 Kbps (kilobits per second) while two operated at 28.8 Kbps. The faster the modem speed, the more

EXHIBIT 2   Equipment Layout

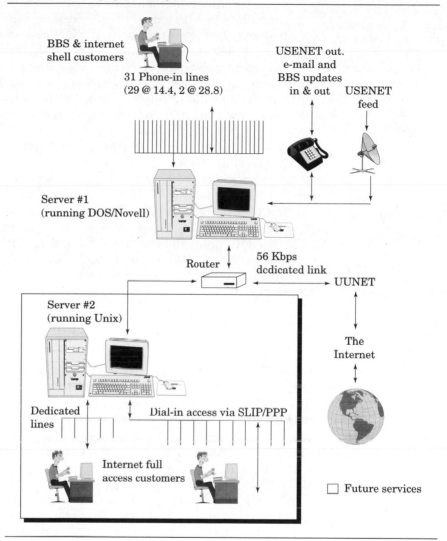

BBS & internet shell customers

31 Phone-in lines
(29 @ 14.4, 2 @ 28.8)

USENET out.
e-mail and
BBS updates
in & out

USENET feed

Server #1
(running DOS/Novell)

Router

56 Kbps
dedicated link

UUNET

Server #2
(running Unix)

The
Internet

Dedicated
lines

Dial-in access via SLIP/PPP

Internet full
access customers

☐ Future services

Source: Company documents.

efficient the line from a user's point of view since he could send more information per second between his computer and CanNet's.

CanNet's Server #1 held CanNet's bulletin board files, along with all its systems software, e-mail systems, customers' accounts, and USENET newsgroup files. The server had three links to the wider Internet:

1. CanNet had a satellite dish on the roof of its office which it used to receive periodic updates of USENET newsgroups. This was a one-way connection (i.e., incoming data only).

2. Server #1 was also hooked up to a modem which used a phone line to access other bulletin boards to update CanNet's bulletin boards, communicate with e-mail systems external to CanNet's, as well as to send outgoing messages to USENET newsgroups. These data exchanges were done periodically, not continuously.

3. The third link was a leased 56 Kbps link to the Calgary node of UUNet, a national Internet access provider. This line had sufficient bandwidth to allow approximately four users to simultaneously download or upload information to the Internet. Plans were underway to upgrade this connection to a T1 link, which would provide 24 times the capacity of the current line (1.544 million bits per second). It was through the connection to UUNet that CanNet customers could directly access the Internet. Because its Internet traffic used some of UUNet's resources, CanNet paid UUNet a fee for this connection. The UUNet connection gave CanNet customers the ability to use Internet standard services such as FTP, Telnet, Gopher, and the World Wide Web. Via Telnet, users could connect to remote computers and access additional Internet services including IRC (Internet Relay Chat), and MUDs (multi-user dungeons).

CUSTOMERS

CanNet's user base had grown approximately four-fold over the past 15 months (see Exhibit 3) and revenues had increased accordingly (see Exhibit 4). The total user base was significantly larger than its paid membership base (approximately 2.5 times larger) since CanNet provided limited time, free trial access to all new users. This promotion mechanism, which was the industry norm for Internet access providers, was necessary to develop awareness among users.

CanNet's membership base had grown largely by word-of-mouth. CanNet's general manager, James Furlong, suggested that CanNet's growth was also due to its excellent customer support. Professional support staff were available from 9 A.M. through midnight, Monday to Friday, for users to call or contact via e-mail. Because either James or Bruce usually provided the support, users had access to knowledgeable, committed staff. New users found this valuable, as they often needed substantial help the first few times they called in order to gain familiarity with the various facilities. However, even experienced users called, often later in the evening, regarding the sourcing of information required for the next business day. Users could access CanNet's services 24 hours per day, seven days per week. The peak usage occurred between 5:00 and 10:00 P.M. on weeknights, with CanNet's system operating at nearly full capacity during those time periods.

EXHIBIT 3   Usage Statistics

Month/Year	Total Calls	User Base	Members	Uploads	Downloads	New Callers	Messages
9/93	5,644	750	250	806	6,023	176	25,000
10/93	6,859	850	319	545	6,314	197	25,000
11/93	9,040	1,050	387	156	6,489	232	30,021
12/93	11,454	1,188	400	281	8,327	312	31,187
1/94	16,530	1,211	478	280	11,529	362	10,494
2/94	19,040	1,415	526	420	14,364	484	81,612
3/94	25,234	1,800	609	346	13,945	385	77,153
4/94	27,000	2,018	587	397	13,642	489	79,623
5/94	27,588	2,082	717	413	14,902	356	82,767
6/94	24,601	2,004	709	645	12,630	235	68,465
7/94	30,601	2,072	729	587	16,532	330	70,124
8/94	30,498	2,341	774	492	17,600	269	62,197
9/94	30,960	2,610	876	513	16,170	408	69,246
10/94	31,123	2,017	924	344	16,575	547	68,421
11/94	35,537	2,549	1,041	297	18,046	537	69,000

Source. Company records.

MARKET AND COMPETITION

Approximately 600,000 potential customers could reach CanNet's dial-in access with a local call to its Calgary office. Given that most of the larger centers in Canada had at least one BBS and/or Internet service provider, few users were willing to call long distance to access a service. Within CanNet's local access area, there were no other organizations offering the same mix of BBS and Internet access. In fact, James had commented that there were perhaps only five firms in North America offering a mix of services comparable to that of CanNet. James also had heard rumors that the two other commercial Internet providers in their area were losing business due to poor service. Both those companies were considerably smaller than CanNet.

David's review of the Canadian Internet Handbook, which provided a fairly comprehensive list of Internet providers across Canada, confirmed that there was little competition in CanNet's area. The only company listed was the one that James believed was shrinking. The fees charged by this competitor were:

- Full Internet Shell Accounts: $45.00 per month
- Electronic Mail/USENET News: $15.00 per month
- UUCP (Unix-to-Unix Copy Protocol) Node: $200.00 plus $15.00 per month

EXHIBIT 4 Income Statement

	Month-to-Date (November)		Previous Quarter (August to October)		Year-to-Date (February to November)	
	$	% Sales	$	% Sales	$	% Sales
Income						
Internet fee revenue	2,877.24	12.1	9,721.99	31.6	16,462.70	16.4
BBS fee revenue	12,321.88	51.8	18,737.55	61.0	65,892.79	65.7
Training revenue	950.00	4.0	1,700.00	5.5	3,350.00	3.3
Renewals	160.00	0.7	290.22	0.9	668.11	0.7
Software sales	365.00	1.5	270.00	0.9	4,200.20	4.2
Miscellaneous sales*	7,128.36	29.9	2.21		9,763.89	9.8
Expenses						
Advertising, prom, & shows	1,860.00	7.8	2,598.72	8.4	9,568.95	9.6
Auto repair & maintenance	0.00	0.0	172.96	0.6	172.96	0.2
Auto gas & oil	9.35	0.0	365.75	1.2	375.10	0.4
Bank charges & interest	114.13	0.5	218.37	0.7	867.11	0.9
Credit card charges	665.22	2.8	1,478.27	4.8	2,790.92	2.8
Loan interest	359.50	1.5	1,089.26	3.5	1,961.65	2.0
Business tax	0.00	0.0	(261.67)	−0.9	536.54	0.5
Delivery expense	101.00	0.4	102.49	0.3	340.53	0.3
Insurance	0.00	0.0	565.72	1.8	2,036.42	2.0
Accounting & legal	282.05	1.2	1,565.34	5.1	2,136.43	2.1
Office supplies	596.96	2.5	623.14	2.0	2,968.69	3.1
Contract services	884.00	3.7	1,612.00	5.2	4,403.50	4.4
Office salaries & benefits	1,754.56	7.4	6,397.88	20.8	13,254.84	13.2
Rent expense	0.00	0.0	1,207.50	3.9	2,352.50	2.3
Unallocated expenses	0.00	0.0	19.93	0.0	1,723.81	1.7
Telephone	3,711.06	15.6	2,112.51	6.9	20,162.85	20.1
Telephone maintenance	0.00	0.0	121.39	0.4	1,051.64	1.0
Utilities	0.00	0.0	0.00	0.0	1,273.37	1.3
Equipment repairs	0.00	0.0	0.00	0.0	684.53	0.7
Software	17.20	0.1	300.00	1.0	1,129.01	1.1
Internet services	0.00	0.0	4,053.93	13.2	12,220.96	12.2
Government loan	0.00	0.0	0.00	0.0	1,600.00	1.6
Travel & meals	0.00	0.0	438.99	1.5	469.54	0.5
Management fees**	24,000.00	100.8	0.00	0.0	24,000.00	23.9
Total income	23,802.48		30,721.97		100,337.69	
Total expenses	34355.03	144.3	24782.48	80.4	108081.85	107.9
Operating income (loss)	(10,552.55)	−44.3	5,939.49	19.3	(7,744.16)	−7.7

*Provincial Government Jobs Program Credit.
**For Bruce Whidden.

Source: Company financial statements.

Nevertheless, some of the articles David had read led him to wonder how long this situation would last. For example, IBM, Microsoft and MCI had all recently announced plans to enter the Internet-provider business. Both IBM and Microsoft planned to include software into their personal computer operating system products which would make it very easy to access the Internet and their respective provider services. Microsoft had said that its planned Internet connection service, called Marvel, would be priced at $4.95 (US) per month. MCI had recently announced its "internetMCI" online service, which was going to include e-mail, a news and database, an electronic shopping mall, and Internet access.

David had also attended a presentation given by Andrew Bjerring, president and CEO of CANARIE (Canadian Network for the Advancement of Research, Industry and Education), a consortium of more than 120 communication companies and research institutions concerned with developing Canada's information superhighway. Bjerring, who was one of the leading architects of Canada's information superhighway and very familiar with Internet activity, suggested that the future of the small Internet provider was shaky, since many large players either had recently entered or were planning on entering the market. He also stated that several telephone companies across Canada had started to offer Internet connectivity services, although neither Bell Canada nor AGT (Alberta Government Telephones) had yet joined the group.

David, reflecting on Bjerring's presentation, wondered whether the exponential industry growth could continue to provide reasonable cash flows for a small independent provider such as CanNet, or whether the large companies would completely dominate connectivity. If this was the case, should CanNet abandon its traditional strengths in favor of trying to develop some emerging niche?

THE INTERNET

The Internet was the world's largest interconnection of computers and computer networks. It was an outgrowth of the old ARPANET computer network, designed in the 1960s and early 1970s by the U.S. Department of Defense to support military research. One of the objectives of the original ARPANET was robustness, so that the network wouldn't be shut down by a few well-placed enemy bomb blasts. As a result, the Internet was a highly distributed network, with no central control site. Another major objective of the early research was to create a common communications protocol with global network addressing capabilities. The protocol developed eventually became known as TCP/IP (Transmission Control Protocol/Internet Protocol). Software implementing the TCP/IP protocol was a common part of the Unix computer operating system. Unix was the operating system used by nearly all Internet-connected

EXHIBIT 5A   The Growth of the Internet—Evolution

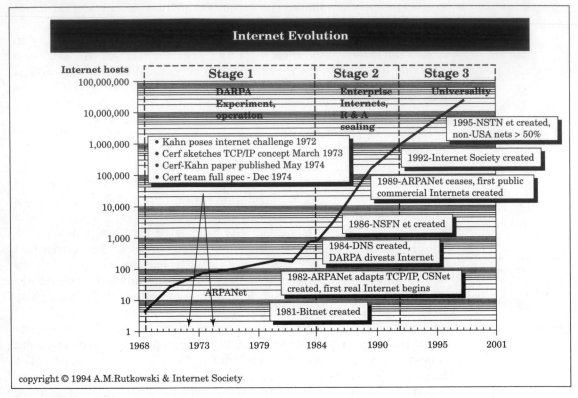

copyright © 1994 A.M.Rutkowski & Internet Society

Source: The Internet.

computers. Unix was an "open standard;" Unix implementations could be run on many different hardware platforms, including IBM-compatible personal computers. Exhibit 5A illustrates some key events in the development of the Internet through 1994.

A variety of information services could be reached through Internet computer-to-computer communications, including libraries, reference databases, newsgroups, and conventional electronic mail (see Exhibit 5B).

At the time that David was evaluating the CanNet investment, the Internet was comprised of more than 4,000,000 host computers located in over 70 countries and on every continent, including Antarctica. Another 150 countries had at least e-mail service or limited forms of Internet connectivity. Traffic on the Internet was growing at the exponential rate of 15 per cent a month and there were no signs that it was slowing down. Traffic on the U.S. National Science Foundation (NSF) backbone portion of the Internet alone was over 20 terabytes (trillion bytes) per month. Estimates of the number of current Internet users

EXHIBIT 5B   The Growth of the Internet—Number of Host Computers

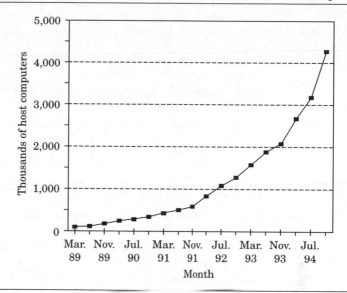

Source: The Internet.

varied from 20 million to 38 million. The variance was large since nobody knew precisely how many people had access to each of the millions of host computers.

In the past, the majority of Internet traffic had been of a research, educational and nonprofit nature. However, that was rapidly changing. In 1993, the number of commercial host computers hooked up to the Internet in the U.S. became larger than the number of nonprofit hosts for the first time. A 1993 Dataquest Inc. survey found that about 22 per cent of the Fortune 500 firms had Internet access, and it was expected that this number would be close to 35 per cent by the end of 1994.

Part of the reason businesses were rushing to get onto the Internet was likely due to the intense media hype regarding the Internet and the information highway. The Internet had been brought to the attention of executives who recognized the potential and began to support efforts to hook up employees. What the Internet offered to companies was a cheap, fast and effective way to exchange information with customers, suppliers and business allies. IBM, for example, relied on the Internet to give OS/2 users and developers around the world a way to download documentation, technical interface specifications, and fixes and upgrades. A law firm in Washington, D.C., used a similar scheme to share files with other firms, saving the cost of photocopying and express-mailing thousands of pages.

According to the articles David had read on doing business on the Internet, some of the services which could make up the coming electronic marketplace included:

- requests for proposals and procurements,
- collaborative engineering and development,
- online employment agencies,
- marketing and advertising, such as electronic yellow pages,
- information services, and
- online shopping.

For such reasons, business writers suggested that connecting to the Internet was an appealing idea for many companies. In the past, it had been very difficult to carry out commercial activity on the Internet, which had originally been designed primarily for university researchers and funded from public sources. The Internet's Acceptable Use Policy (AUP), administered by the National Science Foundation, restricted commercial traffic from using the U.S. Internet backbone.

Recent changes had opened the way for companies to use the Internet. First, a group of Internet access providers, known as the Commercial Internet Exchange, had co-operated to make it possible for commercial traffic to travel across the Internet without travelling over the nonprofit portion of the backbone (thus the AUP was not violated). Second, by mid-1995, the Internet in the U.S. was required to be commercially self-sustaining because the NSF would cease its funding support. At that time the NSF backbone would be taken out of service and traffic shifted to a commercial backbone network. Therefore, the AUP itself would no longer strictly apply.

However, businesses still had to be sensitive to the existing culture of the Internet. Because the Internet had developed primarily as a university research network, most users were opposed to blatant commercial activity such as advertising. The reaction to several companies which had sent advertisements to users' e-mail boxes had been rapid and severe. The companies were bombarded with thousands of nasty e-mail messages (flames) and their fax machines were also tied up by irate Internet users.

Although the Internet's not-for-profit culture discouraged overt commercial activity, including advertising, an informal shop-at-home network had evolved whereby companies such as booksellers, software retailers, florists, and novelty-gift sellers provided product information for network users who chose to look for it. Businesses hoped that users would browse electronic catalogues and place orders online. As long as the companies did not actively solicit business by sending out e-mail to Internet users, they did not seem to violate the culture of the Internet.

By December of 1994, it was estimated that 20,000 companies were on the Internet and almost 2,000 more were joining each month. In part, business growth on the Internet was due to the development of the highly successful World Wide Web (WWW). The WWW, or "Web," had emerged from a project initiated by CERN, the European Laboratory for Particle Physics, near Geneva, Switzerland. The purpose of the WWW project was to combine the techniques of networked information, graphical interfaces and hypermedia to provide an easy-to-use, powerful, global information system. The Web's architecture was designed to enable the seamless linking of multimedia "pages" consisting of text, images, audio or video, irrespective of time, distance or geography. According to Dr. Michael L. Dertouzos, director of the Massachusetts Institute of Technology's Laboratory for Computer Science:

> The key to tomorrow's information market is to make it possible for machines to talk to each other and relieve us of the painstaking details of doing the work ourselves. We aspire to enhance the Web by developing the "bulldozers and backhoes" of the information age, that will work for us—not the other way around, as is often the case today.

The WWW was somewhat akin to the older Gopher service, which had been operating on the Internet since the mid-80s. Gopher, like the WWW, provided hypertext capability—the ability to click on a link in one document and thereby jump to another. However the WWW provided much more as well. Gopher was a simple text-only system, which did not require the use of a graphical interface. Web browsers, such as Mosaic or Netscape, employed a graphical screen to make it extremely easy and fun for a user to navigate the Internet and use it effectively. These browsers permitted jumping from one computer to another by simply clicking on highlighted links on the screen. Images could be imbedded in a web document, as could sound clips and even full-motion video clips. The effortless navigating via hypertext links created the illusion of using one big computer. The growth in the use of the WWW had been phenomenal—3,000 fold in the first year. Exhibit 5C illustrates the growth of the older Gopher service alongside that of the new WWW. The exhibit makes it clear that, as the WWW took off, the less capable Gopher facility has stagnated.

The WWW seemed well suited to fit the needs of electronic commerce. It was easy to lay out full-color catalogues that could include video clips of demonstrations, voice annotation, color images, and so forth. Electronic equivalents of shopping malls had sprung up which allowed users to browse through companies' offerings and place orders online. Book stores, florist shops, computer hardware retailers and travel companies had all found that their sales increased due to their WWW presence.

Another example of the growing business presence on the WWW was the CommerceNet which was introduced in California in April, 1994. Essentially a consortium of members working together to establish standards for conducting business on the Internet, it provided companies with a presence on the Internet, via the World Wide Web. Users of CommerceNet created their own WWW pages and loaded them on one

EXHIBIT 5C   The Growth of the Internet—Gopher and World Wide Web

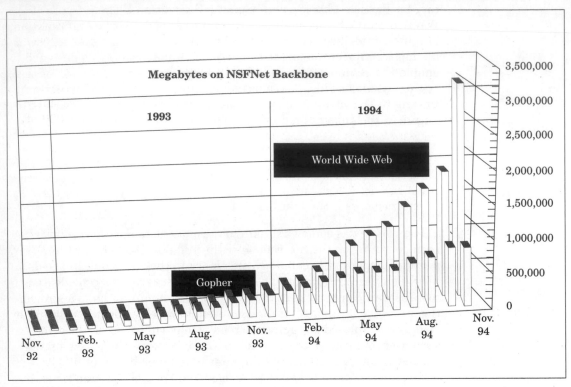

Source: The Internet.

of the CommerceNet server computers. These "home pages" included company information and/or marketing messages that users could view. Internet users could browse a hyperlinked web of formatted pages containing company directories, referral services, catalogues, and product demonstrations. Users could solicit bids, place orders, coordinate production and schedule transportation. CommerceNet promised to streamline procurement, cut costs and shrink development cycles.

While the future for electronic commerce appeared bright, some of the articles David read raised doubts about the immediate commercial viability of Internet-related businesses. Alternative technologies to reach customers, ranging from interactive cable television to videophones or even online services such as America Online, were in the process of being developed. One of these technologies might surpass the Internet as the preferred technology to reach mainstream customers and business partners interested in electronic commerce. If this happened, once these technologies had matured, the Web could well end up as a footnote in the history of computing.

Also, unresolved business questions, such as how many of a company's target customers are actually using or even capable of using the Internet had to be addressed. Companies such as Sun Microsystems (which had built a major presence for its company on the Web in 1993) or Microsoft and IBM (each of which also had a major Web presence) likely had quite a few customers able to use the Internet. However, for companies such as Pizza Hut, Dun & Bradstreet, and even the Internet Shopping Network, there were not many customers on the Internet—at least, not yet. For example, only about 2,000 Internet users presently belonged to the Internet Shopping Network and only about 1,000 of those were regular Web shoppers.

DAVID SAMPSON'S BACKGROUND

David Sampson, 33, was an entrepreneur at heart, even though he had worked in large law firms for four years, completed an MBA, and subsequently worked for three years in the corporate finance department of an overseas stock exchange. He had moved back to Canada with his wife Lisa just before the birth of their first child, 18 months earlier. While overseas, they had managed to save a considerable sum of money, a portion of which was now available to invest in a business. David was looking for a business opportunity where he could take on an active marketing and general management role. He was interested in buying into an existing business rather than starting a new business, given the high failure rate of new businesses. Lisa was also able to contribute to the business. She had earned her MBA from a well-known Canadian business school, and had worked for seven years in business and financial planning. The couple had looked at over 100 business opportunities before becoming attracted to CanNet's potential in the so-called information highway industry.

THE FUTURE FOR CANNET

As part of the evaluation process, David had asked Bruce to indicate his future plans for CanNet. Two aspects of the ensuing discussions surprised David. The first was that Bruce's concrete plans for the company extended out for only six months; many of the other businesses David had investigated had long-range plans covering a period of two to five years. The second unusual aspect was the wide range of possible options available for CanNet to pursue. David wondered if these were simply a reflection of the fast pace of technological change in this new industry, or whether CanNet lacked a sufficient long-term plan.

The plans which Bruce had laid out for David could be broadly categorized into two groupings: expanding the capacity and reach of the existing services offered by CanNet; and upgrading the service offerings and applications available to users.

Under the first category, an immediate requirement was to increase the number of dial-up connections (incoming telephone lines plus associated hardware) by 10 lines to a total of 41 (see Exhibit 2 for a layout of CanNet's equipment). The existing pool of 31 lines, which was reaching its capacity during peak hours, needed to be expanded. The new lines were necessary to keep service and access levels high. As James explained, "If customers get two or three busy signals, they won't call back." Bruce had estimated that the up-front costs associated with adding 10 more lines would be approximately $5,500, consisting of five microcomputers and 10 modems and the hook-up charges for 10 phone lines ($50/line). He estimated the on-going operating costs at $1,200 per line per year.

Once the immediate capacity problems were taken care of, CanNet planned to extend its customer base in a number of different ways. First of all, CanNet was aggressively pursuing new users in its service area through its "participating retailer" program. Under this program, major personal computer equipment retailers were able to offer three months of free access to CanNet's service to all customers buying a modem from their location. The retailers would pay nothing to participate in this program—all they had to do was recommend CanNet as a service provider to their customers.

CanNet also had plans to extend its service to locations outside the immediate Calgary area by leasing telephone lines to connect each of the areas to its central Calgary site. Users in these locations could then access CanNet's BBS and Internet connection via a local telephone call. Bruce estimated the up-front cost of each such leased line at approximately $500, with annual operating costs at $350.

CanNet also planned to offer its service in other major metropolitan areas in Western Canada. When the company became an Internet provider about 15 months earlier, its original expansion strategy was to replicate the Calgary system in new locations, and either operate the new sites as branch locations, or franchise them in return for an up-front investment and royalty. For each additional site, Bruce estimated the up-front cost of setting up to be $40,000 and the on-going operating costs to be $120,000 per year.

More recently, Bruce had looked into the possibility of expanding into new metropolitan markets without setting up a complete site. Rather, he believed it would be possible to simply set up local access for users via an Internet gateway in the targeted cities which would then route the calls to the central system in Calgary, over the Internet. The advantages of this strategy would be lower up-front and operating costs as well as greater control over the service offering. However, it would preclude a franchising approach. He had estimated the costs of the centralized expansion strategy per location at $15,000 up-front and $6,000 per year in operating costs. Part of the up-front cost was an allowance to expand the capacity of the central facilities. Under the centralized approach, CanNet planned to initially offer the service to potential users in Edmonton and then, depending on the success of the Edmonton market, consider expanding the service to other markets.

The second grouping of expansion plans which Bruce discussed with David involved upgrading service offerings and applications for users. In anticipation of providing some of these upgrades, CanNet had already purchased a second server (Server #2 on Exhibit 2) and was in the process of installing Unix on it. As the de facto standard operating system used by Internet computers, Unix was needed to provide the security required for commercial accounts. CanNet had a reciprocal arrangement with a local firm to provide Unix programming and support in return for CanNet's referring its own commercial clients to the firm when they needed assistance with Unix servers. This arrangement meant that the initial server development cost to CanNet would be minimal.

Server #2, a 386 DX40 PC with 16 Mb RAM and a 2.5 gigabyte hard drive, would be linked to Server #1 and the Internet link to UUNet, via CanNet's router (a unit which directs communications among different networks). The system software currently under development for the Unix server would be able to offer customers full TCP/IP connections to the Internet, or either a dedicated or dial-in (temporary) basis. In order for a customer to have full access to the Internet, its machine must have its own Internet address and the ability to conform to the Internet's standard protocol, TCP/IP. For temporary dial-in connections, two similar approaches had been developed recently to allow PCs with modems to connect into an Internet server computer: SLIP (serial line internet protocol) and PPP (point-to-point protocol). SLIP or PPP software assigned dial-in users temporary Internet addresses so they could have full access while they were temporarily connected to an Internet server system. Both SLIP and PPP provided the TCP/IP protocol between machines, needed for communicating with other computers on the Internet. A full access account was necessary to access some of the new Internet services, in particular graphical World Wide Web pages using browsers such as Netscape.

In terms of future plans, the first major item on the list of upgrades was to increase the bandwidth of CanNet's dedicated link to the Internet from 56 Kbps (also known as a DS-0 connection) to 1.544 Mbps (also known as a T1 line). Such an upgrade was required for CanNet to have enough bandwidth to allow its connected users to efficiently access the multi-media and graphical information available on the World Wide Web. The cost of a T1 line was $5,000 per month, compared to $1,400 per month for a DS-0 connection. The major advantage of pursuing such an upgrade was that CanNet would be able to offer high-speed access to the WWW to its users. This, in turn, would open up the possibility for CanNet's corporate clients to advertise their services on the Internet using WWW home pages. CanNet was planning on offering its clients the space for five WWW pages on its Unix server together with a full Internet access account, for about $10,000 per year. For $100 per hour, CanNet would help businesses design their web pages. Although CanNet had not yet marketed this concept aggressively, a number of its business clients were ready to purchase this type of account as soon as it was available, in order to advertise electronically on the WWW.

Another service upgrade CanNet planned for users was an additional package of online information services including: USA Today, sports information, stock market information and other news services such as Reuters. These services could be made available for an additional annual charge of approximately $50 per year per user. The additional operating costs were estimated at about $1,500 per year for CanNet.

After the Unix server had become fully operational so that users had full Internet access (including WWW access), CanNet planned to launch C*NET, allowing secure commercial transactions and payment via the Internet. CanNet was developing C*NET in partnership with the Canadian Information Access Council, a national organization whose mandate was to work with both government and Canadian business to develop the Canadian information superhighway. The main costs for providing such a service would be up-front development and ongoing maintenance by a Unix programmer, estimated at $40,000 per year. The estimated revenue would be $12,000 per year for each participating business.

THE DECISION

It was still unclear in David's mind whether CanNet should pursue such a broad growth strategy in the near future. If its goals were not feasible or desirable, David wondered which options CanNet should focus its efforts on.

As he reflected on all of the information he had accumulated since his initial contact with CanNet and Bruce Whidden, he voiced his main concern:

> I just keep wondering if this business is going to quickly grow like a beanstalk over the next 12 months only to be cut down by a major provider with one swift stroke.

If he decided to go ahead with the business, he was also wondering how much he should invest to get 50 per cent of the company. CanNet had just been breaking even in the last two months of operations (Exhibit 4 contains a recent company-prepared income statement). While CanNet seemed to have a lot of potential, what value should be put on that potential? According to the business valuation methods he had learned during his MBA studies, the value of CanNet's equity was essentially zero. From an asset valuation point of view, the company was technically insolvent (CanNet's balance sheet is given in Exhibit 6).

EXHIBIT 6 Balance Sheet (as of October 31, 1994)

Assets	$	$	$
Current assets			
Cash on hand	(5,520.20)		
Accounts receivable	6,228.08		
Inventory	1,759.45		
Prepaid expenses	739.49		
Total current assets		3,207.02	
Fixed assets			
Fixtures & fittings*	397.04		
Leasehold improvements*	4,373.64		
Computer equipment*	73,958.54		
Alarm system	543.42		
Vehicle	31,722.64		
Office equipment*	6,007.04		
Total fixed assets*		117,002.52	
Incorporation costs	1,500.00	1,500.00	
Total assets			**121,709.34**
Liabilities			
Current liabilities			
Accounts payable	12,013.59		
Taxes payable	1,173.93		
Total current liabilities		13,187.52	
Long-term liabilities			
Business improvement loan	55,157.00		
Due to shareholder A. MacKay	14,522.34		
Due to shareholder J. Ankney	(240.12)		
Due to shareholder B. Whidden	18,004.68		
Long-term lease—Vehicle	23,981.33		
Investor loan	(1,605.42)		
Total long-term liabilities		109,819.81	
Total liabilities		**123,007.33**	
Equity			
Total share capital	(300.00)		
Retained earnings	(997.99)		
Total equity		**(1,297.99)**	
Total liabilities & equity			**121,709.34**

*Net of depreciation.

Source: Company financial statements.

From an earnings valuation approach (there were no proven earnings), the value of equity was zero. A riskier approach would be to look at the future potential earnings of the company as a basis for valuation, based on CanNet pursuing a specific growth strategy over the upcoming year.

While David knew that he would have to prepare a business plan as part of his evaluation, he reflected that the amount of money he invested would ultimately be determined by what CanNet needed in order to buy out the two existing minority shareholders, cover CanNet's short-term commitments, deal with salary accrued to Bruce, and pursue the most promising future opportunities.

As he leaned back in his chair to reflect on the decision facing him, David thought to himself:

> It sure would have been useful to have had some business cases during my MBA which identified the real-life issues faced by an entrepreneur investor entering into a fledgling high-tech venture.

Appendix A

A GLOSSARY OF INTERNET TERMS

Archie   "Archie" is a shortened form of the word "archive." Archie allows one to search Internet-linked computers for file names that contain a string of letters that you designate. Archie searches for an exact string match (a specific file name) or a substring match (part of a file name).

bandwidth   The capacity of a communication line is referred to as bandwidth. The higher the bandwidth, the more information it can carry.

bulletin board systems   Picture a bulletin board "system" at the entrance to a supermarket. An electronic BBS is similar, but uses computers and telecommunications instead. There are over 50,000 BBS in the U.S., most run by hobbyists, who offer simple capabilities such as the ability to post messages for others, or up-load or down-load files. Online services such as Prodigy and CompuServe offer bulletin boards, too, on a variety of personal, professional and computing topics.

e-mail address   An Internet e-mail address has two main sections: the "user identification" and the "domain," separated by an @ sign. The user identification appears before the @ sign and represents the person who is connected with the e-mail address. The domain, everything after the @ sign, refers to the name of the computer the person uses.

electronic mail   E-mail is the ability to send and receive information—primarily textual information—in an electronic format. It is particularly useful for sending information to colleagues and networking with large groups of people.

finger Finger is a utility used in the Unix world to list users on a local system or to list users located on another location on the Internet. Some locations on the Internet also use Finger as a simple method of making information available.

FTP stands for File Transfer Protocol. FTP provides a way for system users to copy public-access files stored on remote computers. The term "FTP" is used as a verb as well as a noun.

gopher A gopher is a computer utility that allows system users to browse a collection of textual information. The contents using the gopher program. Gopher is both a noun and a verb. Using gopher, information may be linked to other related information in a simple form of hypertext (a feature that has been greatly extended by the World Wide Web).

hypertext This is a format for documents wherein items in a given document— e.g., a string of text, or a graphic, or other things, can be set up to link to other places in the same or different documents, stored on the same or other connected computers. In a hypertext document, the user can "jump around" from place to place, without concern about the location or other aspects of the computer on which the documents are stored.

Internet shell account This is a type of access to the Internet. Users use their personal computers to emulate a simple terminal, and access the Internet by connecting to their service provider's system. An Internet shell account gives users access to Internet services such as FTP, but does not give the users their own IP address, so the user's PC does not function as a node on the Internet. Therefore, such a user cannot access higher level Internet services such as the WWW, since he/she is not directly connected to the Internet.

Internet The Internet is the world's largest interconnection of computers and computer networks. Estimates of the number of users, as of December 1994, vary from a low of 20 million to a high of 38 million. It is comprised of over 30,000 networks spread over 78 countries.

IRC IRC (Internet Relay Chat) is best described as a "CB radio" for the Internet. Using IRC, you can participate in online discussions in real time with other Internet users, by typing on your keyboard and reading what others type.

Lynx This is a web browser like Netscape, except that it is limited to viewing and retrieving only text over the WWW. Lynx can be used through a "type 2" internet connection (shell account), unlike graphical browsers such as Netscape.

Mosaic This is a World Wide Web browser, a program that allows one to locate, obtain and display items available over the WWW. It can handle information stored as text, graphics, video or sound. Using Mosaic requires a direct connection to the Internet (or a temporary one via SLIP or PPP). Mosaic is available free through the Internet. Mosaic was the first WWW browser, and set the stage for the phenomenal growth of the WWW.

MUD MUDs (multi-user dungeons) are virtual realities where participants take on virtual roles in the communities. They are like a game but are much more.

Netscape   This is another Internet WWW browser, and recently has become the most popular such browser. Netscape was developed by the same people who created Mosaic, but provides numerous features not available in Mosaic.

online services   Online services offer a gateway to the world of electronic information. By dialling the service with a computer and modem, you can access information such as online bookstores, bulletin boards, travel agencies and banking services. You can also send electronic mail to anyone else who has an account on the online service, or participate in real-time discussion groups. The largest online services in North America include: America Online, CompuServe, Delphi, Genie, and Prodigy. Subscriptions to the Big Three services, America Online, CompuServe and Prodigy, grew to approximately 3.8 million users in the U.S. by the end of 1994 (an increase of over 90 percentage points from 1992).

TCP/IP   This is the Internet protocol which allows packet-switching networks of different kinds to communicate. In order for a computer to have a full Internet connection, it must follow the TCP/IP protocol. TCP (transfer control protocol) refers to how the host machines communicate with each other. IP (Internet protocol) refers to the addressing scheme used by the various interconnected computers. Each host machine must have a unique IP address that is assigned by the Internet administrative body, InterNIC.

Telnet   Telnet is another Internet utility, which can be used to gain access to a remote computer as though you were a local user. Once connected to a remote computer via Telnet, one would normally have to have an account (with a password) on that computer in order to use it further (although some remote computers allow limited "guest" login accesses). Telnet is useful for browsing the holdings of resources such as the U.S. Library of Congress. The term "Telnet" is also used as a verb and a noun.

USENET   USENET is an Internet-based facility for the exchange of information on thousands of topics, referred to as newsgroups. Individuals can choose to subscribe (there is no charge) to any particular newsgroup, read information sent to the newsgroup, and add or "post" information to the newsgroup. Not all providers carry all newsgroups. Newsgroups within USENET belong to a series of categories. The major categories are: biz.—business-oriented topics; comp.—computer-oriented topics; misc.—things that don't fit elsewhere; news.—news and information concerning the Internet or USENET; rec.—recreational activities; sci.—scientific topics; soc.—sociological issues; talk—debate-oriented topics; and alt.—virtually any topic.

UUCP   UUCP (Unix to Unix copy protocol) is a suite of programs—part of the Unix operating system—designed to permit communication between Unix hosts.

Veronica   Veronica is a program that supports the gopher program. Veronica both maintains a current index of gopher menus and allows a user to search gopher menus by keywords. A Veronica search will pull together menu items from many gophers in one customized gopher menu that reflects your search. You can run Veronica from any publicly accessible gopher program; just select it from the gopher menu.

WAIS   WAIS stands for wide-area information search. This search tool allows you to obtain information from data bases that use WAIS software. Like gopher and Veronica, WAIS allows you to search archived data on the Internet through keywords. WAIS is harder and more time consuming to use than Veronica because it searches the full-text holdings of hundreds of computers. Veronica searches for keywords that show up in gopher menus.

WHOIS WHOIS servers are resources that let you search for the Internet address of an organization or individual.

World Wide Web The World Wide Web (WWW) another vehicle for sharing information across the Internet. The WWW began as a project for scientists and researchers to share information in a more powerful and flexible way than was yet available on the Net. It has since evolved far beyond its original target audience, and has become the "killer application" that has made the Internet such a household word recently. The WWW comprises software—for example, WWW server software which runs on specially designated Internet server computers, and web browsers such as Mosaic or Netscape; it also includes the evolving standards for formatting WWW document files.

World Wide Web documents WWW documents (often called "pages") can include text, images, sound information or even moving images (video) formats. They also contain "hot links" (hypertext links) which allow a person to click and connect to some other document presumably related to the one being browsed. WWW documents are generic, in that they should appear pretty much the same on any computer, regardless of what type of computer it is, or what type of browser software is being used to access the document. A document on the WWW contains special codes—called HTML, or "hypertext markup language"—the purpose of which is to instruct the browser programs as to how to display the document on any user's computer.

America Online Inc.: The Portal Era

By Edward A. Stohr, Sivakumar Viswanathan, and Larry White

> *I can buy 20% of you or I can buy all of you. Or I can go into this business myself and bury you.*
>
> > Bill Gates to Steve Case on May 11, 1993; from "aol.com: How Steve Case Beat Bill Gates, Nailed the Netheads, and Made Millions in the War for the Web," Kara Swisher, 1998

INTRODUCTION

For America Online Inc., 1998–99 was another tumultuous year. On December 23, 1998, the world's largest commercial online service was inducted into the S&P500 index, a glowing tribute to its size (a market capitalization of over $147 billion (April 7, 1999)—2.5 times that of General Motors), and position, in an industry that was defining the future. With over 17 million subscribers, AOL's leadership as an online service was largely unchallenged. The nearest rival Internet service provider was nowhere close. Today AOL is one of the strongest brands in cyberspace, with over seven times higher unaided brand awareness than its closest competitors in Internet service.

With the completion of the $10.2 billion acquisition of Netscape Communications Corp. in March 1998, AOL is attempting to redefine the Internet landscape, yet again. According to Business Week, for AOL, the timing couldn't be better.

> The acquisition comes at a time consumers, small businesses and major corporations are grappling with wrenching changes in the way they interact commercially. They are all scrambling to determine the smartest approach to rewiring for the next century, when every facet of business—from procurement, to billing, to human resources, to customer support—will be conducted over the Internet.

However in an industry that moves at "Internet-speed" and where size is no guarantee of success, AOL is faced with challenges that come in different shapes and sizes—challenges that constantly threaten its dominant position. Historically, AOL has not only survived such threats but also succeeded in defining and redefining standards in an industry that has defied standards. But for Chairman Steve Case, who has led AOL to this enviable position from its humble beginnings in the mid-80s, this is no time to rest on laurels. He may have won the battle of the online services, but the cyberwars have just begun, and from early reports they look destined to be long and convoluted.

THE ONLINE SERVICES INDUSTRY

The online services industry traces its roots back to the introduction of time-sharing computers in the early 70s. Companies such as CompuServe, Tymnet, and General Electric's GEISCO allowed customers with "dumb" terminals to connect via slow (10–30 characters per second) telephone lines to large and expensive mainframe computers. Users could access financial and economic databases and also develop and run their own market research and decision support applications. The companies spread geographically by building computer sites ("points of presence" or POPs) in local communities. Customers dialed into their nearest POP to reduce or eliminate telephone access charges.

The personal computer revolution in the 80s provided a more user-friendly interactive environment for access to the timesharing computers and started the era of home computing. The online services industry grew rapidly, with companies such as AOL, CompuServe and Prodigy (which started as a partnership between IBM and Sears in 1984) leading the way. Special communications software is required to access these online services from a PC. At first, this software was distributed to customers on 3.5-inch diskettes. Nowadays, with the increasing sophistication of the software, distribution is often by CD-ROM.[1] The distribution of free software, often bundled with magazines, has been a major marketing strategy for the online services companies. Literally millions of such diskettes and CD-ROMs have been distributed free.

In July 1994, the consumer category of the online services industry consisted of about a dozen large general-interest services led by Prodigy Information Service with about 2 million customers, followed by CompuServe with 1.7 million subscribers, AOL with 900,000 customers, and General Electric's Genie with 350,000 members. These companies provided proprietary content such as encyclopedias, and financial data, and member services, such as e-mail and chat rooms. They generated revenues from a number of sources including subscriptions, advertising, and additional charges for premium content.

The advent of the World Wide Web in 1993 started a revolution that is fundamentally changing industry and society (see Appendix for a history of the Internet and the World Wide Web). A new class of online companies, Internet service providers (ISPs), appeared to provide cheap access to the vast and rapidly growing resources of the WWW. Among other services, ISPs usually support e-mail and allow users to maintain their own homepages. However, they rely on the Internet itself to provide content and other services, such as home banking and electronic commerce. The rapid growth of the Internet and low barriers to entry soon produced a crowded field with thousands of ISPs ranging from mom-and-pop operations that provide local access, to national ISPs such as Netcom, and telecommunications giants such as MCI-Worldcom, AT&T and Bell Atlantic that provide both POPs and transportation on their own networks using standard TCP/IP protocols (see Appendix). In addition, search engines such as Yahoo, Lycos and Infoseek, were created to guide users to useful Web content. To add to the competition, Microsoft Corporation started the Microsoft Network (MSN) online service in mid-1995, quickly becoming a major player with 800,000 customers by mid-1996.

---

[1] If a potential user has access to the Web via browser software (such as Netscape, Internet Explorer, or one of the proprietary browsers offered by the ISPs), the sign-up and downloading of the online service's client software can be done via the Internet.

EXHIBIT 1   Internet and the WWW—Growth

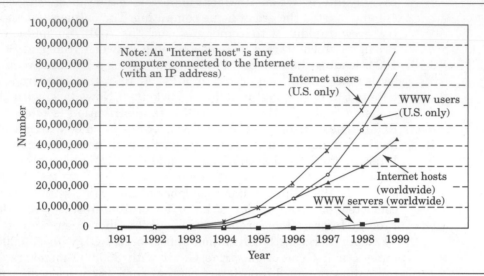

Sources: http://www.commerce.net (1999) and Hobbes Internet Timeline (1999).

The explosive growth of the Web in 1994–95 (see Exhibit 1) took the traditional online services industry by surprise. Online services companies delivered content and programming, using proprietary networks (and proprietary protocols) owned and operated by them. Compared to the WWW, their interfaces and services were stable but unexciting. The Internet was both a threat and an opportunity: a threat because their proprietary networks, content and programming suddenly had a powerful and rapidly growing rival; an opportunity because the growth of the Internet offered opportunities for new markets that were unprecedented in size and scope. Starting in 1995, commercial online services rushed to provide Internet access to their customers. Meanwhile, ISPs and search engines attempted to create user-friendly interfaces and to provide useful content and programming. As a result, the distinction between a "managed" commercial online service like AOL and an ISP has blurred.

By mid-1999, the online services companies (primarily AOL, MSN, and Prodigy) were serving approximately 25 million customers (see Exhibit 2) and receiving income from subscriptions, advertising and electronic commerce. Their primary offerings could be classified under five main categories: access, communications, content, hosting homepages, and electronic commerce (see Exhibit 3 for a sample of AOL's offerings). Despite its rapid growth and popularity, the online services industry is

EXHIBIT 2 Growth in Subscriptions to Online Services

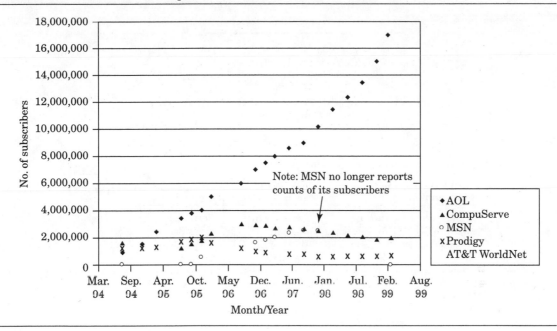

EXHIBIT 3 A Partial List of Features Offered by AOL

Access	Physical access	Access to AOL & Internet
Communication	Online community	E-mail, fax, buddy lists, instant messages discussion groups, interactive chat rooms, bulletin boards
Content	Information	Live news feeds, financial data, sports, personalized portfolio tracking, reference, magazines and newspapers
	Entertainment	Hobby forums, multi-player games, MusicSpace, Hollywood Online, MTV, Cooking Club, Environment Club, Comedy Club, etc.
	Education	Tutoring sessions, education and reference services, including Library of Congress, Smithsonian, Consumer Reports and Compton's Encyclopedia
	Web hosting	Hosting web sites
E-commerce	Travel and shopping	Interactive shopping service at AOL Marketplace featuring goods and services from numerous catalogs and retailers, online auctions.
	Computing	Access to public domain and "shareware" software programs, online computer magazines, etc.
	Other services	Search engines—AOL Netfind, What's Hot, Home Banking, PrivacyGuard, etc.

EXHIBIT 4   Information Industry—Value Chain (illustrative)

Transaction Services

AOL, MSN, Prodigy
CUC International,
Home Shopping Network,
QVC Network,
Netscape, Yahoo, Lycos,
Visa, MasterCard,
Check Free, Cybercash.

Content Providers

Film entertainment	Programmers	Music, games & education	Publishing	Information
Time Warner	Turner	Electronic Arts	Bertelsmann	Dow Jones
Walt Disney	Broadcasting	Broderbund	News Corp.	Bloomberg
Paramount	Viacom	The Learning Co.	Tribune	S & P
Sony	Groupo	Scholastic	Gannett	Moody's
Matsushita	Televisa	Sega, Nintendo	Times-Mirror	Census Bureau
			McGraw-Hill	Mead Data

Transporters

Cable TV companies	Regional phone companies	Long-distance phone companies	Access providers	Wireless communications
Time Warner	Bell Atlantic	AT&T	Netcom Online	Qualcomm
Tele-Communications	NYNEX	MCI	Earthlink	Motorola
Cablevision	U.S. West	Sprint	AT&T Worldnet	AT&T/McCaw Cellular
Comcast	GTE		Uunet Tech.	Racotek
				Fleetcall

Technology Enablers

Computers	Consumer electronics	Software	Storage technology	Semiconductors	Communications
Silicon Graphics	Sega	Oracle	Seagate Tech.	LSI Logic	Broadband Tech.
Sun Microsystems	Nintendo	Sybase	Maxtor	C-Cube, Intel,	AT&T
Hewlett Packard	3DO, Sony	Informix	Optex, EMC	Media Vision	Fujitsu
NCR/AT&T	Apple Comp.	Microsoft		Texas Instruments	NEC

Source: Adapted from Bear, Sterns & Co. Inc. "New Age Media: The Merging of Media Communications, Computing, Consumer Electronics," 1998.

still struggling to define its role and to increase the number of services that are truly valuable to users. Exhibit 4 provides a schematic view of the information industry showing some of the major companies and their role in the industry's value chain. The online service companies are shown in the transaction services category but they are also content providers.

AMERICA ONLINE INC.: THE EARLY YEARS (1985–1996)

In the early days, the commercial online market was largely divided between technical users on CompuServe and business users on Dow Jones News/Retrieval. In 1985, Steve Case and James Kinsey founded Quantum Services Inc. and launched Quantum Link—a useful, affordable, easy-to-access and entertaining online service. The objective was to provide online services for home users. Riding on its initial alliance with Commodore International Ltd., then the largest home PC company in the U.S., Quantum soon offered new services that emerged out of alliances with Apple, Tandy, IBM and other companies. In 1989, the various offerings were folded together under the name America Online (AOL). AOL's content partners were paid 10–20 percent of revenues, depending on how long members spent in each content provider's area. In addition, they received a "bounty" for subscriptions that resulted from their marketing efforts on AOL's behalf. AOL's strategy of leveraging the brand names of its content providers to build subscriptions, particularly at a time when content providers and subscribers had difficulty coming together, paid off handsomely.

AOL started offering Internet access in 1995. Within one year, the number of subscribers increased by more than 200 percent, revenue tripled and its stock price quadrupled in value (see Exhibits 2, 5, and 6).

EXHIBIT 5   Selected Consolidated Financial Data

	Year Ended June 30 (amounts in millions except per share data)				
	1998	*1997*	*1996*	*1995*	*1994*
Statement of operations data					
Online service revenues	$2,161	$1,429	$992	$344	$98
Advertising, commerce, & other revenue	439	256	102	50	17
Total revenues	2,600	1,685	1,094	394	115
Income (loss) from operations	78	(505)	65	(21)	4
Net income (loss)	92	(499)	30	(36)	2
Income (loss) per common share:					
Net income (loss) per share—diluted	$0.35	($2.61)	$0.14	($0.26)	$0.01
Net income (loss) per share—basic	$0.44	($2.61)	$0.18	($0.26)	$0.02
Weighted average shares outstanding:					
Diluted	259	191	215	139	138
Basic	210	191	171	139	114
Balance sheet data					
Working capital (deficiency)	$36	($230)	($23)	$0	$39
Total assets	2,214	833	959	405	155
Total debt	373	52	23	22	9
Stockholders' equity	598	140	513	217	99

Source: http://www.aol.com/corp/inv/reports/1998/10k2.html.

EXHIBIT 6   AOL's Stock Price

Company Name: America Online, Inc. (AOL)   Exchange: NYSE

Sector: <u>Information Retrieval Services</u>

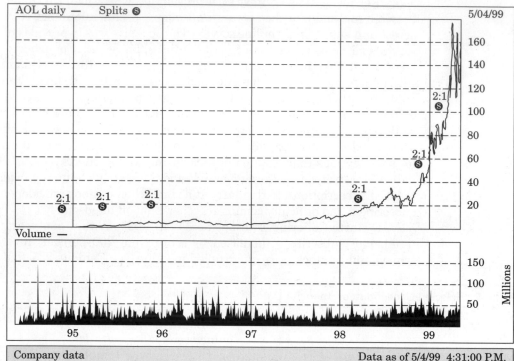

Company data	Data as of 5/4/99 4:31:00 P.M.

Shares outstanding: 1,009,712,014   Market cap: 134.4 Billion

Short interest: 56,942,528 (5.64%)

52-Week EPS: .82   P/E ratio: 155.03

52-Week high: 175.50 on   52-week low: 17.25 on
     Tuesday, April 06, 1999   Tuesday, September 01, 1998

Source: http://www.bigcharts.com.

By mid-1996, America Online Inc. was the runaway leader in the online services industry with over 5 million subscribers. In part, this success was due to its very successful strategy of building the "AOL brand" and its reputation for "user friendliness." However, it faced pressure from the rising popularity of the Internet and from Microsoft's Microsoft Network (MSN), which was rapidly gaining market share.

To keep pace with the growth, and as part of its Internet expansion plans, AOL continuously acquired new technology companies and made

EXHIBIT 7   AOL's Acquisitions, 1994–1999

Date	Target Firm	Price	Target Business
8/94	Redgate Communications	$34m	Makers of multimedia CD-ROMs with online links
11/94	ANS	$35m	High-speed Internet network
11/94	Navisoft	$6m	Web site creation software
12/94	Booklink Technologies	$41m	Web browser and Internet software developer
1/95	WebCrawler	N/A	Search technology
1/95	Global Network Navigator	$11m	Web site
5/95	Medior Inc.	$30.9m	Interactive media developer
5/95	WAIS	$15m	Web server software
9/95	Ubique	$14.6m	Software for chat forums
2/96	Johnson-Grace	$59m	Data compression
8/96	ImagiNation Network	$14.5m	Games sites
9/97	CompuServe	ANS Com.	Online access service
1/98	Personal Library Software	$15m	Search technology
5/98	NetChannel	$29m	Internet-TV technology
6/98	Mirabilis	$287m	ICQ chat technology
11/98	PersonaLogic		Decision-guide technology
11/98	Netscape Communications	$4,200m	Internet browser and e-commerce
2/99	MovieFone Inc.	$338m	Movie listing and ticketing service
4/99	When Inc.	N/A	Internet calendaring and event services
6/99	Spinner Networks Inc.	N/A	Internet music service

alliances with other companies (see Exhibits 7 and 8). In February 1994, AOL formed a $100 million joint venture with German media conglomerate Bertelsmann in an attempt to bring the AOL vision to Europe. Shrewd alliances with partners ranging from the American Association of Retired Persons to MTV helped make AOL the most popular and highly rated online service.[2]

In June 1995, AOL created a separate business to offer Internet access to computer users by acquiring Global Network Navigator (GNN)—a popular Internet site for web-related information. GNN was rated among the best ISPs—on price, ease of navigation, and technical support. In March 1996, AOL announced deals with Netscape Communications Corp., licensing Netscape's Navigator web browser for its main service and for GNN—a move that gave AOL's customers the option of choosing Navigator as their default Internet client. AOL's agreement also gave the service a prominent presence on the Netscape web site and called for cross-promotional efforts.

---

[2]AOL received an Editor's Choice award from *PC Magazine* in 1995.

EXHIBIT 8   AOL's Recent Alliances

Date	Alliance Partner	Alliance Synopsis
2/26/97	Tel-Save Holdings Inc	AOL to get $100m from Tel-Save Holdings Inc. for marketing its long distance service on AOL
7/7/97	NYNEX	Nynex entered into an agreement with ANS to resell AOL to corporations
5/19/98	Eastman Kodak Co.	AOL subscribers to get digitized versions of their photos e-mailed to them
7/1/98	E* Trade Group Inc	AOL to get $12.5m a year for prime placement in AOL's brokerage area
7/1/98	Waterhouse Investor Services	AOL to get $12.5m a year for prime placement in AOL's brokerage area
9/28/98	Real Networks Inc.	Real Networks will license its RealPlayer free of charge to AOL
11/23/98	Inktomi Corp	Provide search technology to ICQ
11/25/98	Sun Microsystems	Collaborate to use and sell e-commerce software and Internet terminals
12/21/98	Dell Computer Corp.	2-year agreement to provide AOL's Internet access and software on its PCs
1/6/99	CBS News	Cross-promotion and CBS News to become exclusive supplier to broadcast news on AOL
2/4/99	Banc One Corp's First USA	AOL to get $500m for a 5-year agreement to market credit cards over the Internet
2/5/99	MCI WorldCom Inc.	CompuServe to provide content to MCI's new online service
2/15/99	Supermarkets Online	AOL & Supermarkets Online signed a deal to offer coupons for leading packaged-goods products
2/15/99	NBC & ABC	AOL, NBC & ABC to join OpenNet—a coalition to force cable companies to open their networks to Internet competitors
3/12/99	SBC Communications Inc.	SBC to market high-speed online access (DSL) to AOL customers in California, Nevada and Southwest

The success of any online system depends crucially on the level of perceived service. How easy is the system to set up and use? How responsive and reliable is the technical support (800 hot lines, online support, user-support groups, bulletin boards, built-in help features of the browser, etc.)? AOL achieved popularity in large part because of its friendly interface and easy set-up. Providing Internet access involved a new set of problems and increased the demand for service. In 1995, AOL established an online Community Action Team to combat online scams, spamming, and inappropriate mail—all problems that are likely to bother users.

It hasn't all been smooth sailing (see Exhibit 9). Despite its reputation for user friendliness, there were periodic breakdowns in service.

EXHIBIT 9   America Online's Tough Climb to the Top

March 1992   AOL, founded in 1985, takes it stock public.

February 1994   Computers clogged by an influx of new members, AOL limits how many members can sign on during peak hours.

August 1994   Members fret over a new AOL twist: advertisements displayed on the service.

March 1995   Competition on two new fronts: the Microsoft Network and Internet service providers.

September 1995   FBI arrests a dozen users for exchanging child pornography on AOL.

June 1996   AOL's president, William Razzouk, departs after four months on the job, after failing to fit in with key executives.

August 1996   Blackout! AOL is shut down completely by technical glitches for 19 hours, angering users.

December 1996   AOL offers a flat-rate price plan: unlimited time for $19.95 a month. AOL is quickly overwhelmed.

January 1997   Besieged by member complaints over busy signals, AOL says it will cut back marketing efforts until it can increase its system capacity and offers $40 refunds to members who couldn't get online.

May 1998   AOL settles dispute with 44 state attorneys general and agrees to provide members with better warnings about price changes.

March 1999   AOL concludes its acquisition of the Internet pioneer Netscape, giving AOL the heavily trafficked Netcenter portal site as well as browser and a formidable electronic-commerce software.

Source: *The Wall Street Journal,* New York, March 19, 1999.

Rapid membership growth occasionally overwhelmed AOL's system capacity, resulting in endless busy signals, frozen screens, and e-mail that could take longer to deliver than the U.S. Postal Service. As early as 1994, when AOL had only 600,000 subscribers, it had to deny access to some customers at peak hours to avert system deterioration. The worst blackout occurred on August 7, 1996, when six million subscribers were left without access to its services for 20 hours due to problems encountered when installing new network routing software. Coincidentally, the next day, August 8, AOL announced that it had become the "first billion-dollar interactive-services company."

AOL has suffered from more than just technical problems. Over the years there were several legal suits against the company, charges of "insider trading," and several incidents involving poor communications with customers. AOL was also criticized for its accounting practices, particularly for its practice of booking its heavy marketing costs as capital expenses to be amortized over a two-year period. In October 1996, AOL decided that it would report marketing costs as expenses in the quarter in which they were incurred. As a result, the company announced a one-time $385 million charge to write down the outstanding expenses that it had yet to amortize.

Towards the end of 1996, America Online restructured its organization, dividing the company into three distinct divisions: AOL Networks (which included the flagship online service), AOL Studios (which created content and services to be distributed on the network), and ANS Communications (which built and maintained the network backbone that most AOL customers used.)

Throughout its history, virtually all of AOL's revenues have come from subscriber fees. Subscribers could access all of the information and services available at the site, including interactive chat rooms, hobby forums, games, personal business services, etc. AOL was an aggressive competitor focused on increasing market share rather than profits. In fact, AOL had scarcely turned a profit although it reached $1 billion in revenues in fiscal 1996 and had been traded on the NYSE since early 1996.

FALL 1996: THE FLAT-RATE PRICING DECISION

Prior to January 1995, AOL's base rate subscription was $9.95 per month, which included five hours of connection time, with additional hours being charged at $3.50 per hour. In addition, AOL had extra charges: $2.50 a letter for sending a printed message to users who did not have an electronic mail account, and $2 a page for sending messages to a facsimile machine. Starting July 1, 1996, AOL offered its customers two different pricing plans: light users could adopt the standard plan of $9.95 per month for 5 hours of access with a charge of $2.95 for each additional hour, while heavy users could pay $19.95 per month for 20 hours of access with a charge of $2.95 for each additional hour.

In the first half of 1996, under severe competitive pressure, other major online service companies, including CompuServe and MSN, and most ISPs such as Netcom and AT&T, introduced a "flat-rate" pricing structure of $19.95 per month for unlimited hours of usage.

In the fall of 1996, AOL's management pondered several issues. How could they make best use of their proprietary content and expertise in interactive services in the face of the burgeoning information content and services available on the Internet? How could they continue to capture market share in the face of the flat-rate "all you can eat" pricing policies of their competition? When could or should they start to make a profit?

AOL decided to meet the competition by switching to a flat-rate pricing policy. The planned date for the switch over to its new flat-rate pricing policy was December 1, 1996. At this time, all subscribers were to be automatically moved to the new flat-rate fee of $19.95 per month for unlimited use. Low volume users, however, could request a separate payment plan whereby they would pay $4.95 per month for three hours of use, with additional time costing $2.50 per hour. In addition, AOL planned to charge $9.95 per month for access to its proprietary content by users who connected to the AOL site from another ISP. Such users do not use AOL's dial-in facilities but have access to all of AOL's content. In announcing the flat-rate pricing decision Steve Case told reporters that "AOL had used price before to achieve its objectives and was not afraid to do so again."

In an effort to handle the expected surge in usage, the company added 12,000 new modems in November 1996, along with more phone lines and more powerful servers for popular online services such as e-mail, chat, WWW publishing, etc. In the last quarter of 1996, 1.2 million new members subscribed to AOL.

On December 1, when the flat-rate price came into effect, the 7 million AOL subscribers overwhelmed the system. Those who were able to obtain a connection on December 1 logged eight million individual sessions, the most ever. On December 2, the company's stock rose $4.625 per share on the NYSE to $39.875.

AOL's decision to switch to a flat-rate fee was not without its critics:

> *America Online has discovered that its officers should not have fallen asleep in those economics courses. They probably failed to hear that decisions are made on the margin.*
>
> "Attention to the Rules of Commerce Could Have Saved AOL a Bundle: Prices Must Prompt Cost-Efficient Use," Donald Ratajczak, *The Atlanta Journal and Constitution,* February 2, 1997

In fact, all was not well. In December, AOL subscribers logged 102 million hours online—up from 45 million in September. AOL's network could not handle the surge in traffic, and many users had to wait endlessly to connect. And because customers were having so much trouble connecting to the service, they tended to keep the line tied-up—in some cases using special software (such as Keep Alive and Ponger) to hang on to their network connections as they did other work or even slept. The average usage per customer more than doubled, to 32 minutes a day. AOL users in three states filed class-action suits against the company, and other frustrated users who were willing to tolerate other snags seemed to have reached their breaking point. Prodigy reported a substantial increase in its subscriptions in the first two weeks of January 1997. According to a press release, 45 percent of AT&T's customers were AOL dropouts, and an estimated 15 to 20 percent of AOL subscribers had more than one online account. Shares of AOL fell 7 percent on January 27 to close at $34 1/4.

Many customers were upset when they were automatically switched to the new plan. On receiving a letter of complaint from 17 state attorneys general, AOL agreed to allow customers to choose their preferred plan and to give retroactive refunds to all customers who asked to switch back to their old plan before April 10, 1997. To help contain the problem, AOL suspended its high-profile advertising and marketing campaign for the month of February and added a temporary disclaimer to its ads disclosing the service's access problems. It also vowed to resolve the capacity problems and pledged a $350 million investment to improve its networks. As of January 1997, AOL's system allowed 250,000 of its 7.5 million users to log on at the same time. AOL's announced goal was to be able to support 400,000 simultaneous users by July 1, 1997 (350,000 dial-up users and 50,000 users who log on through another ISP). AOL added 30,000 modems a month through June 1997, bringing the total to 350,000 modems by July. It also added 600 customer-support people to its staff of 4,000.

In the fiscal quarter beginning in December 1996, America Online reported strong growth in revenue to $409 million, but also a sizable loss of $155 million. In addition to a cash squeeze, one of the major problems facing AOL was the sharp jump in its current liabilities, resulting from the change in accounting procedures mentioned earlier, laying off workers, shutting offices, scrapping outdated marketing materials, and credits and refunds to customers. However, according to analysts, the main reason for the fall in its gross profit margins was the adoption of the flat-price policy for unlimited service. An unexpected increase in new subscribers (from 800,000 in the June quarter to 1.2 million in the September quarter of 1996), free-trial time and increased costs of technical support also contributed to increased costs and depressed margins.

AOL: RECENT HISTORY AND CURRENT STATUS

In March 1998, AOL increased its monthly subscriber fee to $21.95 for unlimited use. Most ISPs continue to charge a flat-rate price of $19.95 per month for unlimited usage, which has become almost an industry standard. However some companies feel that flat-rate pricing is a money-losing proposition as it encourages people to stay online much longer than under the previous metered pricing plans, which charged hourly fees after a minimum monthly threshold of five hours or so. A number of commercial web sites, such as *The Wall Street Journal,* have adopted a tiered pricing strategy. Some content is made available free as a "come-on", while other content, particularly where royalties to a third party are involved, is made available only through a membership subscription or on a fee-for-usage basis. A challenge faced by AOL is to decide which, if any, of its premium services or resource-hungry and popular activities such as multiparty games can be priced separately in addition to the basic subscription.

On September 7, 1997, WorldCom Inc., the fourth-largest U.S. long-distance telephone company, announced that it was acquiring CompuServe Corp. for nearly $1.2 billion in stock, and selling CompuServe's subscription service to AOL. Under the terms of the three-company deal, WorldCom's Internet Services unit, Uunet Technologies took over CompuServe's high-speed telecommunication lines and Internet gateways and also acquired AOL's Internet telecommunications unit, ANS. In addition to CompuServe's 2.3 million subscribers, AOL received $175 million in cash and gained access to an additional 100,000 modems from Uunet. Following the announcement, shares in WorldCom rose $2.25 to $33.75 and shares in AOL rose $6.125 to $76.0625.

AOL made another significant acquisition in November 1998 when it bought Netscape Corporation in a stock-for-stock transaction valued at $4.2 billion. Under the terms of the deal, Netscape's brand and Netcenter portal, which has 9 million registered users, were continued. AOL gained a larger audience and access to Netscape's browser and e-commerce technologies. In addition, Marc Andreesen, the developer of the first WWW browser and founder of Netscape, became AOL's first chief technology officer. Simultaneously, AOL announced a strategic alliance with Sun Microsystems to generate revenues across the Netscape and AOL brands. The objective of the alliance is to build end-to-end e-commerce solutions consisting of directory, security, messaging (e-mail) and collaboration servers running application software that performs e-commerce exchange, procurement, selling and billing. The intention of the alliance is to get to the market first with significant e-commerce functionality.

Brands operated by AOL now include AOL.com itself, CompuServe, Netscape, ICQ (instant communications and chat portal) and Digital City (a portal specializing in local content). Other acquisitions made over the years such as GNN, Ubique and WAIS were absorbed into AOL itself.

To accommodate the above changes, AOL recently reorganized itself into four product groups:

- Interactive Services. Includes the AOL, CompuServe and Netscape's Netcenter services and is responsible for the development of broadband access.
- Interactive Product Group. Manages ICQ, Digital Cities and AOL's interest in Direct Marketing Services.
- Netscape Enterprise Group. Manages AOL's side of the Sun-Netscape alliance.
- AOL International. Responsible for the international operations of AOL and CompuServe.

Exhibit 10 provides some statistics summarizing AOL's current position.

EXHIBIT 10   America Online—Company Highlights

	Year Ended June 30		
	1996	*1997*	*1998*
Total revenues ($ millions)	1,094	1,685	2,600
Advertising and commerce revenues ($ millions)	102	256	439
Online service revenues ($ millions)	992	1429	2,161
Worldwide members	6,198,000	8,636,000	14,605,000
Average hours per AOL member per month (Q4 average)	6.4	18.5	22.1
Maximum AOL simultaneous users	120,000	384,000	692,000

Source: Company highlights, http://www.aol.com/corp/inv/reports/1998.

COMPETITION

> Ask any of AOL's 14 million subscribers why they stick with the service—despite ongoing problems with busy signals, sluggish downloads, and other abrupt disconnects—and you'll probably hear the same answer from all of them: content and chat. Where else can you so quickly and easily commiserate with other harried parents, get the scoop on the hottest Internet stocks, catch up on your magazine reading, or find the latest music tracks? But AOL's reign as king of content is coming under siege. Recognizing the powerful pull of one-click access to news, weather and chat rooms, more and more ISPs are following AOL's lead in hopes of sharing its market success.
>
> "Imitating AOL—ISPs Strive for Easy Web Access,"
> *PC World*, March 1999

Internet Service Providers.   It costs approximately $2 to $3 per subscriber per month for AOL to provide basic telecommunications services. Given this, the telephone companies, with millions of customers, vast distribution networks, and large financial reserves, would seem to have a natural advantage with regard to Internet service. However, they were rather late into the consumer market: MCI Internet was founded in 1995, AT&T started WorldNet and Sprint Corporation entered the ISP market in 1996. The ISP arena is very dynamic. On the one hand, large national ISPs, long distance phone companies, the regional Bells and cable operators are consolidating to build a global presence (for example, the MCI-WorldCom and AT&T-TCI mergers). And, large regional ISPs such as Rocky Mountain Internet and Cybergate are buying up smaller ISPs in an effort to become national providers. On the other hand, the total number of ISPs has grown from 1,500 in 1996 to more than 6,500 in 1999, with

96 percent of the U.S. having access to at least four providers. According to estimates by International Data Corporation smaller ISPs have almost doubled their market share to approximately 16 percent in two years, while the market shares of Microsoft and AOL dropped by 11 points to 56 percent by the end of 1998, with the Baby Bells' share only 3.5 percent.

In a recent survey, *PC World* rated regional and national ISPs on performance, cost, ease of setup, features, support, download times, etc. Exhibit 11 presents the findings of the survey. AOL ranked 15th. However, according to Maritz AmeriPoll, of the homes with Internet access, 55 percent have AOL as their service provider, 12 percent have phone companies, 8 percent have independent ISPs, 6 percent have Microsoft Network, 4 percent have CompuServe, 3 percent have Prodigy and 12 percent don't know!

Under intense competitive pressure, many ISPs have begun to add additional e-commerce services. Experts forecast rapid consolidation as cable and other broadband technologies take hold, squeezing out ISPs that can't provide new types of service or are unable to ally themselves with cable companies.

Portals. Portals are Internet sites that are the initial entry points into the WWW for very large numbers of users. With Netscape's web site included, AOL's network of sites logged 38 million unique visitors in February 1999, while the next most popular portals, Yahoo and MSN, each totaled approximately 31 million unique visitors (see Exhibit 12). While attracting visitors is important, portals add features such as auctions, chat, free e-mail, games, shopping, and compelling content to entertain and educate visitors and prevent them from straying elsewhere. A "sticky" site keeps visitors occupied for a relatively long period of time and is therefore a good place to advertise. Exhibit 13 lists the sites with high stickiness ratings. According to Andromedia, a company that measures Internet traffic, sites that customize the viewing experience to the individual user have longer visits, higher return rates and higher product purchasing rates. For example, Netscape's "My Netcenter" and Yahoo's "My Yahoo!" let visitors customize the site to obtain a selected choice of news items, stock quotes, and so on, whenever they log on.

"E-wallet" technology is another service that can help retain users and encourage repeat visits (see Appendix.) Sites with a widely accepted e-wallet technology can gather valuable data revealing what sells, what doesn't and who the purchasers are across different sites. Portals prefer a centralized wallet that could be used across different online stores. In November 1998, AOL rolled out its wallet technology—called Quick Checkout—and now has several online merchants participating in it. Yahoo! Shopping, which has hundreds of online retailers, also has an e-wallet technology shared by its retailers. However, individual retailers might be wary of letting portals get in between them

EXHIBIT 11 Ranking of ISPs in Terms of Quality of Service

Rank	Internet Service Provider	Coverage Area	Start-Up Fee / Monthly Fee	Summary	Trial Period (hours / day)	High Speed Access
1	AT&T WorldNet www.att.com	National	None/$21.95	World-class competitor, slow responses to e-mail requests	Unlimited/30	ISDN/Cable/DSL/T1/Frame relay/ATM
2	IBM Internet Connection www.ibm.net	National	None/$19.95	Excellent all round, easier to install, monthly fee covers only 100 hours	30/30	ISDN/Cable/DSL/T1/Frame relay/ATM
3	MindSpring www.mindspring.com	National	$25/$19.95	Fast, easy to set-up, backed by on-the-ball support	Unlimited/30	ISDN/Cable/T1
4	Ameritech www.ameritech.net	Midwest	None/$21.95	Nimble performer except for support and ease of installation	None	ISDN/DSL/T1/Frame relay
5	Concentric www.concentric.net	National	None/$19.95	Good features, plenty of overseas access points	Unlimited/30	DSL/T1/Frame relay
6	EarthLink/ Sprint www.earthlink.net	National	None/$19.95	Good support, slow speeds	None	ISDN/Cable/DSL/T1/Frame relay
7	SBC/Pacific Bell Internet Services www.pacbell.net	West	$15/$22	Hard to set-up, but great performance; best in the West	Unlimited/10	ISDN/DSL/T1/Frame relay/ATM
8	BellSouth www.bellsouth.net	South	$10/$19.95	Fast web page downloads	None	ISDN/DSL/T1/Frame relay/ATM

EXHIBIT 11 (Continued)

Rank	Internet Service Provider	Coverage Area	Start-Up Fee/ Monthly Fee	Summary	Trial Period (hours / day)	High Speed Access
9	RCN www.rcn.com	Northeast	None/$19.95	Solid all-round service and good high-technology	None	ISDN/Cable/T1/ Frame relay
10	Voyager www.voyager.net	Midwest	$20/$19.95	Decent showing in all categories	None	ISDN/Cable/DSL/T1/ Frame relay
11	Prodigy Internet www.prodigy.com	National	None/$19.95	Sluggish performance and support, good features	None	None
12	Bell Atlantic Internet Solutions www.bellatlantic.net	Northeast	None/$19.95	Next only to RCN	None	ISDN/DSL/T1/ Frame relay/ ATM
13	GST WholeEarth Network www.wenet.net	West	None/$25	Free access to a cool online community (The Well)	None	ISDN/DSL/ Frame relay/ ATM
14	Microsoft Network www.msn.com	National	None/$19.95	Short support hours and toll-only support line	Unlimited/30	ISDN/T1
15	America Online www.aol.com	National	None/$21.95	Easy setup, poor performance and weak support	100/30	None
16	Rocky Mountain Internet www.rmi.net	Rocky Mountain	$15/$19.95	Limited support hours but reliable service	None	ISDN/DSL/T1/ Frame relay/ATM
17	CyberGate www.gate.net	South	None/$17.95	Hard to install and slower speeds	None	ISDN/T1/Frame relay/ATM

Source: Adapted from "Good Providers—The Best National and Regional ISPs," *PC World*, March 1999.

EXHIBIT 12   Top 20 Digital Media and Web Sites

Combined at Home and at Work (measurement period—February 1999)

Rank	Digital Media / Web Properties*	Unique Visitors (000s)	Web Sites	Unique Visitors (000s)
1	AOL Network (including WWW)	38,144	Yahoo.com	30,674
2	Yahoo sites	31,075	AOL.com	29,602
3	Microsoft sites	30,866	MSN.com	20,489
4	Lycos	29,187	Geocities.com	19,604
5	Go Network	21,897	Go.com	19,334
6	GeoCities	19,926	Netscape.com	18,666
7	Netscape	18,666	Excite.com	15,621
8	The Excite Network	18,081	Lycos.com	14,401
9	Time Warner Online	12,715	Microsoft.com	14,283
10	Blue Mountain Arts	12,632	Bluemountainarts.com	12,632
11	Amazon	10,516	Angelfire.com	11,895
12	Xoom sites	9,730	Tripod.com	11,438
13	AltaVista search sites	9.709	Hotmail.com	11,293
14	Broadcast.com	8.870	Altavista.com	9,709
15	Snap.com (search and services)	8,551	Xoom.com	9,270
16	RealSite portfolio	8,505	Amazon.com	8,669
17	ZDNet sites	8,029	Snap.com	8,551
18	Juno	7,171	Real.com	7,890
19	CNET	6,820	Hotbot.com	7,172
20	Ebay	6,547	ZDNet.com	6,918

*Top 20 digital media and web properties are based on unduplicated audience reach (unique visitors). "Digital media and web properties" include the largest single brands as well as consolidations of multiple domains that fall under one brand or common ownership.

EXHIBIT 13   Sites with High Stickiness Ratings

Rank	Site	Time Spent per Month by Average User
1	AOL (proprietary & web)	5 hrs., 34 mins.
2	Ebay	2 hrs., 3 mins.
3	Gamesville	1 hr., 32 mins.
4	Hotmail	1 hr., 22 mins.
5	Yahoo	58 mins.
6	MoneyCentral	45 mins.
7	Excite	34 mins.
8	ESPN	30 mins.
9	MSN	30 mins.
10	Netscape	25 mins.

and their customers and might prefer to develop their own wallet systems. For example, eToys, a toy retailer, is focusing on its own Express Checkout system, tailored to the company's needs.

Yahoo! is the most popular portal, with 63 percent of the respondents claiming to use the service, while Excite, with 38 percent and Infoseek (Go Network) with 32 percent usage lagged behind. To illustrate the meaning of these figures in another way, Yahoo! recorded an average of 205 million page views per day in the first quarter of 1999, up from 167 million in the last quarter of 98. According to Forrester Research, the top nine portals—AltaVista, AOL, Excite, Infoseek, Lycos, Microsoft, Netscape, Snap and Yahoo—account for a mere 15 percent of all Internet traffic. Yet they attract 59 percent of all advertising revenue on the Internet. Network television, in contrast, attracts 67 percent of all television viewers and 84 percent of advertising. Forrester estimates that overall spending by advertisers will rise to $8 billion by 2002 and that the portal share will be worth $2.5 billion, enough for only three or four portals.

ISPs and other online services apart, AOL is likely to face its toughest competition from traditional media giants (cable and TV networks), content providers and retailers who are quickly moving online, and most importantly have the brand name, the technology and deep pockets to compete. Exhibit 14 compares AOL with traditional media companies as of early 1998. Some of these companies are buying stakes in existing web properties. For example, GE's NBC bought stakes in Snap and iVillage, a specialized web site for women; Walt Disney Co., parent of ABC, acquired a share in Infoseek; News Corp's Fox has an alliance

EXHIBIT 14 A Comparison of AOL with Traditional Media

Media Brand	Circulation	Monthly Fee	Prime-Time Audience	What $500,000 Can Get an Advertiser
AOL	11 million direct subscribers	21.95	625,000	A year of banner ads on AOL's stock page
MTV	73 million cable subscribers	$0.15 to $0.30*	502,000	More than 100 30-second ads during prime-time
NBC	Anyone with a TV set	Zero	10.2 million	A 30-second ad on "Friends" and another on "News Radio"
Newsweek	3.1 million weekly readers	$2.43	3.1 million readers	Five full-page ads
New York Times	1.1 million daily readers	$30.40	1.1 million readers	Six full-page ads and $40,000 in classified ads

*Portion of subscriber fee paid to MTV by cable operator.

Sources: Company data; Paul Kagan & Associates; Competitive Media Research; Nielsen Media Research, 1998.

with Yahoo! Inc.; Walt Disney and Infoseek unveiled a site called the Go Network, with Infoseek planning to spend $165 million through 2003 promoting Go in an aggressive bid to attract the most web traffic.

> *The companies that will win on the Internet are those who have the ability to create content, and no one does that better than we do.*
>
> Jake Winebaum, President, Buena Vista (Walt Disney's online unit),
> *Business Week,* March 2, 1998

Internet firms, realizing the value of "online communities" have also begun to consolidate. For instance, Yahoo! recently acquired GeoCities, a community site with 3.2 million members (Dec. 1998) for $5 billion and Lycos Inc. bought Tripod Inc. for $58 million. Microsoft allied itself with NBC acquired Hotmail, Expedia Travel, CarPoint, HomeAdvisor. It also bought Firefly Network, which has "personalization" technology that monitors consumers' web-usage patterns and recommends products.

Niche Players—Hubs.   In the 1970s and 80s, shopping malls redefined not only how people shopped but also how they spent their leisure time. In a similar fashion, portals with e-commerce capabilities are beginning to reshape the online experience. Because portals try to be all things to all people, they lack focus, perhaps providing opportunities for specialized niche players or hubs. Hubs provide content, commerce and community tailored to a particular audience. For example, Justballs, started in September 1998, offers only balls—footballs, baseballs, cork balls, wallyballs, etc.—and ball-related accessories such as pumps and tees. iVillage is a prominent hub that caters to women on the Web, while eToys is a hub specialized in toys, and is a formidable competitor to Toys-R-Us. The kids' market offers lucrative opportunities for niche players. By 2000, there will be 19.2 million kids surfing the Net, who will spend over $1.8 billion. AOL is the current leader in this market. Since 1994, the company has offered a Kids-Only area featuring homework help, games, and chat rooms. It gets about 1 million 8- to 12-year old visitors monthly. But competition from sites like Walt Disney's Go Network, Warner Bros., and Nickelodeon is becoming more intense.

According to Jupiter Communications "Niche markets are the only markets to succeed in generating revenue from content. Users will not pay for content which appeals to a mass audience." Niche sites usually provide higher quality as well as greater depth in content. Portal sites may have to adjust in the future—possibly focusing on a particular area or constellation of areas as evidenced by the "special-interest" channels being developed by some portals. In a contradictory trend, some large niche players have sought to leverage their customer base and widen their product line. For example, Amazon.com, primarily a book retailer, successfully diversified into selling CDs and videos online, and, more recently, bought a 46 percent stake in Drugstore.com, an online drugstore, and a 50 percent stake in Pets.com, a pet-store startup.

DIGITAL CONVERGENCE

In an increasingly network-centric era, isn't it only natural that the actual network owners should emerge as big time players? Local bandwidth is the key, and AOL and other Internet service providers do not have it. That's not Washington's problem; it's AOL's.

ComputerWorld, February 8, 1999

Technologies such as telephone service and television, which traditionally used analog (continuous waveform) transmission are now becoming digital. Advances in compression technologies allow greater throughput and digital data can be manipulated more easily. The most important impact of "the digitalization of everything," however, is that previously separate industries now have increasingly similar technologies and can compete on each other's turf. On an almost daily basis there are announcements of new alliances, mergers and acquisitions. Some of these deals are vertical (same industry segment) aiming for market size and economies of scale. However, a significant proportion involve companies trying to gain a position in an entirely different segment. A number of examples, such as AT&T's purchase of TCI, were mentioned earlier.

The stock market has placed an extraordinarily high valuation on Internet stocks. For example, in January 1998, the market value of Amazon.com was about $20 billion even though it has never earned a profit, while J.C. Penney's market capitalization was $11.5 billion. The disparity in the valuations of Internet versus non-Internet companies makes it easier for Net companies to acquire traditional companies and other Internet companies than for a traditional media company to acquire an Internet company. As a result, in some deals, a significant part of the payment for equity is promotion. NBC's recent equity stake in women's site iVillage was partially paid for with promotion on NBC and CBS acquired its 22 percent stake in SportsLine USA in 1997 primarily in exchange for promotion on its TV network. Traditional media companies also protect themselves from the cost of acquisition by taking a small stake in an Internet firm with an option to increase its ownership over time for a specified price. For example, in June 1998, NBC acquired 19 percent of Snap for $5.9 million, along with an option to increase its ownership to 60 percent over the next three years for an additional $38 million.

Broadband Internet access—access at speeds 10 to 50 times that of conventional analog modems—is another important impact of digital convergence. AOL has 16 million users using "narrow-band" modems to access its service, but has virtually no broadband access capability. It's not clear how AOL will move to the high-bandwidth world of the 21st century. The competing broadband technologies—cable, digital subscriber lines (DSL), and satellite—are explained in the Appendix. According to Forrester Research, 16 million homes will have high-speed Internet connections by 2002, and 80 percent of them will use cable modems while the rest will use DSL.

Cable modems are currently the leading technology for broadband access with some 300,000 users. AT&T recently acquired Tele-Communications Inc. (TCI), a cable company that holds a 42 percent stake in At Home, the leader in cable-modem services. TCI and its partners potentially give AT&T access to one-third of American homes, enabling it to provide local telephone and Internet access on a mass scale. AT&T also has an alliance with Time-Warner, which is one of the biggest cable operators with more than 12 million subscribers. About 70 percent of Time Warner's systems are modernized to carry voice and data traffic. Time-Warner has its own high-speed Internet access—Road Runner, which had over 125,000 subscribers on October 22, 1998. According to an estimate by investment firm Sanford C. Bernstein & Co., in 10 years 36 million homes will get their phone services delivered via cable. As Comcast's CEO Brian L. Roberts puts it, "We're not just in the cable television industry anymore. We're becoming telecommunications companies."

Digital subscriber lines (DSL) offered by local phone companies use existing telephone lines into the house and offer a faster alternative to traditional telephone modems. Local phone companies are in the process of introducing DSL into various regions within their jurisdictions. In January 1999, AOL allied with Bell Atlantic to offer high-speed Internet access using DSL at a total cost of $40 per month (about the same price charged by cable modem services). Dataquest Inc. predicts that DSL modems will outsell cable modems, starting in 2000.

Meanwhile, widespread Internet access via satellite seems just around the corner.

REGULATION

Under current regulations, cable companies can offer their own online services and force customers who want AOL to pay extra for it. The cable industry argues that unnecessary regulations will diminish the willingness of capital markets to finance the construction of new broadband cable networks. In response, AOL is leading a coalition called

OpenNet, which advocates regulation to open cable-TV lines to all competitors (similar to the open-market standards imposed on local phone companies). The coalition includes MCI-WorldCom Inc., US West, and Mindspring Enterprises Inc. Entertainment companies have also expressed concern that their programs and movies could get locked out of the broadband Internet market.

Online service providers and ISPs currently do not pay access charges to local phone networks. However, the regional Bells contend that online services companies and ISPs should have to pay to connect to their services. They argue that local phone rates are based on the assumption of brief conversations. However, Internet calls tend to last much longer, tying up network switches and requiring the phone companies to upgrade their systems to handle the demand. Computer companies and Internet providers argue that changing the regulations would jeopardize the low monthly rates that have made the Internet accessible to millions of subscribers. The ISPs won a legal victory in August 1998, when an appeals court upheld the FCC's decision to prevent the local phone companies from charging ISPs access fees, similar to those that the local phone companies charge long-distance carriers. However, in February 1999, the FCC ruled that phone calls made to connect to ISPs should be considered long-distance instead of local calls. Although the FCC insists that this ruling would not affect how consumers connect to the Internet or how much they pay, consumer groups argue that this could lead to higher prices for people who access the Internet through services such as AOL.

Finally, a number of states, including New York, have considered new sales and use taxes on the Internet and online information services. This is particularly inviting as industry analysts predict that the value of computer-based electronic commerce will be more than $70 billion a year by the end of the decade. But legal and technical issues, such as the location of the transaction, its monitoring, etc., complicate matters.

AOL'S BUSINESS MODEL: QUO VADIS?

With online price comparisons, automatic grocery shopping and the ability to get whatever we want whenever we want it, 21st century Americans will face a radical reshaping of the consumer culture we have been building since the 1950s.

"The Cyberspace Marketplace," *Time,* July 20, 1998

Several years ago, AOL moved from a passive publishing model, towards "programming," i.e., to providing interactive chat rooms, hobby forums, games and personal business services, etc. With the sale of ANS, its service provider business, AOL planned to model itself after TV with a group of easy-to-use "channels" each based on subjects of interest such as sports, workplace, families and life styles. Visually, a channel is associated with a button on the screen (see Exhibit 15). However, the concept is broader—namely, to deliver real time information associated with the subject area of interest. AOL also decided to move from a revenue stream based largely on subscriber fees towards a more balanced model including revenues from advertising, electronic commerce and hosting of web sites.

"AOL Anywhere" is the label for an important component of AOL's current strategy. According to Steve Case, "AOL Anywhere is the idea that people do not want a separate service at different places." This means that AOL plans to extend Internet delivery to television, cable-TV, wireless handheld devices, and other Internet-enabled devices. AOL's new "Instant Messenger" service, which allows users to interchange messages immediately with friends who are currently online, is consistent with the AOL Anywhere strategy.

AOL's advertising and electronic commerce revenues (reported under "Other Income" in their financial statements) grew from $256 million in 1997 to $439 million in the 1998 fiscal year, accounting for approxi-

EXHIBIT 15   AOL "Channel" Screen and "Welcome" Screen (background)

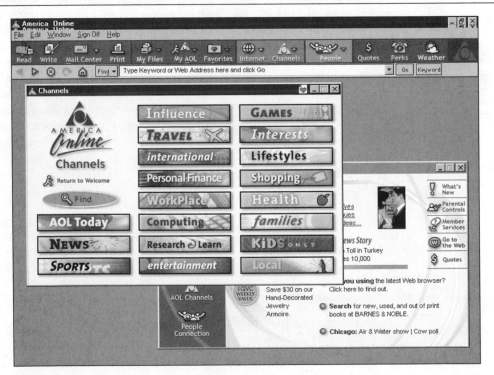

mately 17 percent of total revenues. Similar growth is expected in fiscal 1999. AOL's backlog of advertising and commerce revenues currently exceeds $1 billion.

Advertising is an important source of revenue on the Web. According to Jupiter Research, total advertising expenditure on the Web was almost $1 billion in 1998 but is likely to rise to $8 billion (approximately 4 percent of total advertising expenditures) by the year 2000. As in more traditional media, advertisers pay for exposure—a typical banner ad costs between $10–$30 per CPM (1000s of exposures measured)[3] or $100–$150 per thousand click-throughs (visits to the advertiser's site). There is an interesting duality with regard to advertising: it is common to advertise one's own site both on the Web and in other media in order to increase traffic. This in turn increases the value to others of advertising on your site. The amounts of money involved can be large—Alta Vista is thought to pay $5 million a year to advertise on Yahoo! According to Yahoo!, its mix of advertisers has changed from 85 percent computer-related in 1995 to approximately 80 percent consumer brands in 1997.

According to Forrester Research and Jupiter Communications, Internet sales were about $3.5 billion for the last quarter of 1998 as compared to $1.3 billion in 1997. Total online sales for the whole of 1998 is expected to be around $13 billion. Exhibit 16 lists the top online shopping sites along with the projected online spending by sector for 1999. IDC, a market research firm, predicts that more than one-third of U.S. households will be online in 1999, creating a surge in Internet users to 147 million people. AOL users spent an estimated $1.2 billion with online retailers on its service during the 1998 holiday season—an average of $80 from each of its 15 million accounts. In December 1998 alone more than 1 million customers shopped online for the first time on AOL.

While advertising and online sales malls will grow as sources of revenue, the Web has spawned several other innovative marketing models that are intended to create efficient markets for consumers and form new ways of doing business. Typical examples include: online auctions (eBay, OnSale, etc.), name your own price (Priceline.com), get paid for looking at ads (CyberGold), buy at cost for looking at ads (Buy.com), get a free PC for looking at ads (Free-PC), and band together for volume discounts (Accompany). AOL has alliances with Internet auction companies, OnSale and eBay and is developing its own auction site with help from eBay.

While AOL has built its success as a consumer-oriented company, it is currently exploring avenues to attract business customers. The combination of Netscape's enterprise and commerce software with Sun's

---

[3]Average ad rates for TV are $5 to $6 per CPM, and for a top magazine such as *Cosmopolitan* they are as high as $35 per CPM.

EXHIBIT 16 Online Shopping

Top Online Shopping Sites (1998)

No.	Web Site	Visitors (in millions)*
1	Bluemountainarts.com	12.32
2	Amazon.com	9.13
3	AOL.com**	8.04
4	Ebay.com	5.49
5	Barnesandnoble.com	4.69
6	Etoys.com	3.85
7	Cnet.com	3.45
8	Egghead.com	2.93
9	CDNow.com	2.69
10	Musicblvd.com	2.69
11	Columbiahouse.com	2.45
12	Classifieds2000.com	2.26
13	Beyond.com	2.17
14	Coolsavings.com	1.89
15	Valupage.com	1.82
16	123Greetings.com	1.75
17	Onsale.com	1.49

*Figures are for December 1998, with repeat visitors tallied once.

**Includes web and proprietary shopping areas.

Source: "Where Web Shoppers Stop," *New York Times,* February 21, 1999.

Estimated Online Revenues by Industry in Millions (1998)

Sector	Revenue (in $ millions)
Travel	$2,091
PC hardware	1,816
Groceries	270
Gifts/flowers	219
Books	216
PC software	173
Tickets	127
Music	81
Clothing	71

Source: Jupiter Communications.

Java tools should help AOL build and host corporate web sites (online stores), but it needs to compete with more established hosting services such as IBM and GTE Internetworking.

The volume of users visiting an Internet site is a crucial determinant of the revenue stream that it is likely to generate. Features such as news, weather, chat and games that attract visits can not only increase the number of subscribers but also increase the intrinsic value of other features at the site and the potential for advertising and e-commerce revenue at the same time. AOL's purchase of ICQ Chat, which has attracted 21 million members, obviously increases the scale of AOL's reach to consumers.

To build a business model, AOL's management must therefore consider a number of questions: What is the value of each feature on the site? How can interactive features such as games, music and chat rooms increase revenue? What is the appropriate level of advertising of AOL on foreign sites and in other media? What is the appropriate level of advertising (for others) on AOL's site? What is the appropriate mixture of non-income generating and income generating features, and more importantly, how should these services be priced?

As complex as these decisions are, they must be made in the context of a strategy that will ensure AOL's long-term growth; a strategy that can help AOL maintain its preeminent position in the face of rapid technological and social change and the competition of powerful global companies from multiple industries.

Appendix

THE INTERNET AND THE WORLD WIDE WEB

Formative Stages

The Internet began in 1972 as Arpanet, an experimental network financed by the U.S. Department of Defense. The Internet uses a communications protocol called TCP/IP (Transport Control Protocol/Internet Protocol). TCP/IP breaks messages from the sending computer into discrete variable-length packets of data before transmitting them independently over the network (via possibly different routes) to the receiving computer. Each packet contains the address of the sender and receiver. Advantages of this approach are its simplicity and reliability. In its original form, the Internet supported remote log-in, file transfer, and e-mail. In the early 1980s the Internet was funded by the National Science Foundation (NSF) and was extended to provide free access for educational institutions. In 1989–90, the Internet was opened for use by corporations and the general public. Since the Internet is based on open standards, it has been relatively easy for developers from all over the world to develop software and communication products that provide a wide array of services.

In 1990, Timothy Berners Lee, a British scientist working at the European Particle Physics laboratory (CERN) in Switzerland, developed HTTP (hypertext transfer protocol) to support the publication of documents consisting of text, audio, and video on the Internet. The documents themselves are written in HTML (hypertext mark-up language). The significant advance was that HTML documents residing on computers all over the world could now be linked to each other. The result was called the World Wide Web (WWW).

Building on this structure, Marc Andreesen of the National Center for Supercomputing developed Mosaic, a cross-platform WWW application, in 1993. Mosaic was the "killer-app" that launched what is perhaps the most profound economic and social revolution in history. Mosaic consisted of server software residing on a central computer or workstation and browser software on each client computer. The server software satisfies requests from the clients for HTML documents stored on the server. In 1994, Andreesen and several colleagues started the Netscape Corporation, which develops and distributes Netscape Navigator. For a time, Netscape was the most popular WWW browser with installations on approximately 64 percent of all computers connected to the Internet. However, in 1998, Netscape was overtaken by Microsoft's Internet Explorer (IE) browser, which comes "bundled" with almost all new Wintel and Macintosh machines. (Naturally, IE connects by default to Microsoft Network (MSN), giving MSN a modest advantage in the race with the other online service companies.)

In the year following the introduction of Mosaic, the number of Internet users doubled to over 3 million users. By mid-1999, there were about 70 million Internet users in the U.S. Recent Internet growth has been fueled by the rapid growth of electronic commerce. Commercial applications include providing company information to prospective investors and product information to customers, business-to-business communications and electronic data interchange (EDI), advertising, and consumer sales.

Technology: Access and Distribution

The Internet is, in reality, a network of thousands of sub-networks and millions of computers located all over the world. To provide convenient local access to the Internet, a whole new industry of Internet service providers (ISPs) has arisen over the last few years. ISPs provide local points of presence (POPs) that allow users to connect to the Internet via local telephone service. When a user dials into his/her local POP, the call must be received by a compatible device. Usually, this is a modem (which translates analog signals to digital and vice versa), but in the future, DSL, cable modems or satellite devices will be more common, particularly for commercial users (see below). Currently, modems can handle up to 56 Kbps (thousands of bits per second), but 33.6 and 28.8 Kbps modems are still in use.

The speed of the available modems (or preferably, the support for broadband access) is an important consideration when choosing an ISP. As shown in Exhibit A–1, a typical computer can handle multiple modems. When a call is received, it is allocated to the next available modem for the duration of the session. The number of users supported per modem is a crucial factor in capacity calculations; the industry average for ISPs is between 15 and 20 users. AOL currently has 800,000 modems supporting up to 750,000 simultaneous users sending 34 million e-mail messages and 290 Instant Message communications daily.[4] The power of the server hardware and software is a second crucial consideration in providing capacity. As shown in Exhibit A–1, the computational load is usually divided between a number of servers each performing a specialized function. Because of the enormous computing power needed to connect and store information about millions of users, there is a trend in the industry towards a centralized model of computing. AOL, Amazon.com and other large Internet companies run large "server farms" consisting of dozens of powerful computers. AOL has two such server farms in Richmond, Virginia, capable of handling nearly one million users. A third farm costing $520 million is planned.

By the year 2000, it is estimated that there will be 66.6 million households in over 100 countries connected to the Internet. In the U.S., 25 percent of all households have access to the Internet. With the number of people tapping into the Internet doubling every year, congestion is inevitable. This is particularly the case, because the average "net surf" lasts five times as long as the average telephone call, with 10 percent of Internet sessions lasting as long as six hours.

In the future, a variety of consumer-electronics devices will be wired to the Net: TVs, digital cameras, cell phones, digital pagers, personal digital assistants, even household appliances. A recent trend is to combine technologies to create new appliances and to combine services to provide new experiences for the user. Microsoft's WebTV, a set-top box, which combines television with Internet access, and Interactive TV, which allows two-way communication and gives users the ability to control their entertainment medium and respond to prompts for information, are two examples. These devices, together with Internet telephony and capacity-hungry multi-media applications, such as Internet radio, music and video conferencing, will place even greater loads on the Internet. To avoid delays many companies are building private Internets

---

[4]AOL's 1998 Annual Report.

EXHIBIT A–1   The Structure of the Internet

a. Schematic of the Internet

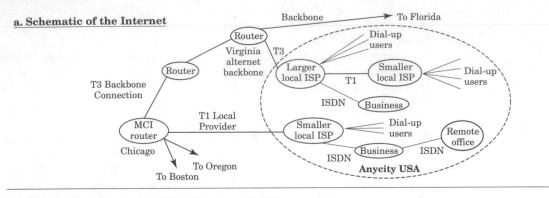

b. ISP Information Architecture/Business Model

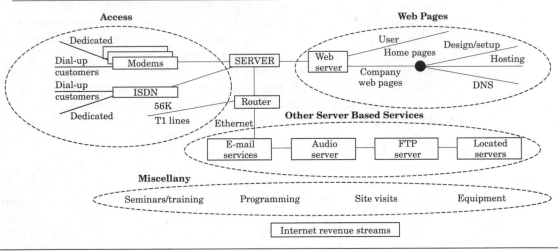

Source: *The Entrepreneurs Guide to Building an Internet Services Company, ISP or Online Business.*

("Extranets") to ensure fast communications with other firms. However, the growth in Internet capacity has been astounding—according to Bill Gates, Chairman and CEO of Microsoft, "the demand for Internet services will be exceeded only by the growth in its capacity." Three companies— MCI-WorldCom (Uunet), GTE Internetworking and Sprint—handle the bulk of U.S. Internet traffic (and all of AOL's).

Broadband Internet Access

Exhibit A–2 shows alternative technologies for connecting homes and businesses to a wide area network such as the Internet. So-called "narrow-band" access employs modems that convert digital signals for the computer to the analog signals that carry voice signals on the traditional

EXHIBIT A–2   The Information Superhighway: Emerging Technologies

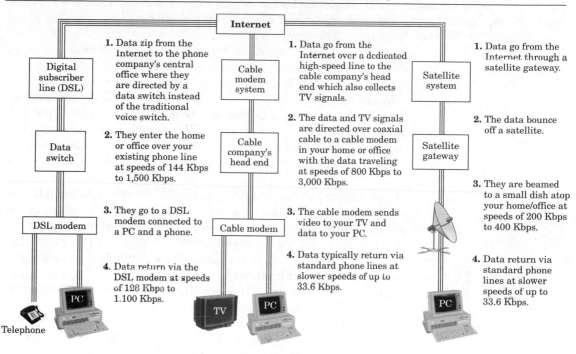

Service	Cost/Month	Speed to Your PC (Kbps)	Speed from Your PC (Kbps)
Modems	$20 to $100*	14.4 to 56	14.4 to 56
DSL Lite	$40 to $100	384 to 1,500	384 to 512
DSL	$40 to $200	144 to 1,500	128 to 1,100
Cable Modem	$30 to $60	800 to 3,000	33.6
Satellite Dishes	$20 to $130	200 to 400	33.6
T1	$1,200	1,544	1,544

*One-time cost.

Source: "Warp Speed Ahead," *Business Week,* February 16, 1998.

telephone system, and vice versa. The remaining technologies in Exhibit A–2 are alternative ways of achieving broadband access, which enables the transmission of data intensive applications such as TV and live video.

T1 service is a private line leased from a telephone company that costs several thousand dollars per month. T1 is often used by businesses to link geographic sites as well as to connect to the Internet.[5]

---

[5]T3 lines have a capacity of 45 megabits per second and are used as part of the backbone of the Internet (see Figure A–1).

Cable modems are up to 50 times faster than traditional telephone modems. Cable networks for delivery of broadband Internet services are expensive to construct. Essentially, a cable network branches like a tree from the cable company's "head end" (central distribution point) through various feeder stations to individual homes. Branches closer to the main distribution point (trunk of tree) serve multiple users and performance can degrade under heavy usage. Cable companies such as Time Warner and At Home have already provided cable modem service in parts of their regions. Cable modems, which currently cost about $40 per month in addition to the normal ISP access fee, are currently the most popular form of broadband access. But, because of the potential billion dollar revenues, the competition from alternative technologies is likely to be intense.

Digital subscriber line technologies (DSL)[6] permit wide band transmission over the twisted pair copper wiring that carries household telephone lines. While transmission rates are nominally lower than for cable modems, DSL will not degrade as more people in the local area connect to the Internet. This is because DSL is a switched technology—a dedicated circuit is maintained between the household and the telephone company's local switch. The local Bell Companies—Bell Atlantic, SBC, and so on—are driving the deployment of DSL.

Satellite communications have been used for commercial voice and data transmission for over 30 years. Today new constellations of satellites costing billions of dollars provide services such as teleconferencing, mobile communications, and direct broadcast of television signals to businesses and homes all over the world. Major projects include Iridium (developed by a consortium led by Motorola) and Teledesic, which is backed by Microsoft among other companies. When it is completed in 2003, Teledesic will provide worldwide connection to the Internet.

Security and Payment Mechanisms

Security was a major concern in the early days of the Internet. Security depends on the development of a number of complex technologies such as a robust data encryption standard, an efficient electronic payments system, and electronic document interchange standards, which would allow companies to exchange purchase orders and forms. These technologies have been developed and deployed very rapidly. Netscape's SSL (Secure Sockets Layer) is currently the most popular mechanism for securing messages such as credit card numbers on the Internet. SSL checks that the connection is reliable, authenticates the client and host

---

[6]DSL comes in a number of forms. ADSL (asymmetric digital subscriber line) is one such form; the name comes from the differential speed at which data is transmitted to and from the home.

machines, and encrypts all subsequent transmissions. MasterCard and Visa International are currently launching a security system designed called SET (Secure Electronic Transaction.) SET authenticates both the merchant and the customer involved in the transaction and facilitates the credit-card approval process.

At most web sites, shoppers fill an electronic "shopping basket" with goods, then proceed to the online equivalent of a checkout counter where they provide detailed personal information—including their name, address and credit-card number. This tedious process has to be repeated each time they visit a different site. Electronic wallets hold customer information (credit-card numbers, address books, etc.) in a secure form either on the user's hard drive or on the merchant's or financial institution's server. Purchases can then be made by simply clicking on an image of the purse.

In addition to securing e-commerce transactions, Internet sites must protect the integrity of the data on their sites and guard against attacks by hackers. Firewalls, combinations of hardware and software that are set up between the Internet and the site's computers, are used to prevent unwanted traffic from entering or leaving the site.

Regulation and Deregulation

Until 1995, the NSF provided some financial support for the Internet and maintained the NSFNet "Backbone"—very high speed communications lines connecting government-sponsored "super computer" centers and major research and educational sites. Since 1995, the Internet has been entirely financed by user fees. The Internet is not really owned by anyone. It is governed by a non-profit organization, the Internet Society (ISOC). Another non-profit group, the Internet Activities Board (IAB), sets technical policies and standards.

The commercialization of the Internet was widespread and rapid and has fundamentally changed its culture. The traditional culture of the Internet emphasized freedom of expression, bottom-up governance, and a spirit of sharing. The Internet user community still jealously guards these values, and the culture of the web is something to be reckoned with by commercial organizations. For example, "spamming"—the broadcast of unsolicited advertising material—is fiercely resisted.

Although the Internet remains largely unregulated, there has been a debate over whether the FCC should provide a forum for public hearings to establish industry-wide ground rules for the Internet, similar to that which it has provided in telecommunications. Government's efforts to regulate Internet information have been most visible in cases of pornography, gambling, and hate speech. There is no consensus on whether existing jurisdictional rules ought to be extended to cyberspace. Privacy is a hotly debated topic, particularly with the rapid rise in Internet use by non-technical consumers. Bills seeking to prevent online service providers and ISPs, such as AOL or Netcom, from selling personal information about their subscribers without written permission, and to require a detailed accounting of the use of computer databases, have periodically been introduced in Congress.

The Telecommunications Act of 1996 deregulated wireless and wired communications in the United States. Effectively, this means that local phone companies can offer one of the services previously offered by long-distance carriers and cable companies. Long-distance companies can enter the local phone business or offer cable services and cable companies are permitted to offer long-distance telephone service or compete with the local phone service. This law, together with the technical convergence on digital technologies discussed in the text, will increase competition and enable completely new services to be delivered.

Chapter 5

Electronic Commerce— Services

In many ways it is services, not products, that fit most naturally with electronic commerce. While products can be ordered and paid for electronically, they can not be delivered that way. Services, on the other hand, can often be paid for and delivered electronically and consumed immediately. Companies such as America Online and *The Wall Street Journal* make money by delivering content to Internet users and access providers for a fee. Other service providers such as financial brokerage houses, news clippers, translation agencies, and travel agents are finding that they can offer services at a lower cost through electronic means than through traditional channels. The vast majority of content providers, however, fail to make money on the Internet. The culture of the Internet has developed around tenets of trust, openness, and volunteerism. The challenge has been to convince users to pay for electronic commerce services (see Chapter 7 for further discussion on Internet payment systems), when so much can be accessed for free. One way businesses have done this is by adding value, or intelligent analysis, to the information they provide.

The chapter's first case is about Open Text Corporation, the company behind one of the Internet's first search engines, the Open Text Index. The case revolves around two basic issues: revenue generation on the Internet and Internet culture. Revenue generation has been, and continues to be, a challenge for most Internet companies. Traditional models such as banner advertising, subscription fees and usage fees have been dominant, but new models are being tried all the time. In order to increase revenues, Open Text came up with a revenue model that involved advertisers paying to have their web sites appear at the top of search engine results when "bought" words were included in the search criteria. It was an innovative approach to revenue generation, and a departure from the traditionally dominant "banner ad" model. The second issue of the case concerns whether Internet culture will allow search engine results, which are generally considered to be a free and "accurate" resource, to be influenced by advertisers. The case also describes the technical aspects of search engine technology, and thus can be used as a primer for a discussion on index, search, and retrieval techniques.

The second case concerns Jobnet, a startup company in the job placement industry. Jobnet's focus is to provide the company's basic services, job matching and placement, using the Internet. Jobnet was confronted with a decision to enhance its ability to service clients in its domestic market. An opportunity to purchase new software and hardware presented itself. However, the software, a "parametric search engine," was nonstandard, in that it had been originally designed for the manufacturing and distribution industries. The specific issue faced by the principals of Jobnet involves decision making when unfamiliarity with technology and differing perspectives have to be reconciled. The broader issue involves the longer-term viability of a job placement company attempting to work primarily through the Internet.

The third case is about Stock Research Group (SRG), a financial services information broker. SRG's primary business is serving as a collection point for information useful to investors seeking to invest in small-cap firms—primarily mining companies. SRG in effect pulls potential investors to its site, then channels them to the specific sites of companies in which the investors may have an investment interest. SRG's revenue comes from the mining companies, who generally pay on an impression basis (i.e., pay for "eyeballs" delivered to their web pages). The resource companies are willing to pay for this, as they are much less likely to attract much investor traffic on their own. SRG is also in the business of developing web pages for these small-cap investment firms, since resource firms generally do not have in-house expertise to create and maintain a web presence. SRG thus represents a new kind of business—the specialized "infomediary," or information broker. Further, SRG is doing quite well financially, something that cannot be said of many web-based companies. The case describes how SRG got to where it is today, and where it hopes to go in the future.

The final case in this section describes Celebrity Sightings, a web-based company that offers services to fans of teenage celebrities. The case describes the creation of the company and its evolution during the first two years of operation. The company provides a forum in which fans can read material about their favorite celebrities, purchase celebrity merchandise, and chat with one another. The company is also a "front" for many celebrity web sites. Special features and promotions, such as interactive chat sessions with celebrities help to attract premium (paying) members. A number of issues are brought up in the case. These include effective web site design, marketing of web-based services, online community building, and the necessity of continuous innovation.

Open Text Preferred Listings (A)

By Professor Sid L. Huff and Mike Wade

It was June 20, 1996, and the marketing team at Open Text Corporation in Waterloo, Ontario were putting the finishing touches on the new "Preferred Listings" service. Senior management had to decide whether to incorporate this service into the company's main product, the Open Text Index, an Internet search engine.

OPEN TEXT CORPORATION

Open Text Corporation was born in the aftermath of a project to index and catalogue the 60 million words and 2.4 million quotations contained in the Oxford English Dictionary (OED). OED project manager, Tim Bray and two University of Waterloo professors, Frank Tompa and Gaston Gonnet, formed Open Text after the project ended in 1989. In its early days, Open Text was, according to Bray, a "low-key, academics-in-the-garage kind of operation" with a superior product, the software used to index the OED, but without the marketing or management skills required to exploit it. Potential clients had trouble imagining any new uses for the product. "When we showed people the OED, they said, 'This is good stuff, but we don't have a dictionary.'" Bray notes, "As computer scientists, no matter how hard we tried to explain the benefits, we couldn't do it."

In 1994, the company brought Tom Jenkins in as president. The 36-year-old electrical engineer had worked in a number of high-tech companies. He had a technical background (his name is on several patents for integrated circuit designs), but his main contribution to the company came from his experience as a sales and marketing manager. When Jenkins got the call, Open Text was just one product, the direct descendant of the OED's search engine. It was a product without a market, and without any change, the venture seemed doomed. But unbeknownst to Jenkins or anyone else at Open Text, the company was actually well positioned to take advantage of the unexpected growth in global networking.

"The Internet came out of nowhere and surprised everybody," said Bray. "Partly through design and, to be honest, partly through accident, our software's technical characteristics applied beautifully to the Internet." Bray recalled the exact moment Open Text changed course. In November 1994, a speaker at a conference that Bray was attending made an observation about the World Wide Web (WWW). He said, "The truth may be out there, but without help, you'll never find it." At that moment the "penny dropped" for Bray—the Web needed a search engine! "I was so excited, I was physically shaking for a couple of days, because I could see right away how it could be done."

Bray's idea was to send robotic software agents crawling through cyberspace, following tens of thousands of links and finding millions of pages of text, then bring them home and index them. Users would be able to search this vast catalogue of information by using key words. The retrieved information would be ranked according to relevancy with the most relevant result at the top of the list. Users could then find the best-fit material they wanted quickly and efficiently.

As Open Text worked to get an indexing software package together for the WWW, it became obvious that others were working toward the same goal. In April 1995, Open Text launched the Open Text Index on the WWW. The Open Text Index was initially designed to showcase the company's information management and indexing software. The product was a huge hit with Internet users as it was easy to use, free and comprehensive.

By the end of 1995, the Open Text Index was getting half a million visits per day and was routinely mentioned in the press as one of the top search engines on the Internet. It became so successful that Open Text management decided to run the Open Text Index as a for-profit center by selling online space to advertisers.

Open Text had many early successes, most notably the exposure it received thanks to its partnership with Yahoo, the definitive WWW catalogue. In the fall of 1995, Open Text agreed to be the main indexing agent and search engine associated with the Yahoo index, a service it agreed to provide free of charge. Management felt that the exposure and recognition Open Text would receive due to its collaboration with Yahoo would justify the running costs. See Exhibit 1 for a description of the difference between a catalogue and a search engine.

In January of 1996, Open Text raised US$69 million in a successful initial public offering (IPO) and joined the NASDAQ index. The stock initially soared but lost value in the following months. Chinks in the Open Text armor started to appear by April 1996. Netscape, who had offered Open Text a spot on its home page, one of the most visited sites on the net, decided to go with other search engines. Newer search engines such as AltaVista and Excite had developed superior products. From being one of the pioneers, the Open Text Index was becoming a

---

EXHIBIT 1 Internet Catalogues and Search Engines

Internet catalogues and search engines are two tools available for Internet users to cut through the vast amount of information on the World Wide Web (WWW). Even though they approach the task differently, both have their uses depending on the nature of the information being sought.

Internet catalogues such as Yahoo are essentially searchable directories. Designed in a tree structure, they allow users to delve deeper and deeper into a particular category, until the desired topic is isolated. At the lowest level, the user receives a series of links relating to the chosen topic. Most Internet catalogues don't actually index the linked web pages. An advantage of this structure is that searches can be refined to include only those topics of interest to the user. Disadvantages are that searches can be slow if there are many branches to go down, and imprecise if directory categories don't mesh perfectly with the categories users are looking for.

Search engines such as Open Text Index are vast databases, holding millions of web pages. These databases can be searched using key words as search criterion. When a search is initiated, the search engine goes through its database of web pages and responds with the most appropriate results. Most search engines respond to search requests quickly, and since many search engines index all the words on a web page, the level of detail is very high. A disadvantage of search engines is the high number of search results that are inappropriate to the search criteria. It is not uncommon for a search engine to retrieve hundreds of thousands of search results, 99 per cent of which are useless, i.e., a high signal-to-noise ratio.

EXHIBIT 2   Open Text Stock Chart (15.1.96–15.6.96)

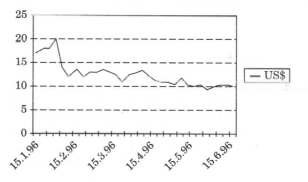

"me-too" search engine. A deep blow came in early June 1996, when Yahoo cancelled its arrangement with the Open Text Index and, instead, signed a long-term agreement with AltaVista to provide its search services. Management felt that the positive brand exposure generated from working with Yahoo did not justify the cost of running the service. Open Text stock dropped by $1 on the news. See Exhibit 2 for share price data for the period.

EXHIBIT 3   What Is a "Spider"?

A "spider" or "web robot" is a program that traverses the Web's hypertext structure, retrieves web pages, indexes them in a database, and then recursively retrieves all documents linked to those web pages. The name "spider" is a bit misleading as it gives the impression that the software itself moves between sites like a virus. This is not the case. A spider simply visits sites by requesting documents from them. This is different from an "autonomous agent," which does travel between sites, deciding when to move and what to do. Autonomous agents can only travel between special servers and are currently not widespread on the Internet.

Spiders allow search engines and other databases to be updated automatically at regular intervals, so that "dead" links in the databases can be detected and removed. Spiders operate continually over prolonged periods of time, often months. To speed up operations, many spiders feature parallel retrieval, resulting in a consistently high use of bandwidth in the immediate proximity. Consequently, some sites do not like to be visited by spiders. To stop a spider from visiting a site, or part of a site, a special file called a robot.txt file can be inserted on the web server.

In general, spiders start from a historical list of Uniform Resource Locators (URLs), especially of documents with many links elsewhere, such as server lists, "What's New" pages, and the most popular sites on the Web. Most search engines and indexing services also allow users to submit URLs manually, which will then be queued and visited by the spider. Sometimes other sources for URLs are used, such as scanning through Usenet postings, published mailing list archives, and so on.

The amount of data a spider indexes depends on the particular spider. Some spiders index just the text in the title section of the web page's underlying code, or the titles plus the first few paragraphs of text. Others parse the entire page, including hidden tags and all text, and apply weightings to different components. In practice, most spiders end up indexing and storing almost everything they come across.

WORLD WIDE WEB SEARCH ENGINES

In June 1996, there were a number of search engines on the WWW. The big names, in order of popularity were AltaVista, Excite, Webcrawler, Lycos, Open Text Index and Infoseek. "Meta" search engines, which would submit a search request to a number of search engines concurrently, were also in existence. All search engines basically did the same thing in slightly different ways. Using "spiders," they combed the WWW by travelling from link to link, indexing the pages they found along the way. See Exhibit 3 for a description of how spiders work. Pages could also be submitted to the indexes by programmers. Some engines only indexed a portion of each web page, others indexed the whole thing, every word on every page. Most search engines allowed users to run advanced searches using Boolean operators such as AND, OR, NEAR and NOT. These helped users to refine searches. Nevertheless, often a search would result in thousands of hits, many of which were not useful to the user resulting in a high signal-to-noise ratio. See Exhibit 4 for a comparison of the top search engines.

EXHIBIT 4   World Wide Web Search Engines

The following chart describes some differences among various WWW search engines.

Category	AltaVista	Excite	Webcrawler	Lycos	Open Text	Infoseek
Case sensitive?	Y	N	N	N	N	Y
Considers phrases?	Y	N	Y	N	Y	Y
Required term operator	+	+	N	N	N	+
Prohibited term operator	–	–	N	N	N	–
Results ranking?	Y	Y	Y	Y	Y	Y
Controllable results ranking?	Y	N	N	Y	N	N
Booleans allowed?	Y	Y	Y	N	Y	N
Proximity operators allowed?	Y(10)	N	Y(range)	N	Y(80)	Y(100)
Subject (directory) searching?	N	Y	Y	Y	N	Y
Refine based on first search?	N	Y	N	N	Y	N
Controllable display format?	Y	N	Y	Y	N	N

All search engines received revenue by selling advertising space on their web pages. It was generally understood in the industry that revenue from this type of advertising was not sufficient to cover operating costs. The search engines ran at a loss in the hope of operating profitably in the future.

PREFERRED LISTINGS

The Open Text Index, like other search engines, made its money from advertising revenue. Advertisers "bought" certain words so that when users included a bought word in their search strings, the advertiser's banner appeared at the top of the page over the search results. For example, a hotel chain might buy the word "travel." If an Internet user ran a search including the word "travel," the hotel chain's advertising banner would appear above the results of the search. In the case of the Open Text Index, advertisers would be charged five cents each time their word was included in a search request.

The marketing team in Waterloo believed that the potential to earn revenue from the Open Text Index was underrealized. In response to many requests from advertisers, they came up with the idea of Preferred Listings.

By buying a Preferred Listing, advertisers would be guaranteed to appear at the top of the retrieved lists of relevant web pages. So, for a fee, a link to the web page of the same hotel chain mentioned earlier would appear at the top of the search results list. This differed from the banner advertising model in a number of ways. For one thing, the paid-for link would look similar to other non-paid-for search results. Also, more than one advertiser could buy each target word.

The top 10 spots on the search result list for each target word would be sold at a sliding fee scale. The number one spot would go for US$20,000 while the number 10 spot could be purchased for US$2,000. The paid-for spots could be renewed at six-month intervals. To make the user aware that the paid-for place would not necessarily be the most relevant, the marketing department decided that it would be fair to mark the paid-for spots clearly as advertising space. This was done using a special icon that would appear next to the paid-for spot. If all 10 of the top spots were bought, then the eleventh spot would actually be the most relevant result of the search.

The potential for revenue generation using Preferred Listings was significant. If a word was completely bought it would generate US$110,000 for the company every six months. If the company could completely sell just 100 words, it would generate US$22,000,000 in revenue in the first year or more than 20 times the previous year's revenue from traditionally placed banner ads.

There was some speculation that allowing advertisers to buy spots on the list of retrieved search results would not be received well by the Internet community. The de facto standard for WWW search engines was for the search retrieval list to be organized by relevancy. The most relevant items would be returned first, and the least relevant would appear last. It was not clear how the Internet community would react if this standard was altered.

Proponents of the plan likened the scheme to the Yellow Pages, where advertisers paid for larger and more prominent listings. Opponents noted that, unlike the Yellow Pages which lists in alphabetical order, a WWW search engine is *expected* to list by relevancy.

The technology to add preferred listings to the Open Text Index was in place. In addition, many advertisers had shown interest in the service. Senior management had to decide whether or not to go ahead.

Jobnet: Finding a Job through the Internet

By Professor Sid L. Huff and Harvey Enns

On June 10, 1996, the senior executives of Jobnet, an Internet-based job placement service, sat in one of their meeting rooms and listened to a presentation by Antaeus Systems Inc., a software reseller, about one of their leading edge products—a specialized search "engine" for use over the Internet. The initiative for the meeting came from Tom van Turnhout, a Jobnet director. Van Turnhout had discovered the software product, and thought it would be a valuable addition to Jobnet's World Wide Web–based system. In van Turnhout's mind, the new search engine had the potential to differentiate Jobnet from other Internet-based job placement services. However, he and the other executives also saw some risks associated with this new initiative. The senior management group had to decide whether the potential rewards justified the costs and risks.

FRESHSTART PARTNERS INC. AND JOBNET: GENERAL COMPANY BACKGROUND

Freshstart Partners Inc. (FSP) was established in 1994 for the purpose of providing a job matching service for employers and individuals looking for employment. The original concept for FSP emerged from discussions between the two founders, William R. (Bill) MacDougall, and James A. Towse. MacDougall had a background in advertising and marketing. In 1971, he started an advertising agency, Marketing Communications. The agency grew and prospered, and in 1992, he sold his share of the company to his partner, and began looking for a new venture in which to invest his energy and resources. Towse's background was in human resources and operational management. He had worked for the past 20 years for Avco Financial Services Canada, most recently as Vice President, Corporate Development. Towse left Avco in 1993. MacDougall and Towse had met some years before, in a business setting. Later, after Towse left Avco, MacDougall sought Towse out to talk with him about teaming up to find a new business opportunity.

The original concept for FSP was a simple variant on the job placement agency idea. With the unemployment rate in Ontario and much of the rest of Canada at nearly 10 percent, MacDougall and Towse felt there must be a strong supply of individuals anxious to find jobs. At the same time, since the economy was doing relatively well, slowly recovering from the recession of the early 1990s, there should be a reasonable demand from firms for employees. They felt the largest opportunities existed in the lower and middle levels of management.

Their original plan was to advertise in newspapers for job-seeking individuals to register themselves with FSP. They would charge a fee for an individual to have his résumé information entered into FSP's database— say, $50. But they would allow an employer to conduct a search on the database for free. An individual looking for work would mail or fax or telephone the necessary information to an operator at FSP's call center in London, Ontario. The information about the person and his or her skills would be entered into FSP's database. Then, an employer (client) seeking to hire someone could contact the call center, specify its needs, and FSP would execute a database search on the client's behalf and forward the resulting information to the client.

MacDougall and Towse felt that the value they would provide would come from being able to select the most appropriate candidates for a particular job, using the capabilities of the database to focus the search. As they noted, an employer placing a "help wanted" advertisement in the paper would be inundated with résumés, and would have to spend a great deal of time sorting through them to determine those most appropriate for the position. FSP would save the employer all that time, by only forwarding résumé information on candidates who fit the requirements.

With that business model in mind, MacDougall and Towse created Freshstart Partners Ltd. in April 1994. MacDougall became the company's President, and Towse the CEO. They were joined in the project by Tim W. Forristal, previously an audit and tax partner with Deloitte and Touche. Forristal was named CFO of FSP. Sheila Dunford also joined FSP in September 1994, with the title of Placement Director. Prior to that she had been an employment counsellor with Human Resources Development Canada. In May 1995, Tom van Turnhout, Vice President of Information Technology and CIO of Chelsey Corporation, was appointed to the Board of Directors of FSP. Initial funding for the initiation of the company came from personal investments made by the company principals, primarily MacDougall and Towse. MacDougall and Towse held joint ownership of the initial shares of FSP. [Exhibit 1 shows a partial organizational chart for the London office.]

MacDougall and Towse saw three types of corporate clients who might use their services. First (and most basic) was the individual company seeking to hire a new employee. While FSP did not charge such companies a fee to search the database at the time, they planned to in-

EXHIBIT 1   Partial Organization Chart for Jobnet

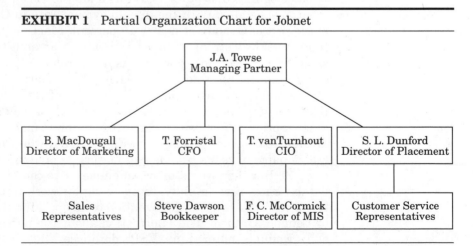

troduce a search fee soon. Second was an organization in the midst of a downsizing or restructuring, wishing to provide a group of employees with a placement listing through FSP. The company could negotiate with such organizations for special rates to add information on such groups of employees into their database. Finally, various government social service agencies such as Human Resources Development Canada, might be willing to negotiate a "mass" placement arrangement with FSP. In particular, MacDougall and Towse realized that the provincial government was launching a major "workfare" experiment to try to get welfare recipients back to work. This project presented a potentially huge opportunity.

A NEW OPPORTUNITY

As MacDougall and Towse pushed ahead to get FSP up and running, a new opportunity soon became apparent: the Internet. They had originally thought that telephone, mail and fax would comprise the company's distribution channels, the means whereby they would obtain résumé information from job seekers and also distribute information to employer firms. They later recognized that a fourth channel, perhaps most important of all, was available to them in the form of the Internet. They felt they could use the World Wide Web (a part of the Internet) to register and bill individual job seekers, as well as to provide employers direct, hands-on access to their database. With that in mind, they created Jobnet, a subsidiary of FSP, in April 1995. The role of Jobnet was to develop and manage an Internet presence for the company's job-matching business.

Although some of the staff did have information technology experience, the principal owners, MacDougall and Towse, did not. Rather, they relied on advice from other officers such as van Turnhout and external consultants, when making information technology decisions. Towse summarized the decision to go the Internet route:

> A lot of job hunters do not yet have access to the Internet. We are gambling on this new technology and that the Internet as a vehicle will be made accessible through other facilities like the library and school systems. The key to Jobnet is, will the Internet become a tool for everyday use? If it goes this way, the business will be a gargantuan success.

MacDougall added:

> Our goal is not to "make money on the Internet." We want to be able to make use of the Internet as a communication vehicle that will be able to reduce our communications costs.

Initially, FSP acquired its own server PC, and contracted with an Internet Service Provider, MCC Systems Inc., to house and maintain the server. At first, Jobnet considered sharing their web site (and server resources) with other firms who also wished to have a web presence, as a way of making some extra money. However, they soon recognized that management of their server and their web presence required closer attention than could be provided under such an arrangement. For instance, under a shared web-site arrangement, when the web site was accessed by a potential client, information regarding other companies' products could appear on the same web page as Jobnet's information. Towse commented:

> Relying on the service provider to provide the level of service required was too risky. The core service functions needed to be in-house. The only competitive advantage is the level of service you provide, so this needed to be controlled. We'd be stupid if we failed to provide the level of service necessary.

Also, MCC wanted to charge Jobnet a hefty fee for managing and maintaining the server. For these reasons, MacDougall and Towse were considering moving the server computer into their own premises, and operating a dedicated, not shared, web site.

Jobnet's web site became operational in February 1996. The original technical work to create the web site was contracted to a graphics company, Virtual Systems. This gave Jobnet an immediate presence on the Internet and also bought them some time to identify a company that could create a more sophisticated "look." In addition, van Turnhout started developing the concept for the database, but it soon became apparent that he required more assistance in this task. Van Turnhout approached Frank McCormick, who had experience in the insurance and services industries, about finishing the development of the database on a contract basis. McCormick, who was enrolled in a software development course, agreed to take on the job of completing the database infrastructure on weekends. McCormick built the forms, queries, and supports necessary for the smooth operation of the database. McCormick was eventually hired on a full-time basis in January 1996. Also, Keith MacDougall, a high school student and Bill MacDougall's son, was brought in as part of a high school apprenticeship to enhance the original web site and database infrastructure.

Once the site was up and running, individual clients looking for a job could register themselves via the web site. Those who did not have access to the Internet could still register by phone or fax or regular mail. Individual clients who were looking for a job had to pay a fee in order to be included in the database. Corporate clients could place job postings on the web site as well as search the database to identify specific skill sets. When qualified candidates were found, companies would arrange face-to-face interviews directly with the individuals. Corporate clients could register for free and use the system's features after a 48-hour verification/security process was completed.

See Exhibit 2 for FSP's financial projections.

EXHIBIT 2   FSP's Financial Projections

Freshstart Partners Inc.
Financial Projections of Earnings
For the Five Years Ended December 31

	Jun–Dec 1996	1997	1998	1999	2000
Revenues					
Registrants—base	$1,155,000	$3,267,600	$4,968,000	$6,952,500	$10,700,000
Employer—connect	$0	$580,000	$1,220,000	$1,464,000	$1,756,800
Contract revenue, net	100,000	200,000	250,000	250,000	250,000
	$1,255,000	$4,047,600	$6,438,000	$8,666,500	$12,706,800
Operating expenses					
Rent	52,000	257,000	273,000	289,000	289,000
Telephone/communications	20,500	75,000	75,000	75,000	75,000
Office	15,000	70,000	70,000	70,000	75,000
Wages and salaries—admin.	47,250	217,000	322,500	322,500	382,500
Wages and salaries—selling	144,550	597,300	775,630	1,096,770	1,523,080
Communications center costs	275,000	466,800	496,800	502,125	642,000
Advertising	383,000	1,089,200	1,545,600	1,641,000	1,641,000
Advertising—initial launch	260,000	250,000	0	0	0
Miscellaneous	25,500	63,000	68,000	68,000	68,000
Total operating expenses	$1,222,800	$3,085,300	$3,626,530	$4,064,395	$4,695,580
Head office expenses					
Communications/systems	50,000	125,000	125,000	100,000	100,000
Advertising	0	75,000	75,000	100,000	100,000
Travel	20,000	30,000	30,000	30,000	30,000
Wages and salaries—admin.	50,000	110,000	150,000	150,000	150,000
Wages and salaries—IT	40,000	175,000	175,000	175,000	175,000
Professional fees	25,000	30,000	35,000	40,000	45,000
Office	10,000	10,000	15,000	15,000	15,000
Rent	14,000	30,000	50,000	50,000	50,000
Managing & consulting fees	300,000				
Management salaries & benefits	210,000	420,000	420,000	500,000	500,000
Depreciation	99,197	127,935	165,439	184,258	193,923
Total head office expenses	$818,197	$1,132,935	$1,240,439	$1,344,258	$1,358,923
Net earnings before income taxes	($785,997)	($170,635)	$1,571,031	$3,257,847	$6,652,297
Provision for income taxes			273,900	1,452,348	2,965,594
Net earnings	($785,997)	($170,635)	$1,297,132	$1,805,499	$3,686,703

Continued

EXHIBIT 2   (Continued)

Freshstart Partners Inc.
Financial Projections of Balance Sheet
For the Five Years Ended December 31

	1996	1997	1998	1999	2000
Cash	$461,131	$1,130,431	$2,357,002	$4,098,758	$7,755,385
Fixed assets					
Computer hardware	113,438	219,438	305,438	403,438	477,438
Computer software	144,063	244,063	344,063	444,063	544,063
Furniture & equipment	82,168	139,168	164,168	189,168	214,168
Less: Accumulated depreciation	(99,197)	(227,131)	(392,570)	(576,828)	(770,751)
Fixed assets, net	$240,473	$375,538	$421,099	$459,841	$464,918
Total assets	$701,604	$1,505,969	$2,778,101	$4,558,599	$8,220,302
Liabilities (cash basis assumed for projections)	$250,000	$225,000	$200,000	$175,000	$150,000
Shareholders' equity					
Common shares	$1,408,002	$2,408,002	2,408,002	2,408,002	2,408,002
Retained earnings	(111,402)	(956,399)	(1,127,033)	170,098	1,975,597
JCP costs	(59,000)				
Earnings for the year	(785,997)	(170,635)	1,297,132	1,805,499	3,686,703
Total shareholders' equity	$451,603	$1,280,969	$2,578,100	$4,383,599	$8,070,302
Total liabilities & shareholders' equity	$701,603	$1,505,969	$2,778,100	$4,558,599	$8,220,302

THE COMMUNICATIONS CENTER

The new company recognized the need for a decent communications center. A location within Jobnet's office was chosen and a Norstar Meridian PBX system was acquired from the former tenants of FSP's office space. It had the capability of accommodating eight work stations with twelve telephone lines devoted to incoming calls. MacDougall and Towse recognized the communications center as a key asset of the company. The communications center performed a variety of services for clients, both job seekers and corporate clients, including handling pay-

EXHIBIT 2   (Continued)

Freshstart Partners Inc.
Financial Projections of Cash Flow
For the Five Years Ended December 31

	Jun–Dec 1996	1997	1998	1999	2000
Cash, opening balance	$254,261	$461,131	$1,130,431	$2,357,002	$4,098,758
Add					
Registrants—base	$1,155,000	$3,267,600	$4,968,000	$6,952,500	$10,700,000
Employer—connect	0	580,000	1,220,000	1,464,000	1,756,800
Contract revenue, net	100,000	200,000	250,000	250,000	250,000
New share issue	1,000,000	1,000,000			
Total cash in	$2,255,000	$5,047,600	$6,438,000	$8,666,500	$12,706,800
Deduct					
Total operating expenses	$1,222,800	$3,085,300	$3,626,530	$4,064,395	$4,695,580
Total head office expenses (excl. depreciation)	719,000	1,005,000	1,075,000	1,160,000	1,165,000
Income taxes	0	0	273,900	1,452,348	2,965,594
Computer hardware	71,000	106,000	86,000	98,000	74,000
Computer software	35,000	100,000	100,000	100,000	100,000
Furniture & equipment	39,000	57,000	25,000	25,000	25,000
Retire (increase) small business loan	(38,670)	25,000	25,000	25,000	25,000
Total cash out	$2,048,130	$4,378,300	$5,211,430	$6,924,743	$9,050,174
Cash, closing balance	$461,131	$1,130,431	$2,357,002	$4,098,758	$7,755,385

ment transactions, providing registration assistance, and providing assistance in finding suitable candidates for those that were unfamiliar with or unable to use Jobnet's search capabilities. As MacDougall pointed out:

> A key to the business was making it easy for clients to register. This company was built around that philosophy. One of our main competitors, JCI, requires clients to register using a kit. Here we want to avoid this by making it simple to register.

OTHER POTENTIAL LINES OF BUSINESS

Jobnet also hoped to provide other services to corporate clients, for example, outplacement services such as referrals to counselling for employees who had lost their jobs due to downsizing. Also, Jobnet wanted to capitalize on provincial and federal employment agencies' budget cuts, by contracting with these governmental agencies for the job placement work they were currently performing. Another prospective service that Jobnet was contemplating was taking over placement aspects of the human resource function for private companies. Jobnet could use its skills to manage all aspects of both external and internal company placements on behalf of client firms. Jobnet also considered the possibilities of adding other search services similar to the real estate and car shopping services provided by competitor, JCI.

Finally, another initiative that Jobnet was pursuing was to partner with a university to provide a "branded" placement service for the university. The university could advertise a Jobnet-like service to their alumni and any alumni taking advantage of the service would perceive it to be a service offered directly by the university. Jobnet could simply provide a tailored web site and tailored responses to 800-number enquiries, thereby essentially putting the university's name on the basic Jobnet service offering. Revenues would be shared between the university and Jobnet.

INDUSTRY PROFILE

The outplacement consulting industry was a $65-million to $75-million-a-year business in Canada in 1995 and had been the fastest growing part of the consulting industry in Canada for the past 10 years. Mac-Dougall estimated that it was a $1-billion industry in North America. Downsizings were beginning to slow down; however, companies were continuing to reorganize as they searched for ways to streamline further. Business reengineering was also providing substantial business for outplacement services, and this was expected to continue for the next few years at least.

Jim Towse perceived major changes taking place in the employment agency/job placement industry in the mid-1990s:

The conventional structure of the industry is changing. Temporary placement agencies such as Olson's and Kelly Services are moving from their traditional niches of placing secretarial support to place middle level managers. The cost structures are also changing and it is becoming more price competitive. Companies are more reluctant to pay the conventional percent of the newly hired person's salary as a placement fee—which could be as high as 50 percent of the annual salary. Conventional placement is dying as a concept. The industry is also fragmented and few companies are utilizing technological support. This is especially true of the way people were being hired and recruited.

MacDougall added:

> Temporary placement agencies were also entering the contract services market. For example, the mail room activities of a major Canadian insurance company were contracted to a placement agency.

A relatively recent change in the industry was the ability of individuals to look for jobs using the Internet. This is described in more detail in the Appendix.

A number of job placement service providers in the United States had begun to utilize the Internet in the mid-1990s. In a recent poll of 435 human resource professionals in the United States, 47 percent said they found job candidates via the Internet. In addition, 31 percent said they searched electronic résumé databases for leads. Online Career Center, a non-profit organization supported by Hallmark, GTE, AT&T, Apple and others, provided the capability to search a résumé database or post an unlimited number of job advertisements free of charge. America Online Career Center focused their primary activities on job seekers but also allowed companies to post job advertisements. CareerMosaic also provided a job posting service and a career resource center for job seekers. Some job matching services were quite regional in their focus. For example, JOBNET provided job matching for those in the greater Philadelphia region. Other examples included JobNet Australia,[1] which provided job matching services in the Australian market. These companies essentially converted paper résumés into electronic form for easy access by potential employers.

CANADIAN COMPETITION

A major Canadian competitor to Jobnet was JCI Technologies, which provided a similar service called JobMatch. JCI Technologies, founded in 1992, had recently added automotive and real estate purchasing capabilities to its suite of services. Human Resources Development Canada (HRDC) had signed JCI Technologies Inc. to establish an online employee pool that matched Canadian job seekers with employers via the Internet. JCI's pilot program with HRDC was initially available at 10 Canadian Employment Centers in New Brunswick and Newfoundland. Job seekers entering those offices were able to sit down with a JCI employee who scanned their résumé into JCI's system and entered additional information about skills and abilities.

---

[1]Neither JOBNET nor JobNet Australia were related in any way to Jobnet, the subsidiary of FSP. The label "Jobnet" was, for obvious reasons, a popular one for such companies.

All of this information was accessible on JCI's national Internet system to employers, who could perform searches for specific skill sets and qualifications. The service was free to job hunters who registered through the Canadian Employment Centers. The federal government paid JCI's normal $25 registration fee only if the job hunter found a job. JobMatch allowed people looking for jobs to place detailed résumés into JCI's electronic database. By spring 1996, JCI already had over 23,000 electronic résumés on file, at $25 a résumé for a six-month period. Also, more than 4,400 companies had registered with JobMatch in order to access their database. JobMatch charged such companies $7 per résumé forwarded to them. JCI had also begun including what amounted to "classified ads" on its web site, which had attracted investment from some of Canada's largest newspaper chains including Torstar Corp. ($6.3 million) and Southam Inc. ($4.5 million).

JCI's goal was to have everyone seeking employment registered on its system. In 1995, JCI had been chosen by Microsoft Corp to be one of its two Canadian content providers for the Microsoft Network, the giant software company's commercial online service. Since starting up in August 1995, Microsoft Network had attracted 500,000 subscribers. That number was likely to grow as sales of Microsoft's Windows 95, which allowed access to Microsoft Network, climbed into the tens of millions. Each network subscriber was able, for a fee, to post his or her qualifications in JCI's database or pull out a résumé from a prospective employee.

The company planned to provide its service internationally. JCI's hope was that individuals would want to be registered on its system whether they were unemployed or employed. According to Geoffrey Edmunds, president and CEO of JCI,

> Being on a system like this is going to become a normal thing for everybody. Whether you're employed or unemployed, it's going to be part of your personal career management. If you're employed, maybe there's an opportunity out there for something better.

FSP'S LONDON OFFICE

Jobnet's principal operations, including its communications center, were centerd in London, Ontario, Canada. In mid-1996, the London office had almost 400 employers registered and over 1,400 clients looking for work registered in the database. Approximately 600 were institutional registrants obtained through Canada Employment Centers, while 800 were individual clients, a number of whom had been registered by corporations as a result of corporate downsizing. Most had registered via fax or telephone. Six individual clients so far had registered via Jobnet's web page.

The registrant database used at Jobnet, unlike JobMatch's detailed résumé, relied heavily on Canada's National Occupation Classification (NOC) system. When registering, clients would have to select between one and five job classification codes which best described the types of jobs they were qualified to perform and had experience in. Employers looking for employees would utilize this classification system to find qualified candidates or post jobs on Jobnet's service.

Even though Jobnet had moved their web server in-house and assumed management of their web pages, they continued to use MCC Systems Inc. as their Internet service provider (ISP). MCC specialized in system integration of hardware, software, and networks. The owner of MCC had been involved in various aspects of the computer business for over ten years and had operated MCC for a number of years. MCC was a preferred supplier for 3COM and Sun Microsystems and acted as a value-added retailer (VAR) for PCDocs document management software. MCC could provide clients with the hardware necessary for any kind of electronic network. This included routers, modems, and other types of telecommunications switches. They also provided software required to perform such tasks as encryption and compression. They provided secure network services for companies such as London Life and Canada Trust. They could also provide a point of presence (POP) on the Internet for companies such as Jobnet. Clients could dial up MCC's access via telephone or modem connections, or via ISDN lines.

MCC's web server had the capability of supporting 200 concurrent users. Jobnet's own administrative server was connected into their web server located on MCC's premises using a dedicated ISDN line. An ISDN connection provided a bandwidth of approximately 128 kbps—about eight times the capacity of a 14,400 bps modem. Jobnet's administrative server comprised a Pentium PC operating at 90 MHz with 32 MB of RAM and a 1 GB hard drive. This was the computer which held Jobnet's main database. This machine ran the Microsoft Windows NT operating system. Jobnet's database was developed using the Microsoft Access database management software. See Exhibit 3 for a simplified system diagram.

LIMITATIONS OF THE REGISTRATION AND SEARCH SYSTEMS

There were some challenges with the existing registration and search systems. For example, at times the NOC classification system was too rigid. Clients looking for work were sometimes forced to choose a classification that did not adequately reflect their qualifications or the type of work that they were seeking. For employers, the classification system had its limitations as well. The types of positions they wanted to fill did not always fall neatly into the existing classification systems. In some

EXHIBIT 3   Simplified Network Diagram

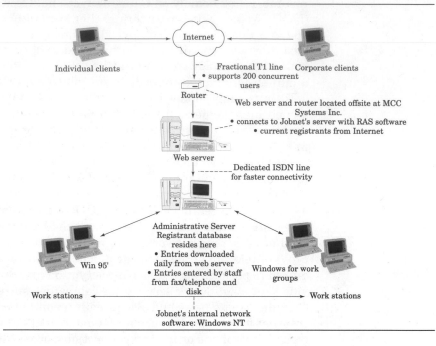

ways, the NOC system was *too* specific. For example, the NOC system differentiated between individuals who could skin fish and those who could de-bone fish. Jobnet currently addressed such difficulties by encouraging employers to call the communication center directly and have a customer service representative assist them with a search or to fill out a registration form for a job placement.

THE PARAMETRIC SEARCH ENGINE

Both MacDougall and Towse believed that a key success factor for Jobnet was to provide quick and accurate service to their clients. One way to provide this was to look at more flexible ways to register both clients looking for work and employers who wanted to register a job posting. Tom van Turnhout had come across a piece of software, called Krakatoa, that was used in the manufacturing and distribution industries. Krakatoa, which had been built using the Java language, allowed someone to define certain attributes about a part and use these defined attributes to perform tasks like locating the part or checking on inventory levels. Van Turnhout thought that the software could be adapted for use by Jobnet. Instead of using the software to define attributes of parts, it could potentially be used to define attributes of clients and job postings to assist in the job-matching process. The hope was that this software—termed a "parametric search engine"—would work in tandem with the existing NOC-based system to provide the results that clients expected of the service.

Krakatoa was different from conventional search and retrieval software because it was not text-driven. In conventional search and retrieval software, a term like "bolt" would have to be entered at the user interface, sometimes accompanied by boolean operators such as "AND" or "OR". In contrast, Krakatoa could find what a user was looking for based on attributes of the item in question. The attributes could be text, or numeric, or even an object such as a picture.

Krakatoa was similar to Microsoft's Windows 3.1 File Manager tree structure concept. The left-hand side of the screen showed the item's classification and sub-classification. Users could "drill down" in the tree structure until the appropriate subclassification was located. On the right-hand side of the screen the attributes of the subclass were then revealed. The attributes from classifications higher up in the tree structure would be inherited by subclasses below. An example from Jobnet's perspective could be a search for a specific engineer. The classification might be "Engineer," and the sub-classification "Chemical Engineer." The attributes of "Chemical Engineer" could be salary range, years of experience, and willingness to relocate. Krakatoa also had the capability to perform conventional text searching of items such as résumés, and thus could combine an attribute search with a text search.

The new software ran on the Unix operating system, and would require an update to the existing hardware utilized by the network. The software would require a Hewlett-Packard or Sun workstation, and additional memory would have to be purchased. In addition, other changes were required if the new parametric search engine were to be utilized. These included: (1) re-training existing staff or hiring new staff, (2) a major change to the system and procedures currently in place, and (3) focus groups would have to be organized to determine the best way to set up the database, to determine which attributes would be salient. In addition, the price for the software was $30,000, and the hardware, training, and information consulting required would cost another $70,000 for a total cost of about $100,000.

Jobnet, via van Turnhout, proposed another option to Antaeus. Antaeus could purchase and install the software on their dedicated server. Jobnet would then rent space on this server, and use a portion of the server for its own database. This approach might cost Jobnet between $1,000 and $1,500 per month and would give Jobnet an opportunity to test out the new software before totally committing to it.

The potential benefits to Jobnet were very enticing. It would be the first Internet job placement service to utilize this type of technology. If Jobnet did it right, it felt it would be able to leap-frog its Canadian competition as well as become a formidable competitor in the international arena. As Tom van Turnhout suggested: "it (the new parametric search engine) would put them in a different league."

The risks associated with this option were also high. For example, the software being contemplated had never been used outside of the manufacturing/distribution arena. Also, the company's future could be jeopardized given the financial commitment required if it was to purchase the software and other hardware components outright.

* * * * *

As MacDougall, Towse, van Turnhout and the others mused over the possibilities, other questions came to mind. Were they ready for this type of move now? Was this type of service going to be the focus for the company in the long run? If not, what kind of business *should* they be in? How would their competitors respond to this kind of initiative? And, could they afford *not* to take the risk?

Appendix

There were four ways[2] to look for jobs on the Internet. First, newsgroups, usually arranged by geographical location, contained job postings for positions. Newsgroups were comparable to electronic bulletin boards containing discussions and information on specific topics. The majority of job postings were placed by employment agencies; others, such as corporations, posted positions also. Newsgroups provided the advantage of isolating specific cities, and allowed users to contact employment agencies that represented hundreds of positions. People interested in jobs could load a résumé on the newsgroup or send electronic mail to a company in response to a posted job. Examples of Canadian newsgroups were: can.jobs (jobs across Canada), tor.jobs (Toronto), ont.jobs (Ontario), bc.jobs (British Columbia), ab.jobs (Alberta), and nb.jobs (New Brunswick).

Second, there were World Wide Web sites specifically designed for job searching. Many of them allowed a user to search for positions by location, job type, or specific skills. Having located a possible job, the seeker could then send e-mail or a résumé to the company in question. In order to locate job-search web sites, a search could be conducted using an Internet search engine such as Yahoo (http://www.yahoo.com), using search terms such as Canada, Employment, Jobs. Another exam-

---

[2]As reported in the Toronto *Globe and Mail,* Saturday, October 14, 1995, by Philip Jackman.

ple was that of Human Resources Development Canada's web site, which allowed users to search for work. That site offered access to the National Job Bank and the Electronic Labour Exchange. These services allowed job seekers to search for vacancies across Canada. On the ELE, users could develop a personal profile that the computer tried to match with employers' needs. If a match occurred, the job seeker was informed by e-mail. The service also provided links to numerous job-searching services on the Internet as well as to Canadian newsgroups that focus on job vacancies.

The third way to search for jobs was to examine web sites of corporations. Many companies' home pages had links to a sub-page which listed available jobs in the company. To discover the web address for a particular company, a person could use an Internet search engine, look for advertisements that listed the company's Internet home page address, or call them directly. Finally, one could conduct a general search using an Internet search engine, and search for the words "Employment" or "Jobs."

Stockgroup Interactive Media

By Professor Sid L. Huff and Rob Attwell

"Our goal is to be a fifty million dollar company in five years," said Marcus New, president of Stockgroup Interactive Media (SRG), an Internet-based investor relations services firm whose physical offices were in Vancouver. Marcus had a great deal to celebrate. Three years ago he had started SRG to develop web sites for junior public companies. The firm had been profitable since its earliest stages, a significant accomplishment considering the money-losing reputation many Internet-based businesses had earned for themselves.

SRG had developed an enviable reputation as a leader in providing investor relations services to junior public companies via the Internet. Recently, however, Marcus and his partner, Craig Faulkner, had found it increasingly difficult to sustain the company's growth, and were becoming frustrated with the operating problems that SRG was starting to experience as it attempted to expand. As Marcus gazed out his office window at the spectacular Vancouver harbor, he wondered how he would achieve the fifty million dollar goal he had set for himself and for SRG.

IVEY   Rob Attwell and Professor Sid L. Huff prepared this case solely to provide material for class discussion. The authors do not intend to illustrate either effective or ineffective handling of a managerial situation. The authors may have disguised certain names and other identifying information to protect confidentiality.

THE INVESTOR RELATIONS INDUSTRY

The investor relations industry served a number of important functions for public companies and investors alike. Investor relations firms worked for public companies, usually as sub-contractors, to make investors aware of the company's stock, to encourage them to invest in the stock and, once the stock has been purchased, to continue to hold the stock. The mission of the investor relations firm was to ensure that the stock was not under-valued by the market and that the price of the stock remained relatively stable. They were also responsible for raising additional interest in the stock when the firm had a good news announcement to make, or when the firm was seeking additional funding.

Investor relations firms were usually paid a monthly retainer by the public companies they represented, plus expenses incurred to promote the stock. However, they made most of their money by cashing in on stock options issued to them, which they were able to exercise after a specified period of time.

The Internet had much in common with financial markets. Both were largely borderless, operated 24 hours a day, and were essentially electronic media. Not surprisingly, the investment community was one of the earliest adopters of the Internet. In spite of this, most investor relations firms had been slow to recognize the potential of the Internet as a source of value to client firms and to their own operations. Rather than viewing the Internet as a way of delivering information to existing and potential investors quickly and at a relatively low cost, it was often seen as having a negative impact on financial markets, as a source of rumors and hype.

JUNIOR PUBLIC COMPANIES

There were at least 3,500 junior public companies in Canada, and over 12,000 in the United States, at the end of 1998. Junior public companies, or "small caps," are classified as a public company with a market capitalization of less than US$500 million. These companies passed through a predictable life cycle, starting with the funding of a new initiative, subsequent rounds of funding, and periods of dormancy and failure. A small minority of such firms became going concerns, grew larger, and graduated to senior markets.

Junior public companies ("juniors") faced a number of challenges not faced by established firms. These companies were usually run by entrepreneurs whose personal wealth was largely tied to the success of the venture. Their primary challenge was that of survival, since they were almost always under-financed. Juniors had a perpetual need to raise money, since their cash flows were usually insufficient to cover their operating costs. As a result, these firms went through regular cycles of promotion and fundraising to sustain operations until their cash flows grew sufficiently to operate the company, or until the company failed altogether.

Given the shoestring nature of their operations, most juniors directed little of their resources towards administration and support. Most operated out of small offices, typically with a staff of three to ten people. Management, product development, marketing and sales activities soaked up most of the available resources. The majority of support services and functions were supplied by outside service providers, with very few of these kinds of functions performed in-house.

Juniors also had difficulty finding additional funding on acceptable terms, since few were closely followed by investment analysts and the business press. It was very difficult for investors to wade through the sea of scattered information about junior public companies and be confident about investing in the firm. As a result, all but the most informed investors tended to avoid investing in these types of firms.

Investors in small-cap stocks (i.e., the publicly traded stock of junior public companies) typically possessed a sophisticated understanding of investing and financial markets. They were usually well informed and up-to-date about developments in the sectors in which they invested. Since comprehensive information about the junior markets and the firms involved in them was not available, investors in the sector obtained information from multiple sources. They also spent a lot of time talking with other investors in the sector, often by attending investment conferences where they could speak to analysts as well as company representatives and management.

Many Canadian juniors found it extremely difficult to gain access and exposure to U.S. investors, the largest pool of risk capital in the world. The opportunity to become known by U.S. investors was limited to a small number of investment shows in major U.S. cities. By the same token, U.S. investors found it difficult to locate good, reliable information about Canadian juniors.

Recently, the Internet had emerged as a channel through which U.S. investors could obtain useful information about Canadian junior companies. Fifteen-minute delayed quotes and charts were available through various investment web sites. Investors were able to "chat" via sites such as The Silicon Investor.[1] And of course any junior which wished to could create a web site to promote the company and its products or services. That was where Marcus New first spotted an opportunity.

---

[1]The Silicon Investor is located at www.techstocks.com. Subscribed users can participate in discussion forums for US$20.00/year. Only subscribed users can post to the site, however read-only use of the site is available to anyone (such users must first register at the site).

MARCUS NEW AND CRAIG FAULKNER

Marcus New graduated with a bachelor in commerce from Trinity Western University, a small private university in Langley, British Columbia. Marcus's career as an entrepreneur started at age 17, when he worked as a branch manager for Triple 'A' Student Painters, a small painting company which hired university students over the summer. Marcus was one of the youngest branch managers ever hired by Student Painters.

In his first summer with the company Marcus's branch produced revenues of over $100,000, and Marcus was named the Western Canadian Rookie Manager of the Year. Marcus returned to Student Painters each summer through his university career, as a branch manager in his second year, and then as a district manager. In his final year with the company Marcus was general manager for the entire Western Canadian division, generating four-month revenues of $1.5 million.

Since the age of 16, Marcus had been an active investor in the stocks of small companies. Through his interest in investing, he had developed a good understanding of financial markets, and particularly the special challenges faced by the juniors. After completing his commerce degree at Trinity, he had the opportunity to join Student Painters full time, but instead looked for opportunities in the financial markets community surrounding the Vancouver Stock Exchange (VSE). He joined a small public relations firm whose main business was the promotion of VSE-listed junior public companies.

Craig Faulkner met Marcus at Trinity Western University. Like Marcus, Craig was an entrepreneur and had been a successful branch manager with Triple 'A' Student Painters. Craig graduated from Trinity and joined Construction Select Software as a consultant specializing in database applications.

THE CREATION OF SRG

Marcus and Craig started Stock Research Group (SRG, later re-named Stockgroup Interactive Media) in 1994, out of Marcus's apartment. The purpose of the original business was to create web sites for junior public companies. Marcus hired Scott Larson, a former classmate from Trinity Western University, as the company's first salesman. Initially Scott was paid on a commission-only basis. The company's first client was Exor Data. Within six months SRG had 15 accounts, and 25 accounts after 12 months, at which point Marcus moved the company's operations into a modest 800-square-foot office in Vancouver's financial district.

From the outset Craig was a minority partner in the business. Initially, he worked for SRG on a part-time basis early each morning and in the evenings after his day's work at his "regular" job. Craig performed all of the technical work in this fashion until February 1996, when he quit his other job and joined SRG full time.

Marcus soon discovered that his clients gained little value from the web sites SRG developed for them, since nobody visited the clients' sites. His first client received fewer than 100 visits to its web site during the first month the site went live. Not surprisingly, the client was unimpressed. It was evident to Marcus that if SRG was to be successful, he had to find a way to channel "eyeballs" to his clients' sites. That, he felt, would be a far more valuable service for his clients than simply designing and maintaining their web sites.

Marcus came up with the idea of a special web site, which he envisioned as an online "world" of financial information for small-cap investors. He chose a name for his concept: Stockgroup. The financial world that Marcus envisioned was based on the concept of a retail shopping mall. The idea was to create traffic, in the same way that a shopping mall establishes traffic that is part and parcel of its offering to its retailers. Marcus's vision was to provide a one-stop site on the Internet, through which investors interested in junior public companies could find all the information about the markets and companies they needed on a daily basis. The entire purpose of this online community was to bring value to his clients by directing traffic from Stockgroup to the client sites, so as to enhance the value of the web site design and maintenance side of the business.

Stockgroup,[2] the small-cap financial "world" envisioned by Marcus, was developed quickly and went live on the Internet in August 1995. Considerable effort was put into developing the initial traffic base. Once Stockgroup went live, everyone involved with SRG spent hours each day trying to build traffic to the site by registering the site with various search engines, establishing cross-links with related financial sites, promoting the site in chat rooms and on subject related bulletin boards, and placing banner advertisements on related web sites.

Stockgroup was also promoted in the mainstream media. Press releases were issued to the local business press and also to the national and international media, which led to a number of feature articles in local business publications (see Exhibit 1). Marcus also recognized that success on the web could be achieved by advertising in print media, which SRG did by taking out small advertisements in the national Canadian newspaper *The Globe and Mail,* as well as in Canada's leading daily financial publication, *The Financial Post.*

EARLY SUCCESSES

Traffic to the site grew steadily. In June 1996, SRG got its first big break when Point Communications, the owner of the popular search engine Lycos, rated Stockgroup the top Internet financial site for that month. A surge of traffic resulted immediately. Following the award the growth of traffic flattened out but did not decline as these new users

---

[2]www.stockgroup.com.

EXHIBIT 1   Article from *Business in Calgary* Magazine about Stock Research Group

---

STOCK RESEARCH GROUP OFFERS INTERNET WINDOW
FOR PUBLIC COMPANIES

By Business in Calgary Staff

"We started Stock Research Group (SRG) in April 1995 to help investors find and research information on small cap companies. We had found that research on Vancouver, Alberta and Toronto small caps was virtually nonexistent and that the Internet provided a medium where the investor could find information at one site."

With that vision and two home computers, company president Marcus New and partner Craig Faulkner began an entrepreneurial project that has led them to open offices recently in Calgary and San Francisco, with plans to open a third branch in Toronto next spring.

While the head office remains in Vancouver, the de facto core of its business is the bastion of Cyberspace and a spot on the World Wide Web accessed at http://www.stockgroup.com.

There, retail investors avidly and anxiously seeking the next Bre-X flier can access a wealth of information: company profiles, investment newsletters, Hot Topics, client products, charting and current quote services, market reports and a wide variety of linked financial sites from across the web and consequently the globe. A point which distinguishes it from other Internet services is that SRG is focusing on smaller cap companies. This said, they do have one client with a market cap of more than $1 billion.

"Rather than focus exclusively on the market cap, we are primarily attracting investors with a certain risk capital who are interested in stocks that are trading below $10," says Karen Hounjet, SRG's Calgary Account Manager.

New characterizes his firm's core services as focused, efficient, cost effective, third party connectivity and marketing strength. "The vision of Stock Research Group is to become a dominant supplier of small cap information in the Internet and to help the investment community learn more about these public companies."

The site has now evolved into a meeting ground where investors receive quotes on a 15 minute delay, the latest stock charts and news releases and Q&A sessions with company executives. The Real Audio button on the site accesses a variety of interviews with company presidents. What they provide is a professional quality interview for computer users to hear. The only prerequisite is a free download of the Real Audio software which users can easily accomplish from the SRG site.

Much of what distinguishes SRG from the myriad of competitive services is the lengths to which the company actively markets to third-party resources. Stockgroup.com is featured on more than 70 other financial sites including Quote Com, UK Financial, Wall Street On-Line and Equity Magazine.

Source: *Business in Calgary,* October 1996.

continued to visit the site. The next big break came in August 1996, when Stockgroup was picked as the Microsoft Network "Site of the Day," and was featured on the MSN member start page. The result was another significant surge in traffic, with a similar retention of the new traffic volume.

Determined to maintain their ranking at Lycos, Marcus and Craig continued to upgrade and develop the Stockgroup site, and consequently managed to hold the top financial site ranking for 17 months straight, until it was bumped to number four, with The Motley Fool site[3] taking over the number one position. In spite of losing Lycos's number one ranking of all financial sites, Stockgroup continued to gain recognition, winning 19 different Internet awards. Exhibit 2 illustrates a web site rating placing SRG's site at the top. Exhibit 3 shows a portion of the home page of SRG's web site as of late 1998.

EXHIBIT 2   Web Site Rating Showing SRG as the Number One Site

Source: Point Review, http://point.lycos.com, March 1997.

---

[3]www.fool.com.

EXHIBIT 3   Portion of SRG Home Page (as of October 1998)

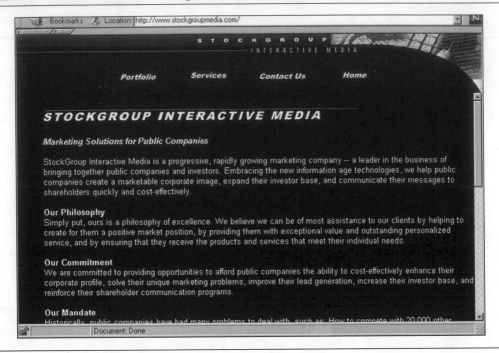

Source: SRG.

SRG'S PRODUCTS AND SERVICES

SRG began business strictly as a web site design and maintenance service for junior public companies. As the client base expanded and a close working relationship developed between SRG and its clients, it became evident to Marcus and Craig that SRG was in a strong position to compete with traditional investor relations service providers. As a result, SRG expanded its line, and developed a portfolio of web-related and non-web products and services. These included:

Web Site Design and Development

From the beginning, web development and design has been SRG's core business and the source of its profitability. In late 1998, web site development continued to provide over 70 per cent of the company's revenues. This service was responsible for bringing in many new clients who at the time had no web presence (although the proportion of junior public companies without a web site was declining continually). SRG's focus on investor relations for junior public companies allowed it to offer a number of specialized products and services tailored specifically for this segment.

Web Site Maintenance Service, Updates, Quotes and Charts

It was essential that information on any investor relations site be kept up-to-date and accurate, in part to comply with securities regulations, and also to maintain good relations with investors. Junior public companies usually lacked the personnel and expertise to update their own web sites in a timely manner. As a result, SRG offered a site maintenance package, which ensured that the client web site was updated regularly. Material changes in the state of the company, new press releases, and other such information of interest to investors were added to each maintenance client's web site in a timely manner.

The maintenance service was a key to SRG's profitability. An initial web site design typically generated a fee of $1,200 to $1,500 on a one-time basis. In contrast, the maintenance package generated $300/month and required considerably less effort, since most of the functions were automated. Each SRG client site used a standard quote and chart format, which was customized to match the client's web site design. Most clients required three updates per month, usually in the form of press releases, which could be uploaded with a template in a matter of minutes. Still, this service was extremely valuable to clients, since they could count on having their web sites updated in a very timely manner. Many small web developers took days just to return client phone calls, and longer to update the sites, while SRG was able to update its clients' sites seamlessly, within hours.

Sector Specific Financial Worlds

Based on the data provided by its member profiles, SRG possessed useful information on the specific sectors preferred by its users. From these data it developed specialized sector-specific sites catering to narrow investor segments, with an emphasis on small-cap stocks. Through these sites, SRG provided information, drawn from the wider market, which it thought likely to have an impact on its clients' companies.

The first such "super site" to go live was DiamondStocks.com, followed by PetroleumStocks.com and, most recently, MiningAuthority.com. The idea behind these super sites was to create "category killers" of investment information for each of these sectors, providing all of the information that investors in the sector need to stay informed and up-to-date.

SRG invested considerable resources gathering accurate data and information about each company in the entire sector. Each of these sector-specific sites contained information about each of the companies in the sector, but featured SRG clients. SRG also sold links to non-client sites. By the end of 1998 the majority of SRG clients in the diamond sector and the oil sector had been listed in the new financial worlds, however only a few non-clients had signed up for the linking service. Marcus was considering hiring a dedicated sales force to sell these links. He was also considering outsourcing sales of this product to a telemarketing firm on a straight commission basis.

Banner Advertising

Stockgroup's large volume of narrowly focused traffic made it a very attractive site for banner advertising. The profile of its users made it ideal for advertising by both offline and online brokerage businesses, junior public companies seeking to gain additional exposure for their stocks, and online and offline financial publications. However, interest in SRG was not limited to the financial world. IBM and Lotus Development Corp. were also regular advertisers at the SRG site.

Advertising revenue had almost no cost associated with it other than the 20 per cent sales commission. The client purchased a given number of impressions for $35 per 1,000 impressions, which was a common rate on the Internet for banner advertising. Once the ad was sold the client would e-mail the banner to SRG's webmaster, who would upload it for rotation on the site. Banner advertising was, however, limited to a few key pages on the site and was restricted from client sites. As a result ad revenue was limited by Stockgroup's traffic.

E-Mail Blasts

Although the Stockgroup financial world was a free site, which did not require registration, users were given the opportunity to register for the SRG Club. These members received a monthly newsletter and periodic information about events and companies in industry sectors that they had specified. This provided SRG the opportunity to sell another product, e-mail blasts, to corporate clients. A client company was usually interested in sending out an e-mail blast when it had a major "good news" announcement it felt would help build momentum for the stock. For $1,500, SRG would e-mail a press release to those of its 21,000 SRG Club members interested in the corporate client's industry sector.

One of the challenges of this product was managing its impact on the SRG Club members. SRG had to balance its desire to gain additional revenue with the tolerance level of the club members for unsolicited information. Too many e-mail blasts per week, Marcus thought, was likely to lead to a lack of effectiveness of the e-mail blasts, an increase in club member attrition and an erosion of club member trust.

Quote and Chart Applications

In order to improve efficiency internally, SRG developed a number of software applets, small downloadable browser applications that could provide certain web site functions such as quotes and charts. It turned out that being able to provide this capability in this fashion gave SRG an important competitive advantage.

Numerous established companies, as part of their corporate web presence, included features on their web sites of interest to potential investors. In particular, investors often wanted to be able to get near-real-time quotes of the price of the company's stock, and to be able to view various graphs of the stock's performance. To provide this, the company's site would normally include a link to a separate quote-and-chart site, outside the corporate site. However, once an investor reached the quote-and-chart site, he or she would often spend time checking the price of other stocks, or would choose to access various other financial information provided at the quote-and-chart site, and might not return to the company's site. As a result, the quote engine site pulled traffic away from the corporate site, effectively stealing its traffic.

SRG's quote-and-chart applets allowed SRG to provide the same service, but actually imbedded the quote-and-chart feature on the client's own site, by reposting the client's quote-and-chart page every 15 minutes. SRG could package its quote-and-chart applet software for its client firms as an add-on to their sites. SRG provided the data feed required by its software through a satellite link at the Vancouver office. Early in 1998 SRG decided to package and to sell the quote and chart applets as a separate product for an annual fee of $1,200.

Electronic Newspaper

Marcus had developed (but not yet implemented) another idea for a vehicle which would draw more users to the SRG site: publishing an online investment newspaper. Since Stockgroup's visitors had the same profile as investors who subscribed to small-cap analyst newsletters which were mailed to the investor via Canada Post, Marcus felt they were a community of people primed to buy such a service online from SRG. Marcus thought an appropriate price for the newspaper would be $9.95 per month. The newspaper would be delivered via a password-protected web site. The web format was chosen instead of an e-mail format to allow for additional banner advertising revenue. As well as an electronic newspaper, Marcus intended to establish a virtual newsstand of newsletters and analyst reports to sell to visitors to the site. Launching the services would require nine full-time staff to write and publish the content and operate the business. The new division of SRG would also need operating capital for office space, computers and startup operations.

Investor Market Place

The first non-web product SRG developed was called the *Investor Market Place (IMP),* a high-quality four-page color brochure delivered as an insert in *The Financial Post* (see Exhibit 4). Space in the

EXHIBIT 4   Example *Investor Market Place* Document

Source: SRG company documents.

brochure was sold to web clients, and utilized text and graphics supplied by the client company. Each edition contained a profile of 24 small-cap companies, and included a detachable postage-paid reply card which prospective investors could fill out and mail to receive more information about the companies listed. The brochure was supported by a web site which contained the same features, along with a direct link to each company.

The IMP service competed directly with Stockdeck, a traditional investor relations service provider. Stockdeck, however, had not yet identified the web as a key to its future success. Over a three month sales cycle SRG's web service sales force cross-sold IMP spots to its existing web clients and targeted non-clients and vice versa.

Investment Shows

One of the most effective ways for junior public companies to reach new investors was by attending investment shows. The shows were designed to give the juniors an opportunity to present their company to investors, and to give investors an opportunity to speak directly to employees of the company, including management.

Companies featured at such shows were charged a fee for space and services in a convention hall. Attendees were charged a registration fee, which was often waived in the interest of ensuring that the event was well attended by potential investors and investment analysts and since the featured companies were the primary source of revenue for the show promoter.

By the middle of 1997, Marcus realized that SRG was in a unique position to compete effectively in this business. It already had a corporate client base of over 300 public companies which were all seeking more exposure to investors at one time or another; many of these clients were regular purchasers of trade show booth space. As well, SRG attracted a large volume of Internet traffic, some proportion of which would surely be interested in attending investment trade shows. Stockgroup site had been generating over five million page views per month, and was visited by over 170,000 unique visitors per month. Furthermore, SRG could use the investment shows to further promote the Stockgroup community, as well as SRG's other services, creating a "virtuous circle" of on- and off-web services.

Marcus decided initially to partner with investment show promoters, thus providing SRG an opportunity to test the strategy with less risk. The success of the first two shows led to the acquisition of an investment show business. This was done in order to leapfrog many of the development stages of this new line of business. The first two shows following the acquisition were successful in terms of attracting companies to feature at the shows; however, both shows were poorly attended by investors.

Full Investor Relations Services

The ultimate extent of backward integration for SRG was to become a full-scale provider of investor relations services. Marcus was considering taking SRG into the mainstream investor relations business in a limited way, since two key clients indicated interest in having SRG handle their investor relations. This was a potentially lucrative business, since companies typically paid a monthly retainer plus expenses and offered a significant number of stock options. However, Marcus was not yet convinced that this was the right move, given the state of the junior markets in Canada, the businesses' lack of scalability and the amount of SRG management time full investor relations might require.

REVENUE MODEL

Unlike the majority of Internet-based startups, SRG enjoyed solid initial revenues, generated primarily through its web site design and maintenance businesses. As a result it did not experience as much pressure to generate revenue from visitors to the Stockgroup web site as it otherwise would have. Marcus continually reminded himself that the purpose of the Stockgroup site was to generate traffic and channel potential investors to SRG's clients' corporate sites, thereby providing added value to client companies in order to sustain the design and maintenance revenues. Still, it was not lost on Marcus and Craig that the large number of visitors to the Stockgroup site was a potential source of revenue in its own right as well. The question of whether and how to generate revenues from the Stockgroup traffic, which had become an investor community with a life of its own, was a nagging issue for SRG.

In the interest of allowing traffic to continue to develop, Marcus and Craig decided that Stockgroup would always be free to the user, based on the firm belief that charging users a fee to access the Stockgroup site was a sure way to kill the virtual community in its infancy (for further information on virtual communities, see the Appendix). As a result almost no revenue was generated from the investors who visited the Stockgroup web site.

As of August 1998 more than 70 per cent of SRG's revenues were generated by fees charged to corporate clients for the design and maintenance of their web sites. Site design fees ranged from $1,200 to $7,500, and maintenance typically cost each client $300 per month. SRG's remaining revenue came from selling banner advertising on four key pages on the Stockgroup site, by selling e-mail advertising (e-mail blasts) which was sent to SRG's 21,000 registered users, and by selling the low-margin IMP to web clients. Revenue from trade shows was only starting to build and the quote and chart software applets had not yet been launched.

EXHIBIT 5 SRG Financial Performance through 1997, and Projection for 1998

Year	Sales	Profit	Net Margin
1995	$78,000	($1500)	(2%)
1996	458,000	110,000	24
1997	1,340,000	152,000	11.3
1998 (est)	4,200,000	800,000	19

Source: SRG.

Less than one percent of SRG's revenue was generated through on-line transactions with visitors to the site. The online transactions that did take place centered on the online sale of two analyst newsletters through the Stockgroup community, which were not produced by SRG. Although Craig and Marcus had not been able to find a way to generate revenue directly from the Stockgroup traffic, they were convinced that it had considerable, and possibly the most significant, upside potential in the long run.

SRG's financial performance projected through 1998 is illustrated in Exhibit 5.

COMPETITION

SRG's unique product and service mix meant that it had no direct competition. However, it did face competition in each of the segments of its business from different competitors.

Web Design Firms

Local web site design firms frequently competed with SRG for the initial development of clients' corporate web sites. The number of these small, local web design companies was growing rapidly. They ranged in size from one individual working part time or evenings at home, to a handful of people working out of a low-rent office. Marcus felt that these design firms were not well equipped to match SRG's range of products and services.

While many such firms competed to do initial web site design work, none was focused on ongoing maintenance, the most profitable service. The difficulty was in convincing clients that ongoing maintenance was important, not just for regulatory compliance, but more importantly to bring their existing or potential investors back to the site regularly.

A number of larger design houses, such as Agency.Com in New York and Cyberplex Interactive Media in Toronto, catered to the needs of

Fortune 500 or TSE 300 companies. These firms had sophisticated services designed to meet their clients' entire corporate web service needs, including investor relations. While these larger firms had the capability to provide a complete range of services, their offerings actually went well beyond the needs (and budgets) of junior public companies; and their services were not tailored to the specific needs of this market.

Traditional Investor Relations Firms

Traditional investor relations firms were not seen as a major threat to SRG, even though they served the same clients and performed some of the same functions. SRG could also be seen as a service provider to these firms, and these firms as gatekeepers to the clients. This industry was quite highly fragmented, and most of the companies were only beginning to see the need to be online, largely as a result of "investor pull" rather than an industry recognition of the Internet as a competitive weapon. Given their relatively unsophisticated understanding of the Internet, the industry remained largely unaware of the potential of virtual communities (such as Stockgroup) as a source of value for clients. Moreover, the industry had not yet perceived the potential threat posed by competitors backward integrating from the Internet— competitors such as SRG.

Online Financial Sites

Investors have been very rapid adopters of the Internet. A number of financial virtual community sites have been developed, and online investors have begun to amalgamate at these investment sites. Popular investment web sites included the Silicon Investor,[4] TheStreet.Com,[5] the Wall Street Journal Online[6] and The Motley Fool.[7]

Portals

Internet portals such as Yahoo, AltaVista, Lycos, Excite and the portal services of Microsoft and Netscape aggregated information and generated content on a wide array of topics, including investing. Portals were increasingly becoming destination sites for many purposes. So far, how-

---

[4] www.techstocks.com.
[5] www.thestreet.com.
[6] www.wsj.com.
[7] www.fool.com.

ever, Marcus felt that these portal sites were less a source of competition than they were a source of traffic through their links to Stockgroup and SRG clients.

THE CHALLENGE OF GROWTH

SRG's success with its web business had led to an array of opportunities, each of which included its own set of challenges. The greatest overall challenge facing Marcus and Craig was that of deciding which opportunities to pursue first, and how to assess opportunities appropriately. However, rapid growth of the business had created a number of challenges and each of the opportunities required cash.

SRG Operations

In less than four years SRG had grown from a two-man company operating out of an apartment, to a $1.3 million operation with a full-time staff of 21 and offices in the financial districts of Toronto, Calgary and Vancouver. All of the computer and communications technology for operating the web sites and the administration of the business was located in Vancouver, while the Calgary and Toronto offices handled only sales and marketing functions. The Vancouver office had moved three times in two years to accommodate new staff, and recently had taken over the adjoining space in its current office building, doubling its workspace to 5,000 square feet. Soon after securing the new space Marcus wondered if it would be big enough.

Management of the daily operations increasingly consumed Marcus's time, while Craig spent most of his time managing the array of computers which ran the site, the data feeds and the networks upon which the site depended. A full-time webmaster administered the content of the SRG web site and managed the design, development and maintenance of client sites with five full-time site designers.

Recently Marcus had become frustrated by SRG's inability to attract and retain qualified staff, particularly sales staff. Turnover of sales and marketing staff required Marcus to devote a considerable amount of his time to recruitment. He was considering hiring a national sales manager whom he could put in charge of managing the sales and marketing functions. He was also considering hiring a human resources manager. However, finding and attracting highly qualified staff was time-consuming, difficult and expensive for a relatively small company like SRG. A very positive sign was that Marcus seemed willing to hand over functions and control to professional managers.

SRG's difficulty in retaining qualified sales staff was driven in part by the competition for sales people due to the robust state of the

Canadian economy, but also by SRG's cash constraints. Since SRG's growth was financed entirely by operating cash flows, it could not offer aggressive salaries. The sales staff had the potential to earn substantial commissions, however, only a small proportion of their salaries was guaranteed. The commission structure put considerable pressure on sales staff to produce in the short term, and made it difficult to attract the most capable sales staff, who were able to command higher salaries and more guarantees elsewhere.

Furthermore, with the growth of the account base for the core business had come the problem of account attrition and the need to secure additional accounts just to "stand still." The problem of account attrition had been exacerbated by the relatively poor performance of juniors in Canada during 1998, following the collapse of the infamous Bre-X mining company.[8] The Vancouver Stock Exchange Index, mainly comprising junior public company stocks, had fallen over 60 per cent during that period. Many junior firms had failed to raise the capital necessary to continue operations, and others had had to scale back their stock promotion (investor relations) activities until market conditions improved. This had resulted in a higher than normal rate of account attrition for SRG.

Need for Financing

SRG was starting to come under cash flow pressure in the third quarter of 1998. Marcus attributed this to a number of factors. The high level of account attrition experienced recently had forced the company to spend additional time and money on customer acquisition and retention. Overhead costs had been expanding rapidly. The Calgary office had been added in October 1996 and the Toronto office in January 1997. Sales volume from these offices had not yet grown sufficiently to cover their costs. Toronto in particular was only producing 50 per cent of its budgeted revenues. Furthermore, the Vancouver office had been expanded and required leasehold improvements. The additional site traffic also meant that SRG's hardware and software had to be upgraded constantly.

The expanding volume of product development initiatives undertaken by SRG was a concern, as it was consuming rapidly increasing amounts of resources. These product and service developments included: the further development of quote-and-chart applets, the development of three additional "category killer" sector-specific financial

---

[8]The web site http://www.brexclass.com/provides information and background on Bre-X, and on the ongoing class action lawsuit.

worlds, and the move into the trade show business. All of the new projects had been undertaken without having secured additional financing.

Raising Additional Financing

According to Marcus, SRG had a number of advantages in raising capital. Most importantly, the firm had been quite profitable for over two years, a rarity among Internet companies. The success of the Stockgroup virtual community, and its high volume of traffic, made it quite attractive, especially in light of the premiums being paid for Internet stocks. Investors also seemed to be rewarding Internet category leaders, such as Stockgroup, with disproportionately high valuations.

In spite of those advantages, SRG had had trouble convincing Canadian sources of funding about the merits of the company. While there had been some interest from Canadian venture capitalists, in general, when it came to the Internet, "[Canadian sources of funding] just don't understand," according to Marcus. "Your best bet is to go to the U.S.," he continued.

For over a year, Marcus had been seeking additional financing to provide SRG the resources it needed to progress to the next stage of development. Both Marcus and Craig spent a lot of their time speaking to everyone they knew in the financial community about financing the business. While the firm had received considerable interest, no major financing agreements had yet been reached. Marcus had been able to secure a line of credit with a major bank for $150,000, secured against accounts receivable and personally guaranteed by Marcus. Recently, Marcus engaged PriceWaterhouseCoopers to assist in securing financing, and to help SRG establish a credible valuation of the firm for the negotiation process.

The need for additional financing was a long-standing issue for SRG; however, SRG's profitability and positive cash flows had, until now, allowed Marcus to wait until he could get additional funding on acceptable terms. For Marcus, acceptable terms meant a valuation which reflected his understanding of the value of the company, and being able to meet SRG's funding needs to implement his vision.

As Marcus returned to his desk, he reviewed his travel agenda for the next two weeks, which would take him to Calgary, Toronto, New York and Seattle. The problems of the business didn't simply seem to be accumulating, but rather to be compounding. Although it had never seemed that there was enough time in the day to put in place all of the plans Craig and Marcus had for the business, it now seemed that there was no longer time in the day even to sustain operations at the current level. Marcus wondered what it would take to get SRG to its $50 million goal.

Appendix

VIRTUAL COMMUNITIES AND THE PRINCIPLE OF INCREASING RETURNS

Virtual Communities

A distinguishing feature of SRG has been its ability to develop and maintain a virtual community of and for small-cap investors. Hagel and Armstrong, in their book *Net Gain,*[9] argue that virtual communities should have five distinct characteristics, all of which are necessary for success.

Distinctive Focus

The community must have a distinctive focus, making it easy for users to understand what they can expect to find on the site and the kind of resources it contains.

Capacity to Integrate Content and Communication

Virtual communities are sources of content and information for customers. Furthermore, they provide an environment for communication between users and members of the site.

Appreciation of Member Generated Content

In addition to providing for communication, virtual communities should provide an environment in which users/members can generate and post content. The community site should facilitate interaction and communication between members.

Access to Competing Publishers and Vendors

Virtual communities comprise an aggregation of information about an entire area of interest for the users/members. In order to provide for the needs of users, Hagel and Armstrong argue that it is essential to offer access to competing publishers and vendors in order to enhance the value of the community for users.

Commercial Orientation

Similar to many other Internet facilities and services, virtual communities originated as volunteer ventures, provided for free or at cost to

---

[9]*Net Gain: Expanding Markets through Virtual Communities,* John Hagel III and Arthur G. Armstrong, Harvard Business School Press, Boston, MA, 1997.

members. Increasingly, however, they have been organized as commercial enterprises; the community organizer seeks a financial gain from the community.

The Principle of Increasing Returns

One of the key elements of the concept of a virtual community is the principle of increasing returns. According to this concept, the larger and more concentrated the virtual community becomes, the more valuable it becomes as a potential source of profits. To this end, a virtual community can develop increasing returns in four ways, according to Hagel and Armstrong. These are:

Transaction Offerings

One way to increase the value of a virtual community is to provide transaction offerings. Users will value the community increasingly if they can act on the information provided in the community immediately.

Content Attractiveness

Hagel and Armstrong emphasize the need for attractive content to increase the value of the virtual community. This can be achieved by offering a comprehensive collection of information about the distinctive focus of the community, content which is updated regularly, to give reason for members to return regularly.

SRG fully understood the need to provide content which was up-to-date, relevant to users and constantly changing to enhance the value of the community to users. To this end the site provided constantly changing news, quotes and charts. Regular news and features were updated every day throughout the day. The information supplied was carefully chosen to meet the distinctive focus of the community; it was very focused and relevant to the members. Links to even more focused and specific information for different users was available at Stockgroup in the form of SRG-developed sector-specific sites, and links to other sector-specific resources.

Member-Generated Content

The third means of increasing returns is to capture user profile information on an individual and aggregate level. On the individual level, this information can be used to customize and tailor the site for individual users to enhance their experience. On an aggregate level the information can be used to determine how to enhance the community for all users. The aggregated information can also be used to attract advertisers and to target advertising to portions of the user group.

Member Loyalty

The fourth way to increase the returns of a virtual community is by continually building user loyalty. This can be achieved by customizing interaction with the user, by encouraging member interaction and by giving power to the user in the purchasing process.

Celebrity Sightings

By Professors Arnoud De Meyer and Soumitra Dutta and Lieven Demeester

INTRODUCTION

Celebrity Sightings provides entertainment on the World Wide Web. In July 1997, after eight months of operation, the site had over 16,000 members with ages ranging from 8 to 25 years. Members visited the site to read the latest stories, see the latest pictures and get the inside scoop from their favorite teenage celebrities. They also visited to chat with each other, shop in the Star-Store, play interactive games or quizzes and participate in announced chats with the teenage celebrities themselves. With the membership growing steadily, Robert Landes, the CEO of Celebrity Sightings believed that the first sponsoring deals that would allow him to cover his costs were in sight.

In an important move, Robert Landes had recently set up a merger between Celebrity Sightings and its main supplier and technology partner, Guidance Solutions. In many ways Celebrity Sightings had become the flagship of the new company. Further building the success of Celebrity Sightings would surely require the best of Robert's extensive marketing and sales skills. More than before, however, Robert now also found himself thinking about how to shape the new company's organization.

THE VISION OF ROBERT LANDES

The idea for Celebrity Sightings had come fairly naturally to Robert Landes. In his function of Chief Marketing Officer at LA Gear, a sport

Source: This case was prepared by Lieven Demeester under the supervision of Professor Arnoud De Meyer and Professor Soumitra Dutta. It is intended to provide a basis for classroom discussion, not to illustrate positive or negative administrative practices. The authors would like to thank Karen Barber, Rob Bynder, Barry Burchell and Robert Landes for their time and their support. Some information has been disguised to protect the interests of Celebrity Sightings. Celebrity Sightings TM is a trademark of Celebrity Sightings Inc. Copyright © 1998 INSEAD, Fontainebleau, France.

shoes and clothing retailer, he had worked frequently with young celebrities in his effort to create brands for a teenager market. Later on, his leadership had been at the source of a new group of designers that focused on interactive multi-media marketing applications. Obviously his attention had been drawn to the Internet and the World Wide Web as an excellent medium for these applications.

While surfing the net for ideas, Robert noticed the multitude of "unofficial" celebrity web pages. He wondered if he would be able to create some attractive content on the web by bundling a set of "official" web pages in cooperation with the celebrities. In his idea, these web pages would contain exclusive and authentic pictures, stories and interviews for fans to read and look at. In March 1996 he started thinking seriously about a market and a competitive strategy for this business idea.

Robert realized that the best market would be the one centered around teenage celebrities. Teenagers, it turns out, have quite an interest in teenage celebrities. In the United States alone, a total of 6 million youngsters read one of several teen magazines whose content is heavily focused on teenage celebrities. Each of these magazines (such as *Super Teen, Tiger Beat, Six Teen,* etc.) is published monthly, bi-monthly or quarterly and costs $3 per copy. Observing also that the TV shows in which these celebrities star have growing audiences all over the world, Robert was confident that there was a promising market.

The web site Robert had in mind would be a mix between a magazine and a fan club but with clear advantages over both. The web site would have some areas of general interest and also special areas for each celebrity. Exclusive contracts with the celebrities would guarantee a lot of authentic material that would generate a sense of closeness that no magazine could copy. In the meantime, because the site would contain information about many different celebrities, it would retain a flavor of independence that is not always present in a fan club.

It was the web technology, however, that would give the site its major advantages. The communication technology behind the web would allow fans to interact through e-mail or through electronic chat, not only with each other but also with the celebrities themselves. Web technology would also enhance the entertainment that would be offered. Alongside text and pictures, the site could also use sound and video to report on the lives of the celebrities. In addition to these multi-media elements, the medium would also allow for all kinds of interactive games, contests or live quizzes. All this with a technology that would make it no harder to reach Australian teenagers than it would be to reach the kids in Beverly Hills. Robert figured he would be able to attract 100,000 surfing teenagers at least.

Robert's vision reached further than the web site however. He believed that he could use the "Celebrity Sightings" web site to create a "Celebrity Sightings" brand. He envisioned Celebrity Sightings print

EXHIBIT 1   Growth in Popularity of the Celebrity Sightings Web Site since Its Launch in December 1996

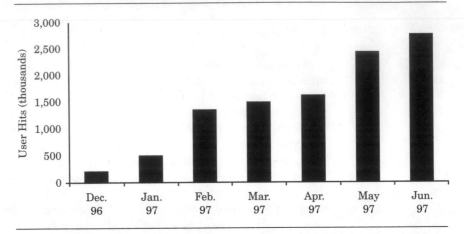

editions, radio and television shows. "Build the proprietary content on the Web and then fan it out to the traditional media," was the picture in his mind.

LAUNCH

The Celebrity Sightings web site was launched November 13, 1997. The web site was designed and implemented in a joint effort between *Bright Interactive,* Robert's own design group for interactive media, and *Guidance Solutions,* a provider of web site design and programming services. Bright Interactive was a spin-off of the Bright Design group and contained all the artistic and creative talent needed to create the "look" and structure of the web site. Guidance Solutions contained the IT experience, programming skills and project management capabilities that were necessary to make the web site into a technical reality.

Present at the launch party were Jonathan Taylor Thomas (ABC's "Home Improvement"), Tatyani Ali (NBC's "Fresh Prince of Bel Air"), Jodie Sweetin and Candace Cameron (ABC's "Full House"), Danielle Fishel (NBC's "Boy Meets World"), Tia and Tamera Mowry (WB's "Sister, Sister"), Larisa Oleynik (Nickelodeon's "The Secret World of Alex Mack") and Andrew Keegan ("Independence Day"). The nine celebrities had all signed two-year contracts with Celebrity Sightings. Also present at the launch were reporters from ABC, CNN, MSNBC and Family PC. The presentation of the web site was a success and reporters all covered the story on their separate networks. In its first six weeks of operation, Celebrity Sightings realized 880,000 user hits and by July 1997 the web site was attracting 880,000 user hits per week (see Exhibits 1 and 2).

EXHIBIT 2   Celebrity Sightings Site Statistics

Many Celebrity Sightings members visit the site more than once a week. When they visit they spend an average of 14 minutes on the site.

Site Statistics for July 1997

Basic members	14,000
Premium members	2,200
User hits per week	880,000*
User-sessions per week	22,000
Average length of user session	14 minutes
Members who chat	400–500

*Among the 10 percent most hit sites on the WWW.

THE WEB SITE

Celebrity Sightings had succeeded in creating an entertaining web site for its members. Both look and content were appealing and the promise of interactive fun had been realized. Exhibit 3 gives an overview of the Celebrity Sightings web site as it was in August 1997 (for changes since then, check www.celebritysightings.com).

On the entrance page, members can enter the site by using their login ID and password. Others can register online to become a member. Members choose between basic membership, which is free and premium membership for which they pay $12 a year. Credit cards are accepted online. Their $12 a year provides premium members with access to the electronic chat facilities, higher-resolution pictures as well as a set of special privileges.

The site is organized as follows. Each one of the celebrities has their own dedicated area, each with a similar structure but with a personalized look. Exhibit 4 for instance shows Chamique Holdsclaw's homepage. A **celebrity's home page** contains pictures, character and lifestyle descriptions, interviews, answers to frequently asked questions, career information, sighting reports and a fan mail section. Premium members can write e-mails to the celebrities. The electronic fan mail is screened and then posted on the site. The celebrities read their fan mail on a regular basis and write an answer to typical or especially interesting letters. Their answers get posted too, for all members to read.

Each of the stars can sell memorabilia in the **Star Store** section (Exhibit 5 shows Jodie Sweetin's store). Most stars offer autographed pictures and posters but some also have T-shirts, caps or even sports bottles. Celebrity Sightings also presents a selection of its own brand-name merchandise such as T-shirts, caps, pictures, videos, etc. Fans can pick out the items they like and order them online.

EXHIBIT 3   Web Site Overview

Entrance

Join the club   Membership registration center. Those who join choose between the free,
                          basic membership and the $12 a year, premium membership.
Open sez me   Members enter with ID and password they chose for themselves while
                          registering.

Home (with an official homepage for each one of the celebrities, see Exhibit 4)

Up-close   In depth look into the life of the celebrity. Topics include dreams, wishes,
                          character etc.
Snap-shots   This section has the latest set of exclusive pictures. Only premium members
                          can see the pictures full size.
Event update   Information about the latest activities of the celebrity and about his or her
                          upcoming schedule.
A day in the life   Report of a one day visit to see the celebrity in action in the studio.
FAQ   Answers to the most frequently asked questions about the celebrity.
Word up   Reports by fans of their own personal "celebrity sighting."
Article archives   Archives of articles that have previously appeared in Up Close, Event Update
                          or a Day in the Life.
Read fan mail   Screened fan mail as well as the celebrity's answers to a few of the letters.
Write fan mail   Option to send a fan mail letter. Only for premium members.

Calendar

                          Table of events. Events include celebrity chats, celebrity appearances, radio-
                          show broadcasts, contests etc. (see Exhibit 7).

Fan Central

Cool list   E-mailed member reviews for movies, TV shows, music, books, places and
                          other stuff.
CS-radioshow   Broadcast and scheduling information for the CS-radioshow on AAHS-radio.
                          Excerpts available on *RealPlayer* format.
The Buzz   Celebrity-centric articles on dating, sports, movies etc.
Chat transcripts   Transcripts of previously scheduled celebrity chats.
Contests   Rules of contests. Announcement of winners and winning submissions.
Comics   Two CS-created characters show up in a new cartoon every week.
Teen-seen   Reports of Celebrity Sightings Special Events, reported by Bazza (online
                          personality created by Barry).

Chat (Premium members only)

Rules of the road   A set of rules are communicated in order to foster a pleasant chat-culture.
                          Because of the young audience specific safety guidelines are also
                          communicated (see Exhibit 8).
Celebrity chat room   In their favourite celebrity's chat room, fans can chat with each other about
                          different topics. Sometimes the celebrity will pay a surprise visit.
Auditorium   The auditorium is a chat room used for planned celebrity chats, games and
                          contests. Members "reside" in the auditorium to participate.

EXHIBIT 3   (Continued)

Games

Fashion puzzles	Players put celebrities in six different outfits by combining the right tops, bottoms and shoes (enabled by Shockwave from Macromedia).
Jig-saws	Players complete jigsaws of their favourite celebrities (enabled by Shockwave from Macromedia).
Other games	Word-games. Matching games (e.g., which nose belongs to which celebrity).

Star Store

Celebrity stores	Each celebrity has a "store" with their own merchandise. Merchandise ranges from signed pictures, posters and T-shirts; with online ordering.

Information Station

Membership information	Membership agreement. Option to change from basic to premium membership.
Instructions for downloading software	In order to fully enjoy the site members need to have (1) the Macromedia Shockwave plug-in for games and (2) the I-chat plug-in for chatting.

EXHIBIT 4   Celebrity Home Page

Each one of the celebrities has an official home page that is part of the Celebrity Sightings sites. Pictured is the home page of WNBA star Chamique Holdsclaw.

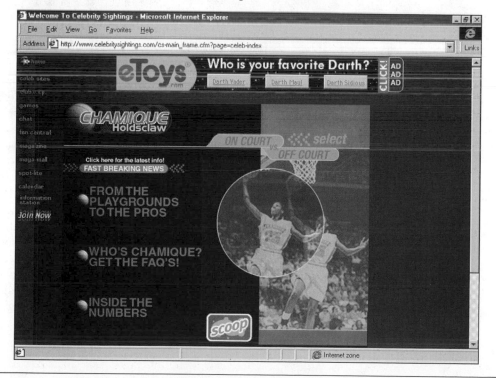

EXHIBIT 5   Jodie Sweetin's Star Store

Just fill in the quantity you want to order and click on "check out" to place your order automatically.

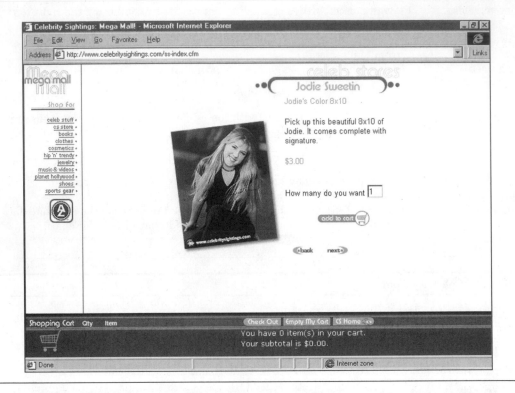

The section called **Fan Central** contains event reports, articles, letters and information not specifically related to one of the celebrities. It caters to the teenage audience by covering topics such as movies, music, dating, etc. In this section Celebrity Sightings goes beyond being a collection of fan clubs and creates an identity of its own.

Another section where a kind of common culture is created is in the "rooms" for electronic **chat.** An electronic chat room is a virtual room that you enter by clicking on the appropriate icon on your screen. Once you enter, your presence is announced to the others in the room and you can see who is there. You can make conversation by typing. As soon as you hit the return key, your words appear on the screens of those in the room. An example of a "chat session" can be seen in Exhibit 6. To make up for the lack of non-verbal communication, you can also use special "emoticons" to do things like "frowning," "smiling" or even "flirting" with someone.

EXHIBIT 6   Transcript of a Moderated Chat Session with a CS Celebrity

Larisa Oleynik; August 19, 1997

*(In the transcript below **Larisa-cs** identifies Larisa Oleynik who stars in "The Secret World of Alex Mack" on Nickelodeon's Cable Network. **Momoney-cs** and **Monkybutt-cs** identify two Celebrity Sightings associates. This chat session was "seen" by online premium members who were in the "auditorium"— chat room. The members in the auditorium could not participate directly in the chat but they were allowed to type questions, which, if selected, were presented to the celebrity.)*

Momoney-cs says, "Welcome back to CS Melissa!!!"

Momoney-cs says, "Ooops"

Larisa-cs says, "Melissa?"

Momoney-cs says, "She's a special CS member Larisa"

Larisa-cs bops Mo-money

Monkybutt-cs says, "So, Mo, lets get this show on the road!"

Momoney-cs presents question #160 from Amyr
  If you were stranded on a deserted island what 3 things would you bring?

Momoney-cs says, "This one is becoming another CS standard question"

Larisa-cs says, "A phone . . . my stereo system and a cute boy!"

Momoney-cs presents question #163 from Crono
  Hey how are yah? do you remember me? Crono? Anyhow WB to CS!!! How was your summer and what did you do?

Larisa-cs says, "I remember you . . . how are you? My summer? I worked all summer . . . now I have some time off"

Momoney-cs presents the speakers with question #212 from Yankees
  What do you like to do in your spare time?

Larisa-cs says, "I like to go and hang out with my friends and go to concerts . . . righty now we are OBSESSED with JambaJuice . . . a juice bar in LA . . . we go every night!"

Momoney-cs presents the speakers with question #205 from So-fly
  Where would you go or like to go if you want to spend time alone?

Monkybutt-cs loves jamba juice too!

Momoney-cs says, "Yummy!!!!"

Larisa-cs says, "I love hanging out on the roof of my building . . . its really calm and relaxing"

Monkybutt-cs says, "On the roof??"

Momoney-cs presents question #225 from Dgol
  Hey, Larisa, Hi) How come you don't come to CS more often? You otta just pop on sometimes, everyone here loves you!

Larisa-cs says, "Ummm I am sorry . . . I just got my powerbook fixed . . . I will try as hard as I can"

Momoney-cs presents the speakers with question #226 from Harmony84
  Larisa are you going to do any movies?

Larisa-cs says, "I would love to, but I have nothing planned right now."

Momoney-cs presents question #224 from Mr_t
  Are you still single (please say yes)

Larisa-cs says, "Um........"

Larisa-cs says, "Maybe"

Momoney-cs says, "Um.......?"

Larisa-cs says, "Maybe not"

Momoney-cs presents question #228 from Jimstark
  What would constitute the perfect date for you, Larisa?

Larisa-cs says, "Just something fun with no awkward pauses would pretty much rule right now."

Momoney-cs presents question #181 from Jimstark
  Larisa, do you think the world will be a better place 100 years from now?;)

Monkybutt-cs says, "Larisa must be typing for herself . . ."

Momoney-cs says, "This is a serious question, requires some DEEP thought......."

Larisa-cs says, "Actually, if it were up to me. Id live 100 years in the past. As much as I love CS, technology sometimes moves toooo fast!"

Larisa-cs says, "Sorry my typing sux"

Each of the celebrities has their own chat room where members can chat with other fans. The announced chats during which fans can interact directly with the celebrities usually take place in a special room called the "auditorium." To make a chat session with a celebrity manageable, the chat is moderated. In this format, all members are made electronically mute but they can submit their questions for screening. The selected questions are presented to the celebrities and their answers come live on the screen for everybody (Exhibit 6 is an example of such a moderated chat session). Another special chat room is the trivia room. In this room weekly trivia contests are organized. Members type answers to live questions and the best or fastest answers are rewarded with celebrity related prizes. All chat facilities are for premium members only.

The **Calendar** section gives a listing of past events (with links to the archives) and a list of announcements to future events. Most items announce electronic chat sessions with celebrities. Others refer to celebrity appearances that are sponsored by Celebrity Sightings. Exhibit 7 shows the events that took place in July 1999.

EXHIBIT 7   Calendar Section of the Celebrity Sightings Web Site

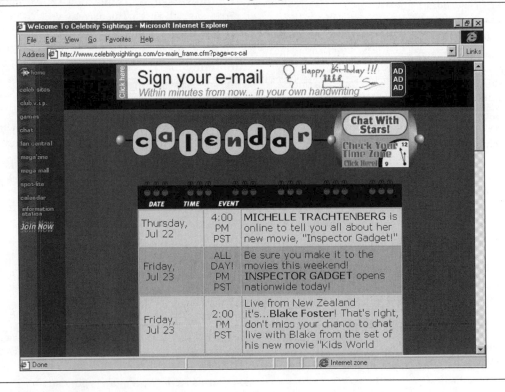

The **Games** section contains a set of celebrity-centric interactive games in which fans can test their celebrity knowledge in a playful way. Most of these games require a special software plug-in which members must download to their computers first.

Guidelines for downloading the plug-ins for the games and for the electronic chat can be found in the **Information Station** section. This section also contains general technical information and a link to the membership registration area.

LEARNING BY DOING

By running, maintaining and further developing the web site the Celebrity Sightings team members learned first hand which capabilities they needed to build further. Technically, operationally and editorially important lessons were learned and decisions taken.

On the technical side, Celebrity Sightings learned to control the complexity of the web site but also learned to create awareness about it. The two-type membership concept and its technical implementation provides a good illustration. In the original design, there were two web sites, one for premium members and one for basic members. This created a maintenance nightmare because every change had to be implemented twice, not only the content but also the underlying browsing logic and database links. After a costly redesign in January 1997 this complex double web site system was replaced by the current one where there is only one web site but where access is controlled for each page. The company also experimented several times with the extent of the privileges granted to premium members. Several sections were changed from "free for all" to "for premium members only" or vice versa. The difficulties in making these changes often surprised those with non-technical backgrounds. After a while everybody learned to think ahead and to work out a proposed change in detail before implementing it.

Operationally, it was quickly discovered that there was a need for specific skills and systems to operate the Star Store. Processes like order-tracking, inventory management and order-fulfillment required operational skills, systems and experience that were not available in the company at the outset. Originally Robert had planned to run the Star Store within Celebrity Sightings, offering the celebrities a 15 percent share in the profit from the store. After realizing the difficulty in building the necessary operational capabilities and considering the priorities, Robert negotiated a different formula with the celebrities. Under the new arrangement, orders are passed on to the celebrities who are responsible for fulfilling the orders and who pay a 15 percent commission to Celebrity Sightings.

On the editorial side, the Celebrity Sightings editors were learning more about the differences between an online magazine and a printed one. It was mostly good news. A big difference is the level of feedback you get from your readers, directly and indirectly. Writing an e-mail is very fast and many Celebrity Sightings' members enjoy giving direct feedback about their experiences with the site. The e-mail link with the "readers" not only generated useful suggestions but also provided encouragement and satisfaction for the Celebrity Sightings team-members who were flooded with positive comments. Indirectly, "readers" provide a lot of information by clicking their mice. After introducing a horoscope feature in their Fan Central section, Celebrity Sightings found out that very few members were interested in it. Only a small number of user hits reached the horoscope. The feature was quickly discontinued. "You quickly find out what works and what doesn't," says the editor in chief. The contact with the readers is much closer than what printed magazines can achieve.

Another important difference with a printed magazine is the fact that there are very few internal delays between a story and its readers because there is no "waiting for the next edition." Celebrity Sightings is often able to bring stories to its readers within a week after the facts. For the magazines, which often have editorial cycles of three months, that would be impossible. The knife cuts both ways however. Without monthly "editions" and deadlines, the natural pressure to have a new set of stories every month disappears. In practice most of the articles on the site range from being "hot off the keyboard" to being several months old and updates are often not as fast as hoped. Because fresh content is crucial in attracting user hits from the growing group of loyal members, a need was felt to create some self-imposed editorial discipline, not only for the writers but also for the programmers who were often needed to bring new content to the site.

A very special and new set of skills Celebrity Sightings had to build was related to the electronic chat. It became clear that the electronic chat element provides real value to a sizeable group of members. Mastering the art of producing a large chat event and creating a safe, pleasant and exciting chat culture was seen as critical.

Members are definitely attracted to the interaction with the stars during the electronic chats. Their positive e-mail responses as well as the recurring presence at the chats were interpreted as strong approval signals. A chat event in April 1997, where several celebrities were online at the same time attracted more than 300 members. Other entertainment in the chat areas is popular too. The weekly live "quiz" easily draws 30–50 members in the chat area and even on eventless nights anywhere from 10 to 30 members can be found chatting on the site. There are also signs of an online culture. One element in the culture is the complete denial of spelling, grammar and punctuation rules in the typed language. In response to a statement, it would not be unusual, for instance, to read something such as "WUT!?" on the screen. Members also look for small ways to express feelings online. The emoticons provided by the chat software are very popular and typed expressions such as "Ouch" or "Joan has a headache" are quite common in the conversations. "In some small way," says the editor in chief, "I believe the online chat activities satisfy some of our members' basic needs."

Providing successful chat entertainment was something that Celebrity Sightings learned by doing. That quite a few things can go wrong in a chat event was illustrated by the first announced chat with Jonathan Taylor Thomas (also known as "JTT"). The first problem was technical. When more than 50 members tried to access the chat room area, the software failed. There was hectic phone traffic between the facilities for the big PR event, the Guidance Solutions office, and the provider of the chat software. Only five minutes before the event was scheduled and after many added stress points for the Celebrity Sightings team, the right parameters in the Unix server were set to the required values. Once the chat had started, it was difficult to organize an orderly and interesting chat. "Our first chat with JTT was a mess," describes one of Celebrity Sightings' main chat moderators. After a few more experiences, Celebrity Sightings eventually became quite good at organizing chats. For chats with 30 members or more, the format of a moderated chat became the preferred solution (see description above and example in Exhibit 6). For smaller groups the presence of an experienced chat moderator was sufficient. Little tricks like typing "Sssssh-hhhhhh" to ask for electronic silence now belong to the toolbox of each chat moderator at Celebrity Sightings. This accumulated experience means that, even after serious comparison, the Celebrity Sightings team can now count itself among the best chat organizers on the Net.

To create a chat culture that is safe, pleasant and exciting, Celebrity Sightings publishes rules and safety tips, enforces the rules and uses online personalities to monitor, guide and stimulate conversations.

When a member enters the chat area he is encouraged to read the safety tips and the rules of the chat (see Exhibit 8). Members are also encouraged to report on infraction of the rules. So far only two people have had their membership retracted because of inappropriate chat behavior and in general the online conversations are nice and good-natured.

To have a more direct impact on the chat culture, Celebrity Sightings team members have created online personalities who participate in chats regularly. They try to foster a non-sexist, non-racist, teenager-friendly chat culture. In a neutral, low-profile manner the online personalities try to stimulate thinking, bring in new ideas and reinforce positive issues in the discussions. As one of the team members stated, "it is not very hard to raise the level of discussion because most online discussions are fairly mindless." The online personalities seem well liked and accepted and clearly add value to the chat experience of many members.

EXHIBIT 8   Guidelines for Electronic Chatting on Celebrity Sightings

Rules of the Road

At Celebrity Sightings we want EVERYBODY to have a great time!

In the chat rooms you can flirt, gossip, joke, banter, flirt, argue, sing, smile, shout and giggle to your hearts content but please don't be offensive or rude to other members 'cuz that is just so un-cool.

If you do encounter people who are bugging you, using foul language or are threatening you in any way here is what you can do: First ask them politely but firmly to stop! If that doesn't work copy and paste the entire message including their screen name and email it to chatguide@celebritysightings.com.

As a last resort members should simply ignore the comments and log off from that chat-room. Any members who are reported to Celebrity Sightings and who continue to break the rules of the road will be given the celebrity boot and their membership will be canceled.

At Celebrity Sightings we want EVERYBODY to be safe! Please take a couple of seconds to read the following tips and make sure you stay street smart!

- Just as you stay away from strangers on the street, be careful about strangers you meet in chat rooms.
- Don't believe anyone who tells you that they are one of the stars featured on Celebrity Sightings.
- Each of the celebrities have been given just one name which they will always use when they are chatting in the rooms. The celebrities are the ONLY people who have access to these screen names ending in "-cs." Other people who have "-cs" in their member names are Celebrity Sightings Staff members.
- Be aware that people are NOT always telling the truth. Sometimes guys will say they are girls and girls will say they are guys.
- If anyone uses nasty language or mentions things that make you feel uncomfortable, don't respond, just log off or ignore them.
- Never ever give your real last name, address, telephone number or fax number to anyone. If someone asks for this information (or for your password), don't respond. Log off and tell a trusted adult and/or Celebrity Sightings Staff at chatguide@celebritysightings.com.
- Remember even if you call someone else's telephone number, with caller ID they can still get YOUR telephone number.
- Never agree to meet with someone you've talked with in chat rooms without asking permission from your parents first.

Celebrity Sightings had clearly succeeded in creating value for its members through the chat facilities. Two issues received continuing attention. Although sizeable as a group, only 20 percent of all premium members participated in chatting. The Celebrity Sightings editor-in-chief felt he needed to understand why the other 75 percent remained silent. Secondly, considering the age group of its members it was very important to do everything possible to secure their safety. The publication of the safety tips was a good first step but continued alertness was necessary.

PARTNERSHIP WITH THE STARS

The contracts with the stars are clearly Celebrity Sightings' main asset. These contracts enable it to create the attractive content that is key to its revenues. The contract is basically an exclusivity agreement for content on the Internet. In exchange for a few commitments and for an agreement on exclusivity, the celebrities receive an interesting set of benefits.

Fifteen percent of membership revenues is divided among all participating celebrities based on the relative popularity of their personal web pages. Through the Star Store, celebrities are also provided with a new distribution channel for their merchandise at 15 percent commission. If they are interested in sharing further in the success of Celebrity Sightings they can become an investor (three celebrities have taken this option). In addition to these extra revenues celebrities benefit in other ways too. Celebrity Sightings offers a set of services, such as free publicity and contact with fans, that celebrities otherwise have to pay for or do themselves. Also, to have some control over what is shown about them and written on them in a prestigious new medium like the Internet is quite valuable to a young star. That they have to share space with other celebrities on the web site is not perceived as a problem. Most celebrities understand that everybody wins in this situation. Robert Landes explains, "It is like a community. Everybody enjoys being part of it."

The young stars sign a two-year contract with annual renewal option after two years. Nine celebrities were signed on at the launch in November 1997, two more were added in the first six months of operation and several others have shown interest. The commitments the celebrities agree to are reasonable but not negligible. They include monthly information updates, one hour of electronic chat per month, two photoshoots per year for exclusive pictures, two interviews per year, two appearances per year and regular cooperation with respect to fan mail. The content that Celebrity Sightings creates this way becomes exclusive property and cannot be distributed without its consent. In addition, the celebrities agree to do this exclusively for Celebrity Sightings. They can still have one-time appearances on other web sites but not without mentioning Celebrity Sightings.

So far there has been no need to enforce the contracts and most celebrities have cooperated enthusiastically. Celebrity Sightings manages these relationships very carefully. Apart from Robert himself, only one other experienced person at Celebrity Sightings deals with the celebrities directly.

MEMBERS

Although nowhere near the estimated potential, the total number of members had grown steadily to a respectable 16,200 in July 1997, 2,200 of which were premium members, and together with the other members they had purchased about \$13,000 of merchandise online. Signals about member loyalty and member demographics provided good news but total member growth had been slower than expected.

About 6 million teenagers in the U.S. read one of several teen magazines whose content is heavily focused on teen celebrities. Depending on who is counting (Killen, Commercenet/Nielsen, Project 2000, Jupiter Communications), somewhere between 25 and 35 million Americans had access to the World Wide Web early in 1997. According to Louis Harris and Associates around 16 percent of all web users are under 25. Independent from them, Jupiter Communications estimates that around 5 million kids are online. This is in the U.S. alone. Morgan Stanley estimates that by the year 2000, 150 million people will be online worldwide.

Even in his most conservative estimations Robert Landes saw himself as the only player in a market with several hundred thousand potential "members" for his web site. How many of the members would be willing to make online purchases? One indication comes from the same survey from Louis Harris and Associates, in which 24 percent of web users respond that they have already used the Internet to make purchases, a percentage that, it is estimated, will climb to 39 percent in 2001.

Members seem to have good potential for loyalty. More than readers from magazines, the members of the Celebrity Sightings web site seem active, responsive and motivated to participate. When asked for contributions to the web site in the form of movie reviews or stories of their personal celebrity sightings, responses have always been surprisingly numerous. It became clear, however, that current members have a rather narrow interest, focused on the celebrities. Most attempts to create interest outside the celebrity sphere were not so successful. Horoscopes on the web site failed to attract readership and a photocompetition to win a Kodak camera received fewer than 30 submissions. A contest, however, in which you could win the jacket that Jonathan Taylor Thomas had worn in his last movie by writing a review of that movie, received hundreds of responses. "We must not forget that our members are generally strongly preoccupied with these celebrities," says the editor-in-chief, "sometimes even obsessed."

The demographics of the July 1997 member base came as a pleasant surprise, both in age and gender. Robert expected to get 8 to 14 year olds and instead the age of members ranged from 8 to 25 with most members between 12 and 18 years old. Robert was happy to get the important group of 18 year olds: "Once you get the 18 year olds, you also get the 12, 13 and 14 year olds." In gender, members were divided 50:50. This was a surprise since 95 percent of all teenagers that buy teen magazines are girls. Since in general more boys use the World Wide Web than girls (70 percent vs. 30 percent), a different proportion was to be expected, but no one hoped to get 50 percent boys. "I think I discovered a new market," says Robert Landes. It seems that, from the privacy of their own rooms, boys are more eager to check out their favorite celebrities than at the newsstand. Danielle Fishel, for example, has a majority of male fans.

Members need a lot of technical support. By July, around 20 messages a day were technical questions. The provision of step-by-step instructions in the Information Station on the web site brought some relief but members still needed a lot of technical help. Someone even had to be refunded his membership fee after it turned out that he didn't have access to a computer.

Looking back, Robert was not unhappy with membership growth. "It is a little slower than I expected though. It took us eight months to achieve what I thought we would do in three."

SPONSORS

In July 1997 there were no corporate sponsors yet. Robert was hoping to get around 14 sponsors at $20,000 a month by the end of the first year. In exchange for their contribution, sponsors would be offered a customized advertising and promotion mix with elements such as chat room or scheduled event sponsoring, banner ads with web interlinks, animated interactive ads, online contests and promotions or co-marketing programs. In addition sponsors would also get priority access to a range of market research programs that could be organized among Celebrity Sightings members.

Although no sponsoring deals had been signed, Robert remained optimistic. The Celebrity Sightings members were a targeted and attentive group of young consumers. Such an audience usually has no problem getting the attention of marketing managers of large consumer companies.

One reason for the slow progress was that advertisers had become more careful about advertising on the Web. After the initial rush many companies were rethinking their web advertising policies and rates. There was a general feeling among advertisers that web advertising rates were too high. In the first quarter of 1997 *Webtrack* reported web advertising rates of between $15 to more than $80 per thousand pageviews (a pageview happens when someone's browser program loads the page in question to be viewed by the user), with destination sites getting higher rates than search engines. In comparison, a 30-second spot on "NBC Evening News" costs around $5.50 per thousand households and a full-page, four-color ad in *Cosmopolitan* costs $35 per thousand paying readers. Obviously web advertisements have some clear advantages in their ability to convey news and information (this happens when a viewer clicks through the ad to receive more information), their ability to change content quickly and in their opportunity for audience response. Add to that the prestige of the medium and the possibility to really select your audience, and it is easy to imagine the advertising power of the Web. Setting the price per thousand pageviews remained controversial, however, and it seemed that advertisers were educating themselves more thoroughly and were waiting for lower rates to be established.

STRATEGIES FOR MARKETING CELEBRITY SIGHTINGS

In his original marketing strategy Robert Landes focused on using Celebrity Sightings' proprietary content and its agreements with the stars to "pay for" advertising in other media.

Celebrity Sightings has a cross-promotional deal with the publisher of seven teen magazines. In exchange for banner ads that allow the user to subscribe to a magazine online, Celebrity Sightings has full-page ads in the editions of these magazines. With AAHS Kids Radio, a national radio station with 9 million listeners, Celebrity Sightings has another interesting marketing deal. In exchange for the appearance of a celebrity on a bi-weekly radio show for children, the show markets the Celebrity Sightings brand and provides recurrent information about the web site on the air. Robert Landes is working on an even more extensive deal for television and cable with Samuel Goldwyn Mayer. The plan is to produce a Celebrity Sightings TV show. Already $125,000 has been put aside to produce a pilot-show in August 1997. More than extra advertising, a successful TV show would also generate extra revenues. "If that pilot gets picked up, we're in the black right away."

Further promotion of the web site can come from celebrity appearances in malls, new stores, special events, etc. So far, Celebrity Sightings has set up two PR events of its own, one at the launch and another one in April. These included the presence of all the celebrities and were mainly directed at getting news coverage in other media. In another event, two celebrities appeared at the opening of a new toy store from FAO Schwarz in Las Vegas. This last promotional event was paid for by the toy store. When more sponsors for these kind of events can be found, they can become an important element in the promotion of the web site.

A second element of Robert's marketing strategy was the pricing of the premium membership. Initially premium membership, with chat privileges, was priced at $5 a month and $50 a year. Fearing after a while that $50 was too high, Robert reduced the price to $12 a year in order to attract more premium members. Lowering the price clearly had a positive effect on the growth of premium members but pricing remained a point of discussion. Another lesson about pricing changes was that they required a fair amount of administration and programming. Weighing the costs and benefits of further price changes clearly received more attention whenever changes were suggested.

Given the slightly disappointing member growth after a few months of operation, Robert decided to expand his original strategy. In April 1997 he started looking for other ways to increase member growth.

In a first step, Celebrity Sightings decided to buy advertising on Yahoo, one of the five most used search engines on the Web. When you buy advertising on a search engine, you usually "buy" a set of words. When a user makes a search for that word, your banner ad will be on top of the results page. Users may then click on the ad to go to your web site. Celebrity Sightings started by buying the names of the celebrities it features. This turned out to be a success. The Celebrity Sightings banner ads obtained a 50–60 percent click-through rate (this is the percentage of users that, after seeing the ad, click on it to go to the web site). The average click-through rates for ads is less than 5 percent. At $15 per thousand pageviews, the Yahoo advertising seemed quite effective. After this successful first step Celebrity Sightings was now considering doing further advertising on the Web.

Another avenue that Robert started considering was to link the Celebrity Sightings web site to another highly successful entertainment web site. Such deals usually involve some form of revenue sharing and Robert started looking carefully at alternative options. Warner Brothers was a viable candidate and had already shown interest.

THE TECHNOLOGY PARTNER

To make the Celebrity Sightings web site into a technical reality, Robert Landes hired Guidance Solutions, a small but growing provider of Internet services. Guidance Solutions was a promising start-up that originally specialized in database to web integration for business-to-business web applications, mainly for midsize distributors and manufacturers. The founders of Guidance were all top-trained engineers or computer scientists with several years of experience in software development and system applications. Their database expertise, in particular, made them stand out in the Internet services market. Guidance Solutions had been looking to expand their services to the business-to-consumer web application market and had expressed an interest in a partnership with Bright Interactive, a group of designers led by Robert and specializing in interactive multimedia applications. With skills that were almost perfectly complementary to the skills Robert had access to in Bright Interactive, Guidance Solutions was asked to make a proposal for the technical realization of the Celebrity Sightings web site.

It was clear from the start that the relationship with Guidance Solutions would not be a supplier relationship at arm's length. Guidance Solutions was to design, select, install, operate and maintain the information technology of Celebrity Sightings, an asset that would be key to its success. The project manager from Guidance Solutions would become almost an integral part of the Celebrity Sightings organization and communication would have to be frequent and intense. Since the stakes were high for both companies, the relationship was seen as a partnership from the outset.

As requested, Guidance Solutions designed and installed a hardware and software infrastructure that could be scalable to a capacity of 1 million user hits a day. The Celebrity Sightings web site is hosted on a Sun Ultra Enterprise with multiple UltraSPARC processors, each with 512-Kbyte UltraCache connected to a T3 line with a direct connection to the Internet. The site was co-developed by Guidance Solutions programmers and Bright Interactive designers with C-based Common Gateway Interfaces, Unix scripts, Javascript, Oracle SQL, Netscape SSL encryption for secure transmissions, Macromedia Director and I-chat interactive chat software. It is an open architecture designed for future growth and scalability. Originally a video and audio-server were included in the plans, but their installation was postponed to limit the investment costs.

Choosing application software is difficult. Functionality, ease of development, availability of technical support are all important but so is browser compatibility. Celebrity Sightings uses Macromedia Director for the interactive games, I-chat for electronic chat and IC-verify for online credit card processing. Carefully selected by Guidance Solutions, these applications are compatible with most common browser software, such as those from Netscape or Microsoft (not all are compatible, however, with the WebTV or America Online browsers). By building relationships with these application software vendors but also by keeping an eye on new innovations or new standards, Guidance Solutions enables Celebrity Sightings to make the most of current technologies and to stay in sync with future developments.

Guidance Solutions also plays an important role in the operation of the web site. It is responsible for the flawless technical operation of the web site and it also monitors and reports on how it is used by members. In addition, Guidance Solutions manages the member database and generates needed outputs from it, thereby taking on a set of administrative tasks and creating important management information.

ORGANIZATION

Celebrity Sightings has a simple organizational structure, where practically all team members work directly with CEO Robert Landes. Robert is an enthusiastic leader and, although simple in structure, his organization has started to incorporate a set of unique skills and organizational capabilities.

As CEO of the company, Robert represents the vision for the company, provides leadership and manages most important external relationships, at least in their initial phases. He is the one who contacts the celebrities, makes the media deals, looks for sponsors and sets up the partnerships. The company's marketing strategy and plan are his and he takes the important steps in implementing the plan.

Barry Burchell is the editorial director. Barry has a strong media background. He has worked as a writer for magazines and as a researcher and producer for radio news. More recently he managed the L.A. office of a British film magazine. He joined Celebrity Sightings in November 1996 and has since then written over 90 percent of all the text that has appeared on the web site. He is the content guru. He does the interviews with the stars, reports on special events and organizes the semi-annual photo shoots to get exclusive pictures. His writing style is very much adapted to the teen audience but his texts clearly testify to a personal devotion to authenticity. He is also the one who manages the relationships with the celebrities and their parents, on a regular basis. Barry is probably also closest to the members. With his online personality "Bazza," Barry hosts most of the chat events and has become an "icon" in the Celebrity Sightings chat rooms. Together with two student interns who work with Barry and who have created their own online personalities, he manages the site's chat events and responds to all member e-mail that doesn't deal with administrative or technical questions.

Rob Bynder is the artistic director. Rob has a creative art background and knew Robert from Bright Interactive. Before joining Celebrity Sightings, Rob managed several projects in which he was responsible for creating the graphic identity of magazines or of corporate PR materials. This included setting up the pallets, style sheets and style guides that enable publishers to create a single unified "look" for their publications. As a freelance designer Rob has also done artwork for interactive applications such as kiosks or CD-ROMs. Rob is responsible for the look and feel of Celebrity Sightings. He did most of the artwork, not only for the web site but also for all PR and marketing materials. Through his work designing marketing materials for Celebrity Sightings Rob also started taking small responsibilities for marketing in general. Among other things, he is now responsible for identifying further advertising opportunities on the Web. Now that most of the design groundwork is finished Rob finds that he can spend more time in other areas, especially since he started to commission out some of the artwork to student interns or freelance designers.

Richard Parr is the production director. Also coming from the creative sector, Richard has the final responsibility for the production of the web site. Where necessary he coordinates Rob, Barry and the programmers at Guidance Solutions.

Mo Whelan is the operations director. She is responsible for the day-to-day operations of the company in the areas of administration, public relations, membership services, and coordination of Celebrity Sightings events. She is the contact person for Celebrity Sightings and handles all promotions on the site. Having degrees in Fashion Design and Business Administration and having worked in an architectural design firm, Mo has the right combination of creative talent and business sense to keep the operations in gear at Celebrity Sightings.

Although theoretically not part of the organization, Karen Barber from Guidance Solutions took on major responsibilities in Celebrity Sightings. As project manager for the technical realization of the web site she has spent about 60 to 80 percent of her time working for Celebrity Sightings since September 1996. Before joining Guidance Solutions in early 1996 she held roles as technical team leader and technical developer in the systems application/business support unit of a large aerospace and defense company. In September 1996, after Robert had shown interest in working with Guidance Solutions, she specified the requirements, made a functional description and provided a cost estimate for the web site that Robert's team had in mind. She selected the technical architecture, made all major software choices and managed the implementation project from start to finish. Even after the launch of the web site, several redesigns of the site and its continuous evolution meant that Karen remained active in Celebrity Sightings. During all this time she managed on average two programmers at Guidance Solutions. The partnership between Celebrity Sightings and Guidance Solutions worked very well and Robert encouraged Karen to be proactive about the continuous technical innovation of the web site.

The people at Celebrity Sightings are all selected for their talent and enthusiasm. Moreover, they all own stock in the company. "Everybody here has a vested interest in the company so I don't spend a lot of time checking in on people's work," says Robert, who sees himself more as an entrepreneur than a manager. "Being one of those one-idea-a-minute guys, I am the one who needs to be managed," he jokes.

Clearly Celebrity Sightings was building some unique skills and organizational capabilities. It was learning how to entertain a teenage audience over the Web. Nobody in the company would claim that they mastered the art yet but confidence was fairly high. A certain proficiency was clearly emerging, both in organizing chat-based entertainment and in creating the type of content that is attractive to teenagers. In another important skill domain Celebrity Sightings was learning how to build long-lasting partnerships with the celebrities. Having grown from nine celebrities at start, to two more after eight months, and several more celebrities considering participating, the Celebrity Sightings team felt it was making strong progress in this area too.

Another aspect of the Celebrity Sightings organization is that people from very different backgrounds need to work together to make the site a success. In the beginning it was clear for instance that the creative people were novices with regard to the technical aspects of a database-linked web site, and that the technical people at Guidance did not fully understand the creative aspects of running an entertainment web site. Not without some difficulties the different experts learned about each others' work, work style and added value. The mutual fine-tuning and cooperation that developed gradually between Robert Landes, Barry Burchell, Rob Bynder and Karen Barber had generated an organizational capability that takes a while to develop.

MOVING FORWARD

In July 1997, the pressure to find a first big sponsor was slowly rising. The business model for Celebrity Sightings depended heavily on revenues from sponsors (see Exhibit 9 for an overview of sources of revenues and costs). Partly because the company was undercapitalized at first, but also partly to compensate for the current lack of sponsors, Robert organized two extra rounds of funding in the first eight months, raising the company's capital to $1m.

In the meantime there seemed to be many opportunities to enlarge and improve member services. One idea was to enlarge the target audience by including sports and music celebrities. This would be especially exciting once the planned audio and video capabilities were installed. One of Robert's dreams was to let bands play live music on the web site.

Another set of ideas involved increasing the "community" features of the web site by allowing members to publish their own homepage and by enabling them to send internal e-mails. The chat rooms demonstrated how much members enjoyed the interactive aspect of the service. By facilitating this effect further everybody could benefit.

Marketing, of course, remained one of the biggest points of focus. Robert kept targeting his energy towards making advertising deals with other media and recently also towards finding other ways to strengthen the Celebrity Sightings brand. More direct advertising on the Web or an important inclusion deal with a high-traffic entertainment site were some of the ways the exposure of the site could be increased.

There was also a feeling that none of this should wait too long. Although no real competitors were on the horizon, it was unlikely to stay this way. Most networks were seriously considering creating an Internet presence for their shows and might also be interested in claiming some Internet time and content from their stars. Also, many other community-based web sites targeting teenagers were emerging and becoming

EXHIBIT 9   Revenues and Costs for Celebrity Sightings

Revenues

Premium memberships	$12 per premium membership	Considering to raise price to $19.95
Corporate advertisers	$10 per thousand pageviews (minimum rate based on current advertising rates on the WWW)	So far no advertisers were found
Merchandise	15% commission on all merchandise sold	In the first 6 months, the star stores grossed $14,000

Celebrity revenue sharing

Premium memberships	15% of membership revenue	Divided among stars according to relative popularity

Web site hosting and development costs

Web site hosting fee	$1,000 per month, includes hardware rental, telecom costs and software costs for operating systems, database systems and CGIs.	Paid to Guidance Solutions, who owns $35,000 hardware setup
Web site development	$25,000 per month for programming and project management fees (average from September 1996 till June 1997)	Paid to Guidance Solutions, who have one project manager and the equivalent of two full-time programmers working for CS

Staff costs and commissioning

Directors	Average of $45,000 per director per year	Currently five directors
Freelance writing or designing	Highly variable	So far less than $1,000 a month
Web site operators	$20,000 per operator per year	Currently one full-time equivalent
Support staff	$20,000 per staff member per year	Currently one administrative assistant

Sofware costs

Software purchases	$20,000 in one time fees	Database software, web-application software, graphic design software, administrative software
Software licenses	$10,000 each year	Most development and design software is licensed per computer. Licensing costs for operational software, such as the chat software depend on the number of supported concurrent streams (users)
Software upgrades	$2,000 per year	Around 20% of original purchasing price

EXHIBIT 9   (Continued)

Office expenses

Office space rental	$20 per square foot per year	$1,500 per month for current office
Travel, supplies etc.	$500 per employee per month	

Advertising and promotion

Advertising on WWW	$10 per 1,000 pageviews	Currently $2,000 per month to Yahoo
PR events	$10,000–$15,000 per event	3 PR events in first half of 1997

increasingly professional (Kidscom, Cyberteens, etc.). In order to become really credible for sponsors, Celebrity Sightings needed to grow further at a steady pace.

THE MERGER

In July 1997, Celebrity Sightings merged with Guidance Solutions. Robert Landes became the CEO of the newly merged company. For Celebrity Sightings the merger brought a couple of important advantages.

Financially the two companies were very complementary. Guidance Solutions was a profitable, low-debt company in the growing but competitive market of Internet services. Celebrity Sightings was a potentially highly profitable business in the entertainment business that needed a little time and resources to grow to viability.

In terms of capabilities, the synergies were very clear. Robert Landes and his creative team brought the sales and marketing experience and the graphic design skills that Guidance Solutions would need to grow its business. The system application and business support experience at Guidance Solutions would be of real value to Celebrity Sightings' growing operations. Having Guidance Solutions programmers and project manager in the same office as the Celebrity Sightings organization would also improve organizational efficiency quite drastically given the need for frequent communication.

Finally, the merger provided important synergies in knowledge generation and exploitation. By merging with a web development firm, Celebrity Sightings could benefit from the knowledge Guidance Solutions was generating by working with other clients. Vice versa, in merging with an Internet entertainment business Guidance Solutions would gain a much deeper understanding for the needs of its clients, thereby improving its competitiveness.

Satisfied with the merger, Robert now needed to think hard about his new role. In the short run he would probably take important sales and marketing responsibilities for the two different companies. In the short run this would probably be the best use of his time, but he also realized that in the long run it would be difficult to keep running around with two different hats. Eventually he would have to redefine his role and reshape the organization of the newly formed company.

Chapter 6

Electronic Commerce— Products

The incredibly rapid rise of the bookseller Amazon.com has served to direct the world's attention to the selling of physical products over the Internet. As noted at the beginning of the previous chapter, the selling of services, especially information services that can be delivered electronically, fits the domain of electronic commerce best of all. Nonetheless, the business press has devoted a great deal of attention to the product side of electronic commerce—with companies such as Amazon.com, Auto-By-Tel, Buy.com, eBay, and so forth receiving much media attention month after month.

One of the distinguishing features of the product side of electronic commerce is the challenge of distribution. While for some purposes the Internet does put a company in touch with the entire world, in fact as soon as that company actually tries to ship a product somewhere it runs head on into the distribution nightmare. Users of sites such as Amazon.com quickly discover that what they save on the price they pay for a book, they lose in payment to FedEx or some other shipper. And when a web-based firm decides to ship beyond its borders, things become even more complex. In a nutshell, when selling physical products via the Internet, geography *matters*.

The first case in this chapter concerns the computer manufacturer and distributor Dell Computer, specifically its online distribution business. Dell has set the pace for successful use of the Internet as a sales and distribution channel. Today, Dell is "eating the lunch" of traditional suppliers such as Compaq, who are late getting into the direct-to-customer game. How Dell got to where it is today provides valuable lessons for anyone thinking of selling physical products through the Internet.

The second case focuses on a type of physical product that practically everyone has shopped for on many occasions: groceries. The case describes a new company, Homegrocer, and the business model this company developed to compete with both virtual and traditional grocery stores. Internet-based grocery stores have existed for some time, predating the advent of the World Wide Web by a number of years. Two of the best-known existing Internet grocery operations are Peapod and Netgrocer. Peapod's approach is to partner with existing real grocery chains, offering an electronic picking service that piggybacks on its partner's existing bricks-and-mortar facilities. In contrast, Netgrocer only handles nonperishable items, and ships continentwide via FedEx, out of a huge central warehouse. Both companies have had considerable difficulty building their businesses and turning profits, for various reasons.

Homegrocer has developed a new approach, in which it is attempting to outflank both Peapod and Netgrocer, by following a "best of both worlds" strategy. Homegrocer handles a full line of groceries, but avoids the extra costs associated with the overhead of a physical grocery chain. By operating out of a warehouse in a "low rent" area of the city, Homegrocer is able to maintain a considerably higher gross margin than its real-world competitors. In addition, the company made the interesting decision to restrict delivery to only 30 miles around its warehouse, despite the fact that demand, at least in theory, could come from much further afield. HomeGrocer's main challenge is building its customer base. This entails changing people's mind-sets, since shopping for groceries in a real grocery store—as opposed to an online one—is a practice that many people find hard to break.

The third case in this section focuses on Good Night Ben, a retailer of high-end children's furniture: cribs, playpens, small beds, and the like. The store's proprietor, Bob Brown, a longtime "computer junkie," developed his company's own web site. Brown has gone further and created sites for other small companies as well. He has also created interconnected sets of web sites—sometimes referred to as "web wheels"—to link various related sites together and create greater volume of business for each participant. Brown also studied the mysterious ways of web search engines and figured out techniques for ensuring that his firm's web site appeared near the tops of the lists returned to people searching for stores such as his. Recently, Brown has discovered the power of the Web for stealing business from competitors' stores in other geographical regions—even though these competitors were supposedly provided an "exclusive" right to sell the manufacturer's products.

The final case concerns an Internet-based auction company, Internet Liquidators International (ILI). ILI was one of the earliest Internet-based auctions, and attempted to differentiate itself partly by specializing in the Dutch auction format. A Dutch auction features a declining price, such that the longer a bidder waits, the cheaper the item becomes, but the greater the likelihood that someone else will buy it first. Internet auctions have received a great deal of attention in the media, with firms such as eBay and OnSale—both competitors to ILI—gaining notoriety. ILI recently changed its name to Bid.com.

Dell Online

By Professor V. Kasturi Rangan and Marie Bell

"It was Michael's idea. He is a visionary in our industry," stated Morton Topfer, Vice Chairman of Dell Computer Corporation, gesturing toward Michael Dell's office across the hallway. "There's no doubt that Dell Online is a huge innovation, just as Dell Direct was a decade ago. But times have changed. We are now a big company, with 1997 revenues of nearly $12 billion and a growth rate of 50 percent over the last three years. We have to be nimble but methodical in how we absorb and build on this new approach of going to market," added Topfer.

In July 1996, Dell Computer had launched its online web site, www.dell.com. The online store mirrored the experience customers had when they called Dell Computer's toll-free 800 number to place a direct order. Site visitors could customize the computer's configuration to suit their needs, noting how those changes improved performance and affected pricing. Additionally, customers could check on the status of their order at their convenience and even receive technical support *online*. The store was open 24 hours a day. The response to the retail store was overwhelming, with hundreds of thousands of people visiting the web site each week and generating millions of dollars of revenue for Dell.

In addition to its online store, Dell also developed Premier Pages, online interfaces with its key corporate accounts. Customers viewed the Premier Pages to get technical help, to access their Dell account executive, or in some cases, to place orders using the customer's preferred pricing and standard configurations. Scott Eckert, the 30-year-old director of Dell Online, remarked,

> Dell's foray into Internet-based sales, marketing and support has been a big win. We're getting a lot of publicity about selling $3 million a day on the Internet—and our goal is to execute half of Dell's sales volume over the Internet within three years. It's also clear that major competitors such as Compaq are attempting to break with tradition and imitate Dell, not only by going direct to the consumer, but also by letting the customer configure his/her product. We need to know how to leverage our initial success into a sustainable competitive advantage.

THE STORY OF DELL[1]

In 1983, Michael Dell, an 18-year-old freshman at the University of Texas at Austin, spent his evenings and weekends pre-formatting hard disks for IBM-compatible PC upgrades. A year later, he dropped out of college to attend to his burgeoning business, which had grown from nothing to $6 million in 1985 by simply upgrading IBM compatibles for local area businesses. In 1985, Dell shifted his company's focus to assembling its own brand of PCs and the business grew dramatically, with $70 million in sales at the end of 1985. By 1990, sales had grown even further to over $500 million and with it Dell's capabilities as a national supplier to Fortune 500 companies. The company now had a broad product line of desktop and portable computers based on the most recent Intel processors and had earned a strong reputation for its products and services.

Dell's success continued through 1992, until in 1993 it faced an operating loss for the first time in its history, despite a 40 percent increase in sales. (See Exhibit 1, on page 228, for Dell's financial performance.) The problems, Dell quickly discovered, stemmed in part from its attempts to sell its products through retail channels, such as CompUSA, Staples, and Sam's Clubs in the U.S. Moreover, quality problems with its laptops had exacerbated Dell's financial woes. While some pundits were questioning Dell's future, the company acted decisively, exiting the retail channel and resolving to re-enter the laptop market only when that product's quality matched or exceeded the quality of the Dell desktop. By 1997, the Latitude, Dell's laptop, had won *PC Computing* magazine's Torture Test twice in three years in addition to winning *Business Week*'s Industrial Design Excellence Award.

Dell's product line evolved with the PC market. In 1997, Dell manufactured two types of desktop systems: the Dimension line that offered high-end technology at value prices, and the OptiPlex line featuring highly reliable network ready systems designed for corporate and institutional customers. Similarly with notebooks (laptops), the Inspiron line offered state of the art technology at aggressive prices, while the Latitude line offered reliable notebooks designed for the office network, equipped with dependable network connectivity. In addition to its desktop and laptop products, Dell introduced its PC/LAN (server) product the PowerEdge in 1996 and workstations in 1997.

By 1996, Dell sales reached $7.8 billion with an operating income of more than $710 million. Dell continued offering its customers high-quality products, value-added services, and reduced costs of ownership. Value-added services included: DellPlus that enabled Dell to install commercial and proprietary software and peripherals to customers'

---

[1]Some parts of this section have been drawn and adapted from HBS case No. 596-058. "Dell Computer Corporation."

specifications: DellWare, a one-stop shopping service of thousands of hardware and software products (Dell maintained no inventory; orders were placed electronically for immediate shipment to affiliated warehouses); and Dell Asset Management where Dell helped customers with leasing packages. To lower the costs of ownership, Dell also worked with its customers on proper software management practices, offered volume license programs, and efficient installation services.

Throughout its remarkable history, nearly all of Dell's sales were to large corporate accounts, medium and small businesses, federal and state governments, and educational institutions. "Home" consumers were only a small proportion of its sales. Almost universally, customers and analysts alike attributed Dell's reputation and success to its unique and distinctive "Dell Direct Model."

The Dell Direct Model

The Dell Direct Model was a very efficient "made-to-order" high-velocity, low-cost distribution system characterized by direct customer relationships, build-to-order manufacturing, and products and services targeted at specific market segments. By and large using print media, Dell's marketing communication ($150 million budget in 1997) attracted the attention of its customers to its Direct model and its inherent advantages. Over time, Dell was able to accurately forecast demand based on marketing communication efforts. For example, Dell's consumer group was able to predict response rates from newspaper ads, catalogue offers, etc. Based on its model forecasts, Dell was then able to accurately adjust sales staffing and production levels to meet demand.

Dell serviced the North American market from its two plants in Austin, Texas. A new state-of-the-art plant that opened in 1997 manufactured Dell's OptiPlex systems, while Dell's original plant, fondly referred to as Braker 12, continued to manufacture Dell's Dimension systems that were targeted at the individual user, Dell Latitude notebooks, and Dell's PowerEdge network servers. The new facility operated with just-in-time materials, a continuous manufacturing flow, and direct shipment capability that increased productivity and ensured consistent, timely order delivery and high product reliability. With the transfer of the OptiPlex capacity, the old plant, which had grown in a haphazard fashion to accommodate ever-increasing capacity needs, was being redesigned along many of the same principles.

Once Dell received an order at its factory, the configuration details were sent to manufacturing, where the order was electronically broken down into a list of parts required to build the computer. When the specification sheet was generated, an electronic bar code linked the system back to its original order number. If the customer called to check on the delivery status, using the order number Dell could tell the customer exactly where the PC was in the assembly process and when the system

EXHIBIT 1   Financial Performance of Dell Computer Corporation ($ in millions)

	1986	1987	1988	1989	1990
Net sales	69.5	159.0	257.8	388.6	546.2
United States	65.5	153.1	318.2	300.3	358.9
Europe		6.0	39.6	88.3	187.4
Other international					
Cost of sales	53.6	109.3	177.3	279.0	364.2
Gross profit	15.9	49.7	80.5	109.6	182.1
Operating expenses					
SGA	10.3	27.4	51.0	79.7	115.0
R&D	1.5	5.1	6.6	17.0	22.4
Total operating expenses	11.7	32.5	57.7	96.7	137.5
Operating income	4.1	17.2	22.8	12.9	44.6
Net income	2.2	9.4	14.4	5.1	27.2
% of Net sales					
Net sales	100.0	100.0	100.0	100.0	100.0
United States	100.0	96.3	84.6	77.3	65.7
International—Europe	0.0	3.7	15.4	22.7	24.3
International—others	0.0	0.0	0.0	0.0	0.0
Cost of sales	76.9	68.5	68.5	71.8	66.7
Gross profit	23.1	31.5	31.5	28.2	33.3
Operating expenses					
Marketing and sales	14.8	17.2	19.8	20.5	20.9
R&D	2.3	3.5	2.8	4.4	4.1
Total operating expenses	17.1	20.7	22.6	24.9	25.0
Operating income	6.0	10.8	8.9	3.3	8.3
Net income	3.1	5.9	5.6	1.3	5.0

would be shipped. If the customer had a service issue after receipt of the system, they could refer to the number on the bar code and the service technician could look up the exact configuration of the system.

After the parts spec sheet was generated the assembly of the computer began. First the motherboard was configured with the ordered micro-processor and the required amount of RAM. Then the other optional parts (disk drives, CD-ROMs, etc.) were assembled into a bin, with workers pulling the needed parts from stock. The bin was forwarded with the motherboard to a five-person cell for the installation of these other parts, wiring to the motherboard, case assembly, and quality testing. The production cells were equipped with computers that provided instant, detailed access to information regarding part

EXHIBIT 1 (Continued)

	1991	1992	1993	1994	1995	1996
Net sales	889.9	2,013.9	2,873.2	3,475.3	5,296	7,759
United States	648.1	1,459.6	2,037.2	2,400.0	3,474	5,279
Europe	241.9	553.0	781.9	952.9	1,478	2,004
Other international		1.3	54.0	122.4	344	476
Cost of sales	607.8	1,564.5	2,440.4	2,737.3	4,229	6,093
Gross profit	282.2	449.5	432.8	738.0	1,067	1,666
Operating expenses						
SGA	182.2	268.0	422.9	423.4	595	826
R&D	33.1	42.4	48.9	65.4	95	126
Total operating expenses	215.3	310.3	471.8	488.8	690	952
Operating income	66.9	139.1	−39.0	249.3	377	714
Net income	50.9	101.6	−35.8	149.2	272	531
% of Net sales						
Net sales	100.0	100.0	100.0	100.0	100.0	100.0
United States	72.8	72.5	70.9	69.1	66.0	68.0
International—Europe	27.2	27.5	27.2	27.4	28.0	26.0
International—others	0.0	0.1	1.9	3.5	6.0	6.0
Cost of sales	68.3	77.7	84.9	78.8	79.9	78.5
Gross profit	31.7	22.3	15.1	21.2	21.1	21.5
Operating expenses						
Marketing and sales	20.5	13.3	14.7	12.2	11.3	10.7
R&D	3.7	2.1	1.7	1.9	1.8	1.6
Total operating expenses	24.2	15.4	16.4	14.1	13.1	12.3
Operating income	7.5	6.9	−1.3	7.1	7.2	9.2
Net income	5.7	5.0	−1.3	4.0	5.1	6.8

configurations and setup. Dell found that the high-volume cell production lines improved the plant's capacity and also more easily integrated DellPlus program components allowing for even greater customization for customers. The cell-based production in the new plant was significantly more efficient than the old plant which had operated as a traditional assembly line. For example, there was a reduced need for quality checking at several points in the line as the members of a cell worked as a team to configure the system and test it before it left the assembly area.

After all the options had been installed in the manufacturing cell per the spec sheet, the system was sent to the software loading zone, where the appropriate software, including operating system software, application software, and diagnostic software, were loaded into the hard disk of the system. After all the software was loaded, the system was sent to a "burn-in" area where it was powered and tested for four to eight hours before being packed into a box and sent to the packaging area. There, the completed system was boxed along with peripherals such as a keyboard, mouse, mouse pad, and the manuals and floppy disks for all the installed software.

Despite earning some of the industry's highest quality awards in the PC industry, Dell was constantly striving to improve its products. For example, recently "Michael Dell became obsessed with finding a way to reduce his machines' failure rate."[2] He believed the key was to reduce the number of times there was human interaction with the hard drive during assembly and insisted that the number of "touches" be significantly reduced from the existing levels of 30 per drive. When the production lines were re-configured, the number of touches fell to less than 15 and soon after the rate of rejected hard drives fell 40 percent, and the overall failure rate for Dell PCs dropped 20 percent.

The Dell process became a model of efficiency for the industry. The entire process from order receipt to product shipping required only about 36 hours. Incoming parts were pulled through the system and ordered on a just-in-time basis, with Dell's direct model operating on 13 days of inventory, versus the 75 to 100 days in the typical indirect model. This was an improvement over Dell's prior standard of 30 days of component inventory, with suppliers carrying a buffer stock of 45 to 60 days. Indeed, when the plant was designed, an extensive area had been allocated for parts storage, but six months after the plant opened, Dell planned to convert much of the area to production space, adding an additional line to the four already in operation. Dell's ability to operate on a just-in-time basis was facilitated by its suppliers, who warehoused the bulk of their components within 15 minutes from the Dell factory. Dell had been able to reach these agreements by reducing the number of suppliers, buying from just 47 companies rather than the 204 it had purchased from in 1992. An industry observer commented on the advantages of Dell's pull system.

> While machines from Compaq or IBM can languish on dealer shelves for two months, Dell doesn't start ordering components and assembling computers until an order is booked. That may sound like no biggie, but the price of PC parts can fall rapidly in just a few months. By ordering right before assembly, Dell figures his parts on average are 60 days newer than those in an IBM or Compaq machine sold at the same time. That can translate into a 6 percent profit advantage in components alone.[3]

Shipping was contracted out, with multiple shippers delivering the systems anywhere in North or South America. In 1997, in another process innovation, Dell stopped accepting delivery of monitors for its

---

[2]"Dell Turns the PC World Inside Out," *Fortune,* September 8, 1997.
[3]"Whirlwind on the Web," *Business Week,* April 7, 1997.

PC orders. Instead, when a system was ready for shipping, Dell sent an e-mail message to a shipper. The shipper pulled the appropriate monitor from supplier stocks and scheduled the monitor's arrival to the customer for the same date as the PC. The result was about $30 savings in freight costs per display.

Post shipment, if a customer called in with a problem, the first level of support was provided over the telephone. Dell employed nearly 1,300 technical support representatives who could be accessed by phone at any time. Given the nature of the product, this was very effective in taking care of service problems that required hand-holding customers and walking them through standard trouble-shooting procedures, and indeed solved the problem in nine out of ten cases. If the problem was one of defective parts, Dell had third-party maintenance agreements with service companies (office automation vendors such as Xerox) who sent technicians to solve the problem, with most problems being resolved within 24 to 48 hours. Michael Dell explained,

> We first introduced the concept of build-to-order in the PC industry. We were also the first to introduce on-site service. We knew that our corporate customers and experienced individual customers had needs that weren't being filled by the traditional retail channel.

The Dell Customer

Dell broadly segmented its customers as either "transactional" or "relationship," with about 40 percent being relationship, 30 percent being transactional and the rest being a blend of both. Table A below shows Dell's major customer segments. Transactional customers were individuals or businesses who, even if purchasing a large volume of computers,

TABLE A   Dell's Market Segmentation*

Market Segment	Buying Process	Ratio of Outside Reps to Inside Sales Reps
Enterprise (>18,000 employees)	Relationship	1:1
Large corporate accounts (2,000–18,000 employees)	Relationship	1.3:1
Preferred accounts (400–2,000 employees)	Relationship	1:3
Business systems div. (2–400 employees)	Transactional	All inside
Dell catalogue sales	Transactional	All inside
Federal government	Mixed	1:1.5
Education	Mixed	1:2
State & local government	Mixed	1:1

*The data in this table has been disguised.

thought of each purchase individually. For the transactional customer the economics of the purchase was the key variable. The transactional customer usually bought from a variety of vendors over time, always looking for the best PC for a particular application focusing on specific factors such as performance, specifications, features, bundles, reviews, and awards. The transactional customer consulted information sources such as reviews, editorials, advertising, as well as word of mouth in the buying process, relying on previous brand experience only as an indicator. Dell's business systems division (BSD) that served small businesses, catalogue sales (DCS) that served consumers, portions of higher education and the federal government were examples of transactional segments. Dell's main competitors in this segment were companies such as Gateway 2000, and Micron Electronics, and the retail channel. One Dell executive summarized, "On the transactional side of the business, you need to 'acquire' the customer every time they buy a system; the only difference is that they're much more educated the second time than the first."

Traditionally, Dell had steered clear of the neophyte transactional customer, especially the individual consumer who tended to pay lower prices and, lacking a technical user-support group found in the larger business setting, tended to have more intensive service requirements. Morton Topfer added, "Consumers at retail don't know what they are looking for, other than price. We, on the other hand, like to sell to the educated consumer." As a result, Dell tended to market toward the higher end of the segment that attracted a more computer-sophisticated customer.

"Relationship" customers thought of computer purchasing as a multi-dimensional process, regardless of whether they were purchasing 5 or 500 computers. Unlike the transactional customer, the relationship customer was less price sensitive (although the customer may buy at low price points) and tended to focus on factors such as reliability, vendor strength, and standardization of products. Relationship customers got their information from sales people, industry analysts, conferences, and trials and testing. Relationship accounts included the Enterprise, Preferred Accounts, and federal government contracts segments. Dell's major competitors in the Relationship segment were Compaq, IBM, HP, and other leading brands that sold to the customers through VARs (value-added resellers) and national resellers. For example, Vanstar, a major reseller of Compaq's product, would offer its customers a complete computing solution, including Compaq computer hardware, peripherals, installation of standard and proprietary software, and on-site service.

Relationship customers were a key component in Dell's success story. While few large customers signed exclusive purchase agreements with a single vendor, Dell had achieved remarkable penetration of the relationship customer base, with a 25 percent penetration of the Fortune 500 companies, 10 percent penetration of the next largest 5,000 companies, and an 8 percent share of the 15,000 companies with 200–2,000 employees. In the medium and small business segment with nearly a 5 percent penetration of the 7 million accounts, Dell had made impressive gains in the last few years. As a hardware manufacturer, Dell was at a competitive disadvantage against VARs and national resellers that offered a full range of hardware (both PCs and peripherals) and software (off-the-shelf and customized). Dell had overcome these shortcomings in two ways. First, it recognized that it needed to be more than a "pure" hardware vendor and developed its own range of value-added services such as DellPlus that installed commercial and proprietary software and Dellware, a one-stop shopping service of a full range of hardware and software products. Moreover, Dell had contracted out, but maintained accountability for, its service for large accounts to third-party service providers such as Digital Equipment Corporation that had nearly 20,000 field service people. Second, Dell focused on the economics of the overall account, judiciously applying the 10 to 15 percent price advantage earned by its direct model to both win new accounts and deepen penetration of existing accounts.

Transactional customers were given the option of paying for their purchase using a credit card or being charged in full on delivery. In the case of Relationship buyers, payment was usually effected through corporate purchase orders, credit cards, or lease agreements, resulting in a significantly longer payment cycle. Overall, the larger the volume per account, the higher the gross margins for Dell in the Relationship segment. The ability to generate cash from its orders was another example of Dell's process velocity. Especially on the transaction side, Dell converted the average sale to cash in less than 24 hours by tapping credit cards and electronic payment. By comparison, Compaq, which sold primarily through dealers, took 35 days and Gateway, 16.4 days.

Dell Salesforce

Dell organized its business into four regions, the Americas, Europe, Japan, and Asia, with a president within each region responsible for all operations. Each of the four regions, in addition to a worldwide business development group and other specialized functions such as legal and engineering, reported directly to the Office of the Chairman. As seen in the organization chart (Exhibit 2), reporting into the regions were senior vice presidents responsible for manufacturing, individual business units, and other functions such as public relations and finance. Within the Americas (which represented 65 percent of Dell worldwide sales), each of the nine business segments was grouped into broader departments that reported to the group vice president. Each business segment retained its own sales, marketing, operations (information systems, sales order entry, collections, etc.), human resources, and legal departments.

EXHIBIT 2   Dell Computer Corporation Organization

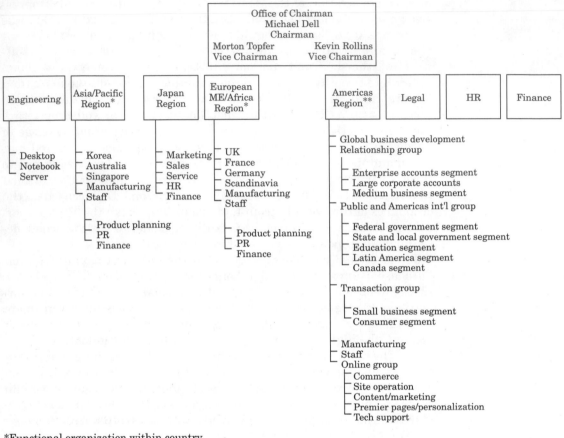

*Functional organization within country.

** Functional organization within segment.

Outside of the Americas, the organizational structure differed slightly. For example, Asia and Europe had a traditional country management structure, with the country vice presidents reporting into the president for the region. Within the respective countries, Dell typically had a functionally based organization, although it was increasingly moving toward the business unit approach used in the Americas. For example, in France, rather than having nine business unit organizations, there was a transactional segment and a relationship segment.

In the Americas, Dell sold its products using a sales organization that resided within the business units. Relationship segments employed teams of outside and inside sales reps, with the exception being the consumer and small business development segments which used exclusively inside sales reps. In 1994, Dell had about 300 field-based sales reps and a similar number of inside telephone reps. By 1997, that figure had grown to over 2,000 reps, with about 40 percent of sales reps assigned to the relationship segments, 25 percent to the transactional segments, and 35 percent assigned to those segments that were a blend of both relationship and transactional customers. The outside rep, known as a field Account Executive, was dedicated to customers in a region and was responsible for understanding the customers' information technology environments and service needs and selling them customized product and service solutions. Additionally, the 1,300-person technical support group was divided into three groups (consumer/small business, public sector, and enterprise/large/preferred) and reported directly to the group vice president.

The inside sales reps were paired with field reps and dedicated to common Relationship accounts, while inside reps in the Transactions segment acted independently. They were responsible for order processing and handling inbound sales calls. When a customer called in, the telephone sales rep was able to quickly call up their sales history online and guide the customer accordingly, accessing eligibility for discounts or corporate-mandated product configurations that the callers might not have been aware of. The inside reps were also responsible for the "up-sell" at the time of purchase—selling the customer a higher-end system with a richer mix of software and peripherals. Inside sales reps received variable compensation based on the gross margin of the goods they sold, with typical quotas averaging $4–6 million in revenue in the transaction segments.

The role of the sales rep changed significantly depending on the type of customer being served. An inside sales rep, in either the small business or consumer segment, was an active selling agent significantly influencing the buying decision as the customer often looked to the sales rep for technical advice. For example, a sales rep's recommendation for a faster CD-ROM or the inclusion of a Zip drive was often accepted by the customer, increasing Dell's margin on the system. By contrast, in the case of an enterprise customer, the purchasing company's information services personnel had pre-determined the specifications of the systems their employees were permitted to order. Moreover, attempting to achieve homogeneity in their installations, these customers actively discouraged any deviations from the prescribed standards. As a result, the inside sales rep's function was more focused on correct order entry and understanding the customer's requirement on product and delivery.

Similarly there was a difference in the roles and responsibilities of the outside sales reps depending on the size of the relationship customer they served. For the Enterprise and large accounts, the outside sales rep was the single point of contact for the customer. The sales rep was responsible for acquiring the account and actively maintaining it—developing specifications, following up on problems, etc. By comparison, the outside sales rep in the preferred account segment who handled as many as 10–15 accounts, was responsible for acquiring the account and then monitoring its satisfaction and growth at regular intervals, leaving the primary contact with the customer to the inside sales rep. One Dell executive described the role as "setting up the account and then getting out of the way."

PC Distribution Channels

In the late 1990s, PC distribution channels remained fragmented, with major manufacturers using a variety of channels to bring their products to market. Despite the proliferation of channels, by the mid 1990s, four fundamental means of distribution had evolved for the distribution of PCs: direct, consumer retail, indirect business sales through VARs, and indirect business through national resellers. (Table B provides an overview of the three indirect channels.) Dell was the only major manufacturer to focus solely on the direct channel. Almost all other manufacturers used one or more of the three other channels to distribute their products, ignoring the direct channel. For example, in 1996, Compaq sold almost exclusively through indirect distribution channels which included top-tier or master distributors, regional distributors, resellers, and retailers. In addition to these four major distribution methods, there were variations including Gateway's recent attempt to develop direct retail outlets in high volume locations such as shopping malls. The three non-direct channels are described below.

Retail. The retail market was dominated by national chains such as Circuit City, Best Buy, and CompUSA. Product flowed from the manufacturer to the national chain's distribution centers and then consumers and small businesses. This channel usually sold standard product offerings primarily to individual consumers and small businesses. About 30 percent of the U.S. market was sold through the retail channel.

TABLE B Major PC Distribution Channels (excluding direct channels)

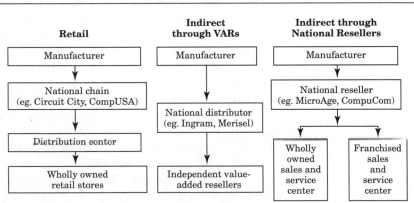

Indirect through VARs. In this channel, product flowed from the manufacturer to master distributors to independent value-added resellers (VARs). In 1996, there were three master distributors in the U.S.—Ingram Micro (sales of $12.0 billion), Tech Data (sales of $4.6 billion), and Merisel (sales of $5.5 billion), carrying approximately 100,000 items and directly or indirectly supplying the full range of all hardware, software, and peripherals for the PC industry. The master distributor emphasized product distribution, leaving system integration or value-added systems to the VARs. For its part, the VARs had direct relationships with mostly business customers, providing system integration, service, specialized software, etc. Approximately 15 percent of the U.S. market was distributed in this manner.

Indirect through National Resellers. The other significant distribution flow for business PCs was through national resellers such as Entex Information Systems, Vanstar (sales of $2.2 billion), CompuCom Systems (sales of $2.0 billion), and MicroAge (sales of $3.5 billion), who purchased PCs from the manufacturer and distributed them through their own wholly owned network of retail store fronts and sales & service organizations. Similar to the VAR, the national reseller's strength was its ability to customize systems to meet individual customer needs. For example, a national reseller receiving an order for 100 systems with sound cards and 56.6 modems, ordered the systems from the OEM, installed the necessary upgrades, reassembled the system, tested it, and sent it for sales to the end user. This channel accounted for approximately 33 percent of the U.S. market.

Competition in the PC industry was intense. With increased market maturation, vendor margins had fallen from 35–40 percent in the early 1990s to close to 20 percent in 1996, and were forecast at 15 percent for the future. In 1992, the top ten vendors accounted for approximately half of the PC market. By 1994, consolidation from increased price competition left the top ten with a 65 percent share. In the $85 billion U.S. market in 1997, Compaq was the leader with about 18 percent share, Dell was second with about 10 percent, followed by Packard Bell-NEC and IBM tied at 8–9 percent. Hewlett-Packard and Gateway had about 6 percent share. Vendors faced "feast or famine" demand cycles that were increasingly difficult to predict. Given the cyclical nature of the industry, inaccurate projections led to either product gluts and obsolete inventory in distribution channels or product shortages. This was exceptionally risky in an industry where manufacturers traditionally guaranteed their dealer networks against price changes. For example, if the cost of chips or components fell, a manufacturer reimbursed its dealers for the price reductions on systems already in the channel and bought back any unsold inventory.

With the success of its Dell direct model and its recent Internet application, and declining industry margins, many vendors were moving toward a build to order model. (See Exhibit 3 for a

EXHIBIT 3   Industry Trends

The PC market was divided into three main product segments: desktops, notebooks, and network servers. The PC server market was the fastest growing segment of the PC market, with a 32 percent increase in shipments from 1995–1996. This high margin segment (with margins 30–50 percent higher than PCs) had traditionally been dominated by Compaq, Hewlett-Packard, and IBM, with a combined 54 percent share. However, volume growth and margin strength had attracted new competitors such as Dell, Gateway, and Digital Equipment. With improved features such as larger screens, faster speeds, and lower prices, laptops were becoming more popular, with a 23 percent annual growth rate forecasted through the year 2001. Further, laptops were increasingly viewed as replacements for desktop PCs. (In 1994, approximately 20 percent of U.S. portables were used to replace desktops; by 1997, it was forecasted to reach 30 percent.) The desktop market was forecasted to grow at 14.5 percent and was characterized by fierce price competition as the PC had been transformed into a commodity-like product characterized by Intel processors (used in 85 percent of PCs worldwide) and Microsoft Windows (used in 83 percent of PCs worldwide) operating systems. See Table 3A below for recent industry sales by product and by leading manufacturer.

TABLE 3A   Computer Industry Sales by Product and Leading Manufacturer (in thousands of units)

	U.S. 1995	U.S. 1996	Worldwide 1995	Worldwide 1996
Desktop PCs	18,269	20,222	49,611	57,893
Portable PCs/Tablets	3,583	4,777	8,483	10,908
Servers	343	457	1,032	1,437
Total	22,195	25,456	59,126	70,238
	U.S. 1995	U.S. 1996	Worldwide 1995	Worldwide 1996
Compaq Computer Corp.	2,790	3,449	6,079	7,214
Dell Computer Corp.	1,034	1,775	1,824	2,838
Gateway 2000	1,155	1,608	1,337	1,990
Hewlett Packard	870	1,365	2,092	2,954
IBM	1,858	2,235	4,803	6,140
Total	7,707	10,432	16,135	21,136

Source: Dataquest

In 1997, many analysts characterized the PC industry as increasingly mature in both the home and business PC segments. Supporting this assertion was the stalled penetration of home PCs, with 38–40 percent of U.S. households owning a PC. Further, with over 50 percent of households with incomes over $50,000 owning a PC, replacements and upgrades rather than new systems were becoming important. Research in early 1997 indicated that 32 percent of consumers who bought a home PC were first-time buyers compared to 49 percent for the same period a year earlier.

With increasing saturation of the home PC market, several manufacturers had developed an entry level PC with a sub-$1,000 price point. Featuring an older Intel processor and slower peripheral speeds (in items such as modems and CD-ROMs), the product was targeted at the less affluent household. Leading the way were AST's $997 product that was shipped to Walmart in 1996 and Compaq's Presario 2120 at $999 which was introduced in 1997. By the end of 1997, the

EXHIBIT 3   (Continued)

PC market was bipolar, with recent estimates suggesting that approximately 33 percent of the market was sales of these sub-$1,000 "bare-bones" systems and 66 percent was sales of fully loaded, state-of-the art PCs selling between $2,000–$2,500.* For many, the introduction of the low-end products was a double-edged sword. On the one hand, estimates suggested that PC penetration rates could reach 53 percent by the year 2001 driven by low-end sales. On the other, many also attributed the low-end PCs to increasing price declines (in the first nine months of 1997, the average retail selling price of a PC fell from $2,400 to $1,500) and margin erosion (margin on low-end machines was 10 percent rather than 20 percent). Further, some analysts were also concerned that these systems could cannibalize the corporate market, where corporations were demanding cheaper and simpler machines for their networks.

On the corporate side, penetration was also high with an average of 1.1 PCs per deskworker (including mobile salesforces) in North America and .8 PCs per deskworker in western Europe and Asia Pacific. Rather than installing new PCs, mid to large size businesses were upgrading their installed base to new systems featuring either Pentium or Pentium Pro processors. In December 1996, however, 75–80 percent of corporate systems still used processors slower than Pentium processors.** Large corporations were becoming slower to adopt new technologies. Buying decisions were shifting from departmental levels to senior levels in the organization, and with the size of investments they were increasingly incorporated into budget cycles. Additionally, increased consideration was being given to the time necessary to make changes, in evaluating new systems, and training. As one industry observer noted, "The old success model, in wide-open, green-field markets, in which suppliers could 'ship and run,' dumping PCs at the corporate customer's or reseller's loading dock and quickly moving to the next stop is obsolete. The corporate PC business is becoming a replacement business."†

*New Cheap PCs Are Shaking Up the Industry," *The Wall Street Journal,* September 10, 1997, p. B1

**"Microcomputer Industry Outlook," Paine Webber, January 10, 1997.

†IDC Executive Insights, June 1997.

brief description of other industry trends.) One industry observer commented,

> The runaway success of Dell Computer's direct sales model and the trend toward Internet ordering are forcing many of the world's major PC companies to rethink how they do business. . . The distribution and manufacturing models that most have favored since the industry's inception in the early 1980s—a combination of internally built products and outside distributors, dealers, resellers, and retailers—is being unpicked. In its place—a fluid model under which manufacturing is spread across outside contractors, distributors/dealers, and the company itself, with more emphasis placed on selling directly to the customer.[4]

In July of 1997, after failing in two attempts to purchase Gateway (one of Dell's strongest direct competitors), Compaq announced its new build-to-order manufacturing process, and established direct sales

---

[4]"Direct Action," *Computer Business Review,* June 1, 1997.

teams and telephone centers that would ship Compaq computers direct to the customer. However, by early September, Compaq's system was already showing strain. One observer noted,

> The era of mass customization is fast arriving in the PC industry. Everyone in the supply chain from manufacturer to distributor is redefining their respective roles, and the final assembly of systems is one role clearly gravitating towards the channel.[5]

For its part, other industry leaders such as IBM and HP were transferring a large proportion of their PC assembly to a select group of distributors and dealers. In its Authorized Assembly Program (AAP), IBM began shipping "bare bones" systems into the channel for configuration to order assembly, hoping to become more responsive to demand, to better manage inventory, to lower the risk of product obsolescence, and to reduce the manufacturing costs of its products. To be part of the AAP, IBM required that the distributors and dealers be certified, use IBM assembly and testing procedures, and use only IBM original parts. Early results suggested that the AAP program resulted in higher product quality—the system was assembled all at once, rather than being "touched" by VARs adding components as needed. Similar to the Dell experience, IBM found that the fewer times the box was opened the less likely the defects would creep in.

Many vendors recognized the risks inherent in going direct to the customer, especially as many believed that the direct model could only reach 30 percent of PC customers.[6] Bill Ramsey, VP of manufacturing strategy and technology for Compaq, remarked,

> By no means is Compaq abandoning the channel, but if it is to fight back against Dell and other direct PC vendors it must have the same advantages and mirror their business practices. It is a calculated risk because we must do so without upsetting the channel, because the Dell model for all its efficiencies can only cover so much of the market. You need the channel if you want to get to them all.[7]

DELL GOES ONLINE

The mid 1990s saw a dramatic leap forward in the use and functionality of the Internet. Once the domain of academic researchers characterized by cumbersome code, the "Net" became mainstream when user-friendly browsers made it possible to search the Internet for information and send and receive mail electronically. The pioneering work by Netscape Communications in the early 1990s had devotees "surfing the Net in increasing numbers and attracting the attention of

---

[5]"Debating the Meaning of Assembly—When Terms Break Down," *Computer Reseller,* August 25, 1996, p. B15.

[6]"Direct Action," *Computer Business Review,* June 1, 1997.

[7]Ibid.

both the PC industry and the business community overall." In May 1995, Bill Gates, CEO of Microsoft Corporation, penned a memo, "The Internet Tidal Wave," in which he stated that the Net was the most important single development since the PC.[8] With that he announced a major drive to bring Microsoft into the realm of the Web.

Similarly, Michael Dell had become drawn to the "buzz" about the Internet, envisioning it as the ultimate extension of the Dell direct model. Indeed, by the early 1990s Dell had begun experimenting with the Internet in response to customer demand, delivering online technical support and order status information. As his vision for the Internet grew, Michael Dell established a small team of about nine people to explore using the Internet as a means of communicating with customers, delivering information, and selling its products. This team was led by Scott Eckert, a Harvard MBA, who at that time was Executive Assistant to the Chairman, working on special projects reporting directly to Michael Dell.

As the team investigated the Internet they became increasingly convinced that it was a viable channel for Dell's products. In 1996, there were 20 million users worldwide, with the number of users expected to double every year. Moreover, Dell's key customers, business users, were major drivers of the Internet, with 82 percent of Fortune 500 companies providing their employees with Internet access, and 64 percent of Fortune 500 companies having developed Intranets (internal communications networks). The U.S. market was an early adopter of Internet capabilities, with 65 percent of U.S. businesses with 50 or more employees either planning to use the Internet or already online, compared to 45 percent of German companies and 28 percent of French companies. Almost universally, industry observers predicted a surge in electronic commerce driven by the Internet. By the year 2000, one industry observer forecasted $67 billion per year in business-to-business Internet commerce.[9] Another prediction was that 46 million Americans would be purchasing goods and services electronically by the year 2000.[10]

Many at Dell were excited by the online prospects, believing that the Net was a natural extension of Dell's direct business model—"the ultimate direct medium for the next generation of the direct model that Dell had pioneered." Moreover, industry analysts suggested that few PC vendors were as well positioned as Dell to take advantage of the Internet opportunity—unencumbered by an existing distribution channel, Dell could go direct to the customer as usual, but others had to use a different medium to go direct. One analyst remarked, "Dell has been positioned for something like this since its beginning. They can migrate what they do in the real world to the Web easily without upsetting any of these existing sales channels."[11]

---

[8]*Business Week,* July 15, 1995.

[9]"Suited, Surfing and Shopping," *The Economist,* January 25, 1997, p. 59.

[10]"In Search of the Perfect Market," *The Economist,* Survey of Electronic Commerce, May 10, 1997.

[11]"Dell Tailors Web for Business," *Inter@ctive Week,* June 9, 1997, p. 19.

In late 1995, the team began designing an online retail store and technical support vehicle for Dell's products. After interviewing potential vendors to build an online ordering system, Dell found that there were few players out there with the technology and turned to in-house programmers to build a program, ultimately called the configurator, to support the design and ordering of a Dell system online. By the end of the first quarter of 1996, the online system began to take shape.

TRANSACTIONAL BUSINESS ONLINE

In late July 1996, Dell began conducting business through its Internet site. Almost immediately Dell began selling $1 million per week through the Web. Once customers logged onto the site and configured the system that best suited their needs, they had the option of purchasing the system using a credit card. After ordering the system, the customer could use "dell.com" to track the order's status from the time it was entered in the system, through to the manufacturing process, and then to shipping. Once shipped, dell.com was linked to shipping partners who assigned the system an air bill number that tracked delivery of the system. In addition to the purchase functionality, the site contained complete service and support data, with 35,000 pages of troubleshooting information—the same information used by Dell's technical representatives to solve hardware and software problems over the phone. Dell served its online customers with 12 sales reps and two order processors dedicated to processing Internet orders.

Once the customer sent the order to Dell over the Internet, it was received by an order processor who classified the order into a market segment and routed it to that segment's e-mail (electronic mail) box. There, a member of the order processing and sales rep team qualified the e-mail order. If the order was complete it was keyed into the sales order system and routed to the factory for system assembly in exactly the same process as any other order coming into the Dell system. If the order was incomplete, the sales rep called the customer for the missing information and once the order was complete, entered it. Approximately 20 percent of the orders that Dell received from its online retail store were complete. About one-third of incomplete orders were attributable to customer concerns over security and were, therefore, lacking credit card information.

Additionally, if customers had a technical support question they could reference Dell's technical support manual, the same one used by Dell's telephone-based service reps. Further, customers could download upgraded information, such as new printer drivers, through the web site.

Six Months—$1 Million/Day in Revenues

By December 1996, more than 150,000 customers were visiting the web site each week, generating sales of approximately $1 million per day. According to Scott Eckert, "I think everyone sensed that the Internet could be a big win for us, but I don't think anyone really envisioned that it would be this big this soon."

By mid-December, the online team was anxious to know more about these customers, so Dell commissioned a market research study to understand customers' perceptions and purchase and usage behaviors in order to develop a profile of its Internet customers. In December 1996, Dell conducted 104 telephone interviews among customers from the Business Selling Division (small business) and the Dell Catalogue Sales (individual consumer) division who had purchased a Dell computer and used the Dell web site to obtain product and pricing information. In the survey, about half the participants were business users and the other half residence users. Nearly 44 percent of customers purchased directly through the web site, 37 percent started with the Web but ended up calling a sales rep to purchase the computer, and the remaining 19 percent used the web site directly to purchase but had also contacted a sales representative for supporting information.

Business customers were more familiar with Dell, with 45 percent of business customers having purchased from Dell before, while only 19 percent of residential customers had previously purchased from Dell. Mirroring Dell's product mix, both business and residential customers were more likely to purchase a desktop PC, with portable PCs being most popular among business customers.

Although residential customers were more likely first-time Dell customers, only 12 percent were actual first-time buyers, with 32 percent purchasing their new PC as an additional PC and 56 percent purchasing it as a replacement PC. Most residential customers indicated that the primary intended purpose of the PC was for personal use (34 percent), business use at home (34 percent), entertainment use (26 percent), or educational use (22 percent). Residential users were frequent Internet users, with 63 percent indicating that they spent one hour per week or more on the Web for professional/business purposes and 60 percent indicating that they spent in excess of five hours per week on the Internet for personal use.

TABLE C Customer Reaction to Dell.com

	Business $n = 51$	Residential $n = 53$	Directly through Web $n = 46$	Called Rep to Purchase $n = 38$	Both—Web Purchase and Calls $n = 20$
Likelihood of purchase without web site	67%	74%	74%	63	75%
Intent to use web site for next purchase (somewhat/very likely)	78%	66%	80%	76%	45%

Dell found very high levels of satisfaction among its customers with almost all customers stating that they were satisfied or very satisfied with their purchase. As seen in Table C on page 243, while levels of customer satisfaction were high, most customers indicated that they would have purchased a Dell computer even without having access to a web site. But the same consumers also indicated that they intended to use a web site for their next purchase occasion.

When customers purchased through a sales rep after initially having accessed the web site, most were able to finalize their purchase with fewer telephone calls than a typical customer that had not used the web site. More detailed findings from the study are outlined in Exhibit 4.

By the spring, Dell Online was convinced that the Internet was a big win. However, to fully capitalize on its efforts, the Online Group believed that it needed to generate some excitement in the market to legitimize the Internet channel for the industry, and more importantly to drive incremental volume for Dell. To capture the media's focus, the Online Group began developing an aggressive PR plan. The team then spent the next 60 days trying to get corporate approval for the plan. Scott Eckert recalled,

> We were convinced that Dell Online represented the ultimate extension of the Dell Direct model. To get the momentum in the market, we needed to make a statement. One million dollars a day in revenue was that statement. Internally, however, there was some resistance. Dell was always conservative and had never released individual segment sales information. Moreover, some counseled that it would be better to build a solid lead in the fledgling Internet channel before making a splash in the market. But we were convinced that we already had a solid lead and that making a splash would benefit the Dell Online effort in many ways. For example, we were convinced that the press coverage would help educate the market and move it in Dell's direction. Further, the excitement created by the press would help drive Dell Online internally. It was not until Michael Dell supported our plan that the wind shifted in our direction.

Three More Months—$2 Million/Day Revenue

In May 1997, Dell conducted a follow-up customer research study (Wave II) to the research conducted in December 1996. To qualify for the study, participants were required to have used Dell's web site to obtain product and pricing information prior to purchasing, and had to have purchased a Dell personal computer within the last 90 days. The study comprised 150 individual customers (DCS—Dell Catalog Sales) and 150 business customers (BSD—Business Systems Division). (Detailed findings from the customer research study are outlined in Exhibit 5.)

EXHIBIT 4   Online Research—First Wave, December 1996

	Business n = 51 (%)	Residence n = 53 (%)
Q. Did you make the actual purchase using the web site directly, or did you obtain information from the web site and then contact a sales rep to make the purchase?		
Web directly	47%	42%
Called sales rep	33	39
Purchased on Web but also called	20	19
Total	100%	100%
Q. How did you learn about being able to purchase through the Dell web site? (note multiple responses permitted)		
Visited site	61%	40%
Friends or colleagues	10	21
Saw advertisement	24	26
Other	4	13
Q. What other brands did you consider, but not purchase?		
Compaq	20%	13%
Digital	2	2
Gateway	20	32
Hewlett Packard	7	4
IBM	2	2
Micron	12	24
Midwest Micro	2	2
NEC		2
Packard Bell	4	4
Toshiba	2	4
Other	10	2
None	33	48
Q. Which of the following best describes your usage of Dell's online order status capability?		
Have used in the past	72%	80%
Plan to use	12	8
Have no plans to	16	6
Don't know	—	6
Q. Which of the following best describes your usage of Dell's online technical support capability?		
Have used in the past	38%	20%
Plan to use	31	40
Have no plans to	31	38
Don't know	—	2

Data disguised.

EXHIBIT 5   Dell Online Customer Research Study—Wave II, May 1997

	BSD (150)	DCS (150)		
Other brands considered: (multiple responses)				
Gateway	33%	59%		
Micron	27	29		
Compaq	21	15		
HP	7	13		
None	33	19		
Use of online order status capability				
Have used in the past	54%	56%		
Plan to use	23	22		
Have no plans to	20	19		
Don't know	3	3		
Use of online technical support				
Have used in the past	37%	34%		
Plan to use	50	54		
Have no plans to	12	9		
Don't know	1	3		

	BSD (150)	DCS (150)	Web Site (82)	Sales Rep (218)
Product purchased (multiple responses)				
Desktop	82%	93%	88%	88%
Portable	18	7	11	13
Servers	13	0	9	6
Likelihood of purchase without web site				
Yes	66%	62%	58%	67%
No	25	22	29	21
Don't know	9	16	13	12
Likelihood of purchase next PC using a manufacturer's web site?				
Very/somewhat likely	65%	67%	87%	58%
Neither likely nor unlikely	17	16	11	19
Somewhat/very unlikely	17	14	2	20

Data disguised.

Many of the research results were consistent with the earlier findings. Most respondents were experienced computer users, with only 8 percent of DCS customers indicating that this was their first PC purchase. Customers reported high levels of satisfaction with the web site, with close to 90 percent of all customers indicating that they were satisfied or very satisfied with the process.

Additional information gleaned from the second study concerned the way customers found the web site. Approximately half of the customers indicated that they had not seen any information directing them to the web site, with about 24 percent citing ads in computer publications and an additional 8 percent indicating that ads in general business publications had directed them to the Dell web site. On the service side, those that used Dell's technical support (approximately 100 of the 300 surveyed) did so to resolve problems. (25—DCS, 18—BSD customers), fix hardware problems (10—DCS, 22—BSD), and download current drivers (4—DCS, 18—BSD).

By June 1997, sales at the retail site had risen to $2 million per day with over 250,000 site visitors per week. The majority of orders generated were from the consumer and small business segments. Logging onto the site, customers were able to place orders electronically with the full range of services that were available over the telephone, including product information, order status, and product support. Within the Dell site, customers evaluated multiple product configurations and obtained instant price quotes, enabling the customer to configure the best possible system given their budget and performance requirements. Dell updated its pricing on the web site daily to ensure that its prices reflected the realities of an ever-changing PC market.

Dell Online with its millions of dollars in revenue quickly became the talk of the electronic commerce world. Internally, however, there was little knowledge of it beyond the Online Group and senior levels of management. To communicate this information to the company, the Online Group conducted a campaign of "internal evangelism." Bill Morris, Senior Online Marketing Manager, remarked,

> When Dell issued its press release announcing $1 million in revenue per day over the Internet, few people inside the company knew about commerce on the Net. Sales and service departments didn't understand its implications and there was some fear about the Net automating their jobs away. As a result we conducted a substantial internal education campaign. We would go into the cubes and high traffic choke points and plaster them with posters and information about Dell Online.

Six More Months—$3 Million/Day Revenue. What Next?

By the fall of 1997, sales had grown to $3 million in revenue per day. In typical Dell fashion, the Online group had already modified the site to make it more functional for Dell and its customers. For example, when logging into the site, customers now self-selected themselves into a customer segment (e.g., home/home office, small business, government, education, etc.). The site then guided customers to those products that would be the most appropriate for their particular use. The customer, however, retained the ability to configure, price, and purchase any of Dell's systems. The customer self-segmentation was also beneficial to Dell's purchasing system as the customer order was now directly routed to the business unit's e-mail box, eliminating the need to centrally sort the orders into business segments.

The online approach had been readily accepted by the DCS and BSD divisions. By year-end 1997, a large proportion of DCS revenues were attributable to the online channel. After some initial concerns, sales reps quickly came to view Dell Online as a big boost to their productivity. David Hood, vice president of the DCS group, remarked,

> At first the reps were worried, but they saw that the site was a source of highly qualified leads. They could close sales with fewer calls. With our growth rates there was enough business for everybody. We still have a few challenges. The back end of the business is still antiquated, with completed orders going from e-mail to reps and then to order entry. We're working on creating an automatic link from the e-mail to order entry. Additionally, we haven't been able to develop the metrics to forecast demand from online marketing activities. Unlike conventional marketing communication where we could accurately predict our lift from promotions, people find the Web in so many different ways.

Similarly BSD was enthusiastic about the benefits of Dell Online. "We are currently selling a significant portion of our business through the online store," remarked Philip vanHoutte, "and our sales people are excited to work on the online telephone queue. We had initially used our less experienced reps on the online queue, but have found that our experienced reps are able to better upsell online customers."

The success of Dell Online also brought organizational changes. Scott Eckert, the Director of the Online group, saw the need to have online resources resident in each of the business units. As a result, the Dell Online group focused on delivering the tools and technology for the Internet site, with each business segment having its own resources devoted to delivering the online content for their segment. Scott Eckert's core group of about 35 people did most of the application programming, coordinated with outside design agencies, and maintained the server farms, the backbone of Dell's online operations. Eckert reflected,

> Once Dell Online was up and running, it was a natural progression to move online resources into the business segments. They know their customers and how to communicate with them; we didn't want to become a bottleneck. However, with Michael Dell's ambitious goal of having 50 percent of revenues online, some functions need to stay centralized. The central online group creates Dell's overall Internet strategy, coordinates our world wide Internet team, builds the applications and ensures that the technology is state-of-the-art and robust. Additionally, we set the standards for the dell.com site to ensure a standard look and feel for every customer. But if we were to attempt to do everything here, my budget would have to grow exponentially. That would not be an efficient nor effective way to scale the business.

Cost Savings: Transaction Business Online[12]

Beyond sales generation, one of the most anticipated elements of Dell's Internet commerce was the savings that it could generate over the sales and service cycle. Firms such as Cisco Systems, a $7 billion hardware provider and systems integrator for enterprise system computers, had created a splash in the market with reported savings of over $500 million, representing 8.3 percent of revenues. Many at Dell were eagerly anticipating similar savings levels.

Using data from early 1997, the Dell Online group had identified two potential areas of cost savings: salesforce efficiency and service efficiency.

Salesforce Efficiency.   As seen in Table D below, the Internet model resulted in fewer number of calls to sales reps with an overall higher close rate.

In addition to the call efficiencies, the sales reps associated with the Internet model were also able to achieve higher cost savings resulting from higher sales quotas. For example, a sales rep assigned to close sales (on the phone) which originated from a web site visit was able to carry 1.5 times the monthly quota as a traditional sales rep. Also, the order processor who handled electronic orders coming in over the Internet was more efficient. The current Internet sales rate of $3 million per day was a considerable proportion of Dell's sales in its DCS and BSC divisions. Thus the savings in the salesforce could be potentially enormous.

Service Efficiency.   Service efficiencies inherent in the Internet model represented additional potential savings for Dell. Each quarter,

---

TABLE D   Economics: Direct v. Online

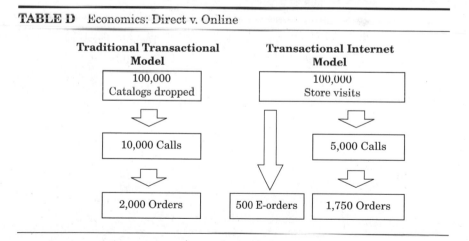

	Traditional Transactional Model	Transactional Internet Model	
	100,000 Catalogs dropped	100,000 Store visits	
	10,000 Calls		5,000 Calls
	2,000 Orders	500 E-orders	1,750 Orders

---

[12]While the data presented in this section of the case are broadly representative, all of the details have been disguised.

Dell received approximately 200,000 visits to its web site to check order status. Likewise, Dell logged 500,000 technical service visits a quarter and 400,000 file library downloads. Each of these transactions would have cost $5 to $15 on the telephone, thus representing significant savings.

A different approach to calculating service efficiency suggested that the savings may have to be adjusted for an "easability" factor. The logic of this argument was that not all visits to the web site could be assumed to be in lieu of a telephone call. A study revealed that some web visits were the result of ease of access and use. Absent the Web, the customers would not have placed a phone call to clarify or seek the service (be it order status, technical service, or download request); especially for lower-level inquiries. Some internal estimates, therefore, suggested that service efficiency may be somewhat smaller for each of the three components. Table E below shows potential savings for every 100 customer visits.

In addition to the above, Dell Online had also identified other savings opportunities. For example, replacement of hard copy manuals with electronic downloads represented a potential savings of millions of dollars per year. On the technical support side, there were opportunities to reduce talk time by electronically uploading system information to Dell's technical support team before the start of the service call. A Dell Online executive explained, "An average technical support call lasts about 10–15 minutes, with the first minute spent on diagnostics. If we could have the customer submit the diagnostics over the Internet to the technician, we could save over 10 percent of the talk time associated with the call."

TABLE E   Internet Service Efficiencies

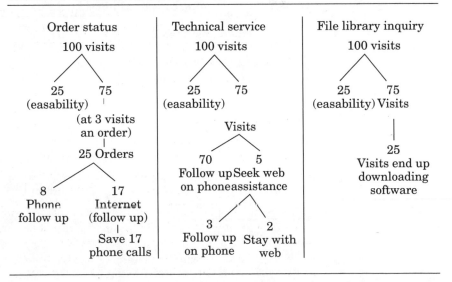

Dan Murray, the finance manager for Dell Online, remarked,

> While there are differing views about how we should measure the savings from our online efforts, it's important that we establish a measurement system. For example, to make measurement easier, we assigned separate telephone numbers for calls originating from Internet site visits so we can differentiate and analyze those calls from the traditional calls that come through the system. Unless we have a measurement system, we'll not understand the use of the online system as a planning tool and we'll never understand the cost savings. At this time, we understand the salesforce efficiencies but need to further exploit the potential in the service delivery side.

RELATIONSHIP BUSINESS ONLINE

In addition to its retail store, Dell had also developed and launched over 200 customer-specific web pages for its large customers, allowing them Internet access to password-protected, customer-specific information about Dell's products and services. The customized pages, called "Dell Premier Pages^{SM}," allowed customers to configure, price, and buy systems at approved, discounted prices, track orders and inventory through detailed account purchasing reports, and access contact information for Dell account and service and support team members, including telephone numbers, e-mail addresses, and pager numbers. Initially, Dell focused on its largest platinum accounts (with Dell sales greater than $10 million) and then its gold accounts (sales $5–10 million). Given recent advances in Internet technologies, Dell anticipated expanding its Premier Pages, offering at a minimum a simplified site for every customer who had an agreement with Dell.

In developing its Premier Pages, Dell took a ground-up development approach analyzing the customer's interaction with Dell before, during, and after the sale; during the product evaluation, negotiation, and specification phases. As part of that process, Dell discovered that the majority of its customers wanted two tiers of access for its users. The first tier of access was general access for the customer's employees who wanted to obtain general information about company-approved offerings, product configurations, order status, and pricing. The second level of information was more specific and included account sales data, detailed service information for internal "help desk" personnel, and Dell team account telephone and pager numbers. One Dell manager remarked on the development of the Premier Pages,

> From the very beginning we knew that the Internet was an opportunity. We're a direct company and the Internet is just like the phone or the fax. In doing our research, customers told us that they wanted Dell to be just like a bank. For the vitally important transactions, customers want to talk directly to someone; otherwise they prefer to use an ATM.

Dell's first level of development was, "Just the basics, capturing who to call for what, and e-mail and pager numbers. Although rudimentary, the development proved key in demonstrating a commitment to the delivery of cutting edge technology to customers. Although customers didn't quite know what to do with the Premier Pages at first, they did believe that it demonstrated our willingness to invest in them," remarked an Online team member. The process for a Premier Page customer to order a PC from Dell varied according to the customer. Some corporate customers had a "blanket" purchase order number so that orders went directly to Dell, while other customers routed purchasing to an internal purchasing department who created a purchase order and then sent the order to Dell.

Increasingly, Dell's customers saw the Premier Pages as a management control tool. Purchasing offices, attempting to control PC purchases, viewed the web pages as a means of enforcing product standards in increasingly decentralized business environments. Additionally, Dell's customers saw the site as a means of reducing work loads, answering routine queries regarding order status, product configurations, and basic user help functions. Dell found, however, that actual usage of the Pages in the site companies was mixed. "It's not a case of build it and they will come," remarked Tom Martin, Dell's director of Global Business Development. "Customers need to promote the site internally, before they become aware of it and actually start using it."

But some customers had already begun to perceive its benefits. For example, Detroit Edison, a longtime Dell customer, found that its Premier Pages were an opportunity to move quickly to electronic purchasing. They used Dell's web site, dell.com, to get required information on Dell's products and services and to configure systems. According to a Detroit Edison representative:

> We have cut a week of processing time, improved the delivery sequence, and made ordering easier. . . . We can monitor orders online, plan installations, and we're never stuck with unexpected inventory. And Dell maintains an exact history of what we have purchased in a database accessible throughout our site.[13]

While many viewed Dell's Online capability as a means of reducing the cost of ownership to customers as opposed to direct savings for Dell, a key benefit of the Premier Pages was the administrative operational support it gave to the sales rep team. With the amount of data available online, reps could allocate more of their time to selling systems rather than dealing with operational issues such as order status, pricing configurations, etc. According to Tom Martin, "A sales rep's active selling time could increase two or three-fold with the online model. In the traditional direct model, a sales rep spent 45 percent of his/her time on operational matters, 15 percent of his/her time on active selling and the

---

[13]Excerpt from Dell public relations document.

rest on travel. In the online environment the time spent on administrative details could fall to 15 percent with 45 percent of time focused on selling activities." Surprisingly, the online model had proved difficult to "sell" internally, especially in the Enterprise market segment. Tom Martin added,

> We needed to convince the sales execs that the online model was a sales facilitator for the account team—that we weren't trying to take sales away from them. Many of them saw a loss of account control with the online system. Before, everything about the account was under their control. We have tried to focus the sales reps on the need to focus themselves on high value-added activities that really generate sales and leave the less value-added activities like the spec sheet and order status issues to the Internet.

Just as the Online store evolved so too did Dell's Premier Pages. In the fall of 1997, Dell began development of revised Premier Pages that could scale to thousands of pages using Active Server Pages (ASP) technology. Dell developed Dell-specific software tools that allowed sales team to create dynamic Premier Pages tailored to individual account needs. Rather than creating a static site, in less than 24 hours, using ASP a sales team could create a new Premier Page site and update it on demand. Michael Swart, Senior Online Manager responsible for Premier Pages remarked,

> The development of the new tools is a real breakthrough, creating a scaleable product for Premier Pages. We've already begun working with 500 customers who immediately saw the value of the Premier Pages. Over the first quarter of 1998 we are conducting training and awareness sessions for all account sales reps to bring them up to speed regarding how Premier Pages can be developed and how the sales teams can use them to extend relationships with existing customers and create a differentiating factor with potential new customers.

STRATEGIC DECISIONS

Michael Dell himself had thrown the gauntlet to his management team. "There is no reason why we cannot do at least 50 percent of our business over the Web the next few years," he had said. "That would obviously mean that we have to creatively extend and build on our direct business model."

But such a thrust also raised related strategic questions. Many senior managers had begun to see the value of the Net in the consumer and small business segments, remarking, "With dell.com we're in the consumer market now. We finally have a channel that is consistent with our Dell Direct model and the market is huge. What's more, we can accelerate our global expansion without the need for capital investment in a sales organization. Indeed, as a reflection of the changes in Dell's consumer business, the Dell Catalogue Sales (DCS) division had been renamed Dell Home Sales (DHS).

Some managers, however, were still reserving judgment until they saw the promised windfall cost savings offered by the Internet, while others were wary that a jump into the consumer market would lead to the maelstrom of the sub-$1,000 PC that would ultimately erode Dell's profitability in both the consumer and ultimately the business markets. Additionally, some other managers were also less certain that the same market opportunities existed with larger customers in the Enterprise and Preferred Accounts markets, still struggling to understand how the Online Model delivered incremental value to both Dell and these customers.

While some saw the Internet as a huge opportunity, others in the industry saw it as a doorway for competitors to finally attack the Dell Direct model.

> Dell faces greater challenges than ever. Its price edge is gradually eroding. It has yet to prove that users in many countries are willing to buy direct. And its competitors fully understand the trick that's driven Dell's success.[14]

In contrast, senior management at Dell was enthusiastic in emphasizing the importance of the online effort. Morton Topfer concluded,

> We have continually demonstrated our commitment to adding value for our customers and stockholders. In the space of three short years our stock has climbed 2,000 percent and our ROIC[15] is 186 percent. We see the online initiative along with our initiatives in servers and workstations as critical in our drive towards continued growth and profitability for Dell.

Homegrocer.com

By Professor Sid L. Huff and David Beckow

---

[14]"Now Everyone in PCs Wants to Be Like Mike," *Fortune,* September 8, 1997.
[15]Return on invested capital.

"We're using only three trucks, we own ten, and we have yet another ten on order. We had better be right about this thing." Mike Donald had reason to be concerned. Having spent three years and four million private investor and venture capital dollars (including over $100,000 of his own money) to build the Pacific Northwest's first online, Internet-based grocery store, he was finding that new customers were signing on more slowly than expected. "We're learning that Homegrocer is a deep sell," noted Donald as he bit his lip and glanced across his desk. He was referring to the fact that winning new ongoing customers was proving to be a lot more difficult than simply letting people know that Homegrocer was open for business.

A NEW BUSINESS MODEL

"What makes Homegrocer unique is that it turns the traditional e-commerce business model on its head," exclaimed Terry Drayton as he headed to yet another meeting with investors. "Whereas the traditional Internet business model promises massive economies of scale and efficiency gains through its access to a worldwide market, Homegrocer is trying to make the model work while focusing on only a few square miles of territory."

Located in Bellevue, Washington, Homegrocer consisted of a warehouse facility plus an Internet web site that allowed wired consumers to log on, purchase groceries via credit card, and have them delivered to their door within 24 hours. Customers could not actually walk into the Homegrocer building, but instead had to order everything over the Web. Corporate offices and the sole distribution center were built into a warehouse the size of a Boeing 727 hanger (see Exhibit 1). Every morning trucks pulled into the loading bay of the warehouse, where each was loaded with the groceries of approximately 30 to 40 customers. Trucks were filled by pickers who wore a Borg-like prosthetic that stretched from their forearm down to the end of their fingers. The LCD screens on their wrists instructed them where to go in the warehouse and what to pick. Upon picking the item, they scanned it with the laser mounted onto the end of their index finger. This approach allowed the company to keep a real-time inventory of every item in the warehouse that, in turn, enabled a very efficient just-in-time replenishment strategy.

As the trucks were being loaded with their day's worth of deliveries, a sophisticated routing computer was determining the most efficient route for each truck. This route plan was provided to the driver, who then left to make his deliveries. The routing system was a third-party purchased system, essentially the same system currently used by UPS. Homegrocer had plans to enhance the system by adding a global positioning component that would continuously update the location of

EXHIBIT 1   Homegrocer's Warehouse and a Homegrocer Delivery Truck

trucks to the routing system. That would allow the routing system to make adjustments for local traffic conditions as well as current vehicle locations. Effectiveness of the routing system was important because customers could choose any 45-minute window in which their groceries were delivered. To date the company had delivered groceries within its requested envelope approximately 98 per cent of the time.

Mike Donald elaborated,

Orders from customers come right into our server. They are then transferred to our software supplier in Vancouver. He then takes the orders off the server at midnight, converts them, and sends them back down to us. Once we get an order, it's put into the routing system, the routes are developed, items are sent out to the picking system and the orders are picked in a certain sequence and are put on a truck. The actual charge for the order is calculated after the order is picked and scanned, so that customers are only billed for what they receive. Trucks go out at about one P.M., and continue delivering up until nine o'clock at night. You get a copy of the order when it's delivered. The customer has to be home to accept delivery. However, customers can schedule delivery times, in 45-minute windows, when they place an order.

COMPETITION

Homegrocer was not the first Internet-based grocery delivery service to begin operation. Several other players, including Netgrocer and Peapod, had been operating for some time. NetGrocer (see Exhibit 2A) offered national service, but only sold shelf-stable products. Orders took four to five days to be delivered via courier. Netgrocer offered low prices on many products.

The Peapod approach was somewhat different (see Exhibit 2B). They focused more on building their expertise in the software and logistics surrounding Internet grocery home delivery. They contracted their expertise to existing grocery operations, such as Safeway, who wished to

EXHIBIT 2A   Netgrocer's Web Site—Opening Page

Source: http://www.netgrocer.com, November 1998.

EXHIBIT 2B Peapod's Web Site—Opening Page

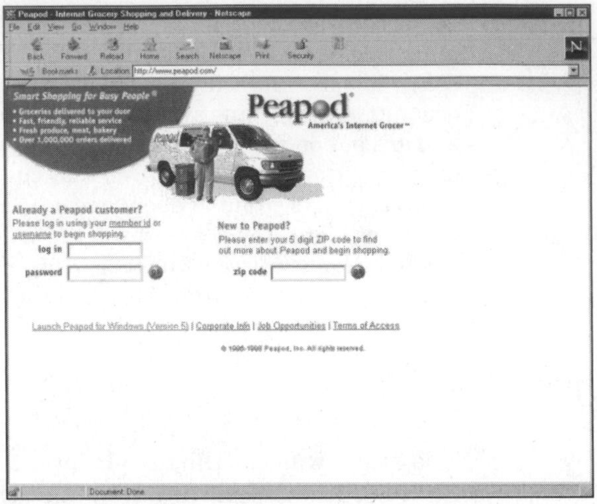

Source: http://www.peapod.com, November 1998.

---

enter the Internet home delivery market. An existing grocery chain entering the Internet delivery business benefited from two key competitive advantages. First, since the existing grocery outlet already served traditional customers, further utilizing the facility to serve the home shopper produced little additional operating cost. Second, existing grocery chains such as Safeway had both a recognizable name and brand equity which new startups such as Homegrocer lacked. Nonetheless, differences between the traditional grocery business and this new business model remained vast.

Donald commented,

> Building a grocery store on the Internet is a very different business from running a traditional grocery business. There is a tremendous amount of integration work to be done in order for the software components to function together properly. Also, the labor component must be minimized. Without automated ordering and automated routing, you need too many people to perform basic clerical operations. Delivery and picking accuracy fail if you have people on phones and by the fax machine, and the whole labor component gets out of hand very quickly. So it's really critical that you get the right systems and software in place from the outset.
>
> People ask me what are the barriers to entry? They try to tell me that everybody's going to be in this business in the course of a year. Well, the most likely competition is the regular grocery chains, but they're so busy doing what they're trying to do to maintain market share they don't have the time or the people to think about it. They're all grocery people. They don't have the technical expertise to understand this new type of business. Companies that

are out there running grocery businesses are nowhere near ready to jump into the Internet on their own. One thing we've learned is that the biggest barrier to entry is just the overall complexity of the task.

HOMEGROCER ADVANTAGES

Homegrocer was unique because it eliminated many of the costs associated with the traditional retail setting. For example, a traditional grocery store would normally be located in a desirable retail district in close proximity to customers. It therefore bore the high costs associated with its location (premium rents both for the store and for sufficient parking, high property taxes, etc.). Homegrocer, on the other hand, was located in a much less expensive industrial district; hence it was not subject to the same high costs as would be mandated by an appropriate retail setting.

Homegrocer also benefited from not having to position stock for retail display. In a conventional grocery store, large displays of produce had to be kept cool by refrigerators that pumped cold air straight through the produce and into the store. Because Homegrocer customers only saw an online display of groceries they were buying—not the real thing—there was no need to store inventory in this fashion. Produce was stored in a large walk-in refrigerator, which was much more efficient than conventional store storage, and resulted in substantial power savings. Also, because large amounts of inventory were necessary to make an attractive display, greater inventory levels—with correspondingly higher carrying costs—were required by traditional grocery stores. Further, regular stores incurred more spoilage (which must be written off) than did Homegrocer with its JIT system.

Finally, Homegrocer was able to deliver a superior product to the consumer. Donald elaborated, "We don't order the perishable products until our customers have ordered them from us. As a result, we have the freshest product available. The produce is better, the fish is fresher, and the meat is restaurant quality."

The savings possible through the kind of system Homegrocer had established were substantial. Traditional grocery store chains operated with a 28 per cent gross margin, but carried just 1 per cent or less to the bottom line. While Homegrocer achieved the same 28 per cent gross margins as its rivals (its groceries were priced to sell neither at a premium nor a discount), Mike Donald anticipated that its efficiencies should allow it to carry almost 7 per cent to the bottom line. Hence, in theory, Homegrocer should be about six times as profitable as a conventional grocery store.

While the potential savings and efficiency gains inherent in Homegrocer's system were enticing, up-front costs were substantial. Design of the Homegrocer web site alone cost the firm over US$750,000.

Considering most successful electronic commerce sites redesigned their web sites from the ground up every few years, this was a rather significant cost that a conventional grocery store would not incur. As well, Homegrocer's fleet of refrigerated delivery trucks represented another cost most "bricks-and-mortar" grocery stores did not face.

THE TECHNOLOGY

Because of management's lack of IT expertise, Homegrocer outsourced all software and back office system development efforts. Back office and administrative software was purchased largely off the shelf and then modified. Design and maintenance had, to date, been outsourced as well. However, this was beginning to change. Management had begun to realize that, to gain some control over its future development potential, the firm had to take closer control over its IT. According to Donald, effective integration of various technologies formed a substantial barrier to entry, which served to keep traditional grocery stores out of the online delivery business. To that end, the company had begun to hire in-house developers to reduce its reliance on external IT consulting and development firms. While this practice was adding to overhead in the short term, management felt that development of this capability "in house" would help the firm develop a sustainable competitive advantage.

MANAGEMENT

Homegrocer was the brainchild of Mike Donald's forum group in the Young Entrepreneurs Organization. The group met occasionally to discuss business opportunities and challenges. Initial discussions about the viability of an Internet-based grocery store took place at Bridge's Pub in downtown Vancouver, following YEO Forum Group meetings.

Mike Donald was also President of Concord Sales, one of the largest food brokers in British Columbia, and had worked much of his life in the grocery trade. Over the years he had developed a deep understanding of the grocery business.

Donald was joined in the venture by Terry Drayton, another YEO member. Drayton had been working with Loblaws in Ontario to develop home delivery of groceries (without the use of the Internet). Drayton had recently divested himself of Crystal Springs Water Co., a company he had founded ten years before, and was looking to move his career in a new direction. The water business had given him a solid understanding of distribution and home delivery. An MBA with a penchant for academia, he had recently enrolled in UBC's Business Ph.D. Program. However, after he had rediscovered the idea, four more years in school gave way to the excitement of a new business startup.

Mike Donald also asked a friend of the family with a history of high-tech experience, Ken Deering, to come in and help create the system structure. Drayton came on board as President of Homegrocer, Donald as Executive Vice President. Donald and Drayton became equal partners; Deering, not having the financing of the others, remained on as an employee.

FINANCING ISSUES

Homegrocer began on a shoestring, with Mike Donald, Terry Drayton and seed investors funding the first $300,000. As the company business plan began to take shape, James Wilson approached private investors and VC firms in hopes of raising the approximately four million dollars the project required.

One impediment to financing the startup was the initial choice of geographic location. Because the principals all resided in BC, Vancouver seemed a natural location for the company. However, potential investors disagreed. Donald explained,

> We went to San Francisco to a big trade show and we talked to some investment companies who said, "Yeah, that's a really good idea, where are you starting out?" We said, "Vancouver," and they said, "Why there?" We said, "Well, that's where we live." They would say, "Okay, whatever," and then off they would go, and we'd never see them again.

At one point, a potential institutional investor suggested that the same deal in a "techno-sexy" town, such as Seattle or Santa Barbara, would make the deal significantly more attractive. In addition, the favorable tax environment offered to firms (and resident employees) in the U.S. further enhanced the financial appeal of the deal. Donald observed,

> As soon as we changed it to Seattle, everybody perked up and loved the idea. We figured the U.S. was the place to be anyway, because in Canada there may be a handful of cities you can do well in, while in the U.S. there are hundreds.

Furthermore, Mike Donald was of the opinion that if they couldn't make the Homegrocer business work in the Seattle area, with its high proportion of Internet-adept, high-tech-oriented workaholics, it seemed unlikely it would work anywhere.

Some of the initial financing was secured very creatively—by finding people who were willing to work for free initially. According to Donald,

> In October 1996, we brought in a few people who were out of work at the time. We were lucky to find a delivery guy who would work for nothing and accrue his salary. There were software programmers who worked for nothing with the understanding that once we started to bring in some money, they would start getting paid. The project is so exciting and has so much potential that people wanted to volunteer. The consultant who came in to be our project manager we have now hired on permanently.

On more than one occasion, the firm was technically insolvent, and relied on small injections of equity from the principals, as well as services in kind from employees. However, the firm managed to stay afloat and the principals continued searching for a more permanent source of growth financing.

Drayton was able to arrange meetings with a number of VCs. The jewel was Kleiner Perkins, a highly respected high-technology venture capital firm. The merits of a "Kleiner" underwriting went well beyond the funding provided per se. The prestige and respect within the e-commerce and investment banking community that accrued from a Kleiner deal, often exceeded the actual financing provided, severalfold.

Kleiner did not come quickly, however. "These folks take the due diligence process pretty damn seriously," remarked Donald with a wry grin. In fact, the entire first round of financing was obtained through local "angel" investors, plus a major contribution from an Australian friend of Terry's, whom Terry had earlier helped with a business venture in Australia. The need for a major VC like Kleiner still existed, however. Eventually, Kleiner completed its due diligence process and was satisfied Homegrocer would be a good investment. A special secondary round of financing was opened to accommodate them. As a result, more than twice the projected financing needs were raised. As it turned out, that was fortuitous, because the company experienced major cost overruns on its software development, and other parts of the business plan needed to be accelerated. As well, with Kleiner on board, Homegrocer's ability to raise more funds inexpensively in the future was greatly enhanced.

START-UP AND GROWTH

Homegrocer was located near Seattle in Washington State partly because the local market contained one of the densest "wired" populations anywhere. Home to a host of high-tech firms led by Microsoft and Boeing, the Bellevue area provided an ideal testing ground to prove the new business model. Homegrocer opened for business in May 1998. Within a month it had acquired approximately 300 customers. A customer was defined as someone who ordered groceries online three times per month, and purchased at least $75 per order (orders under $75 were subject to a $10 delivery fee).

To break even, Mike Donald estimated that the company needed 4,000 such customers. Significant profitability would be achieved when the firm attained between 5,000 and 7,000 customers. Growth projections were based on the current numbers drawn from the wired community as well as projected Internet usage growth over the next several years.

Homegrocer's five-year plan included opening 30 outlets across the U.S. Expansion was to begin up and down the West Coast, and then spread eastward. Donald expected that the expertise they developed in the initial Bellevue site would reduce both the start-up costs and the learning curve associated with each new location. Further, the proprietary back-end computer technology, as well as the firm's web site, could be duplicated at very little cost, making additional location start-up costs dependent almost entirely on building and improvements.

Donald believed the greatest challenge to getting the necessary customer base was that each new customer acquisition required a very "deep sell." When asked to explain he responded,

> Because it (ordering groceries online) is such a drastic change in behavior, it demands that you completely change a certain aspect of your way of life. Grocery shopping is not only enjoyable to some people but it's also pretty systemic. People go to the store not knowing what they want. They rely on the trip to the store to trigger whole patterns of behavior. A lot of people today would argue that couples with both people working would rather just sit at their terminal at work during their coffee break and click on your site. . . . For sure, those people are easy to get. But if you're just a couple, you're not buying enough groceries to make it worthwhile. We need couples with families. Some of the findings that are coming out of other projects across the country are that people on the Internet shop three or four times and then they start to long for the grocery store experience, they miss it. You've got to be able to make the shopping experience fun and be able to bring new items out to people. The goal is to get three shops a month. If we can do that, we're successful.

The Homegrocer opening web page, at http://www.homegrocer.com, was quite simple. There was a dialogue box requesting a username and password for current customers, and there were hyperlinks directing prospective customers to both a signup page and a quick tour of the web site. The rest of the site was designed as one might expect, with category hyperlinks, which, when clicked on, brought up individual category items. Some individual products were accompanied by a picture, while others were not. Exhibits 3A and 3B illustrate pages from the company's web site.

The ideal customer for Homegrocer was a family of four. Such families were most likely to place individual grocery orders in excess of the $75 minimum. To encourage new customers to try out Homegrocer's service, first-time customers could order any quantity of groceries they desired and have them delivered free of charge. After that, Homegrocer charged a $10 delivery fee for orders less than $75. The groceries themselves were priced comparably with average walk-in grocery stores. There was some concern at Homegrocer regarding the effect of charging a substantial delivery fee for smaller deliveries, and the firm's pricing approach was a matter of continuing

EXHIBIT 3A Homegrocer's Web Site—Opening Page

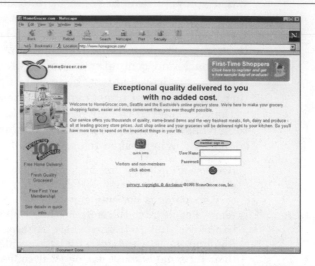

Source: http://www.homegrocer.com, November 1998.

EXHIBIT 3B Homegrocer's Web Site—Typical Grocery Shopping Page

Source: http://www.homegrocer.com, November 1998.

debate. Homegrocer also planned to charge an annual $35 membership fee, but to entice customers, waived the fee for the first year. Whether they would implement the membership fee idea remained to be seen.

In an attempt to generate traffic to the web site, Homegrocer advertised its services in the newspaper as well as through direct mail. It also benefited from its large, easily identified delivery trucks (see Exhibit 1) roaming the streets delivering groceries. Homegrocer directed its drivers, when not delivering groceries, to distribute door hanger advertising in targeted neighborhoods. They also occasionally directed the drivers to simply drive around the Bellevue neighborhoods when not otherwise occupied, so people would see their trucks and become familiar with the logo and name. A smattering of other advertising options had been proposed, but none had been implemented yet, as management was unclear about which promotional options made sense for them.

Homegrocer also looked for ways to utilize the informational aspects of the Internet to better serve its customers. One idea they had implemented was the online recipe. A customer could create a personal recipe and save it on the Homegrocer site. Later, clicking on the recipe would automatically load all the necessary ingredients into the customer's shopping cart. Homegrocer also offered its own recipes that customers could try out.

Despite all these efforts, drawing in new customers had proven to be difficult. Consumers seemed reticent to try the service for the first time. There were several possible reasons for this. The first was that customers might be reluctant to transmit credit card information over the net. Second, there might be a general perception that groceries purchased online were not as fresh as groceries picked up at a store. A third reason was that customers might actually crave the shopping experience, and that a virtual shop precluded the enjoyable impulsive, inspirational purchases made at a conventional grocery store.

It appeared to Donald that potential new customers had to visit the site several times before making the decision to sign up and try out the service.

THE ROAD AHEAD

Recent studies by Forrester Research, Andersen Consulting, Jupiter Communications and The Yankee Capital group all pointed to rapid growth in the Internet grocery business (see Exhibit 4). Unfortunately, these studies did not indicate which approach would win the day. Were firms like Peapod, which piggybacked on existing conventional grocery stores, going to be the big winners? Or would firms like Netgrocer, dealing only in non-perishable goods but offering a wide

---

EXHIBIT 4   Recent Forecasts about the Internet Grocery Business

---

Online Grocery Shopping Projections
September 21, 1998

Analysts are predicting that online grocery shopping could be worth as much as USD1 billion by the year 2000. Andersen Consulting reckon that the market for groceries and retail items such as stamps and photographic services could reach USD85 billion by the year 2000.

Meanwhile in another case of disparate projections, Jupiter Communications predict that online grocery revenue will reach USD2.2 billion by 2000 while The Yankee Group put that figure at over USD6 billion.

Netsmart recently conducted research which showed that the primary reason people would shop online was for convenience (68 per cent). Sixty-six per cent were attracted by the idea of 24-hour access; 60 per cent said it would save time; 57 per cent said it would save money; and 47 per cent were attracted by the idea of comparing prices from the comfort of a PC/Web application.

Source: Excerpted from *The Industry Standard,* newsmagazine of The Internet Economy, http://www.thestandard.com.

Online Grocery Market Will Remain Tiny
October 2, 1998

The sale of groceries online is predicted to generate USD10.8 billion by 2003 but the fledgling industry still has a long way to go before making an impact on the overall grocery market, according to Forrester Research.

While the amount of money that will be spent buying groceries online will increase dramatically on a year-to-year basis, by 2003 this will still only account for 2 per cent of the whole grocery market.

Forrester noted that geographic location, lack of significant demand, delivery fees and a lack of stability in the market were factors impeding the growth of online grocery shopping. The market is expected to remain "tiny" for the next five years despite a projected 92 per cent growth rate.

Convenience is the main attraction of online shopping and consumers will not be prepared to surf the Net for each brand item on their weekly shopping list.

Forrester predicts that sale of specialty goods online will overtake general grocery sales. As the majority of online consumers are in a high-income bracket, there is a healthy market for online luxury items. To realise profitable growth, online supermarkets will need to expand on their basic service and anticipate the consumer's every need.

Source: Excerpted from Forrester Research, http://www.forrester.com.

range of products and servicing the entire country by shipping long distances, be the winners? Or was Homegrocer's approach, providing a full line of groceries via a lower-cost warehouse, the right solution? Or perhaps all three?

As July turned into August, Mike Donald wondered what lay ahead for the firm. Did their assumptions under this new business model still hold? Was the pricing model the right one? Would senior management's lack of IT experience, and the decision to outsource software development, prove to be a constraint down the road? Would financing for expansion continue to be as readily available in the future as it had been in the past? Finally, what would it take to get new customers to try the service in sufficient numbers, and subsequently become permanent customers? And these were only the obvious questions. Several more subtle issues lay just beneath the surface.

Good Night Ben

By Professor Sid L. Huff and David Kolterman

In December 1998, Bob Brown, the owner of Good Night Ben, a baby furnishings store, was reviewing the server logs that recorded the traffic on his web site. The site had experienced a heavy volume of traffic. Brown believed that his web presence had generated between 20 per cent to 50 per cent of his 1998 business, and had enabled him to access some new markets. As he sat reviewing the logs, he thought about ways to extend his Internet efforts in order to generate even greater revenues.

THE BABY PRODUCTS INDUSTRY

Baby product sales were driven by the births of babies, and especially first-borns, since most families re-used most of their baby furniture and equipment with later children. Many of the purchasers were new parents, but a substantial number were the relatives of new parents who wished to help provision the child's room, or give gifts. Baby furniture and accessories were sold by department and discount stores such as Sears and Wal-Mart, by big-box retailers such as Toys-R-Us and IKEA, and by specialty retailers such as Good Night Ben. There was also a significant, but unorganized second-hand market, and a lot of "hand-me-downs" within families.

The mass merchandisers focused primarily on low and mid-priced functional furniture that was manufactured by a small number of companies. Childcraft Industries was the largest maker of children's beds, cribs and furniture, and held a large share of the American market. In Canada, Storkcraft held a similar position, with distribution through the major retailers. The specialty stores tended not to carry these mass-market lines, but focused on more expensive lines of furniture and bedding that featured very high quality materials, finish and aesthetic appeal. These products were intended for parents to whom taste and refinement were important considerations. They were produced by small manufacturers throughout the United States and Canada. The Canadian industry was concentrated in Quebec. The Canadian manufacturers had benefited greatly from the North American Free Trade Agreement (NAFTA), which allowed them to export their products duty-free to the United States. That, together with the relatively weak Canadian dollar, had enabled them to increase their share of the American market for high-end baby furniture.

In the United States, manufacturers used a system of protected dealer territories, in which only one or two specialty stores were awarded dealerships in each major market. This enabled the maintenance of higher prices and margins for both retailers and manufacturers. The Canadian urban population was concentrated in a small number of centers, which made it less worthwhile for the manufacturers to set up and maintain exclusive dealer territories in Canada. Of the major high-end manufacturers, Ragazzi made minimal efforts to market in Canada while Morigeau and Lepine did not use protected territories. As a result, most Canadian retailers carried products made by all of the major manufacturers, and price competition was strong.

GOOD NIGHT BEN

Good Night Ben was a baby products retail store located in London, Ontario, a city of 326,000 people. There was one other store like it in London, though there had been as many as five others in previous years. Good Night Ben derived its main revenue from the sale of baby and children's furniture, cribs, crib bedding, playpens, baby carriages, strollers and car seats. In addition, it sold child-care accessories such as bassinets, bathing basins, breast pumps and nursing supplies, crib toys and room decorations.

After a successful career in sales with a large truck manufacturer, Bob Brown decided he wanted a change. His wife, Linda, had started a successful home-based business making crib bumper pads. Linda Brown's contacts with her baby store customers convinced the Browns that baby products retailing was an attractive business. They chose to open their store in London because they had both lived there during college and liked the city. Taking advantage of a fast-rising real-estate market of the 1980s, in October 1987 they sold their home and invested the proceeds in inventory and fixtures for an independent baby and children's furniture store.

Bob and Linda Brown both worked full-time in the store. They had one full-time and one part-time assistant, and a bookkeeper who came in once a week. Business increased rapidly during the first three years, doubling in the second year and rising another 25 per cent the third year. The store reached break-even and began to generate profits. However, during the recession of the early 1990s, business declined and the profits turned to losses. It became a struggle to keep the business open. During this same period, five other directly competing stores had opened in the London area, a market too small to sustain them all. Eventually, four of the competitors either closed or went bankrupt. This factor, combined with a move to a more prominent location and improving economic conditions, resulted in a 50 per cent increase in business and restored profitability for Good Night Ben.

In the spring of 1998, Brown changed his pricing policy significantly. He had originally tried to carry the most popular lines of merchandise at prices that matched those of his large competitors (Toys-R-Us, Wal-Mart). He found that this usually meant razor-thin margins and low profitability. He switched to a high-margin philosophy, no longer attempting to compete head-to-head with major retailers. Instead he began featuring high-end merchandise that they typically did not carry. He raised his margins by 7 per cent on average. The selling margin on merchandise in this business was typically 30 to 40 per cent. He had calculated that if he raised prices by 7 per cent, as long as sales did not drop more than 20 per cent as a result, he would improve his profits. In the event, sales remained level, but only because Internet-derived business compensated for the in-store decline.

Brown had experimented with mail-order sales, but had found that customers really had to see and touch the furniture to appreciate the quality that justified the higher prices. Few were willing to buy on the basis of photographs in brochures or on web pages. He also found that furniture shipped in small quantities often arrived damaged, leading to extra time and effort to pursue claims against shipping companies. He therefore defined his market as the range within which he could comfortably deliver the furniture himself, which was effectively the territory between the metropolitan Detroit area and Toronto. He would accept mail orders from other parts of Canada, though he did not actively pursue them. A note on his web page explained this:

A Note to International Browsers

Good Night Ben's web page has been designed to advertise our retail store. London is located within a two-hour drive of Toronto, Buffalo or Detroit. Good Night Ben has a beautiful showroom where all our products are displayed. The store is staffed by the most knowledgeable staff in Canada. We deliver anywhere in Canada at reasonable costs. We also deliver into Southern Michigan. Delivery cost quotations are available on request. At this time we have decided not to pursue other international business. We will mail out catalogues and information only to customers in Canada and Southern Michigan. Please browse our page, visit us in London and e-mail us with any comments. We are always happy to hear from our friends around the world. We have several customers that drive to London from Southern Michigan and Upstate New York. The exchange rate is very attractive. $1.00 Canadian is approximately $.68 U.S. All the furniture we sell is either American or Canadian made and can be taken into the United States duty free.

PROMOTION

Brown had regularly spent approximately 3 per cent of his sales revenue on newspaper and Yellow Pages advertisements, divided roughly 50/50 between the two. He eventually came to the conclusion that the newspaper ads weren't effective, and in January 1998 he stopped placing them. He continued to use Yellow Pages ads, placing a display ad in the London directory and small text ads in all the other Southwestern Ontario phone directories. These ads cost $700 per month.

At one point, Brown conceived of the idea of creating a mail-order business sideline which would offer smaller, easily shipped baby products to mid-sized communities that didn't have a baby-products store. He bought a scanner, intending to produce a catalogue. As he refined his idea, he realized that, with a minimum print run of 10,000 copies at a cost of $1 per copy, plus another $1 per copy in distribution costs, and the need to rent a mailing list, the cost of beginning the catalogue operation would run between $20,000 and $30,000. Brown doubted that he could sell enough suitable merchandise to recoup the investment, and he shelved the idea.

Among other promotional techniques, Brown had tried ads in hospitals, without noticeable response, and he had used the services of Welcome Wagon, which distributed promotional gift packs to pregnant women and new mothers, also without success. He had also tried a direct mailout to a list of previous customers, and he felt that it was the most successful promotion technique (besides the Internet) that he had used, though he also believed that it hadn't paid for its costs.

By December 1998, his main promotion techniques were the Yellow Pages, the visibility of his storefront location, a reliance on word-of-mouth, and the Internet. Brown had found through studies he had done that 80 per cent of his customers came to him through referrals, and he considered word-of-mouth to be his most important source of customers. The Internet was also becoming a valuable source of business for him.

GOOD NIGHT BEN ON THE INTERNET

Brown's first computer experience was gained at the start of the 1980s, on a Radio-Shack TRS-80 in the offices of his former employer. Brown found himself fascinated with computers, intensely curious about how they worked as well as about what they could do for him in his business.

Through a company-sponsored purchase plan, he soon had an IBM PC-XT of his own. He introduced spreadsheet analysis at work, and used his PC to do the accounting for his wife's home business. When the Browns opened their baby furniture store, the accounting was computerized from the beginning. Brown bought desk-top publishing software and began making his own promotional material. In 1994, he heard about CompuServe, and signed up for an account. Shortly after he signed with CompuServe, the company began offering Internet connectivity to its subscribers, together with the Spry Mosaic web browser. One day, a newsletter arrived from CompuServe that described how to set up a World Wide Web (WWW) home page, and explained that the home page service was included free with the basic subscription. Brown downloaded the recommended HTML editor (Homepage Wizard) and began creating his own simple home page on the World Wide Web.

Soon after, he submitted his home page's address, or URL (http://our world.compuserve.com/good_night_ben.html) to a few WWW search engines, and was soon receiving an e-mail a day, sent by people who had visited the site. Convinced that people did visit his site, he developed it further, featuring products in the store. He submitted his site to Yahoo for indexing, and he began to think about structuring the site to make it easier to find by people who were trying to search for information about the products he sold.

It occurred to Brown that if people were to use a search engine and enter key words such as "baby," "crib" or "stroller," the words would be too common and the search engine would return thousands of sites, many of them completely irrelevant. Brown's site would be buried in the large collection of "hits" such a query would return to the browser. For example, "baby" might return song titles from music sites and "crib" might return games and farm equipment as well as children's furniture.

He decided that the way to allow more people to find his site was by having it indexed using words that were unique to his industry. Brown thought that the most unique and meaningful words in the baby furniture industry were the brand names of the best-known quality manufacturers. He featured those names prominently on his web pages so that they would be picked up and indexed by the "spiders" used by automatic search engines.

In contrast to automatically indexing search engines such as AltaVista, the popular search engine called Yahoo was indexed by people according to subject content as indicated by a site abstract submitted by the site owner. For Yahoo, then, instead of submitting a site abstract that might have said "baby furniture store in London, Ontario," Brown submitted: "Goodnight Ben, quality brands including Morigeau, Perego, Ragazzi." The consequence of this strategy was that a search for any of these brands, using any of the major search engines, returned Brown's web site within the first couple of screens. Brown's volume of e-mail rose dramatically.

Most of the e-mail Brown received asked for prices on baby furniture. Since people searching the net could now find Brown's web site more easily than they could locate the baby product manufacturers' sites, some of the e-mail asked for help getting replacement parts for broken products. Though most of the e-mail originated in North America, it also came from many other countries around the globe.

Brown found that most people were not prepared to buy high-end baby furniture on the basis of a picture seen on the Internet. E-mail did not lend itself to the personal salesmanship required, and almost none of the e-mail resulted in sales revenue. Therefore Brown stopped answering e-mail, and bought an 800 toll-free number that would connect people calling him from the markets he was interested in; that is, all of Canada and Southern Michigan. He featured the 800 number on every web page, and received a couple of calls each day.

TRAFFIC MEASUREMENT

Brown was convinced that the level of e-mail activity revealed only a small portion of the traffic his site received. He was interested to find out the actual number of unique visitors to his site. Usually this kind of information would be derived from log files kept by the web-page server. In Brown's case, the web server was owned and operated by CompuServe, and the log files were not available to him. Brown's solution was to use a free web-counter service. Brown chose Webside Story, and included a special link to Webside Story on his web page. Whenever potential customers downloaded that page, their browsers would automatically make a request to Webside Story's server as well as CompuServe's server. This request would run a small program on Webside Story's server that would record the time and date that Brown's page was downloaded.

Each viewing of a page was called a "hit," or an "impression." Multiple downloads of a given page by the same person would be recorded as multiple hits. In order to determine how many different *people* viewed a particular web page, Webside Story's server would also send out "cookies" to peoples' browsers that would enable Webside Story's program to detect repeat visitors. Webside Story could thereby provide not only gross hit counts but also counts of unique visits.

Brown (or anyone) could retrieve statistics on the usage of his web site by visiting the Webside Story site and looking them up. The Webside Story counters revealed that Brown was receiving about 4,000 unique visitors per month on the good_night_ben.html page hosted by CompuServe. (See Exhibit 1 for a sample Webside Story report.)

SELLING "EYEBALLS" AND SITES

It was clear to Brown that, as gratifying as all the web-traffic might be, it was not generating much revenue for the store. He thought there must be a way to exploit the traffic, since it represented people with an active interest in baby products. WWW traffic that might not be of much value to a small baby furniture retailer in London, Ontario, might be worth something to other retailers or national manufacturers of, for example, baby food. With this concept in mind, Brown set out to create a general baby-related products web site, which would attract lots of viewers. He thought that he could sell space on this site to interested advertisers. This was called "selling eyeballs." He called his new site www.babybusiness.com, and registered the domain names goodnight ben.com and babybusiness.com with the official Internet name registry in the United States.

For his babybusiness.com web site project, Brown chose a local Internet service provider, selected for its technical ability, high-speed net connection, and fast, reliable servers. It was important to Brown that his pages download swiftly, and that his site never be unavailable. Brown also kept his original site at CompuServe, because recently it had become increasingly difficult to obtain a listing on Yahoo, and he wanted to avoid causing any disturbances that might result in losing his Yahoo listing. He believed that the Yahoo listing was the key to his traffic volume, likening it to having a billboard on a major highway. He was not successful in getting Yahoo to list www.babybusiness.com, so he created a link on his CompuServe good_night_ben site, pointing to his "babybusiness" site, in order to draw traffic to it. He also placed links and information about all the major manufacturers on this site without charge in order to draw traffic. Then he took all the same steps he had taken to get good_night_ben prominently featured: he submitted it for indexing by all the major search engines, and continued in his efforts

---

EXHIBIT 1   Sample of Webside Story's Output

Global Information Monitoring:	Account ID G25153786

http://ourworld.compuserve.com/homepages/good_night_ben/

Total Number of Hits	98,511
Total Impressions	86,111
Total Unique Visitors	57,633
Total Reloads	12,400
Average/Day	189
Average Uniques/Day	126
Average Reloads/Day	27
Local Time	Wed_Oct_7_20:06:26_1998
Counting Since	Thu_Jul_10_17:48:57_1997
Last Reset	Thu_Jul_10_17:48:57_1997
Last Impression	Wed_Oct_7_20:05:49_1998
Last Unique	Wed_Oct_7_20:03:12_1998
Last Reload	Wed_Oct_7_20:03:23_1998

Today's Statistics

Impressions	186
Unique Visitors	120
Forecasted Impressions	222
Forecasted Uniques	143
Reloads	40
Average Impressions/Hour	9
Average Uniques/Hour	5
Average Reloads/Hour	1
Returns Within 1 Hour	66
Returns After 1 Hour	0

Highest Rated

Date Jul 21, 1998		350
Hour	11AM	52
Day	Tuesday	350
Month	July	8,311

For Webside Story statistics on the Good Night Ben page on CompuServe, visit:
http://w12.hitbox.com/wc3/stats.cgi?G25153786

For Webside Story statistics on Babybusiness.com go to:
http://w20.hitbox.com/wc/stats.cgi?H27278696

---

to get a listing on Yahoo. Again, he placed major manufacturers' brand names prominently on his web pages so they would become search engine key words that would point to his site. He was also beginning to employ meta-tags in his pages. (Meta-tags were collections of descriptive words that formed part of a web page but that were not displayed in the browser screen; rather, the text was used to indicate key words to search engines, or to document the web pages.)

His next initiative was to offer to create web sites for other baby furniture retailers in other geographical regions. To pursue this line of business he formed a partnership with the operator of an Internet service provider. Brown was responsible for designing the sites, the ISP operator was responsible for hosting the sites and for any technical programming work required, and they were both responsible for promoting the enterprise at trade shows and through web advertising. They shared the revenues equally. For $800 he and his ISP partner would register a domain name for the new site, host it on the ISP's servers, create the web pages and content, scan the photos and create links to the new site from the babybusiness.com site. The monthly fee for hosting and links was $80. (All fees are in U.S. dollars.) Brown did the graphic design and content creation himself, and was now using Microsoft Frontpage for web page layout. He found that he could create many of these sites rapidly by basing them on the design of his own site, then customizing them for his clients. He recommended to his web site customers that they feature their web addresses on all their other promotional materials—their ads, business cards and yellow pages—just as he did himself.

Brown developed an alternative offering in which he created a much simpler site for $250 and hosted it for $50 per month. Those who wanted only an ad on babybusiness.com were charged $120 per year (see Exhibit 2). So far, several stores had signed up for web site creation and hosting, and a few advertisers had placed ads. By October 1998, revenue from web hosting and ads amounted to $800 per month.

By working with an ISP, Brown now had access to server logs. That allowed him to track statistics for all the pages of his new site and he could track the traffic of his web site customers as well. Babybusiness.com was receiving hundreds of hits per day, and his web-hosting customers were each getting several thousand hits per month on their own pages.

Brown promoted his web site design and advertising activities through his own web pages, at trade shows, and through his extensive network of personal contacts in the business. His ISP partner assisted with these promotion efforts. He and his partner were finding that it was difficult to sell web site links or ads to suppliers, but that retailers were receptive.

THE U.S.-BASED CUSTOMERS

Meanwhile, Brown's own web sites were providing information to prospective customers, and those who were interested in possibly purchasing would find the 800 number on the web site and call his store. Many of these new customers were people from the Detroit area.

Brown had found that people generally weren't interested in purchasing high-end baby furniture without inspecting it personally. Detroit, however, was serviced by several baby furniture dealers, one of

---

EXHIBIT 2   The Baby Business Web Site Rate Card

(All fees are stated in U.S. dollars)

Baby Business has a steady flow of qualified visitors, all looking for information on baby products. Become part of the Babybusiness success story by choosing one of the following Packages.

Package 1 {Full program}—This program is for clients who do not have a web presence and wish to use babybusiness.com as their main World Wide Web marketing point.

Web site creation (see template examples) multiple pages designed—$500 and up.
Domain name registration (yourname.com).
Web site hosting $80 month (one year contract).
Links in babybusiness.com directory under both Retailers or Manufacturer and up to five Products category areas.
E-mail address (myself@yourname.com) available directly or forwarded.

Package 2 {Brochure program}—This program provides an entry level web offering for smaller businesses. Specifically for single products or groups of products/services.

Web site creation (see template examples) one page only—$250.
Your URL listed as a subdomain of babybusiness.com (www.babybusiness.com/-yourname).
Links in babybusiness.com directory under Retailer or Manufacturer and 1 Product category area.
Web site hosting $50 month (one year contract).
E-mail address (yourname@babybusiness.com) available directly or forwarded.

Package 3 {Link program}—This program is designed to provide a marketing link to an existing web site to take advantage of the babybusiness.com directory image.

Link in babybusiness.com directory under Retailer or Manufacturer or 1 Product category area— $125./yr.
Banner ads—this program provides our clients with advertisement opportunities on the babybusiness.com web site to promote their own web sites. Charges are made for banner design and for clickthru's or impressions. Details available upon request.

---

whom had a large showroom in which all the lines Brown carried were attractively displayed. Shoppers would sometimes visit such a showroom in their immediate area, see and inspect various items and lines of furniture, judge the quality, decide which items they liked, and then go home and use the Internet to find where they could get it at a lower cost.

That's when they would find Brown's site, and place a call to his store. Due to the higher margins maintained in the United States through the exclusive dealer territories, the favorable currency exchange rate and the non-applicability of the Michigan state sales taxes on Brown's sales, he could always offer such callers very attractive bargains, while still selling at an above average mark-up himself. This Southern Michigan business had come to account for between 20 per cent and 50 per cent of Good Night Ben's sales.

THE FUTURE

It had occurred to Brown that the American business might not last forever. The exchange rate could become less favorable, or the Detroit dealer could discover the situation and complain to the manufacturer, who might take action against Brown, perhaps by cutting off Brown's supply. Brown's philosophy was that being a small businessman was like going down to the beach each day, picking up a surfboard and trying to catch a wave. Today: this surfboard, this wave. Tomorrow: maybe another surfboard and a different wave. For now, Brown was determined to ride the wave he was on as far as it would go.

Brown also wanted to ride the big Internet wave as far as it would take him. Had he overlooked other good Internet-related business possibilities? Had he exploited those that he had identified to their full potential? Could he further increase the revenue generation possibilities of his web sites? Could he make money on the Web, even if the special situation with regard to the Detroit market were to disappear?

Internet Liquidators: www.internetliquidators.com

By Professor David Shaw and Paul Kedrosky

Late one cool afternoon in November of 1996, incoming jets sparkled in the setting sun as they set up for final approach to Toronto's Pearson Airport, and Paul Godin, Internet Liquidators Incorporated's (ILI) President, wondered which one was his. Godin had spent much of the past month on planes as he simultaneously tried to jump-start his new Internet-based Dutch auction, looked at a high-profile slate of potential equity partners, opened a U.S. headquarters, and as his ILI co-sponsored a North America–wide anti-drunk-driving campaign—all of this and the newly public ILI had not yet been in business for six months or turned a profit.

ILI's online Dutch auction was attracting interest, but it wasn't taking off as quickly as Godin had hoped. He wondered if he should join forces with another online company, like America Online (AOL), CompuServe or the Microsoft Network (MSN), or look at other ways of getting the less than one-year-old ILI increased exposure, or perhaps even rethink what ILI was doing. In the rush-rush world of the Internet, one year meant ILI was already exiting adolescence and would very soon have to stand on its own.

At face value, a deal with an online service looked like a good way of getting ILI going in a hurry. Online services like AOL and CompuServe together had more than 10 million subscribers, all of whom who could be tipped off to that night's auction action if one of them backed ILI. But a deal would mean giving up, he estimated, at least 10 percent of ILI now, with an option to give up much more over the next three years if the business worked. In addition, while Godin wanted to avoid giving any online service an "exclusive" on ILI's content, that might not be saleable. Finally, while cash would always be welcome in ILI's shrinking coffers, any deal with one of these large online companies would undoubtedly mean major changes in small and entrepreneurial ILI with its 12 employees.

But traditional online services weren't the only possible partners. New services were springing up—Microsoft and AOL, respectively, had announced Cityscape and Digital City, the electronic equivalents of a local newspaper. These new services were sure to be at least as thirsty for content as their big online brethren.

Other partners were possible, perhaps companies like Wal-Mart or Zellers, major retailers who sold many of the same products as ILI, albeit through stores rather than through online auctions. Retailers, however, could bring their own problems. While a Zellers might understand retail, not every Zellers customer was an online user. And Zellers or Wal-Mart might even see ILI as competition rather than as a potential ally. At the same time, Godin knew that ILI could always soldier on alone, at least for a little while. While that might mean higher offers from future suitors, that could also mean disaster if ILI burned through its remaining cash without finding its stride.

If there was to be a deal, it would come down to the full terms, not just the cash. Godin needed a clear sense of his requirements. What did he want? How much did he want for a piece of ILI? How much could he realistically get? And who should approach who?

INDUSTRY BACKGROUND

Dutch Auctions

By the late 19th century, Dutch farmers knew they had a problem: their flowers and produce were popular, yet they weren't making as much money as they thought they should. Frugal buyers were playing sellers off one another—negotiating lower prices with one seller under the implicit threat that if they didn't sell at that price, someone else just down the road would. And to make things even more difficult, growers were finding it increasingly difficult to sell to individual buyers, yet still find time to tend to their fields.

One day in July 1887, a cauliflower grower came up with a solution that stuck: the Dutch auction. The shrewd farmer set up shop and announced that his produce would drop in price until it was all bought. The farmer's auction worked. In the excitement of the auction, the farmer got the best possible price from the assembled buyers, and the prices were better than he would have obtained by selling to individual buyers. His auction quickly became popular, spreading across Holland until every Dutch village had its own auction for perishable products.

Since then, Dutch auctions had been used all over the world, but nowhere were they embraced the way they were in Holland. But wherever they were used, the principles remained the same: as time ticked down, the price declined and the number of units remaining were sold off until there were no units left or time ran out. That simple format proved to be remarkably effective. The Dutch auction had some real advantages. For example, like any auction, it played buyers off against each other, thus giving sellers better prices. It also introduced "gaming," an element of chance and excitement, something that many people found exciting. A buyer had to remain vigilant as the price dropped—waiting too long before locking in a price might mean that there was nothing left.

The Internet and the World Wide Web (WWW)

The Internet was the world's largest interconnection of computers and computer networks. Created in the 1960s but only really reaching critical mass in the late 1970s, it was a collection of electronic highways and cities, large and small, over which data flowed among a mind-boggling assortment of computers and countries. If someone used the Internet exclusively for e-mail, the Internet seemed to be an electronic post office, shunting their messages across the street or around the globe. For someone else who was wandering the World Wide Web (WWW)—a new point-and-click way of travelling the Internet—then the "Net" was a huge television network, brimming with all sorts of channels (called WWW sites), from the vital to the silly: from CNN's latest headlines to pictures of exploding Pop Tarts. Whatever it was, the Internet was growing like topsy. From less than 300 computers (called hosts, in Internet parlance) in 1982, it had grown to almost 13 million hosts by mid-1996—a 115 percent annual compound growth rate. From its origins in academia, and mostly in North America, the Internet had grown to comprise more than 150 countries on every continent, including Antarctica. And the number of hosts was doubling every 12 months

EXHIBIT 1   Internet and WWW Growth

Number of Internet Hosts		*Number of WWW Hosts*	
Aug. 81	213	Jun. 93	130
May 82	235	Dec. 93	623
Aug. 83	562	Jun. 94	2,738
Oct. 84	1,024	Dec. 94	10,022
Oct. 85	1,961	Jun. 95	23,500
Feb. 86	2,308	Jan. 96	100,000
Nov. 86	5,089	Jun. 96	230,000
Dec. 87	28,174		
Jul. 88	33,000		
Oct. 88	56,000		
Jan. 89	80,000		
Jul. 89	130,000		
Oct. 89	159,000		
Oct. 90	313,000		
Jan. 91	376,000		
Jul. 91	535,000		
Oct. 91	617,000		
Jan. 92	727,000		
Apr. 92	890,000		
Jul. 92	992,000		
Oct. 92	1,136,000		
Jan. 93	1,313,000		
Apr. 93	1,486,000		
Jul. 93	1,776,000		
Oct. 93	2,056,000		
Jan. 94	2,217,000		
Jul. 94	3,212,000		
Oct. 94	3,864,000		
Jan. 95	4,852,000		
Jul. 95	6,642,000		
Jan. 96	9,472,000		
Jul. 96	12,881,000		

Source: Network Wizards, http:www.nw.com.

with no sign of a slowdown (see Exhibit 1). Internet traffic grew commensurately. Traffic on the National Science Foundation (NSF) part of the Internet was over 20 terabytes (trillion bytes) per month—the equivalent of 33 million King James Bibles. The number of Internet users was the subject of much speculation, but there could be little doubt that the number had grown from under 500,000 users in 1990 to somewhere in excess of 25 million users by 1996. The WWW was one of the main catalysts of all this growth. By making the Internet more graphical, by shielding Internet users from all the underlying disorder, the WWW was growing even faster than the Internet itself. From a humble beginning in mid-1993 with only 130 WWW "channels," the WWW part of the Internet had grown to more than 230,000 channels by mid-1996—and was doubling every six months (see Exhibit 1).

Doing Business on the WWW

For a long time government funding of parts of the Internet, especially in the U.S., meant that the Internet was not open for business. But this changed in mid-1995 when the NSF, facing a cash squeeze of its own, and seeing the Internet getting along fine under its own power, ceased direct funding support. With that government restriction out of the way, the Internet's ceaseless geometric growth might have spurred businesses to think more seriously about how to make money on the Internet, but there were other problems. Perhaps the most important was the Internet's culture itself.

With the Internet's origins in academia and research, its users had long frowned upon commerce being transacted on its wires. To be successful, businesses had to find less overt ways of hawking their wares. For example, Internet industries began to pop up for booksellers, software retailers, florists and novelty gifts—and these businesses sold their products, for the most part, by word of mouth. But the ever-expanding WWW finally overwhelmed even this barrier. No culture that had grown as fast as the Internet's WWW could remember last year, let alone the Internet's misty, government sponsored (and commerce-free) origins decades ago. The tidal wave of new users washed away the Internet's cultural memory and, along the way, its aversion to doing business.

So what kinds of business could be done on the WWW? One study[1] suggested the following list:

Online storefront;

Internet presence—a company that helped other companies build WWW sites or WWW advertising;

Content— any fee-based or sponsored searchable database;
- Mall—a collection of various for-profit ventures;

Incentive site—a sort of "teaser" approach where high-gloss content, even public service information, attracted users to a commercial site; and
- Search agent—a site that helped users find and keep track of changing information on the WWW.

---

[1]Hoffman, D. and Novak, T. "Commercial Scenarios for the Web: Opportunities and Challenges," *Journal of Computer-Mediated Communications,* 1:3, pp. 17–23.

Internet Security

But the skeptics kept tumbling out of the woodwork, most of them pointing to the same problem: security. "Security is the number one obstacle to doing business on the WWW," opined *The Wall Street Journal.*[2]

There were (at least) two security-related problems. The first: How do you keep private things private on the Internet? The Internet had long been the computer equivalent of a rural telephone—anyone with the interest and wherewithal could listen in when and where they pleased. Encryption was the answer, but two competing encryption standards were proposed. That issue was resolved in early 1996 when two of the major Internet software vendors—Microsoft and Netscape—and the two major credit card companies—Visa and MasterCard—after much partisan bickering, finally threw their weight behind a single security standard: Secure Electronic Transactions (SET).

The second problem was convincing consumers that the Internet was safe for the forces of commerce. Months and months of media-drumbeating about the Internet's flawed security had made consumers skittish about handing out their credit cards to eager Internet-based businesses. The situation was analogous to locking someone in a room for a few weeks with a copy of the movie *Jaws,* and then inviting them out for a quick swim off Martha's Vineyard. There were few early takers.

But even with the consumer nervousness, the total amount of business (at this stage, mostly companies investing in creating an Internet presence) attributable to the Internet was large. One study (by industry researcher ActiveMedia) suggested that $436 million in business was related to the Internet in 1995. The same study predicted that $46 billion in business would be done by the end of the century. These were tough numbers to ignore. Especially given the demographics reported for Internet users: they were young, educated, and had ample disposable income (see Exhibit 2).

ILI BACKGROUND

History

"I always liked auctions," said Paul Godin, ILI's President. He just hadn't planned on turning auctions into a career. The basic idea—marrying the Dutch auction concept with Godin's background in consumer products and electronics—had been taking shape in Godin's mind since the late 1970s. But it was only when he saw the Internet taking off, and, in talking to people, learned more about the WWW, that he decided he had finally found the missing piece—the Internet: add Dutch auctions to the WWW and you had global auctions.

---

[2]Clark, D. "Virtual Safety: All Sorts of New Technologies Aimed at Easing Consumers' Paranoia about Buying on the Net," June 17, 1996, p. 21, Sec. R.

EXHIBIT 2   Internet Demographics

Age

Average age across all users is 35.0 years old (median: 35.0 years old), four years older than the last survey in October.

There are significant differences between European users and U.S. users, with the European population being younger (average age 31.2) than the U.S. (average age 35.7).

- There were no significant differences between women's and men's age profiles. The average age for women is 35.2 vs 35.0 years old for men. 42 percent of all surveyed women are between the ages of 30 and 45, while only 37 percent of the men fall into the same range.

The youngest users are European (average age 31.2), with the eldest being Prodigy users (average age 40.0).

Gender

Overall, 15.5 percent of the users are female, 82.0 percent male and 2.5 percent "Rather not say!" The actual numbers are 2,020 women, 10,668 men, and 318 non-responses.

- Compared to the last survey, women represent a six percent increase and men an eight percent decrease. The last survey did not have the "Rather not say!" option.

In the U.S., 17.1 percent of the users are female, 80.3 percent male and 2.6 percent "Rather not say!" There are proportionately more males (91.6 percent) than females (7.2 percent) in Europe than the U.S.

The percent of users (2.5 percent) who chose not to respond to this question via the "Rather not say!" option, is relatively stable across other similar types of sensitive questions, like Disabilities (2.4 percent).

For Prodigy, 19.1 percent of the respondents are female, with 78.8 percent male. These ratios more so reflect the ratios outside the Web and also suggest that as more major online services join the Web and Internet, more balanced female/male ratios are likely to occur. The U.S. and Prodigy ratios also indicate that the U.S. is integrating women more quickly into the user population than other parts of the world.

Number of Dependents

There are more users with two dependents (16.9 percent) than users with one dependent (15.5 percent). Only 7.9 percent report having three or more dependents.

- Of the users with no dependents (61 percent over all groups), Europeans have significantly fewer number of dependents.

Prodigy users typically have more dependents, with 20.9 percent having two dependents, and 9.8 percent having three or more dependents.

- Overall, female users report having fewer dependents than males—63.1 percent for women vs. 60.0 percent for men with no dependents.

Education

While the U.S. users are more likely to have a college degree (36.0 percent vs. 25.4 percent), European users are more likely to have Master's (27.7 percent vs. 18.8 percent) and Doctoral degrees (13.7 percent vs. 4.06 percent). While the percentages may differ, there are no significant differences between European and U.S. response profiles.

Continued

EXHIBIT 2   (Continued)

Both the U.S. and Europe have the nearly same percent (1.8 percent) of users who have completed grammar school. This population of younger users has increased from the last survey.

Compared to the second survey, these users have fewer advanced degrees, but the same number of college graduates (34 percent).

More women have college (37.4 percent) and Master's (24.0 percent) degrees vs the men users (34.3 percent college and 18.7 percent Master's). Though more men have Doctoral degrees (7.84 percent men vs 4.4 percent women), there are no significant differences between response distributions across gender.

Income

This was the most sensitive question asked in the general survey, with 15.7 percent of the respondents choosing to select the "Rather not say!" option—nearly seven times higher than other similar questions.

The below analyses were performed by the Hermes team. The Hermes team develops and analyzes the consumer attitudes and preferences portions of these surveys.

- The overall median income is between $50,000 and $60,000 U.S. dollars, with an estimated average income of $69,000.

- European respondents continue to lag in income, with an average income of $53,500 U.S. dollars.

- 18.3 percent of the women surveyed would "Rather not say!" their income, whereas 14.5 percent of the men chose this response. This, nearly one in five, non-response interferes with robust gender comparisons between incomes.

Statistical examination of the response profiles for women and men do not show significant differences with respect to income.

Occupation

Computer (31.4 percent) and Educational (23.7 percent) occupations still represent the majority of respondents. Professional (21.9 percent), Management (12.2 percent), and "other" occupations (10.8 percent) fill out the other categories.

As expected, there is a high degree of dependence between income and occupation. Europeans tend to be predominantly in Education (36.4 percent) and Computers (33.4 percent), whereas the U.S. sample contained mainly Computer (31.1 percent) and are about equally divided amongst the Professional (22.9 percent) and Educational (21.6 percent) professions.

- There are fewer women than men in Computers (26.5 percent women vs. 32.4 percent men) and Management (10.5 percent women vs 12.7 percent men), but more women fall into the "other" occupation category (15.7 percent women vs. 9.9 percent men).

- Educational and Professional occupations show marginal differences between gender.

Source: *The Hermes Project* (http://www-personal.umich.edu~sgupta/hermes) third annual survey, July 1995.

With Internet-based Dutch auctions as its concept, ILI was incorporated in late 1995 and, with $2 million in the bank, it opened its doors for business in the Spring of 1996. Most of the principals had backgrounds in consumer goods, particularly in consumer electronics such as stereo equipment and cellular phones. See Exhibit 3 for brief biographies of company officers and directors.

Technology

The core of ILI's online auction was a WWW site and custom software written for ILI by contract software developer, Focus Technologies Networks in Mississauga, Ontario. The software was a combination of hypertext markup language (HTML), for the site's appearance, and Java (Sun Microsystems' new Internet-based programming language), for the inner workings of the auction itself. The software ran on a high-performance Alpha workstation from Digital Equipment Corporation (DEC); the workstation was capable of handling 50,000 transactions per hour.

When a user connected to ILI's WWW site he or she would see ILI's logo and a brief explanation of Dutch auctions. The user could then choose between, as appropriate, one icon for U.S. customers and another one for Canadian customers. "We thought about running the same auction in both countries," said Godin. "But for various reasons, including taxes, customs' regulations and logistics, we decided to run two separate auctions." The ILI auction had the same core components as its Dutch namesake. There were three continuously updated counters: a unit counter that showed the number of units remaining; a time clock that counted down as auction time ran out; and a price display that showed the price's steady decline over time. While it was uncertain how much of the preceding constituted an ILI innovation, ILI had gone ahead and applied for various patents and copyrights to protect both the appearance of the screen (the three timers) and the algorithm for how the underlying software managed all the transactions in real-time.

At present, ILI ran everything over a dedicated ISDN (128 Kbps) link to the remote Mississauga site where it kept its DEC Alpha server (see Exhibit 4). (For security reasons, the server was kept off-site and that location was secret.) From that remote site a fractional T1 (up to 1.544 Mbps) link connected ILI's server to the Internet. As the number of transactions per hour began to heat up, the company moved to a new Mississauga location where it had full access to a high-speed T3 line (44 Mbps).

The Auction

A user could watch an auction in progress without entering any personal information, but they had to register for the auction by entering mailing and credit card information if they wanted to buy. Before

---

EXHIBIT 3   Management and Director Biographies

Paul Godin—President

Mr. Paul Godin, founder of Internet Liquidators, was most recently a Senior Vice President, Corporate Sales and Marketing, for Completely Mobile Inc., a Canadian company, which designs and markets wireless data systems. He had extensive marketing and management background spanning twenty years in retail and wholesale electronics and computer markets.

Before joining Completely Mobile, Godin was Vice President and General Manager of Casio Canada Inc., makers of calculators and household electronics goods. From 1990 to 1993, Godin served as Vice President, Sales and Marketing, for Alpine Electronics of Canada Inc., and prior to that he privately consulted to Canadian Airlines, H.J. Heinz, and Clarion Canada.

Godin built his technical background as Director of Corporate and Client Services with Star Data Systems of Markham, Ontario. From 1986 to 1989 he helped Star Data through its start-up phase to an installed base of 5,000 users.

Godin had travelled extensively in Asia, the U.S. and in Europe. He counted among his charitable endeavours being a board member and the treasurer for BACCHUS Canada, a non-profit organization dealing with student wellness.

Jeff Lymburner—President, ILI U.S.A.

Mr. Jeff Lymburner was President from 1990 to 1995 of Completely Mobile Inc., a company that he started and grew to five retail outlets.

In the 1980s, Lymburner held senior positions with responsibilities for advertising, purchasing, store management, sales management, and strategic planning for Multitech Warehouse Direct, a national consumer electronics chain. Lymburner helped build this retail chain from the start-up level to some 50 stores and annual revenues in excess of $100 million. He left the position of National Manager Corporate Sales for Multitech to start his own business.

Lymburner was a former President of the Cellular Industry Dealer Association and was currently a member of its executive committee, as well as being President of the Bell Mobility Dealers Association.

Robert W. A. Joynt—Vice President Merchandising, U.S.A.

Mr. Robert Joynt was most recently Vice President of Sales and Marketing for Logitech Electronics Inc., and prior to that President of Koss Limited and Vice President of Koss Corporation. Joynt spent the preceding 18 years in the consumer electronics industry.

Nathan Freedman—Director of Technical Operations

Mr. Nathan Freedman was from Completely Mobile's Wireless Data Division, where he worked from 1989 to 1996 and was most recently the Technical Director. He worked with clients on providing turnkey solutions for field force automation. He had experience with many Microsoft computer products and operating systems, including Microsoft Office, computer network protocols, voice and data communications, web page design, Microsoft Windows NT, and Internet communications.

T. Christopher Bulger—Chief Financial Officer

Mr. Chris Bulger was a partner with HDL Capital Corporation. From 1991 to 1993 he was Vice President of Finance with Erin Maax Canada Corp., and from 1981 to 1988 he managed the business turnaround and ultimate sale of Murray G. Bulger & Associates Ltd. His corporate finance background comes from 1988 to 1991 in the merchant banking group of Central Capital Corporation, and he began his career in 1980 as a Research Analyst with Midland Doherty Ltd. Bulger is a CFA and holds an MBA from the European Institute of Business Administration (INSEAD).

EXHIBIT 3 (Continued)

Brent Bowes—Corporate Controller

Mr. Bowes was most recently a senior accountant in the mergers and acquisitions group of Deloitte & Touche, a professional accounting firm. Prior to joining Deloitte & Touche, Mr. Bowes had manufacturing and consumer sales experience in a variety of managerial roles.

Dr. Duncan G. Copeland—Director

Dr. Copeland was a consultant in information management with Copeland & Co. He was a past professor of Information Management at The University of Western Ontario's Ivey School of Business. Copeland had consulting practice in introducing new technologies to financial services firms in both the U.S. and Canada. Dr. Copeland was the co-author of *Waves of Change: Business Evolution through Information Technology*.

Frank Clegg—Director

Mr. Clegg was President of Microsoft Canada. He is an International Vice President, Director of Microsoft International and has managerial responsibility for Canada and U.S. control region.

EXHIBIT 4 ILI Operations

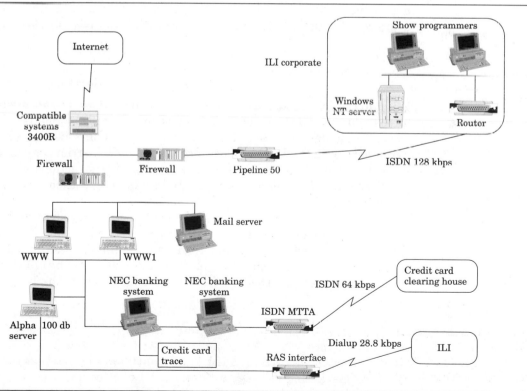

entering the auction they were free to look at information on what products were coming up for sale and information on how ILI ran its auctions—as well as information on ILI's online security precautions.

The basic auction screen comprised five elements: three continuously updated counters, a picture of the product up for auction (with a short description), and an icon to be pressed when a user wanted to lock in his or her price. The counters were arrayed across the bottom of the screen, from left to right they were: the number of units left, the price, and amount of time remaining. The time would tick down in preset increments (usually around 10 seconds) and as it did, the price would fall by similar increments.

For example, in a recent auction, a single Northwestern golf club was auctioned. Advertised as having a $99.00 retail price, the auction clock started ticking with five minutes on the clock, a price of $90, and with six units available. Every seven seconds the display was updated to show the number of units left and the new price. This process continued until all the units were gone, or, in this case, until time ran out. At present, ILI ran only two auction sessions per day: one at lunch time and one in the evening from 7:00 P.M. to 10:00 P.M. The original plan was that until there was sufficient interest, ILI wouldn't run Dutch auctions all day long. But Godin had recently decided to alter that plan. He would run traditional, "Yankee auctions" in off-hours, perhaps, he hoped, building site traffic. Yankee auctions were traditional auctions: users could register bids and prices rose rather than fell.

Security

With all the commotion about Internet security, ILI knew that it would have to do its utmost to placate nervous consumers. ILI signed up both Visa and MasterCard as credit card payment suppliers, and it reached agreement with the Bank of Nova Scotia to clear Visa transactions and with the Bank of Montreal to clear MasterCard transactions. ILI was the first Canadian company to get the banks behind them for online credit card clearance.

On its WWW site, ILI also allowed users to enter registration information into encrypted electronic forms using appropriate browsers (i.e., Microsoft and Netscape), or to register offline by calling a 1-800 number. Godin hoped that this would placate consumers by offering an alternative to sending their credit card information over the Internet.

Sales and Marketing

Newness meant uncertainty. ILI knew that it would be important to make its marketing message as simple and non-technical as possible. It reduced the focus on the technology and put more emphasis on benefits like free and simple access to significant discounts on brand name products. ILI put out that message in flyers distributed to homes in major Canadian cities, in radio advertising, and on its WWW site itself. The company also put "banner" ads to be run on high-traffic WWW sites like Pathfinder, Lycos and Yahoo.

As time went on, ILI envisioned running specific advertising programs for specific times of the year. For example, it would create special programs just for Christmas, or for Mother's Day or Father's Day. While the initial roll-out was for Canada and the U.S. only, Godin was already receiving e-mail messages from people in other countries who had found ILI's site. For example, he had recently received a message from someone in South Africa who had been interested in the ILI auction. As Godin told the South African, ILI was already planning to go outside North America, perhaps to Europe as early as 1997.

In addition to being a good corporate citizen, ILI was always looking for ways to stretch its marketing dollars. It had recently signed up with Recording Artists, Athletes, and Actors Against Drunk-Driving (RADD), a student-oriented initiative aimed at increasing awareness about the perils of drunk-driving. With such stars on board as Phil Collins, Elton John, and Hootie & the Blowfish, ILI felt confident that RADD would make a big splash. As part of its involvement with RADD, ILI would host the RADD WWW page, as well as having ILI's WWW address and name on the bottom of posters that would blanket more than 3,000 universities and colleges across North America. Godin knew that the purchasing power of students was open to question, but he hoped that RADD would give him some inexpensive marketing—as well as raise ILI's profile among potential consumers.

The other side of ILI's marketing equation required getting the word out to suppliers. For the auction to work, ILI needed a steady stream of products that it could offer to consumers. To get those products ILI had a team of dedicated salespeople (two at first, that grew to six, and there would be more later) that called on manufacturers and retailers to explain the ILI auction and get them to sign up as suppliers. As a supplier, a company would provide ILI with products at the right times and prices for ILI to include them in its auction.

On the flip side, ILI was working on creating cross-promotions with suppliers, convincing the suppliers that they could help ILI promote its auction and, thereby, help both ILI and themselves as their larger advertising budgets attracted more users to ILI's auctions. "The U.S. has more early adopters," said ILI's Jeff Lymburner. "They aren't afraid of new ideas like this, and we think it will be a good place for us to focus." With that in mind, in September of 1996 ILI opened a U.S. headquarters and sales office in Tampa, Florida. Why Tampa? "I like Tampa," said Lymburner, who had moved there. "And given the nature of our business, location doesn't matter too much."

Distribution and Logistics

ILI was almost a virtual corporation. Not only did it not manufacture anything, ILI did not even take title to the goods that it sold until they were sold to the end-user and received by ILI at its distribution center. "We want to remain flexible," said Godin. The company had one warehouse in Toronto for product distribution and another in Atlanta, Georgia. The warehouses themselves were provided under contract to ILI. Management of those warehouses was outsourced—in Toronto to R.V. Storage, and in Atlanta, Georgia, to A.E.I.

ILI turned goods around in a hurry. Each day manufacturers were told what products and quantities had been sold in the previous day's auctions. Those products had to be shipped immediately to ILI's warehouses. Within hours of arriving in the warehouse, goods were put onto Purolator or UPS trucks, both of which maintained a terminal at the warehouses, and shipped to the person who had bought them. ILI allowed no inventory to be kept overnight at its warehouses.

As much as possible, ILI had automated this process. For example, when a user locked in a price during the auction, ILI's software automatically calculated shipping charges and all applicable taxes to the customer's address based on the customer's zip code or postal code. That way customers received goods as quickly as possible but were never surprised at the price tag. The shipping and price policies did create some interesting problems. "When we first started shipping products," said Lymburner, "Paul [Godin] had to go down to one of our suppliers' warehouses near Windsor and measure boxes with a ruler." ILI's couriers shipped by size and weight, not information that all manufacturers could give ILI.

COMPANY FINANCIALS

Paying for the Business

ILI received a percentage of the retail price of every product that it sold. For example, if a product sold for $100, ILI might get $10 for having auctioned the product. ILI kept its $10 and remitted the balance to the manufacturer. More specifically, actual commissions paid to ILI ranged from 6.5 percent (for electronics) to 14 percent for casual outerwear. ILI, in effect, received commission payment immediately; it only remitted payment to the manufacturer when the actual product showed up at its Toronto or Atlanta warehouse.

While the Dutch auction was ILI's initial core business, it was also running a "cyber mall" on its WWW site. Promoted as the first true factory-direct online mall, visitors would see a list of various product categories, from sporting goods to clothing and computer equipment.

Users entered the mall by clicking on any product category that looked interesting. By doing that, they could see the names of companies that were offering selected products through ILI's mall. By clicking again on the name of a company, users saw a list of the actual products and prices up for sale in that category from a given manufacturer. If a product looked interesting, a user could click on it for more information and for a small picture. And if what they saw looked like it would fit the bill, clicking on a "Purchase" button would bring the user into another screen where they could confirm their personal information and their interest in purchasing this product.

"Until the auction business takes off," said Godin, "we're going to see if we can't supplement the business with the cyber mall."

A Public Company

Just before opening for business, ILI went public in a reverse takeover (RTO). In a share exchange agreement dated May 15, 1996, ILI completed an RTO of Avonlea Capital Corporation, a shell company listed OTC (over-the-counter) on the Canadian Dealing Network (CDN). The deal resulted in the issuance of 8,877,500 shares and 1,750,000 warrants of Avonlea in exchange for 6,377,500 purchased common shares of ILI and 2,500,000 units of ILI. There were two types of units. Series A units were debentures convertible to 1,000,000 common shares of ILI, and 1,000,000 ILI warrants. Series B units were debentures convertible to 1,500,000 common shares of ILI and 750,000 ILI warrants. All of these debentures converted at the closing of the deal on May 28, 1996. Total consideration for the deal was $7,102,000, made up of $0.80 per common share and $0.80 per unit attached.

In addition to making their shares considerably more liquid, ILI thought that "being public might make it easier for companies to deal with us," explained Godin. He added: "As well as giving us access to equity markets to raise money." The RTO was a somewhat unusual move for a technology company and, for various reasons, including, said Godin, "mistakes by the market-maker in our stock," the market didn't respond well to ILI's new status (see Exhibit 5).

ILI offered its managers and directors an assortment of shares and options. For example, after the RTO, executives of ILI controlled 49.5 percent of ILI's shares. Of those shares, approximately three million were put into performance escrow and held by a lawyer. The ILI Board set up four performance objectives upon completion of each of which the three million shares would be released to management in equal amounts. First, the ILI WWW site needed to be delivered on time. Second, the WWW site had to be delivered within budget. Third, ILI management had to establish 100 product suppliers willing to ante up for the online auction. Finally, management had to meet a specific revenue

EXHIBIT 5   Stock Performance (ILI Share Price—May 25 to November 3, 1996)

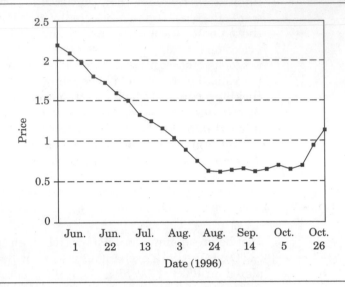

Date (1996)

target by October 31, 1996. While the first three conditions were met, the last condition was later modified to make the date December 31, and to add that in the alternative, management would have to raise one million in additional capital from an appropriate outside investor by the same date.

The Business Model and Forecasts

ILI forecast that revenue would be seasonal, with approximately 30 percent to 40 percent of yearly sales coming during the Christmas season, and equally as much coming from the holidays, like Mother's Day, Father's Day and Valentine's Day. The company forecast gross revenues of $27 M for 1996 (corresponding to about $3.6 M in ILI revenues), and looked for $73.3 M in revenues ($9.7 M to ILI) next year, all on the way toward $135 M in gross revenue ($18 M to ILI) by 1998.

Based on these forecasts for the cyber mall and, more importantly, the online auction, ILI estimated a break-even of approximately $100,000 per month of ILI revenue. More than half of ILI's operating costs came from salaries, but close to half of ILI's were commission-driven and their salaries should rise and fall with actual business.

Historical Operating Results

A set of recent financials is included as Exhibit 6.

OPTIONS

It was a busy time for ILI. On the one hand it was rolling out its auction across North America; at the same time it was trying to maintain the always delicate balance between spending cash to get business, and conserving cash to stay in business. All the while, Godin and ILI's management and Board of Directors wrestled with an assortment of options, partners and ideas for getting ILI flying. Godin and partner were the largest shareholders and had appointed most of the current Board: they wanted—and needed—ILI to succeed.

The Online Services

If the World Wide Web was analogous to a collection of television channels, then online services were like television networks that created their own private channels and then charged for access to those channels. These services knew the online market and knew how to make it easy for non-technical people to get online.

But their future wasn't all roses. Critics argued that the days of proprietary online services, like AOL, were already numbered. They argued that consumers didn't need all that hand-holding, that Internet-based software had already caught, if not surpassed, the best that online services had to offer. The implication? By joining forces with an online service, ILI might be consigning itself to a technological backwater. Perhaps if ILI could stick things out a bit longer on the Internet it might find itself amply rewarded. Godin was looking at the two biggest online services, AOL and CompuServe. Did one of them make more sense than the other as a partner?

AOL

The way Godin saw it, AOL might be just the ticket. As the largest and best known online service, it was already successful at selling goods and services to its six million subscribers. And AOL had stated repeatedly that it was trying to create or buy new kinds of content—new services that would keep subscribers entertained and online. AOL definitely knew how to funnel subscribers and get their attention. But AOL had detractors. It had been in the news for its controversial billing practices (an

EXHIBIT 6   Internet Liquidators International Inc.

(formerly Avonlea Capital Corporation)
Consolidated Financial Statements
(Unaudited—prepared by management), August 31, 1996

Assets, 1996
Current
Cash and short-term investments	$288,971
Accounts receivable	79,148
Other receivables	36,856
Deposits and prepaid expenses	36,295
	441,270
Capital Assets	528,090
	$969,360

Liabilities
Current
Accounts payable	$308,964

Shareholders' Equity
Share capital	2,025,954
Deficit	(1,365,558)
	660,396
	$969,360

Revenue, 1996
Fees and other income	$37,488

General and administrative expenses
Advertising and promotion	360,590
Depreciation	72,828
Filing fees	9,374
Investor relations	53,529
Office and general	143,729
Professional fees	189,502
Salaries and consulting	385,586
Travel and entertainment	62,762
	1,277,900
Net loss for the period	(1,240,412)
Deficit, beginning of period	(125,146)
Deficit, end of period	(1,365,558)

EXHIBIT 6   (Continued)

(formerly Avonlea Capital Corporation)
Consolidated Financial Statements
(Unaudited—prepared by management), August 31, 1996

Net Inflow (Outflow) of Cash Related to the Following Activities, 1996

Operating

Net loss for the period	$(1,240,412)
Items not affecting cash	
Depreciation	72,828
	(1,167,584)
Change in non-cash operating working capital items	147,708
	(1,019,876)
Investing	
Purchase of capital assets	(536,788)
Financing	
Issuance of common shares (net of financing costs)	1,774,754
Net cash inflow during the period	218,090
Cash, beginning of period	70,881
Cash, end of period	$288,971

ongoing class action suit protested AOL's practice of rounding time spent online up to the nearest minute). Internet users turned up their collective noses at AOL's heavy-handed marketing tactics and looked askance at AOL's censorship of what its users could say while online. There was even a highly vocal Internet-based community of AOL critics.[3]

Would ILI get lost in the shuffle if it were folded into billion-dollar AOL? And what would it mean with Frank Clegg, Microsoft Canada's President, on ILI's Board?

And there were cautionary omens about AOL's deal-making. In June of 1995, AOL announced an $11 million (U.S.) deal to buy Global Network Navigator—a subsidiary of publishing company O'Reilly & Associates — to create its own Internet service provider. One year later, a management exodus at GNN, firings and general confusion about GNN's overall direction had led Brainerd of *Wired* magazine to call the GNN/AOL tie-up "a failure directly traceable to Steve Case, AOL's CEO, lack of vision."

---

[3]Of the many WWW sites and newsgroups devoted to AOL bashing, the best known and most comprehensive was located at http://www.aolsucks.org.

In addition, there were signs that AOL itself might not be in the best shape. In October of 1996, AOL took a $385 million restructuring charge—more than five times as large as AOL's cumulative pre-tax earnings in the preceding five fiscal years combined. The charge came as AOL simultaneously introduced flat-rate pricing for unlimited use—an attempt to stem the flow of AOL subscribers to cheaper Internet access providers. The charge also marked the elimination of a controversial accounting practice, one wherein AOL amortized subscriber-related marketing expenses over two years rather than expensing them as they were incurred. Long-time AOL critics welcomed the move, calling AOL's reported profits a "house of cards."[4]

CompuServe

CompuServe was the oldest online service, started in 1979. With approximately 3.2 million subscribers, CompuServe targeted the more experienced PC user in both the home and office. Its focus was on breadth and depth of professional and business oriented content. CompuServe provided over 2,000 content areas such as finance, current events and online reference, as well as approximately 900 managed forums where subscribers with similar interests could meet and discuss subjects of interest. CompuServe had an affiliated company in Japan called Nifty-Serve. It had 1.7 million subscribers.

CompuServe had lost some of its momentum of late, most of that going to competitor AOL. CompuServe was trying to address its problems by moving aggressively to the Internet and by locking up exclusive arrangements with content providers. For example, it had reached an early deal with Pathfinder, the umbrella under which many of Time-Warner's publications appeared on the Internet, to host a subscriptions-only version of that site.

But some people had suggested to Godin that ILI's online auction might work better in Japan than in North America—and CompuServe was the only one of the Big Three with a significant Japanese presence. Godin wondered if that wasn't something he should be thinking more seriously about.

Microsoft Network

The smallest of the Big Three online services, with only 750,000 subscribers, MSN had changed considerably since it was first announced in late 1994. Microsoft's original plan had been to create a direct com-

---

[4]Sandberg, J. "America Online Plans $385 Million Charge—About-Face on Accounting Raises Hard Questions about Past, Future Net," October 30, 1996 p. 1.

petitor to AOL and CompuServe, complete with the similar proprietary network of telephone connections. But the Internet had changed all of that. Proprietary online services, like MSN, looked increasingly anachronistic by early 1996, and Microsoft changed with the times. It announced that MSN would migrate to being WWW-based—all future content would be accessible through the Internet, albeit only with a paid subscription to MSN.

With Frank Clegg on ILI's Board of Directors, all options Microsoft-related had to be taken seriously. But even without Clegg, ILI would have looked very closely at MSN. Microsoft might have been a late arrival to the online scene, but there was no doubting its staying power: Microsoft's war chest was larger than many of its competitors' annual revenues.

More Online Options

The traditional online services weren't the only options. Both Microsoft and AOL had announced big plans to roll out the electronic equivalent of local newspapers in cities across North America. Godin wondered if either of these new services might not make more sense than an online service.

On the other hand, for all the excitement about Cityscape and Digital City, they were unproven concepts. Recent Digital City launches in Washington and Los Angeles seemed to be going well, but it was early in the game. Maybe people would take to them, but maybe people might just stick to their morning paper and leave Cityscape, Digital City, and, more importantly, ILI, out in the online cold.

Digital City

In mid-summer, AOL announced Digital Cities, a series of local guides for 88 cities. AOL planned to spin off Digital Cities, an in-house service started in the fall of 1995, in a handful of target markets, into a nationwide provider of local news, weather, traffic, sports and other information in 88 areas. The Tribune Company would have a minority stake in the Digital Cities venture and use its current newspaper operations to help AOL launch services in Chicago, southern Florida, and Hampton Roads, Virginia. Access to local Digital City news would be free to AOL subscribers.

AOL wanted to be able to produce, as well as deliver, original content to the growing readership of professional online news and information services. "There's a potential for building billion-dollar media franchises directly on the Web," said Adam Schoenfeld, President of research company Jupiter Communications. "It's an opportunity we haven't had since the dawn of television."

As the last of the proprietary online services to stake out Internet turf, AOL was attempting to augment its dwindling online services revenue with this new offering.

Cityscape

Microsoft announced that in 1997 it would offer competitive online city entertainment guides, one designed to help residents get the most out of their cities. The project, code-named "Cityscape," would combine Internet technology and entertainment content published by editorial teams based in each city. Cityscape would be supported by advertising and available as a free service on the World Wide Web and as a featured offering on MSN. The debut guide, for Seattle, was scheduled to be online in the first quarter of 1997. By mid-year, it would be joined online by entertainment guides for New York, Boston and San Francisco, with 10 to 15 cities worldwide expected to be online by the end of the year.

"Cityscape will feature information about movies, restaurants, music, arts and local entertainment events," said Michael Goff, Editor in Chief of Cityscape. "We're going to go far beyond listings to forge a new type of local entertainment service using technology and editorial expertise to speak to each resident individually," Goff said, referring to the personalization technology that will allow the editors to filter content and tailor recommendations based upon a user's personal interests or location. "In fact, we'll have as many front pages as we have users."

Microsoft also announced that Cityscape would have relationships with a variety of local companies that provide additional talent and resources. For example, Seattle associates include Quickfish Media Inc., publisher of *Seattle Weekly* and *Eastsideweek,* and Sasquatch Books, publisher of the top-selling *Best Places* guidebooks. Microsoft said that it was always looking for new alliances where they made sense.

Retailers

In brainstorming their options, Godin and Lymburner had come up with other ideas too. With their background in consumer goods, not surprisingly, the two had thought about tying up more closely with traditional retailers like a Wal-Mart or a Zellers. Those companies knew the ins and outs of moving products at the right price and in big volume. If ILI got closer with one or more of those vendors, there would be one big marketing machine at ILI's disposal. Like so many of ILI's options, there was no easy answer here either. While retailers know retail, they don't know the online world. Would picking up a flyer in a store translate into a visit to ILI's WWW site? It was hard to know, but ILI's early experience with sending out flyers to homes in large cities across Canada had been a bust. But maybe retailers wouldn't even want anything to do with ILI. It was entirely possible that they might see ILI as a potential competitor, not a potential partner. Perhaps opening up to Zellers or Wal-Mart would only tip ILI's hand to these potential competitors. The next thing ILI knew, it might be faced with more online competitors rather than new resourceful allies.

Expansion

With the Tampa office now open, ILI was already thinking about Europe. It would need more bandwidth and bigger servers, but it was virgin territory. If ILI could get an early toehold, "it could mean big bucks," as Lymburner said. More bandwidth and faster servers would be expensive though. New Alpha workstations started at $75,000 and went upward; high-speed communication lines were in excess of $1,000 per month. But ILI's concept really hadn't yet been tested with crowds of users trying to take part in a big auction. It was hard to know, on a technical level, how well the auction would work on a much larger scale. ILI tests suggested that the system would be able to handle the load. But would the real work be different? Would, for example, lag (the time it takes a signal to travel the Internet) make an auction unworkable with large numbers of people?

Perhaps more importantly, ILI faced big language problems. Dealing in North America meant dealing in English. Opening for business in Europe meant a dizzying array of new languages. That meant time and that meant money.

Status Quo

While it sometimes didn't get much attention, Godin knew there was always the option of doing nothing at all, or at least not giving up any of the company yet. ILI could keep working to raise its profile and to build a clientele. Maybe ILI was right on the cusp; maybe a few more months of word of mouth would take ILI over the top. If so, then the next round of suitors would have to look a lot deeper in their wallets: ILI as a demonstrably viable business would be worth a lot more than it was at present as a young company with a very short track record.

But the status quo felt like a big gamble. Godin thought that many of the options he was looking at could get ILI going faster than ILI could do it alone. Maybe the bottom line was that ILI had a good idea, but it was still too early to make ILI work as a stand-alone Internet-only business.

Financing

All the while, ILI, like most startups, needed cash. Godin knew that he could always issue more equity. He estimated that ILI needed at least $4 M; that would mean issuing approximately 3.3 M shares at the current $1.20 share price. Would there be a market for such a large issue? Godin also knew that debt, at least not a significant amount, was not an option. ILI's limited operating history, as well as its variable cash flows and few assets, would turn most banks into shrinking violets. Not to mention that debt would sorely constrain ILI's flexibility.

Time Running Short

Something had to happen. Perhaps a whole bunch of somethings. Godin felt pressure to get ILI moving; things changed so quickly on the Internet that interesting ideas could go through an entire life cycle from fresh to old in the space of months. He had to attract enough people to ILI's online auction so that the concept would go from interesting to profitable. But what would it take? If it was to be a new partner, what were ILI's terms? What could he live with? It was time to prove that the Dutch auction concept could be as viable in the new pastures of the Internet as it had been in the fields of Holland back in 1887.

Chapter 7

Internet Payment Mechanisms

The term "killer app" has been used on many occasions to describe this or that Internet application. None, however, is perhaps more deserving of that title than an application to facilitate payments over the Internet. The Internet is replete with buyers and sellers, but it lacks a well-accepted, secure, and accessible payments system. This has been noted by many as a key stumbling block to increased commerce on the Internet. Many applications have tried to fill the gap. By mid-1999, over 80 different payment mechanisms were vying for online business.

Most Internet payment schemes fall into one of three categories: credit card applications, check or debit applications, and electronic cash applications or smart cards. Some systems are very sophisticated, requiring special software or hardware. Others are extremely simple, requiring nothing more than an Internet browser. Some use powerful encryption, others use little or no security. Some are designed for very small transactions, typically less than a cent, while others only work efficiently with higher-valued transactions. Credit card applications are the most popular Internet payment systems but suffer from perceptions of poor security and cannot easily handle small transactions. Check or debit applications are becoming popular for such transactions as online bill and mortgage payments, but most systems are proprietary, often restricting clients to a single financial institution. Electronic cash and smart card applications have the advantage of being designed specifically for the Internet but have had difficulty attracting the critical mass of buyers and sellers necessary to make themselves viable.

The first case of this chapter looks at an Internet payment systems pioneer. In 1994, First Virtual Holdings Incorporated (FVHI) developed a credit card–based system for use on the Internet. What made the system unique was that users didn't have to divulge their credit card numbers to merchants or anyone else. Instead, to make purchases, buyers would use an alias provided to them by FVHI. The advantage of the system was that buyers could make secure online transactions using only an Internet browser and e-mail. No extra software was needed. However, FVHI was not alone in chasing this market opportunity. The company was competing against much better known and better financed competitors. The case includes elements of information systems and strategic management.

The last two cases deal with Mondex. Mondex is an electronic cash application that resides on a smart card. Smart cards have a number of advantages over credit and debit cards. In addition to a magnetic strip, they contain a tiny computer that allows them to store data and carry multiple applications. They can also support chip-to-chip transactions, meaning that two card holders can exchange value without having to go through an intermediary such as a financial institution. Mondex cards can be used in specially modified pay phones, vending machines, and parking meters. In this respect, they resemble cash. But unlike cash, Mondex can be used to make purchases online.

Mondex Canada owns the license to promote Mondex in Canada. Both cases take the perspective of the director of marketing communications, whose responsibility is to organize the roll-out of Mondex. The case outlines the many roll-out options as well as other strategic decisions to be made, such as which applications apart from Mondex, if any, should be placed on the smart cards. The Mondex (A) case includes aspects of information technology, marketing and strategic management. The Mondex (B) case is set a few months after the first. Unexpectedly, one of the main sponsoring financial institutions pulled out of further active cooperation with Mondex, and the pilot test program already underway had to be canceled. Usage of the Mondex cards in the pilot site was below expected levels. The director must decide what steps to take next. The case is a good example of the management of new-technology diffusion.

First Virtual Holdings Incorporated (A)

By Professor Sid L. Huff and Michael Wade

First Virtual Holdings Incorporated (FVHI, www.firstvirtual.com) Chairman and CEO Lee Stein was driving along the San Diego Freeway thinking over the last 36 months. He felt satisfied that what was so recently just an idea, was now a reality. He knew that he was riding the crest of a wave, one which was about to change the face of commerce. It had become accepted wisdom that commerce on the Internet would blossom and flourish. The only real questions were when—and, after the dust settled—who would be left on the playing field? By any standard, the progress made by the company he co-founded had been spectacular. First Virtual had become one of the most recognized names in the nascent world of online commerce. The First Virtual Internet Payment System (FVIPS) had proven itself to be secure and efficient. Nothing, however, was guaranteed in this business, and Stein worried whether his company had the backing and the resources to make it through the inevitable industry shakeup.

LEE STEIN AND FIRST VIRTUAL
HOLDINGS INCORPORATED

Stein had not always been in the information technology business. In fact, by trade he was an accountant and lawyer. While Stein was attending the Villanova University School of Law in Pennsylvania he saw an episode of the Merv Griffin show between classes. The guest was Hollywood producer Allan Carr, who talked about his business manager. A career as a business manager sounded "pretty cool," recalls Stein, who began knocking on doors in Hollywood after working for Coopers and Lybrand. "I was pretty highly trained," he said. "And there was no downside. All somebody could say was no."

Before long, Stein created his own company and signed his first client, Bo Goldman, an Academy Award–winning screenwriter for *One Flew Over the Cuckoo's Nest* and later a Golden Globe winner for *Scent of a Woman*. Other well-known clients followed, including Gene Hackman, Matthew Broderick, Rod Stewart, Journey and Men at Work.

Stein was developing his entertainment practice in Beverly Hills when his wife, a CPA and then just 24, developed a degenerative inflammatory disease of the spine. The couple was devastated, but refused to accept the prognosis and began exploring alternative remedies, including practices from the Far East. Some remedies were just "kooky California" ideas, but primarily through yoga, she was able to conquer the disease. Eventually, the two studied meditation in Kathmandu with a Tibetan lama, as the experience with the illness led them to re-order their priorities to health and family.

By the mid-1980s, the couple sold their entertainment business and moved to San Diego. Stein became involved in a number of real estate ventures. He also acted as chairman of the San Diego Stadium Authority, home to the Padres and Chargers. A self-described "techno-junkie," Stein was travelling to New York City when he began asking questions of a fellow traveller who was using a wireless device to communicate with the Internet. The other traveller was Einar Stefferud, a computer-savvy Internet veteran, MBA and expert on global messaging systems, who later jointly founded First Virtual with Stein. "He came out of a whole different world. And worlds collide. So we had to invest some serious effort in understanding each other, but we've always worked as a team," says Stefferud.

Along with Stein and Stefferud, the other founding members of First Virtual were Nathaniel S. Borenstein Ph.D., the primary author of MIME, the Internet standard for multimedia and multilingual mail messages, and Marshall T. Rose Ph.D., a leader in the development and implementation of key global Internet standards. For a biography of the four founders, see Exhibit 1.

Despite Stein's non-technical background, Stefferud credits Stein with the leadership role in bringing forth ideas during the founding group's initial meetings in early 1994, and then in developing First Virtual's business plan. "Lee became the hub of all the spokes to carry it forward," as Stefferud put it.

Stein recalled those early discussions:

> I was told that what we wanted to do was impossible. I was reminded that a lot of people had tried to build Internet commerce concepts before, and none had ever really worked. But I kept asking a series of questions, until somebody turned around and said, "Yeah, that could work." And then they turned my broad, goofy, upside-down concepts into reality.

Initiated by Dr. Borestein, the original idea was simple: sell jokes by electronic mail on the Internet. "Every time you turned on your machine, there would be a joke waiting for you. If you liked it, you'd pay a penny. If you didn't like it, you'd pay nothing," Stein explains. A penny a day collected from millions of Internet users could add up to significant numbers, the team realized. But the hang-up was the lack of a payment system. All four recognized the need for a secure, simple and widespread payment system for goods and services over the Internet, which led them into the business of electronic payment systems.

The company was built from the ground up to be a true virtual business. Its founders were based in San Diego, Orange County, Silicon Valley, New Jersey and Michigan. The company had no physical offices for its first 15 months of operation. In fact, for awhile no two members of the company had the same zip codes or area codes. Their business cards contained only e-mail addresses and phone numbers. The servers were set up in a high-security EDS facility near Cleveland; work-at-home customer service representatives were hired to answer customer service requests by e-mail while the data lines were routed to an MCI facility in Atlanta; marketing was handled from Washington D.C.; public relations was based in San Diego. The company itself was registered in Cheyenne, Wyoming. Certainly not your typical organization.

EXHIBIT 1   First Virtual's Founders

Nathaniel S. Borenstein, Ph.D.   Primary author of MIME, the Internet standard for multimedia and multilingual mail messages. Borenstein has served as an advisor to national and international agencies. He is a member of the Electronic Frontier Foundation, holds a Ph.D. in computer science from Carnegie-Mellon University and is the author of two books on multimedia and software.

Marshall T. Rose, Ph.D.   Dr. Rose is a leader in the development and implementation of key global standards for electronic messaging and network management. He is the author of seven highly regarded books on Internet technology. Dr. Rose holds a Ph.D. in information and computer science from the University of California, Irvine and is the former area director for network management on the Internet Engineering Steering Group, one of a dozen people responsible for overseeing the global Internet standardization process.

Einar A. Stefferud, M.B.A.   A key contributor to the development of the global Internet since 1975, he is considered to be one of the leading experts on global messaging systems. He has been active in international standards activities through the American National Standards Institute (ANSI) and the International Federation of Information Processing. Named by *Communications Week* as one of the top 10 visionaries in the computer-communications industry, he is an adjunct professor of information and computer science at University of California, Irvine, and holds an MBA from UCLA.

Lee H. Stein, J.D.   An attorney and accountant, he also serves as chairman of Stein & Stein Incorporated, a California-based firm which provided management services to luminaries in the entertainment and music industries. He has been a successful investor in West Coast real estate. He has served as chairman of the Jack Murphy Stadium Authority, San Diego, California and a director of the Scripps Foundation for Medicine and Science, La Jolla, California.

Source: First Virtual web pages: www.firstvirtual.com.

Although the arrangement was flexible and allowed the founders to remain in their physical locations, the initial employees decided to consolidate most of the company's day-to-day operations in San Diego in late 1995. They found that the more mundane aspects of the organization were hampered by physical distances. It was more difficult, for example to maintain employee morale, schedule meetings, keep people up to date and so on. Stein noted,

> There wasn't a big problem when individuals or small groups worked remotely, they would check in regularly so there would be a constant dialogue.

The problem was when clusters of people worked together at a remote site. We would miss all the hallway and water cooler talk.

President Keith Kendrick added, "e-mail is no substitute for face to face meetings in any company, even one as 'virtual' as us." By the summer of 1997, the company employed 96 people organized into five functional groups under CEO Stein and new President Keith Kendrick, and ran all of its day-to-day operations from San Diego.

FVHI launched its first major product, the First Virtual Internet Payment System (FVIPS) in October 1994. By September 1996, the FVIPS was being used by 2,650 merchants and 180,000 consumers in 166 countries.

The First Virtual Internet Payment System (FVIPS)

The FVIPS is based on the principle that no method of data security is truly secure, and that only non-sensitive information should be sent over the Internet. Using the FVIPS, buyers can make purchases using their credit cards, yet never send their credit card numbers over the Internet.

The first step for those who want to use the FVIPS is to send credit card information to First Virtual by traditional means, namely telephone, fax or mail. They are then assigned a "VirtualPIN," which is a series of alphanumeric characters. They use the VirtualPIN as an alias for their credit card numbers to make purchases on the Internet.

The system works as follows. When making a purchase, the buyer sends his or her VirtualPIN to a participating online vendor. The vendor then forwards the buyer's VirtualPIN along with the amount and a brief description of the purchase to FVHI. FVHI uses the buyer's VirtualPIN and its internal network to look up the buyer's e-mail address.

First Virtual then sends an e-mail to the buyer confirming the amount of the purchase. The buyer returns the e-mail to FVHI either confirming the sale, "Yes," or not, "No." If the sale is confirmed by the buyer, FVHI charges the buyer's credit card for the amount of the transaction (via a network not directly connected to the Internet) and sends a confirmation number to the vendor. The vendor then closes the transaction and provides the service, or in the case of goods, ships the merchandise to the buyer.

The buyer also has the option of replying with the word, "Fraud." If a buyer replies to a confirmation request with the word, "Fraud," the sale is automatically cancelled and the matter is turned over to FVHI for investigation.

At no time during this process is the buyer's credit card information typed into a computer connected to the Internet. Nor does any sensitive information pass through the vendor, further reducing the chance of fraud.

Unlike competing systems, the FVIPS does not rely on encryption of data, nor does it require the buyer to use special software or hardware to function. First Virtual's founders envisioned credit card companies having the ability to automatically create and distribute VirtualPINs, thereby creating mass distribution and eliminating the need for the consumer to take any action.

Merchants who wish to become sellers using the FVIPS can sign up at the company's web site. First Virtual has two categories of merchants: Express Merchants and Pioneer Merchants. Express Merchants are typically larger and more established with existing credit card merchant accounts; Express Merchants also have to pass First Virtual's credit approval process. Pioneer Merchants, on the other hand, are typically smaller merchants that might not otherwise qualify for a credit card merchant account.

Merchants pay First Virtual 29 cents per transaction plus 2 per cent of the transaction price for each sale. Express Merchants receive payment from First Virtual after 3–4 days. Pioneer Merchants are paid after 90 days (the legal limit in the U.S. for reversing credit card charges).

As of September 30, 1997, the company had processed over 430,000 FVIPS transactions and had registered more than 3,800 merchants and 240,000 consumers in over 160 countries.

SECURITY

Lee Stein commented on security concerns:

> We may be subject to a one-off attack. In such an attack, a person would have to eavesdrop on a consumer's electronic mail to intercept his or her VirtualPIN. But since the VirtualPIN can be used only with the First Virtual system, the attacker would have to be able to intercept the user's electronic mail, read the confirmation message from First Virtual's computers, and send out a fraudulent reply. A single user can be targeted, but a large scale attack would be very difficult. . . [t]here are too many packets moving . . . to too many different machines.

Director of Development Winn Rindfleisch described the FVIPS as procedural security, not technical security. "Many people think we're anti-encryption, which isn't true at all. In fact, we use encryption and digital signatures when we send messages to our merchants so they know the message is coming from First Virtual." Director of Strategic Business Initiatives Chris Wand added, "If we thought we needed encryption, or that buyers would be comfortable using it, we'd have it. Our challenge in this area is to create a system, which combines convenience for the user, along with a sufficient number of built in 'levels of inconvenience' to deter hackers and minimize the risk of wide spread, automated fraud."

Furthermore, Stein pointed out, "If somebody's account is compromised, the worst thing that happens is that the consumer notices the fraudulent transaction on his or her credit card bill and declines the charge. Put it this way: Our charge-back ratio, which is usually tied to fraud, is extremely low." Stein added,

The biggest misconception is that the words "security" and "encryption" are identical, or even closely related. A more balanced perspective on discussions of Internet commerce can often be obtained by replacing "computer" and "encryption" with "automobile" and "door lock." The mere existence of a door lock does not imply that the ignition keys (or a wallet) should be left inside the car. In general, it is safest to lock your car *and* remove your valuables. Similarly, while encryption can provide a modicum of additional security on the Internet, it is far more important to consider what is being encrypted, and not to encrypt anything that is better kept off the Internet in the first place. In the system we developed, the worst case would be that a single user's account is compromised; in encryption-based systems, however, if a criminal cracks the code, the consequences would be widespread and catastrophic.

FVHI is so confident that its system is safe that it has published the means by which a hacker could break in, though none has yet been able to do so. To prove that sensitive data is susceptible to being intercepted before it is encrypted, First Virtual wrote and distributed a program that simulates how a hacker could circumvent most encryption systems by monitoring keystrokes and checking for input that resembles credit card information. On security concerns, Stein concluded,

We have two advantages over our competition. First of all, technically, we have the right stuff. Our scientists have come up with a significant number of patches to deal with the difficulties of achieving reliable, automated e-mail communications across a myriad e-mail client programs, hundreds of ISPs and loosely implemented e-mail standards in over 160 countries. Our technicians can answer virtually any questions users might have. Fortunately, we don't get many, which brings me to my second point. Unlike other systems out there, ours is simple to understand and simple to use. If you know how to send and receive e-mail, you can buy and sell on the Internet using First Virtual. Other companies have a heck of a time explaining complex encryption mechanisms, public/private keys, key lifetimes and so on to their customers, most of whom are Internet novices.

"Their electronic mail protocol is a pretty low-tech solution to doing Internet commerce, but it has the advantage that it's pretty easy to understand exactly what the likely risks are—unlike some crypto-gizmo protocols," said Alan Bawden, a computer researcher in Cambridge, Massachusetts. "There are risks, the biggest probably being that you have to trust them (First Virtual) with your credit card number. But I probably take a bigger risk when I hand my credit card to the teen-age clerk at the local hardware store."

Stein put it more bluntly: "There has been so much noise out there about this coming software encryption stuff. We believe in encryption and use it here at First Virtual—all of our employees use public key encryption on a daily basis. But the truth is that many users can't even figure out how to use web browsers, let alone turn on and use sophisticated features like encryption."

STRATEGIC ALLIANCES

From the beginning, FVHI's founders recognized that making good strategic alliances with established industry players was critical to its success. They realized that the winners in the race for the Internet commerce market would not necessarily be the companies with the best products, but those who had the largest share of the market. With this in mind, they strove to develop relationships with the biggest and the best in the business.

Strategic Investors:

First USA Paymentech, Inc.

- The third largest processor of bank card transactions in the U.S., processing US$30.9 billion in sales volume and 574 million transactions during 1996.
- Agreed to offer a free 90-day trial VirtualPIN to its credit card customers.
- A First Virtual investor.

Next Century Communications Corporation

- Marketing and lobbying firm specializing in direct response marketing, promotional and fund-raising campaigns.
- A First Virtual investor.

Sybase, Incorporated

- Sixth largest independent software company in the world. Developer of database, middleware and tools products for four major client/server market segments: new media, online transaction processing, mass deployment and data warehousing.
- A First Virtual investor.

GE Capital Corporation

- Diversified financial services company with assets of over US$185 billion. Provides mid-market and specialized financing, specialty

insurance and a variety of consumer services such as car loans, home mortgages and credit cards.
- A First Virtual investor.

First Data Corporation

- Provides credit card and other information processing services to financial institutions, government agencies, insurance companies, merchants and consumers through its network in 120 countries around the world.
- 5.9 billion credit and debit card transactions processed and revenue of US$4.9 billion in 1996.
- A First Virtual investor.

Online Commerce Providers:

Microsoft Corporation

- Microsoft Corp. chose the FVIPS as one of the payment methods for its new Merchant Server software. The Merchant Server software offers easy-to-use templates and other tools to minimize the development costs associated with Internet storefront development. It allows merchants of any size to build an online presence.

Sun Microsystems, Inc.

- The FVIPS will be a "Java cassette" included in the latest version of the Java Commerce Toolkit. The toolkit is a set of software tools used by Java developers to create Java language-based commercial projects, such as online shopping malls, home banking and electronic brokerage.

The Vision Factory

- The Vision Factory's most well known product is Cat@log, a software package used by professional developers to design and operate web-based storefronts.
- The Vision Factory will integrate the FVIPS as a payment method in the latest version of Cat@log.

First Virtual Customers:

InterNIC

- The FVIPS was chosen to provide online payment for InterNIC domain name registration services.

The Electronic Frontier Foundation (EFF)

- The EFF represents and protects civil liberties of Internet users. The organization has been at the forefront of legal and policy battles to ensure that individual rights are protected online.
- The EFF chose the FVIPS to process online donations.

Saatchi and Saatchi

- Saatchi and Saatchi teamed up with FVHI to create the VirtualTAG, an interactive point-of-sale banner. The VirtualTAG is a multilevel banner that allows potential buyers to purchase products and services without leaving the Web page on which they found the banner.

OTHER INTERNET COMMERCE PAYMENT SYSTEMS

By the beginning of 1996, there were dozens of payment systems vying for a place in the Internet commerce spectrum. Some specialized in very small transactions, called micropayments, typically a few cents or even fractions of a cent. These systems were primarily designed to pay for small amounts of information, generally one-time access to a particular web page or site. Other payment systems incorporated traditional payment means such as credit card or cheque but provided strong security features to allow safe passage of sensitive information. Still others, were proprietary systems that required users to open accounts with special online banks.

Micropayment Systems

Millicent, NetBank and Digicash are three companies that have designed systems to sponsor micropayments. These payments might be made to purchase up-to-the-minute financial data, download a daily joke, picture, newspaper or magazine article or other online information, much of which is currently free.

Millicent was developed by Digital Equipment Corporation to facilitate anonymous microcommerce online. (Digital defines microcommerce as purchases of less than one cent.) Millicents come in "scrips," which are basically small, transitory, prepaid accounts that can be purchased from participating "brokers." A scrip worth, say, $5 is sent to a vendor, who returns a new scrip worth $4.995 in return for allowing the user to view the contents of the vendor's web page. Since the dollar amount of each transaction is small, no elaborate security features are built into the Millicent system.

NetBank offers a similar system where users trade Netcash certificates anonymously online to purchase low value goods and services. The Netcash certificates can be purchased and redeemed from NetBank, a Maryland-based company.

Digicash, based in the Netherlands, offers "ecash" and "cyberbucks" to pay for online goods and services. Unlike Millicent and Netbank, Digicash uses complex encryption algorithms to encode its ecash and cyberbucks when travelling over the Internet. As a consequence, larger anonymous transactions are possible. Digicash is also a leader in card security technology and is working with Visa and MasterCard on a smart card design.

Cybercash

Cybercash uses encryption technology to allow real-time secure credit card transactions, electronic cheques and microtransactions on the Internet. The company has support from the Internet Architecture Board, the World Wide Web Consortium, CommerceNet, the Electronic Funds Transfer Association, Netscape, First Data Corp., and the National Automated Clearing House Association.

The system is based on the "Cybercash Wallet," a browser plug-in, through which users can make purchases using their credit cards, electronic cheques (see below for a description of the PayNow electronic cheque system) or electronic cash for small purchases. Credit card purchases are made using data encryption and digital signatures compatible with the emerging Secure Electronic Transaction (SET) standard. Cybercash and Netscape have collaborated closely to develop a secure payment system for Netscape's new line of SuiteSpot servers and Communicator browsers. Cybercash embarked on a widespread television advertising campaign in the summer of 1997.

PayNow

The PayNow Secure Electronic Check Service is a system that allows Internet users to pay for goods and services online using their bank chequing accounts. Bank account numbers are encrypted, then sent across the Internet to vendors who, in turn, pass them along to a clearing house that debits the user's bank account for the value of the purchase. In early 1997, the system was being used to allow utility company customers to pay for recurring monthly expenses online. By the end of 1997, the system is expected to be able to handle the purchase of services and hard goods, as well as peer-to-peer and business-to-business transfers.

Smart Cards and Mondex

Smart cards look like regular credit or debit cards except that they include a tiny computer chip imbedded in the card itself. This chip can be used to store and process information of various kinds. On the Mondex smart card, the chip stores a binary representation of actual cash, along with the user's digital signature. Hence, this type of smart card is often called a "stored value" card. When inserted into a special reader device connected to the user's computer, the card can be used to download funds from the user's bank account. These funds can then be spent online or offline in regular stores, or transferred from card to card using a small transfer unit. The idea behind smart cards is to create a system as convenient as cash, but far more secure. While the use of digital signatures makes the cash stored on such a card more secure than conventional cash, nonetheless, if a person loses their stored value card they have lost the cash that was stored on it.

The leader in the stored value cash cards is Mondex. Mondex is 51 per cent owned by MasterCard and 49 per cent owned by a consortium of British and International corporations, including: National Westminster Bank, Ulster Bank, and Midland Bank, Scotiabank, Credit Union Central of Canada, The National Bank of Canada, Bank of Montreal, Canada Trust, Le Mouvement des caisses Desjardins, Toronto-Dominion Bank, Royal Bank of Canada, Canadian Imperial Bank of Commerce, The Hongkong and Shanghai Banking Corporation, Wells Fargo, AT&T, Chase Manhattan, First Chicago NBD, Australia and New Zealand Banking Group, Commonwealth Bank of Australia, National Australia Bank, Westpac Banking Corporation (Australia), ANZ Banking Group (New Zealand), Bank of New Zealand, Countrywide Banking Corporation, The National Bank of New Zealand, ASB Bank and Westpac Banking Corporation (New Zealand).

The key components of a Mondex chip are an 8-bit CPU, a 16K ROM, 512 bytes of RAM (and 8K EEPROM for data storage). The Mondex chip has a clock speed of up to 10 MHz and is about 20 mm square.

The first Mondex product specification was issued in April 1994. Currently more than 450 companies in over 40 countries are working with these specifications to develop cards and compatible products such as point-of-sale readers, bank cash machines, desktop readers and wallet-size balance readers.

Mondex cards have sophisticated security features built into the design to help prevent unauthorized use or duplication. Cardholders have unique "digital signatures" and have the ability to "lock" their cards when they are not being used.

Mondex cards are currently in the advanced trial stage. One such trial is going on in Guelph, Ontario. At the end of July 1997, there were over 7,500 cardholders in Guelph, or one in 20 residents. To date, about

$1,000,000 of electronic value has been issued to the cardholders. In March 1997, the first full month following the launch of Mondex, the average amount of electronic cash issued on a daily basis was $15,339.

Smart Cards are not expected to be in widespread circulation until mid- to late 1998.

Proprietary Systems

Many servers and Internet service providers (ISPs) such as Prodigy, CompuServe and America Online (AOL) operate their own proprietary online payment systems.

Traditional Payment Methods

Many users mistrust information sent across open networks such as the Internet. There will continue to be a large percentage of Internet users who will avoid purchases on the Internet entirely, preferring to stick to more traditional methods of payment such as telephone, fax, mail or face-to-face.

There are also users that are comfortable sending payment information over the Internet either using security features integrated into popular web browsers such as Netscape Communicator and Microsoft Internet Explorer or with no security at all.

The Secure Electronic Transaction (SET) Standard

The SET standard is a technical specification for securing credit card transactions over the Internet. The SET specification is jointly being developed by Visa and MasterCard with input and support from IBM, Microsoft, Netscape, Oracle, GTE and VeriSign. The system is based on advanced encryption technology to encode credit card information, and uses digital signatures or certificates to identify credit card holders. (See Exhibit 2 for a description of public key encryption and digital certificates.) The integrity of the system is designed to equal a traditional point-of-sale purchase in which the buyer, merchant and credit card are physically present. Most suppliers of electronic commerce software have made a commitment to build in support for SET-based transactions.

Once widely released, the SET standard is expected to be popular with merchants since traditional credit card processing fees will be reduced, perhaps by as much as one per cent.

Constant delays in the final end-user introduction of the SET system have caused tensions to emerge between the co-sponsors. MasterCard is using a prerelease version of the SET standard in certain markets,

---

EXHIBIT 2   Public Key Encryption and Digital Certificates

In a public key system a key pair is mathematically generated, consisting of a public key and a private key. The key pair is generated so that a message may be encrypted with one key and decrypted with the other (either key can be used for encryption). The message *cannot* be decrypted using the same key that was used to encrypt it. Each user's public key is usually made widely available to anyone wishing to send an encrypted message while the user's private key is kept secret.

For example, if Frank wishes to send an encrypted message to Tony, he would encrypt his message using Tony's public key. After the message has been encrypted using Tony's public key, it can only be decrypted using Tony's private key. Not even Frank could get his message back.

The great advantage of this kind of cryptography is that, unlike conventional cryptosystems, it is not necessary to find a secure means of transmitting the encryption key to the intended recipient of the message. Another useful feature of such cryptosystems is the ability to "sign" messages by encrypting them with the sender's private key. Anyone can then decrypt the message with the sender's public key, and can be sure that only the owner of that public key could have encrypted the message (with the corresponding private key). This is referred to as providing a digital signature.

For example, not only does Frank want to send an encrypted message to Tony, but he wants to assure Tony that it is really he who is sending the message. So, Frank encrypts the message using Tony's public key then re-encrypts it using his own private key. When Tony receives the message, he first decrypts it using Frank's public key, thus proving that it could only have come from Frank, then he decrypts the message itself using his own private key.

In practice, it is not usually necessary to encrypt an entire message in order to insure a digital signature—rather, a small portion of "signed" data attached to the full message is sufficient. This approach is often termed a "digital certificate."

---

while Visa recommends its credit card holders not to use the system until the final product is released. Technical problems have delayed SET's debut, which was originally slated for late 1996. SET is now not expected to be rolled out until mid-1998.

MARKETING

First Virtual had a three-fold strategy for marketing the FVIPS to buyers and merchants. First, through press releases and traditional PR channels, FVHI hoped to attract the attention of journalists who would then publicize the company in the press. So far, articles concerning First Virtual and CEO Lee Stein have appeared in *Business Week, Newsweek, Fortune,* the *Economist,* the *New York Times,* the *San José Mercury News* and more. Second, the marketing department targeted large transaction processors who might be interested in extending their business online. Third, they targeted third-party integrators such as AOL, and large ISPs.

However, it should be noted that for much of its history, First Virtual lacked a formal marketing and sales effort. Part of the reason for this was that First Virtual believed it was essential to have a stable, scalable infrastructure in place before significant marketing was undertaken. First Virtual did not want to be in a position of not being able to meet demand.

FINANCIAL INFORMATION

For the year ended December 31, 1996, FVHI revenues increased over 250 per cent to $696,000 from $198,000 for the year ended December 31, 1995. Revenues for the year ended December 31, 1996, include $150,000 in consulting revenues received from a strategic partner. Net loss for 1996 was $10.7 million as compared to a net loss of $2.3 million for 1995. Net loss per share was $1.25 based on weighted average shares outstanding of 8,524,068, as compared to a net loss of $0.30 per share for 1995 based on weighted average shares outstanding of 7,599,106. See Exhibit 3 for FVHI's Statements of Operations and Exhibit 4 for FVHI's Condensed Balance Sheets.

Commenting on the results, Chairman Stein said, "We are at an exciting stage in the development of our company. First Virtual sees a market opportunity in providing solutions for Internet commerce. We are using a portion of the Initial Public Offering (IPO) proceeds to develop both the technology and the organizational infrastructure necessary to take advantage of this opportunity."

EXHIBIT 3   First Virtual Holdings Incorporated Statements of Operations

	Three Months Ended December 31		Year Ended December 31	
	1996	*1995*	*1996*	*1995*
Revenues	$197,604	$110,672	$695,866	$197,902
Operating expenses				
Marketing and sales	1,091,539	104,314	1,836,545	346,400
R&D	1,747,770	339,951	3,248,958	530,809
G&A	2,126,807	263,007	6,431,286	1,522,784
Total op. expenses	4,966,116	707,272	11,516,789	2,399,993
Loss from operations	(4,768,512)	(596,600)	(10,820,923)	(2,202,091)
Int. income (expense)	58,886	(15,833)	130,983	(67,890)
Net loss	(4,709,626)	(612,433)	(10,689,940)	(2,269,981)
Net loss per share	(0.54)	(0.07)	(1.25)	(0.30)
Shares used in				
per share computation	8,769,491	8,668,046	8,524,068	7,599,106

First Virtual received its major initial financing from several strategic investors including First USA Paymentech, GE Capital and First Data Corporation, who together invested $12.5 million between December 1994 and August 1996. First Virtual Holdings Inc. went public on the NASDAQ exchange on December 13, 1996. The offering was for 2 million shares at $9.00 a share. The gross amount raised by the offering was $18 million ($15 million net), and the stock price closed at $9.00 after the day. Exhibit 5 charts First Virtual's stock price from December 1996 to October 1997.

Even though IPO Network ranks First Virtual among the bottom 10 percent of offerings in 1996 and 1997, CFO John Stachowiak notes that bad timing was mostly to blame.

EXHIBIT 4   First Virtual Holdings Incorporated Condensed Balance Sheets

	Year Ended December 31	
	1996	*1995*
Assets		
Current assets		
Cash and cash equivalents	$17,127,971	$2,091,651
Short-term investment, available-for-sale	200,000	
Accounts receivable	88,278	—
Prepaid expenses and other	83,840	10,953
Total current assets	17,500,089	2,102,604
Furniture and equipment, net	1,964,635	304,320
Information technology, net	59,226	113,333
Organization and other costs, net	105,798	50,569
Deposits and other	62,809	4,000
Total assets	$19,692,557	$2,574,826
Liabilities and stockholders' equity		
Current liabilities:		
Accounts payable	$1,626,198	$513,893
Accrued compensation and related liabilities	372,739	8,170
Accrued interest	196,340	100,340
Deferred revenue	64,683	
Current portion, amount due to stockholder	400,000	—
Other accrued liabilities	576,077	—
Total current liabilities	3,236,037	622,403
Amount due to stockholder	312,500	—
Notes payable to stockholders	1,200,000	1,200,000
Total stockholders' equity	14,944,020	752,423
Total liabilities and stockholders' equity	$19,692,557	$2,574,826

EXHIBIT 5   Share Price in US$ Per Share

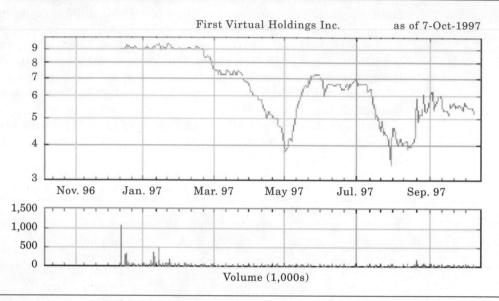

First Virtual Holdings Inc.   as of 7-Oct-1997

Volume (1,000s)

Source: Yahoo! http://quote.yahoo.com. © 1997 Yahoo! Inc.

The final months of 1996 were a bad time for technology stock offerings. The euphoria generated over a number of high profile IPOs earlier in the year had fizzled. Investors were becoming more cautious about investing in new technologies. Besides that, while we were on the road promoting the offering about a week before the IPO, Allen Greenspan came forward and issued a warning about unsustainably high stock prices. This sent the market reeling. Two other companies about to go public dropped out, but we hung in there. Against the odds, our placement was completed.

CURRENT ISSUES AND PLANS FOR THE FUTURE

FVHI had achieved remarkable growth since its inception. The FVHI user base and transaction volume had doubled about every six weeks. As part of a continuing development program, the company planned to internationalize the FVIPS to include multiple language and currency support, to develop better support for microtransactions, better support for the sale of hard goods, add additional mechanisms for buyers to pay into and sellers to receive payment from the FVIPS system. They also planned to open the system to participation by multiple processors and acquirers in the banking world.

The company was also exploring future products which were complementary to the FVIPS model. One area where the company had invested a significant amount of R&D was the VirtualTAG (www.virtualtag.com, www.virtualadz.com). The VirtualTAG was an interactive, multi-level Internet banner advertisement. Because it was multi-layered, a buyer could make purchases through a VirtualTAG without leaving the page on which they found it.

Despite the growth and the new product ideas, First Virtual's future was certainly not guaranteed. The company was still a long way from profitability. Widespread acceptance of the FVIPS would be necessary to guarantee its success, and the market was crowded with alternate payment schemes and players. It was still to be determined whether the FVIPS was the payment system most suitable to the Internet of the future. Questions remained about the tradeoff between security and convenience. How much convenience would consumers be willing to sacrifice for security? Despite FVHI's successes, retail electronic commerce on the Internet had been below most analysts' expectations.

As he exited the freeway and approached First Virtual's offices, Lee Stein wondered briefly where the company would be next year at this time. Stein knew that in an Internet-based business such as his, one year was equivalent to five to ten years in a "real" business—so trying to think a year ahead was long-range planning indeed.

Mondex Canada (A)

By Professor Sid L. Huff and Michael Wade

It was June 5, 1998 and Richard Thomas, Director of Marketing and Communications for Mondex Canada, switched his phone to voice mail. He needed some uninterrupted time to think. The item which needed the most thought was the one which had been put off while lesser, but more urgent, matters were dealt with. The issue was how to manage the national roll out of Mondex in 2003–2004.

WHAT IS MONDEX

"Mondex", or the Mondex electronic cash application, residing on a smart card,[1] was the size and shape of a regular credit or debit card. A key feature that distinguished a smart card from either a credit or debit card was a small chip embedded on the card. This chip was essentially a computer, containing a CPU, memory and software. The chip allowed value to be stored right on the card. This differed from debit, credit and other "magnetic strip" cards, where information relating to the transaction and user was contained not on the card itself, but on a remote computer, accessible through a data network, to which the card merely provided access. Mondex electronic cash cards allowed "off-line," or direct card-to-card transactions, affording it cash-like flexibility. Mondex was specifically designed as a substitute for cash for small, everyday purchases.

Value could be loaded onto a Mondex card from automatic teller machines (ATMs) or from specially designed home or public telephones which had been outfitted with a Mondex interface unit. Value could also be transferred from one card to another, using a special Mondex "wallet," a simple and relatively inexpensive gadget that would accept two cards and would allow users to control value transfers from one to the other. The value that could be held on a Mondex card was potentially infinite, but was restricted by the card-issuing financial institutions for most consumer class cards to $500 or $1,000. Assuming the infrastructure was available, Mondex value could be used like cash to pay for everyday items such as transit fares, telephone calls, parking meters, coffee and other consumables.

Mondex cards were designed to withstand normal extremes of cold and heat, damp, X-rays, electrical interference and wear and tear. A sophisticated security system consisting of both hardware and software components made it extremely difficult for the card to be forged or tampered with. Basic Mondex cards also had the ability to store more than one currency. More advanced Mondex cards also could support applications other than cash, such as database storage, access control to buildings, and so forth.

See Exhibit 1 for a picture of a Mondex card and chip. The Mondex wallet and cash tracker are shown in Exhibit 2. See "Mondex: Technical Note" for more information on the Mondex card and Mondex value system.

---

[1]Strictly speaking Mondex and smart card are two different things. Mondex Electronic Cash is one of potentially multiple applications residing on a smart card.

EXHIBIT 1   Picture of a Mondex Card and Chip

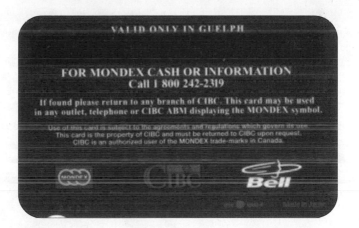

THE HISTORY OF MONDEX

At a meeting on March 2, 1990, the Mondex concept was first outlined by Tim Jones, Deputy Director of Payment Services at Britain's National Westminster Bank (NWB), and Graham Higgins, Manager of NWB's Card Strategy Group. Tim Jones explained:

> We began looking at stored value cards, but couldn't make the business case. The need to account for every transaction was holding us back. We eventually concluded that the answer was to develop a system with no settlement for individual transactions. The economics of a transaction model with no

EXHIBIT 2   Picture of a Mondex Wallet and Cash Tracker

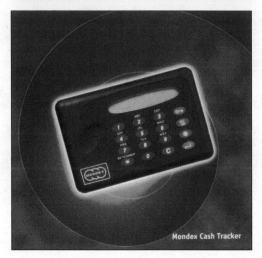

settlements were very desirable—the lack of computing and communications overhead would permit transaction payments of a fraction of a cent. It might also provide a new mechanism for management control within the firm. Rather than managing to budgets, all expenses within the firm, no matter how small, could be immediately settled in cash. This was the kind of concept breakthrough that we had been looking for.

The significance of the initiative was recognized by NWB, which assembled a small team to develop the idea. During the recession of 1991, the Mondex project was almost cancelled due to budgetary constraints and the temporary loss of Tim Jones, but strong support from senior management and the NWB board kept the project alive. The development team worked closely with major industry players such as Dai Nippon Printing, Hitachi, Matsushita Electric, and Oki Electric on the development of the necessary cards and devices. The first trial of Mondex, then known as the "Byte Card," was conducted in March 1992. The cards were distributed to 6,000 NWB employees to be used in the bank's cafeteria. The Mondex development team and its partners worked in secrecy until the official announcement of the development project was made in December 1993.

The first regional consortium to buy into the Mondex scheme consisted of NWB, Midland Bank (another large UK bank) and British Telecom. The subsequent merger of Midland Bank and Hong Kong & Shanghai Banking Corporation (HKSB) brought the latter group into the Mondex circle. HKSB was granted franchise rights for Mondex in Hong Kong, and for a variety of other Asian countries including China, India, Indonesia, Macao, Singapore, and Thailand. Another bank, the Bank of Scotland, also joined the UK consortium.

After the technical specifications had been ironed out, the Mondex card was ready for its first widespread trial. This trial was conducted by NWB, Midland Bank and British Telecom in Swindon, England, beginning in July 1995.

THE SWINDON TRIAL

Swindon was chosen due to its modest size, representative population, and proximity to London's Heathrow airport. The Mondex Swindon pilot commenced on July 3, 1995, with the first electronic cash transaction observed by journalists and TV crews from 15 countries. Some 6,000 cards were requested by consumers in the first months, with over 700 retail outlets accepting Mondex. Swindon's role was in part to act as a global showcase for Mondex technology. Mondex executives estimated that the launch in Swindon generated more than five million dollars worth of free advertising for Mondex worldwide.

The pilot required implementation of a new payment infrastructure within the town of Swindon. Consumers were provided with the Mondex cards themselves, with Mondex "wallets" for transferring value to other cards, and also with a small device for allowing a Mondex user to read the value stored on his or her card. In Swindon, the Mondex value reader was provided as part of a key chain, to emphasize the everyday necessity of having a reader nearby. The two banks provided 20 Mondex-enabled ATM machines. In September 1995, 12 Mondex-enabled ticket machines were installed in six car parks. In October, British Telecom introduced 200 Mondex-compatible payphones to Swindon (in street kiosks and shops) and 2,000 Mondex-compatible private phones

(1,000 in homes and 1,000 in shops and offices) which acted as Mondex cash points. In January 1996, card readers were installed in 80 metropolitan buses which then offered reduced fares to Mondex users.

By the end of May 1996, there were over 10,000 cards in circulation, a penetration rate of 24 per cent of the banks' 43,000 local customers. Although some press coverage suggested growth of the scheme was slower than anticipated, Ron Clark, Chief Executive of Mondex UK, found the results very satisfactory:

> The figures that are coming out of Swindon are well ahead of what was achieved with cash dispensers and credit cards . . . at the same stage.

The average size of a value loading transaction from a bank account to a Mondex card had risen from £10 at the beginning of the trial to between £25 and £30 by May 1996—roughly the same as a typical ATM withdrawal. Most Mondex purchases were for less than £5. Supermarkets were the site of the highest value use, followed by department stores and gas stations.

In 1998, new trials were conducted at universities in York and Exeter. In a trial at Aston University, multi-application cards were used, including electronic cash, access control to campus buildings, student voter registration, library privileges, and student identity card. However, only one application, Mondex electronic cash, resided on the chip. The other applications used a photo, ID number, bar code or magnetic strip.

MONDEX AROUND THE WORLD

Mondex International sold the right to manage and promote Mondex to a licensee, usually on a country-by-country basis. Although there were no restrictions regarding who could purchase a Mondex country licence, they were usually purchased by banks or other financial institutions. Although the licence holder needn't be a financial institution, each country's Originator—the financial agent that governed the Mondex value system in that country—had to be owned 51 per cent or more by financial institutions.

The purpose of this structure was to ensure that Mondex was introduced by strongly committed institutions, and that those institutions had an incentive to make Mondex available to other local institutions as it became established. Mondex International provided initial support services to these institutions as required; often it assisted in discussions with banking authorities, legislators, retailers and consumer groups.

Mondex International owned the exclusive licence to the intellectual property rights and patents of Mondex. Mondex International was also responsible for the technical development (including security), and the regulatory management and governance of Mondex on a global level.

Mondex International was responsible for ensuring that all Mondex cards around the world were compatible and interoperable. Once a Mondex national licensee was established, Mondex International played a very limited role in the development of Mondex in that country.

The licence rights for Canada were announced in May 1995. The Royal Bank of Canada was the first to sign on. Soon thereafter, the Royal Bank split its investment in Mondex with the Canadian Imperial Bank of Commerce. In the United States, Wells Fargo (one of the Mondex USA licensees) began a trial involving 90 employees and nine retail outlets around their San Francisco head office in August 1995. By July 1996 those figures had risen to 1,000 employees and 22 retail outlets.

On November 18, 1996, MasterCard International and Mondex International announced that they had signed a letter of intent for MasterCard to acquire 51 per cent of Mondex International, and for MasterCard to adopt Mondex International's technology as its future choice of strategic chip platform. The remaining 49 per cent was to be owned by Mondex International member financial institutions around the world. Mondex CEO Michael Keegan noted:

> This means that Mondex will be in more pockets and purses, in more countries, more quickly than we had previously planned. MasterCard's participation greatly enhances the resources by which Mondex International can leverage its technical leadership and speed the international implementation of the Mondex platform.

Later in 1996, a group of seven major U.S. organizations announced that they were establishing Mondex USA Services Inc. to commercially develop and implement Mondex in the United States. As a separate company from Mondex International, Mondex USA would be owned by AT&T (through the wholly owned subsidiary AT&T Universal Card Services), Chase Manhattan, Dean Whitter Discover (NOVUS), First Chicago NBD, MasterCard, Michigan National Bank and Wells Fargo. By mid-1997, Mondex International was operating through local affiliates in the UK, the U.S., Canada, Australia, New Zealand, Hong Kong, Israel, Central America and South Africa.

In the latter part of 1997, eight of the world's leading silicon manufacturers and smart card companies from the USA, Europe, Japan and Australia led by Mondex International, joined together to introduce MULTOS—an "open," high-security operating system for smart cards. MULTOS would give issuers of applications the capability to install multiple applications, such as Mondex, in up to five different currencies, data storage (for such things as a health card or a driver's licence data), secure access entry (e.g., for access to offices or opening garage doors), and loyalty. The development of MULTOS was considered critical for the successful implementation of Mondex worldwide. The operating system was expected to be in widespread use on Mondex cards by early 1998.

Also in 1997, Dai Nippon Printing, Gemplus, Hitachi, Keycorp, MasterCard International, Mondex International, Motorola and Siemens announced their agreement to form a consortium—named MAOSCO—to drive the adoption of MULTOS as an industry standard and to manage its on-going development. In 1977, MAOSCO, in partnership with leading smart card manufacturers, announced the creation of a global supplier network in readiness for the mass market deployment of MULTOS. At SmartCard '98, an industry conference, American Express announced that it was joining MAOSCO. See "Mondex: Technical Note" for more information on MULTOS and MAOSCO.

February 25, 1998, marked the first successful completion of an international electronic cash transaction, when MasterCard CEO Robert Selander used a Mondex card to pay U.S. dollars for a breakfast in New York. The Mondex card, which had been issued by HKSB and already carried Hong Kong dollars, was loaded with U.S. dollars at a Chase Manhattan ATM in New York.

THE BENEFITS OF MONDEX . . .

. . . For Financial Institutions

For the banks and other financial institutions, Mondex carried a number of benefits including low transaction costs, strong security, potential new sources of revenue and reduced fraud. Dealing with cash was a large expense for banks. A typical cash withdrawal at a branch bank teller cost slightly more than $1.00. Card and cheque transactions were cheaper, but still more expensive than Mondex, mainly because most Mondex transactions occurred off-line, and, therefore didn't need to be recorded and accounted for by the banks. To compare, a typical credit card transaction cost banks $0.27, a cheque cost $0.11, a debit card or ATM transaction cost $0.06, while a Mondex transaction or an online Internet transaction cost banks about $0.01. The majority of transaction processing costs were associated with salary expenses and operations overhead. Since the Mondex system was largely automated, and thus, cost efficient, there was a clear incentive for financial institutions to adapt existing transaction and data processing systems to incorporate Mondex standards.

Mondex reduced the security risk associated with fraud and counterfeiting. Existing cheque, debit and credit card operations were prone to fraud and abuse through forgery and direct duplication. The smart card physical security and on-board encryption of a Mondex card significantly narrowed the possibility of abuse.

The ability of Mondex to carry multiple currencies and applications provided financial institutions an opportunity for new sources of revenue. For example, banks could charge third-party vendors who wanted to add additional applications to Mondex cards such as keyless entry, data storage, extra currencies or loyalty programs. On the cost side, multiple application cards could save financial institutions money by requiring them to issue fewer cards. For example, financial institutions could issue one card containing Mondex, credit and debit applications, instead of three separate cards.

Finally, chip cards provided greater flexibility in terms of changing the imbedded data. For example, if a basic data element such as a person's name changed, the chip cards could incorporate the change, whereas the stripe card would have to be discarded and a new one acquired. As well, the chip on a stored value card was more durable than a magnetic strip. Typical magnetic strip cards such as debit or credit cards required replacement every two to three years. Smart cards had a five- to seven-year lifespan.

. . . For Merchants

As long as the up-front infrastructure costs were not too high, Mondex had been welcomed by merchants in most pilot programs. The card alleviated many of the hassles of dealing with cash. It offered faster and more secure transactions. Cashiers did not have to worry about change errors, verify cheque signatures, or wait for authorizations. Instead of the 2 to 5 per cent of gross sales demanded by credit card companies, merchants would be charged rates similar to a debit card transaction but without the telecommunications cost (the final cost structure of Mondex to merchants was yet to be determined). Merchants didn't have to worry about bad cheques, and since the Mondex cards in the POS terminals could be set to "receive only," the risk of employee theft was reduced. Furthermore, since Mondex transactions were card-to-card, a merchant did not have to pay a per-transaction fee, as was the case with debit and credit, though a fee would be charged when a merchant transferred his or her Mondex value to a bank account.

Mondex also lent itself well to use in unattended settings such as vending machines, pay phones and parking meters as well as partially attended settings like transit systems. Mondex value was more easy to collect than coinage and less prone to loss or theft.

. . . For Consumers

The main benefit of Mondex for consumers was to avoid the hassles of using cash, such as fumbling for change or pockets full of coins. Mondex cards could be loaded up with value from home, avoiding a trip to the bank or ATM to get cash. Since cards could be locked, Mondex value was secure. Although, to begin with, Mondex was "another" card in an already full wallet or purse, the card held the potential to carry multiple applications, such as debit or credit, and thus provide added value and reduce the total number of cards carried. Finally, consumers could track their spending patterns, affording them better control over their expenditures.

. . . For Internet Commerce

Some industry analysts suggested that Mondex might be the "killer application" that would open the door to Internet commerce. The search had been on for some time for an effective Internet payment system. The challenge was to come up with a scheme which was secure and easy to use. In comparison to credit cards, which were by far the most widespread Internet payment conduit, Mondex offered some important benefits. Mondex value could easily be transferred over the Internet. The merchant would receive payment immediately, while the consumer could conduct the transaction anonymously, and with potentially greater security. Also, Mondex allowed "micropayments" of one or a few cents at a time; theoretically, fractions of a cent worth of Mondex value could be transferred economically. Third-party vendors were already designing and testing equipment which would allow Mondex cards to be used with personal computers and internet connections to facilitate online sales and purchases.

OTHER STORED-VALUE CARDS

In the mid-1990s, the vast majority of stored-value card products in use were telephone cards. Beginning in 1986, France's public telephone system began to use memory-only stored-value chip cards as a way to reduce vandalism and potential theft from pay phones. More than 30 national phone systems worldwide had since adopted the cards. According to some estimates, single-purpose cards such as those used for telephone calls accounted for 90 per cent of the 370 million stored-value cards issued worldwide. Thus, although widely used, most stored-value cards had a limited purpose, and were not a general-purpose replacement for cash. Apart from Mondex, there were two other large-scale stored-value bank cards, Proton and Visa Cash.

By mid-1997, there were more Proton stored-value cards in circulation than Mondex and Visa Cash put together. The main reason for the Proton card's success was its penetration of a single market. Proton was founded by Banksys, a consortium of 60 banks that operated Belgium's electronic-payments network. The combination of bank cooperation and government support enabled Proton to gain widespread acceptance from both merchants and consumers across Belgium. In order to expand beyond Belgium, Proton signed a licensing deal with American Express and entered into a joint venture with a Malaysian company to distribute its cards in Asia. Banksys sold the Canadian rights to the Proton card to the Bank of Montreal, Canada Trust and the Toronto Dominion Bank, who established a North American trial in the Canadian city of Kingston under the trade name "Exact." This trial began in 1996 and was completed by mid-1998. All three financial institutions have since migrated over to Mondex.

The Proton system differed from Mondex in that each transaction was settled individually at a central processing center, thus necessitating a network infrastructure much like credit or debit cards. The advantage of this approach was that if a Proton card was lost, the value on the card could be traced and reimbursed. The disadvantage was that card-to-card, or off-line transfers were impossible, and transaction tracking and reconciliation costs could make small purchases unprofitable. Also, each Proton card only supported a single currency, reducing its attraction to travellers.

Visa Cash, a consortium of Visa International and 65 financial institutions including Citicorp, had issued 1.6 million cards by the summer of 1997. The Visa Cash card differed from Proton and Mondex in that it existed in two forms, disposable and reloadable. The disposable form worked very much like a telephone card: once the value on the card was used up, the card was thrown away. Reloadable Visa Cash cards could be reloaded from ATM machines, member banks or through specially designed telephones very much like the Mondex card. Visa Cash cards differed from Mondex in that there was no "Originator," or central settling body; instead, each member financial institution managed its own Visa Cash value. Person-to-person or card-to-card transfers were not permitted under the Visa Cash system.

By mid-1998, the Visa Cash card was in the advanced trial stage, with pilot programs conducted by Scotiabank in Barrie and Vancouver, Canada and by Citibank in New York City. A trial using $10, $20, $50 and $100 disposable cards was also conducted in Atlanta during the 1996 Olympic summer games. Initial results from the trials were satisfactory. In May 1998 the President of Visa hinted that the Visa Cash card would adopt the MULTOS operating system being used by Mondex, thus making the two cards, and associated hardware, compatible.

Visa Cash appeared to be following a saturation strategy, worrying less about the technical integrity of the card, and more about number of cards issued. For example, Visa International paid for most of the expenses of Visa Cash trials, which provided an incentive to financial institutions to proceed with trials. Mondex, in contrast, had spent a good deal of time developing and testing MULTOS, its operating system, preferring to "get it right" before full-scale launch. In addition, Mondex International, and its majority owner, MasterCard International provided mostly a regulatory rather than financial support function. Visa Cash was expected to be a formidable global competitor to Mondex in the future. Even though Scotiabank joined the Mondex Canada consortium, it still planned to support its Visa Cash program.

THE CANADIAN MARKET FOR SMART CARDS

The value of outstanding Canadian coins and bills with a face value of $10 or less was roughly $5 billion. Those coins and bills circulated, and each one could be used many times a year. Thus, the total value of the transactions involving the stock of coins and bills in circulation was a multiple of the $5 billion face value. It was the cash transactions of roughly $20 or less that the sponsors of Mondex were targeting. Of all payment methods in Canada, cash was used in the largest number of transactions but accounted for only a small share of the total value of all transactions. Studies estimated that between 50 per cent and 75 per cent of transactions—by number, not value—were in cash.

According to a 1995 telephone survey commissioned by the Bank of Canada, cash transactions accounted for roughly 20 per cent of the expenditures, by value, of the average adult in Canada, compared with roughly 63 per cent for cheques and 17 per cent for credit and debit cards. A similar survey in 1984 revealed that cash transactions accounted for 36 per cent of consumers' expenditures and chequing for 57 per cent. Use of credit cards doubled between 1984 and 1995. This came despite the introduction of in-store debit cards in 1990. The introduction of debit cards took market share away from cash and cheques, but spurred the use of credit cards—primarily because both work through the same terminal devices, and because of the growth of innovations such as special affinity cards.

What do the changing patterns in the use of cash, cheque, credit and debit cards mean for Mondex? The rapid rise in the use of credit cards has largely been accomplished through an extraordinary extension of credit to consumers. In fact, the revolving debt of consumers, which is dominated by credit card debt, had more than tripled between 1985 and 1995 to $35 billion. The increased share of cheques probably stemmed from factors outside the financial system. For example, housing had commanded an increasingly larger share of household income, and the overall share of chequing rose because households typically paid their mortgages and rent with cheques. The use of debit cards, which were only being used as ATM cards in the mid-1980s, flourished in Canada during the 1990s.

Total consumer expenditures in Canada in 1995 were in the neighbourhood of $500 billion. This estimate suggested that, at 20 per cent of the total, cash accounted for roughly $100 billion of consumer expenditures. Thus, capturing even a modest share of cash transactions could lead to substantial market gains for Mondex. For every 1 per cent of cash transactions that stored-value cards replaced, issuers would sell 1 billion dollars worth of card value.

Three markets were commonly cited as potential major users of Mondex cards: fast-food restaurants, unattended machines, and convenience stores. Canadian consumers spent more than $20 billion in those three markets in 1994. A very large percentage of meals in Canada were consumed at fast-food restaurants. According to industry data, consumers spent $9 billion on fast food in 1995, up from $7 billion in 1990—an increase of 28 per cent. In addition to the large sales volume at fast-food restaurants, which made that market a likely prospect for Mondex, the market was dominated by a relatively small number of chains, all of which had name-brand recognition. Their offering the option of paying with a Mondex card, even on a regional basis, could positively influence the acceptance of Mondex by consumers.

Industry observers described vending machines as one of the largest potential markets for stored-value cards. Operators of vending machines believed they lost millions of dollars in sales annually because potential customers lacked exact change. According to industry statistics, sales from vending machines had grown steadily in nominal dollars during the 1990s. In 1994, consumers spent $4 billion in vending machines that offered products or entertainment (video games and jukeboxes), up from $3 billion in 1986. Including sales from vending machines owned and operated by soft-drink companies, overall vending machine sales were well over $5 billion.

Operators of vending machines had an added incentive to use stored-value cards: to lower their high rate of theft. Industry rules of thumb suggested that between 7 per cent and 12 per cent of revenue was lost because of theft by employees or outsiders. Especially threatening were thieves who obtained duplicate keys and systematically skimmed sufficient funds to reduce the vendor's profitability but not enough to draw attention. Other unattended machines such as pay phones, parking meters and transit systems also constituted a promising market for Mondex.

Convenience stores, either attached to gasoline stations or free-standing, were a common site for small retail purchases and, therefore, provided a good opportunity for the use of Mondex cards. According to industry estimates, sales of goods other than gasoline at convenience stores totalled $6 billion in 1994, up from $4 billion in 1984. The express checkout line at supermarkets was also cited as a strong potential marketplace for Mondex. Mondex was a fast and convenient form of payment and lent itself well to the modest amounts usually spent in the express line. Yet another possible application of Mondex was loyalty programs. Loyalty "points" could be stored on a Mondex card in a fashion somewhat akin to cash.

MONDEX IN CANADA

Royal Bank of Canada (RBC) and Canadian Imperial Bank of Commerce (CIBC) were the original licensees of Mondex in Canada. Mondex Canada was formed by RBC and CIBC to oversee the development of Mondex in Canada. By mid-1998, Mondex Canada members had increased from two to ten financial institutions, including: RBC, CIBC, Scotiabank, Bank of Montreal, Toronto Dominion Bank, National Bank of Canada, Hong Kong Bank of Canada, Canada Trust, Credit Union Central of Canada and Le Mouvement des caisses Desjardins. These institutions among them held 95 per cent of the financial assets on deposit in the country.

In June 1998, Mondex Canada had eight full-time employees. See Exhibit 3 for an organizational chart. Mondex Canada used advertising agencies, accountants and lawyers for much of the specific day-to-day work. Most of the client-side and network administration work was done by Mondex Canada member financial institutions, not Mondex Canada itself. For example, RBC had 25 full-time office staff and 30 systems integration staff devoted to Mondex.

Mondex Canada was funded by its members. The amount contributed was based on a formula related to shared cash, or the relative value of cash dispensed at Automatic Teller Machines. The amount contributed by Mondex members to Mondex Canada ranged from $50,000 to $2 million.

The main functions of Mondex Canada were to act as intermediary between member financial institutions, to host Mondex-related committees, develop and promulgate operating regulations and guidelines, provide an interface to the media, control national Mondex standards, protocols, trademarks, brand and logo, and oversee national Mondex marketing policy and market research. It was Mondex Canada's responsibility to ensure that Mondex in Canada operated smoothly and efficiently, with the maximum of cooperation and the minimum of confrontation from its member financial institutions, who normally were fierce competitors.

EXHIBIT 3   Mondex Canada Organizational Chart

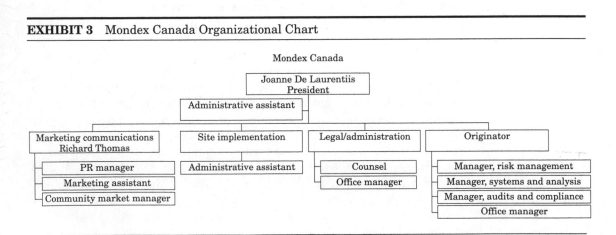

THE GUELPH TRIAL

Mondex Canada's first major undertaking was a pilot program in Guelph, Ontario, which was launched on February 13, 1997, in conjunction with CIBC, RBC, Credit Union Central of Canada and Bell Canada. Merchants in Guelph were encouraged to place Mondex terminals, which were provided free of charge by the sponsors for the period of the trial, next to their cash registers. Numerous households in Guelph were sent Mondex cards, Mondex wallets and information on their use.[2] They were also provided with some pre-loaded "free" spending money to get them started. Two hundred and fifty pay phones were outfitted to accept Mondex value, and 650 specially designed home phones which could download Mondex value were sold to consumers.

At the time, Guelph was the world's largest community-wide Mondex trial. In the first year, the trial grew to include more than 560 merchants, 12,000 cardholders and $2 million of electronic cash issued. The number of card holders and merchants participating in the pilot was beyond original expectations. However, the amount of Mondex value actually used was less than expected. This suggested that many participants had tried the card but few had become regular users. Mondex Canada and the sponsor financial institutions continued to support the Guelph trial through 1998. They even sent all Mondex card holders new Mondex wallets to replace the original ones, which had proven difficult to use.

Cindy Pearson, Community Market Manager for Mondex Canada, noted:

> There's no doubt this community has been recognized as a true international showcase for Mondex and the future of electronic cash. The Mondex Center has been host to well over 8,000 visitors from Canada, the U.S., Latin America, Hong Kong, Korea, UK, Israel, Australia and New Zealand. And in September, Guelph was host to an international forum for suppliers and developers of the electronic cash industry.

See Exhibit 4 for excerpts from newspaper articles describing the Guelph trial.

In March 1998, plans were announced to introduce another Mondex trial in the city of Sherbrooke, Quebec, to begin in the spring of 1999. These dates, however, were contingent on the wide-scale release of MULTOS, the multi-application smart card operating system. MULTOS was expected to be incorporated on Mondex chips by January 1999.

------

[2]The Royal Bank of Canada issued a Mondex card to all their Guelph customers between 18 and 65; CIBC followed a pull strategy, in that their customers had to actively request a card. Royal and CIBC had approximately the same number of customers in Guelph. In the end, both achieved about the same rate of usage of Mondex.

EXHIBIT 4   Newspaper Articles on Mondex

A CITY WHERE CASH IS IN THE CARDS

Toronto Globe & Mail, December 3, 1997

The Southern Ontario city of 95,000 is the site of a 10-month-old test of both Mondex's technology and consumers' reaction to it. The project has sped along faster than the association had anticipated, with 10 per cent of Guelph's population signed up months ahead of schedule. . . .

Nine out of ten local businesses—including laundromats, taxis and the beer store—are equipped to handle the cards. Even city buses and parking meters accept them, something that isn't feasible with credit or debit cards.

That's because of a fundamental difference in the way the Mondex card and its plastic cousins operate. Purchases made with a credit or debit card are supposed to be authorized by the institution that issued them, as a security safeguard and a guarantee of payment.

There's no such authorization with Mondex, however, because the cash balance is stored in a chip on the card itself. Each retailer has a machine that contains a "merchant card" with its own microchip. This card communicates with the consumer card, then transfers the appropriate cash.

This small technological difference has two big consequences for the Mondex system. First, there is no need for a physical link between the machine processing a purchase and the card-issuing institution, allowing the cards to be used in otherwise impractical locations. Individuals can even transfer funds between themselves using an electronic "wallet."

Even more important, the costs are lower because each transaction doesn't have to be authorized, making it financially viable for the cards to be used for very small purchases.

. . . So far, the Guelph test is exceeding the targets its backers—including Royal Bank of Canada and Canadian Imperial Bank of Commerce—had set earlier this year. Mondex Canada was hoping to sign up 8,000 to 10,000 card holders by February 1998, a goal it topped five months early.

. . . Despite his ardour, Mr. Lasko—an information technology worker—says many of his friends are leery about getting a Mondex card. He says security is a concern for some, but he points out that he can electronically lock his card, making it much more secure than the cash it is designed to replace.

Privacy is another worry, he says. "I've always embraced technology, but a lot of my friends are worried because it's somewhat traceable."

Mr. Lasko's friends are not alone in wondering how much of the trail might be left by use of a Mondex card. Part of the concern might stem from the card's ability to keep a running record of transactions. Individual cards have a record of the past 10 transactions and merchant cards contain a record of the past 300.

Both Royal Bank and CIBC are adamant that they do not—and will not—examine those transactions, except in specific cases of suspected fraud.

Privacy advocates are still wondering how much information Mondex and its members will be gleaning from users.

MONDEX TRIAL GETTING MIXED RESULTS

Toronto Globe & Mail, December 9, 1997

Ten months into the Guelph pilot, a random survey shows reaction to the electronic cash card varies widely.

"Will that be cash or Mondex?" That's the crucial question on trial here in Guelph, where the stored-value Mondex card—an electronic alternative to carrying bills and coins—was launched in February. The answer so far is anything but clear.

EXHIBIT 4   (Continued)

MONDEX TRIAL GETTING MIXED RESULTS (*Continued*)

Toronto Globe & Mail, December 9, 1997

Imagine never having to fumble for change to feed the parking meter and never having to face the line up at the automatic teller machine (ATM) for spending money. Imagine your pockets or purse free of weighty coins. For the proponents of Mondex, those are some pretty big pluses.

But far from everyone in the city of 100,000 is buying into the concept. A random survey of shoppers and retailers shows opinion skewed from highly enthusiastic to adamantly opposed.

At the area's biggest shopping center, the Stone Road Mall, both Sue Ricketts, owner of the Compucenter store, and Dan Brown, owner of the Kernels outlet, are firm believers.

"It's been a success from the start as far as I'm concerned. As a merchant, the less cash-handling I have to do, the better, and I can make the transaction in only four seconds," says Mr. Brown. About 10 per cent of his business now is paid for with Mondex, he says.

Ms. Ricketts handles only about four or five such transactions a week, but she believes the convenience of a cashless card will catch on. "As long as the banks keep my costs down for using it, I'm all for it," Ms. Ricketts says.

But to Steve Stasiuk, manager of the Threadz clothing store across the aisle, Mondex is a non-starter. The store opened in August, but so far he's declined offers of a transaction machine from Mondex Canada.

"When we first moved in, we saw all these stores with Mondex and thought, 'Wow, we'd better get into it, too, if we want to do business in Guelph.' But feedback from my customers shows that they prefer to use debit and credit. So far, not one person has asked for it."

Mondex Canada maintains that 90 per cent of retailers take the card but because "Guelph is so close to other cities, people using Mondex still need cash in the other pocket, so the utility is not there as much as it might be," says Royal Bank vice-president of stored-value cards, Al McGale.

WHERE CASH ISN'T KING

The Financial Post, September 27, 1997

Eight months after the full-scale start-up of the pilot test of the Mondex stored-value card in Guelph, Ont., the jury is still out on whether the electronic purse is on the way to being a success.

The Mondex test is crucial to the success of electronic money in Canada. Now that all the big banks, plus Canada Trust, the Caisses Desjardins, Hongkong Bank of Canada and the credit union movement support Mondex, virtually all of Canada's stored-value eggs are in one basket.

Visa has started up a pilot test of its Visa Cash card in Barrie, Ont., in conjunction with Bank of Nova Scotia, but Mondex is the clear leader now that everyone—including Scotiabank—has signed on with them. Even the Exact card test in Kingston, Ont., based on Proton technology from Belgium, is switching over to Mondex sometime next year.

With Mondex, users load cash value on the electronic chip contained on their card. They can do this at an automatic teller machine, at one of the 250 specially equipped pay phones in Guelph, or at one of 2,500 special home phones that have been distributed to interested users throughout this city of 100,000.

When they make a purchase, the card is inserted in the vendor's terminal, and the value is transferred from the buyer to the merchant.

Continued

EXHIBIT 4   (Continued)

WHERE CASH ISN'T KING (*Continued*)

The Financial Post, September 27, 1997

The pilot in Guelph is designed to test equipment and systems, along with public reaction. The banks running the test—Royal Bank of Canada and Canadian Imperial Bank of Commerce, along with one local credit union—will ask users how much they will be willing to pay for electronic cash. However, during the test the service is free to customers and merchants.

Electronic cash is accepted at about 570 retail outlets, and at other locations.

- All Guelph city buses carry terminals to let riders pay their $1.50 exact fare by card.
- Parking meters are being switched to make them card-compatible later this fall.
- Two of Guelph's taxi companies take Mondex in their cabs.
- Vending machines in city-owned locations are being converted to accept Mondex.
- Companies are being encouraged to accept Mondex in their cafeterias

Even one corn stand in the country just outside Guelph accepts the cards. And beer stores in the city not only accept the card for purchases, but also can load money back on the customer's card when bottles are returned.

Some enthusiasts even pay their kid's allowances with Mondex, says Dave Creech, the Guelph city administrator who has been a strong proponent of the pilot. The system allows person-to-person transfers, and thus kids can get electronic money from their parents and use it to pay for bus fares or purchases at corner stores.

So far, about 7,500 cards have been handed out, and they are accepted at retailers ranging from Eaton's and Sears to corner stores and restaurants. Mondex claims that 90 per cent of Guelph merchants who do a high volume in cash transactions accept the card, but a random survey of retailers in the city suggests that number is inflated somewhat.

According to Mondex, more than $1 million has been loaded on cards since the test began in February. While that's an impressive number on its own, in a city the size of Guelph it's a drop in the bucket compared to the overall commerce that takes place.

In interviews with a couple of dozen retailers, it's clear that there is considerable ambivalence toward the Mondex test.

At one end of the spectrum is Dianne McCrimmon-Hall, owner of the Santa Fe Marketplace craft shop. She does not accept Mondex and has no intention of doing so.

Since the test began last winter only two people have asked if she accepts it, she says, so there is no incentive for her to join, even though she would get the terminal hardware free for the time being.

McCrimmon-Hall notes, however, that she was not an early supporter of the Interac debit card system, but she eventually came around and debit now makes up almost 50 per cent of her sales.

De Laurentiis noted:

> Eventually we expect to see all Canadians have access to this exciting new way of paying; however, as with the introduction of any new payment product, it takes time to bring this new system into the lives and operations of consumers, merchants, and the financial institutions. Mondex Canada's plans have always been to expand the Mondex system to other communities at a logical and prudent pace.

THE NATIONAL ROLL-OUT OF MONDEX IN CANADA

Richard Thomas was Mondex Canada's Director of Marketing and Communications. Before joining Mondex Canada, Thomas worked for Glenayre Electronics, a large telecommunications company, first in Vancouver and later in Charlotte, North Carolina as Director of Corporate Marketing. He had also worked as a management consultant with the Business Communications Group, and taught Business Communications at Concordia University in Montreal. Before that he worked as an advertising executive for Ogilvy & Mather in Toronto.

Along with member financial institutions, it was Thomas's responsibility to plan the national roll-out of Mondex in Canada. There were many variables to plan for, and no international precedent to follow. Britain was the furthest ahead on Mondex development, but nevertheless had only reached the advanced trial stage. Many issues pertaining to the roll-out still needed to be resolved. One such issue involved figuring out how best to segment the market for the national roll-out.

GEOGRAPHICAL SEGMENTATION

In looking at the roll-out geographically, Thomas had identified four possible alternatives. The first alternative was to expand on a site-by-site basis in so-called "B" markets. "B" markets were defined as secondary markets, usually self-contained communities with populations between about eighty thousand and a million people. Guelph was a B site. New sites could be added on a continuing basis until all the "kinks" had been worked out of the system. The second alternative was to expand in "corridors." A "corridor" was defined as an area of demographic consistency, perhaps a group of cities surrounding a major highway or waterway, a commuter zone, or an area linked by common industry or geography. The third alternative was to target one or all of Canada's "A" markets, Toronto, Montreal and Vancouver, and expand from there. The fourth alternative was to target a single province at a time and expand province by province.

There was also the possibility of pursuing more than one alternative concurrently, or sequentially. For example, it would be possible to start with "B" markets, then corridors, then "A" markets. Or it might be possible to target the "A" markets first, then the corridors and finally the "B" markets. Alternatively, the whole country could be targeted at once with all regions being focussed upon equally.

A related issue was whether to change the Mondex image to reflect the specific culture and norms of each particular region, or to maintain a consistent and clearly defined image of Mondex nationwide.

SEGMENTATION BY USER TYPE

Another decision was how, if at all, to segment the market by target user. Should all potential users in a specified geographical area be targeted? Or should there be some effort made to segment potential users, and specifically target a particular segment? In Britain, university students were specifically targeted in two separate trials in York and Exeter. It was felt that this segment would be more likely to embrace the new technology and applications associated with the Mondex card. Alternatively, the whole "early adopter" demographic could be targeted. This demographic generally, but not exclusively, included middle to upper-income, educated, 18 to 34 year olds. Another approach was to target consumers who didn't have access to debit cards or credit cards.

PRODUCT CATEGORY SEGMENTATION

Yet another segmentation decision to be made was whether or not to target specific product categories. Mondex cards and devices might be ubiquitous within a specific geographic area, but marketing resources could be focused on specific product categories. For example, Mondex Canada could decide to specifically target its marketing efforts on transit applications like buses, trains, taxis, stations and airports. Alternatively, it could focus on convenience stores, coffee shops, vending machines and other locations where small purchases were common. Internet merchants were also an area that many industry insiders had identified as a good potential market for Mondex, mainly due to the lack of viable alternative payment systems. Or the decision could be made to spread marketing resources equally among all categories.

ADOPTION COSTS

The costs associated with the widespread adoption of Mondex in Canada were staggering. Infrastructure changeover costs, Mondex card and peripheral costs and promotional expenses would run into the hundreds of millions of dollars. Most of the infrastructure costs would be borne by Mondex member financial institutions. For example, the cost of making a single ATM machine Mondex-compatible was estimated to be at least $10,000. New full-service ATM machines cost between $60,000 and $80,000. This alone could cost banks hundreds of millions of dollars nationwide. The Mondex cards themselves cost about $15 each, and promotional costs were estimated to be between two and ten million dollars per year during the roll-out period, depending on the markets, consumers and merchant categories involved. During the trials, Mondex Canada members had paid for all the merchant terminals, while users received the cards and used them free of charge. Thomas knew that member financial institutions were acutely aware of the high cost involved in Mondex, as well as the uncertain payback.

Merchants faced a significant cost to make their stores Mondex-compatible. A simple Mondex terminal for use in a corner store cost about $500. A Mondex-compatible vending machine module cost between $1,000 and $1,200 installed, and had a lifespan of approximately 20 years. New devices and training costs for national retailers would add up to millions of dollars. Merchants would have to pay a Mondex usage fee, still to be determined, but probably in line with what they currently paid to process debit card transactions.

Users would be required to purchase Mondex peripherals such as wallets and readers, which cost between $10 and $15 each. They would also have to pay to use the Mondex card, perhaps through a loading charge or monthly use fee once the trial period was completed. Thomas wondered how consumers and merchants would react to these charges.

ROLL-OUT TIMELINE

Another issue Thomas was grappling with was the Mondex roll-out timeline. The period from 2003 to 2004 had been identified as a target date for the roll-out to be completed, but this period was by no means definite. The possibility existed of conducting the roll-out more, or less, rapidly. On the one hand, there was pressure to move quickly. Vendors of Mondex-related devices such as point-of-sale readers and wallets wanted Mondex to be rolled-out quickly so that they could market the products they had designed and produced. It was felt by Mondex Canada that the availability of third-party–produced Mondex devices was essential to Mondex's success. If the roll-out were put off too long, the vendors would look elsewhere to spend their research and development dollars. Also, the longer the roll-out was put off, the greater the opportunity for Visa Cash, Proton and other competitors to move into the market first.

On the other hand, there was a risk of making embarrassing and costly mistakes if the roll-out was rushed. The Mondex Canada member financial institutions were cautious and aware that they had never previously failed in the launch of a major new initiative such as Mondex. Interac was a good case in point. Interac governed and regulated the ATM/debit system in Canada, including all standards and protocols for ATM machines and debit terminals. Many felt that Interac had been such a phenomenal success because the organization and roll-out had been planned very carefully. Some financial institutions were more anxious to roll-out Mondex than others were.

MONDEX BRAND POSITIONING

Yet another issue to be dealt with before the roll-out could commence was Mondex's brand positioning beside other bank cards such as debit and credit cards. Competing with other plastic cards was unavoidable, since both were broadly classified as alternative cash payment systems. The Mondex card was clearly being targeted as an "attractive alternative for small everyday cash purchases," on the low end of the card spectrum, items up to about $20. Debit cards occupied the middle of the spectrum, with items from approximately $20 to $80 ($45 average), and credit cards occupied the high end, accounting for items above $50 ($75 average). But the possibility of cannibalization clearly existed. Research showed that debit cards were being used in ways that the banks didn't consider when the cards were launched as an alternative to cheques. For example, debit cards were being used to purchase one dollar chocolate bars, while at the same time they were being used to purchase high-cost items such as furniture, traditionally in the domain of credit cards.

Richard Thomas noted:

> We envision Mondex being used as an alternative to cash for small everyday purchases. For example, consumers might use their Mondex card in the express line at a supermarket, but would use their debit card in the regular line. Having said that, in the final analysis, it will be the consumer who decides how Mondex will be used.

MONDEX APPLICATIONS

There was some concern whether or not consumers would accept yet another card in their wallets. Since the Mondex card was considered a "non-continuous innovation," not an improvement or extension of something that already existed, the chance of consumer rejection could not be discounted. There had been some tests of a Mondex "combo" card which had a chip on the front and a magnetic strip on the back. The card could be used as both a Mondex and debit card. Such a card was being planned for the Sherbrooke trial in 1999. Some Mondex Canada member financial institutions had shown interest in this concept, while others were less enthusiastic. There was also the possibility of developing a combo card offering Mondex, debit and credit all on one card, although this had never been done before. Richard Thomas wondered whether the combo card approach would help speed Mondex's acceptance, or hinder it.

The pending release of MULTOS, the stored-value card operating system backed by Mondex International, would allow financial and non-financial applications such as database and remote entry to exist on a single card. For example, a Mondex card could contain cash value, loyalty points, air miles, foreign currencies, health information, driver's licence information, office entry, garage door opener and other applications. These extra applications could increase the consumer attraction of the smart card on which the Mondex application resided. For instance, a university campus Mondex card could be a cash card, a meal plan card, a student card, a photocopy card, a telephone card, and a library card, as well as provide keyless entry to a computer lab and so on. Multi-application cards, however, could add to the administrative cost and complexity of the roll-out process. Also, widespread release of a fully functional multi-application card was thought to be several years away.

Thomas noted:

> The ability of a Mondex card to carry multiple applications and currencies is a definite advantage over what exists today. Most people will admit to having far too many cards in their wallets. With MULTOS, Mondex has the potential to be an attractive application residing alongside many other potential applications, all on one or two cards. The financial institutions are excited, but at the same time nervous, about getting into areas removed from their core "financial" business. On the one hand, they can place Mondex, debit and credit on a single card and also sell card "real estate" to other vendors, such as store loyalty programs or transit authorities. On the other hand, they worry about how such programs will be managed. They don't want to be getting into the business of supporting other vendors' currencies. The issue of whether or not to add non-electronic cash applications to the first generation of Mondex cards is an unsolved one.

Thomas wondered about the roll-out of Mondex in Canada and the many decisions that still had to be made. Timelines needed to be drawn up and marketing strategies needed to be devised. One recent survey[3] of introductions of high-technology products suggests that failures were caused by problems with marketing and management rather than with technology. Still, Thomas felt sure that, in 10 years, most Canadians would be carrying a stored-value "chip" card around in their pockets, wallets and purses. He also believed that that card's stored-value application would be a Mondex application. In his view, Mondex's backing and momentum were virtually unstoppable. He just wasn't sure "how to get there from here."

---

[3]Chris Clugston, "High-Tech Demands Own New-Product Push," *Electronic News,* December 4, 1995, pp. 33–38.

Mondex Canada (B)

By Professor Sid L. Huff and Michael Wade

It was 4:30 P.M. on October 23, 1998, and Richard Thomas, director of marketing and communications for Mondex Canada, closed the door to his office, took a deep breath, and sat down. He paused to think about the ramifications of the meeting that finished a few moments previously. He knew the news wasn't good, but couldn't be sure how much of a setback it was. He reviewed his notes. Three of the Mondex member financial institutions had decided not to join the Mondex trial already underway in Guelph. In addition, one of the participating members had chosen to drop out of the trial. Faced with this situation, Mondex Canada, along with the remaining Guelph trial participants, had decided not to renew the trial after its scheduled completion on December 31, 1998. See Exhibit 1 for a newspaper account of the decision.

All in all, it hadn't been a good month for Mondex globally. A few days before, a large Mondex trial in Manhattan's Upper West Side was closed due to poor consumer and merchant response. Much of the trial's failure was blamed on the infamous reticence of New Yorkers to embrace new technologies. However, pundits also cited the failure of Mondex and Visa Cash, both participants in the trial, to provide sufficiently strong reasons for consumers and merchants to use the cards. Plans for another Mondex trial in New Zealand had been scrapped due to bank reluctance and perceived consumer indifference.

Thomas knew that part of the reason why results from the Guelph trial were disappointing was that Guelph was not very geographically isolated. Approximately one-third of Guelph residents worked outside the city every day, and another one-third came from outside the city during a typical day. Residents who worked outside the city were not able to use their Mondex cards, so for them a Mondex card turned out to be an *addition* to cash instead of a *substitute* for cash. Non-residents who worked within the city had not been issued cards in the first place.

Thomas also knew that Mondex member financial institutions had other things on their minds. For example, a perceived softening in the Canadian economy had caused some institutions to focus on core businesses; the Year

EXHIBIT 1   Mondex Pulls Plug on Guelph Pilot Project

THREE KEY BACKERS REFUSE TO BACK TEST FOR CASH CARD

Susanne Craig and Richard Blackwell
The Globe and Mail, Saturday, October 31, 1998

Cash card pioneer, Mondex Canada, has pulled the plug on its much-ballyhooed Guelph pilot project after failing to tee up financial support from three of its largest members.

The association, which is comprised of Canada's 10 major financial institutions and is part of an electronic commerce program involving 50 countries around the world, decided to end the Guelph experiment because three of its key backers—Toronto-Dominion Bank, Bank of Montreal and Canada Trust—would not join the Guelph test, launched in February 1997. As well, one of the biggest financial supporters of the Guelph project, Canadian Imperial Bank of Commerce, told Mondex last week that it was pulling out because the initiative lacked critical mass. This setback will delay the national roll-out of the Mondex card, which at one point was expected to occur by the end of this year. "All of us are still committed to Mondex. It is just not going to happen now," said Marlene Boyaner, CIBC's vice president of smart cards.

The Mondex system enables consumers to load cards equipped with computer chips with electronic "cash." When the cardholder buys something, the dollar value of the purchase is transferred to the merchant's card or terminal from the buyer's card. Royal Bank of Canada and CIBC brought the Mondex technology to Canada from Britain in 1995. Then, in 1997, Bank of Montreal, TD Bank, Canada Trust, Bank of Nova Scotia, National Bank of Canada, the credit unions and Caisses Desjardins came on board to form Mondex Canada.

TD Bank, Bank of Montreal and Canada Trust previously backed another card that was tested in Kingston, Ont. Insiders at the banks said they learned all they needed from that test, so joining the Guelph experiment didn't make financial sense.

An enormous amount of money and time was poured into the Guelph project, which is scheduled to end officially on December 31. For instance, the city converted hundreds of parking meters to be Mondex-compatible and hundreds of merchants installed Mondex terminals. City officials could not be reached for comment yesterday. Joanne De Laurentiis, president of the Mondex Canada Association, said while certain Mondex members are "facing resource constraints," it will not stop the planned test of the project in Sherbrooke, Que. "This does not change the status of the Mondex organization at all," she said. "They [Mondex Canada] are still committed to the Mondex purse as a product and fully committed to moving it forward as a product."

Royal Bank and Mouvement des Caisses Desjardins are the only backers of the Sherbrooke project. CIBC said last week it would not participate, citing the same reasons that it gave for ending its commitment to the Guelph pilot.

Ms. De Laurentiis said Mondex will not roll out the technology if it incorporates only stored cash. What Mondex needs, she said, is to add other forms of payment to the card, such as credit or debit. "That is part of what we learned in Guelph: You don't just go out and roll out a new form of payment on its own. The retailer wants one terminal at the point of sale." The card that will be used in Sherbrooke will combine stored electronic cash and a debit card.

Melanie Rigney, editor of U.S. publication *Smart Card Alert,* said news that the Guelph pilot is ending isn't good for Mondex. "Canada was supposed to be the showpiece for Mondex International. Can Mondex Canada hold its banks together? CIBC, one of the founders of Mondex Canada, now is not going to participate in Sherbrooke. This isn't good news."

2000 problem was demanding significant technical and financial resources; and proposed megamergers between large banks in Canada were the focus of intense press and regulatory scrutiny. Mondex was, at least temporarily, being put on the back burner.

Despite some disappointing usage statistics, Mondex Canada had learned a great deal from the Guelph trial. For example, contrary to expectations, Mondex cards were being used mostly in grocery stores and restaurants and less so in variety stores and for parking, vending machines and transit applications. It was also noted that a core group of users who were using their Mondex cards frequently had surfaced. Many in this core group used specially designed home phones to load value on to their Mondex cards. Indeed, these Mondex-capable home telephones seemed to be a key to success for Mondex.

Notwithstanding the decision to cancel the trial in Guelph, Mondex Canada, along with Royal Bank and Caisses Desjardins, a Quebec bank, had decided to press ahead with plans for a Mondex trial in Sherbrooke, Quebec. It was felt that Sherbrooke was isolated enough to avoid some of the dilution problems associated with the Guelph trial. The Sherbrooke trial would use a combo card that incorporated debit (stripe card) and Mondex on a single card. A further trial planned for Kingston, Ontario, was scrapped.

Richard Thomas wondered what to do. The Guelph experience suggested that a geographic segmentation strategy, where Mondex cards could be used ubiquitously within a defined geographical area, was not the way to go. It seemed clear to him that a different strategy was necessary, perhaps one that was more focused on a particular type of Mondex application. However, he was not sure what that strategy should be. He also wondered if positioning Mondex as a "substitute for cash" was part of the problem.

Chapter 8

Financial Services and Electronic Commerce

This chapter discusses electronic commerce from a financial services perspective with two cases: a very large insurance company considering strategies for selling insurance over the Internet, and a large bank struggling to find the right mixture of Internet and telephone banking and more traditional financial servicing.

Both cases look at firmly established bricks-and-mortar institutions with long histories and stable, well-capitalized business models facing both threats and opportunities on the Internet. For hundreds of years, financial institutions have been literally that—institutions upon which entire economies and governments have relied. How will electronic commerce affect these bedrock businesses? What do these firms have to offer businesses and consumers in the electronic marketplace? How should these firms position themselves to add financial value in electronic commerce?

The previous chapter addressed electronic commerce in terms of Internet payment mechanisms. This chapter takes electronic commerce one step further. Traditionally, banks have been the central exchange medium for nonbarter economic payment. Although cash and goods physically traded hands, money in various forms was invariably channeled into or through banks and other financial institutions. But banks have long stopped dealing primarily with physical money, in favor of exchanging funds with customers and among themselves electronically. With Internet businesses and consumers exchanging electronic payments, will the need for intermediary financial institutions be reduced?

The first case in the chapter is about Metropolitan Life. In 1998, Metropolitan Life's first vice president of Interactive Commerce faced a plethora of decisions in charting MetLife's strategy for e-commerce. He wanted to move quickly into conducting web-based commerce, but he had to consider executive support, infrastructure requirements, disenfranchisement of the sales force, fast-moving competitors, and the frenzied rate of technological change. The case covers many start-up issues, but from the perspective of a large, established business.

The second case concerns new distribution channels of Dominion Trust. Dominion Trust, one of the five largest, full-service banks in Canada, wanted to be a strong player in virtual banking with a nationwide, full-service, Internet banking web site—even though there were many doubts about the Web's profitability. They faced many issues, including how to price the service to bank customers, how to compete with the growing number of competing virtual banking services, and how to add value to virtual banking. They also had to consider the option of partnering with vendors or service providers.

Metropolitan Life Insurance: E-Commerce

By Professor Scott L. Schneberger and Murray McCaig

A study by Ernst & Young LLP revealed that despite considerable spending on Internet ventures, most financial companies don't have a clear idea of what they're doing or why they're doing it. Only 1 per cent of the companies listed "selling more products and services" over the Internet as a top e-commerce goal. Thirty-three per cent listed retaining existing customers and 23 per cent cited reducing operational costs as driving forces behind their Web strategies.

Meanwhile, 40 per cent hadn't coordinated their Web offerings with their other distribution channels, and 70 per cent had not come up with a pricing strategy for their e-commerce efforts. Still, financial companies are budgeting twice as much money for e-commerce this year as last, and by 2001, they predict they'll spend about 14 per cent of their technology budgets on Internet commerce.[1]

Deep in thought, Richard Painchaud gazed out the window of the train on his return trip in June 1998 from Metropolitan Life Insurance Company (MetLife) headquarters in Manhattan. Richard was contemplating the difficult questions posed to him by Jim Valentino, the Senior VP of Corporate Marketing.

---

[1] *Wall Street Journal,* September 9, 1998.

In 1995, as MetLife was assembling the Interactive Commerce department, Jim had asked Richard what he knew about the Internet. "Not much, I'm a marketer. Why?" That honest reply got Richard appointed as first VP of Interactive Commerce (IC), a position that was originally considered to be low stress. Richard's initial mandate was simply to create an informational web site that would feature MetLife's extensive Life Advice® program for customers.

At that time, developing an information-based web venue had required only limited coordination with other business units and departments. Moving the web venue to the next level where it could generate revenue as a fully transactional (see Glossary of Terms) and interactive site would require complex integration and interaction with many departments. Between coordinating departmental integration and trying to keep up with the unprecedented rate of change in the Internet, Richard's position became one of the most demanding roles of his career. As he looked out on the countryside, Richard wondered what strategy he should take both internally and externally to answer Jim Valentino's most difficult question, "When is this thing going to make money?"

Richard knew he needed to have a comprehensive solution in the works by year-end that clearly demonstrated to upper management that the MetLife web venue was moving towards profitability. To meet this deadline, he figured he had two months to lay out his strategy.

METLIFE

MetLife was a mutual company that had been a leader in the life insurance industry since its inception in 1868. The MetLife family of companies currently had offices throughout the United States and operations in North and South America, Europe and Asia. Its prized team of associates worldwide served millions of people. In the United States, MetLife served 86 of Fortune's top 100 companies. MetLife was the second largest North American life insurer (behind Prudential) with over $1.6 trillion of life insurance in force as of December 31, 1997, and ranked 15th on the Fortune 500 list in terms of assets (Exhibit 1).

MetLife was established by Simeon Draper, a New York merchant, following the Civil War. From its inception, aggressive sales were a MetLife hallmark. The company even imported polished British salesmen in the early 1900s when no suitable Americans could be found.

Throughout the 1900s MetLife experienced consistent growth in a highly regulated, and thus stable, environment. The most significant changes were becoming a mutual company, owned by policyholders, in 1915 and expanding to Canada in 1924.

Beginning in 1970, MetLife began to make some major organizational changes beginning with decentralizing its operations by setting up a number of regional service centers across the country. By the end

EXHIBIT 1   Fortune's 1997 Corporate Rankings (Top 45 Ranked by Assets)

| | *(in millions)* | | | |
Company	Revenues	Profits	Assets	Employees
1. Fannie Mae	$ 27,777	$ 3,056	$ 391,673	3,500
2. Travelers Group	37,609	3,104	386,555	67,250
3. Chase Manhattan Corp.	30,381	3,708	365,521	69,033
4. Citicorp	34,697	3,591	310,897	93,700
5. General Electric	90,840	8,203	304,012	276,000
6. Morgan Stanley Dean Witter	27,132	2,586	302,287	47,277
7. Merrill Lynch	31,731	1,906	292,819	56,600
8. Ford Motor	153,627	6,920	279,097	363,892
9. NationsBank Corp.	21,734	3,077	264,562	80,360
10. J. P. Morgan & Co.	17,701	1,465	262,159	16,943
11. BankAmerica Corp.	23,585	3,210	260,159	77,000
12. Prudential Ins. Co. of America	37,073	610	259,482	79,000
13. General Motors	178,174	6,698	228,888	608,000
14. TIAA-CREF	29,348	1,227	214,296	4,824
15. Metropolitan Life Insurance	**24,374**	**1,203**	**201,907**	**44,979**
16. Federal Home Loan Mortgage	14,399	1,395	194,597	3,200
17. American International Group	30,520	3,332	163,971	40,000
18. First Union Corp.	14,329	1,896	157,274	43,933
19. Lehman Brothers Holdings	16,883	647	151,705	8,340
20. Bankers Trust New York Corp.	12,176	866	140,102	18,286
21. Hartford Financial Services	13,305	1,332	131,743	25,000
22. Bear Stearns	6,077	613	121,434	8,309
23. American Express	17,760	1,991	120,003	74,000
24. Banc One Corp.	13,219	1,306	115,901	56,600
25. First Chicago NBD Corp.	10,098	1,525	114,096	33,962
26. Cigna	20,038	1,086	108,199	47,700
27. State Farm Insurance Cos.	43,957	3,833	103,626	72,655
28. Wells Fargo & Co.	9,608	1,155	97,456	33,100
29. Washington Mutual	7,524	482	96,981	19,880
30. Exxon	122,379	8,460	96,064	80,000
31. Aetna	18,540	901	96,001	40,300
32. Norwest Corp.	9,660	1,351	88,540	55,729
33. Nationwide Ins. Enterprise	12,644	806	87,830	29,051
34. Fleet Financial Group	8,095	1,303	85,535	32,317
35. New York Life Insurance	18,899	651	84,067	7,003
36. Intl. Business Machines	78,508	6,093	81,499	269,465
37. Allstate	24,949	3,105	80,918	51,400
38. American General	8,927	542	80,620	16,200
39. Lincoln National	6,437	934	77,175	8,120
40. PNC Bank Corp.	6,859	1,052	75,120	24,814
41. KeyCorp	6,568	919	73,699	24,595
42. U.S. Bancorp	6,909	839	71,295	25,858
43. Northwestern Mutual Life Ins.	13,430	689	71,081	3,818
44. Loews	19,648	794	69,577	29,747
45. BankBoston Corp.	6,727	879	69,268	21,500

of the decade, MetLife had head offices in seven cities across the United States. At the same time, regional computing centers were established in four different cities.

By the end of the decade, the flaws of MetLife's decentralization program became apparent. Spreading out the company's bureaucracy had caused frustration among employees, and the sales staff was defecting at a rate of about 40 per cent per year—very high turnover for MetLife. In 1979, a major effort was begun to reduce bureaucracy, and the number of managers between the chief marketing officer and the sales representatives was reduced from six to three over the next five years. Executive vice president Pierre Maurer, in charge of the reorganization, told employees in 1983, "Always wage war against paper—it's the greatest waster of management time and energy." This began the trend towards centralization of operations at the Manhattan, New York–based corporate headquarters.

Deregulation of financial services throughout the 1980s gave impetus to a number of new subsidiaries and products. During this period, MetLife acquired numerous financial service operations; many of these, like Century 21 real estate, were unrelated to their core insurance business. By the late 1980s, the trend was towards globalization of financial markets. In keeping with this trend, MetLife initiated operations in Tokyo, Spain, and Taiwan.

MetLife undeniably had one of the most effective sales forces in the industry. MetLife placed immense value on this sales force, because it was central to the company's competitive position. Many of the senior executives in the organization had been involved in sales at one point in their careers, which further reinforced their commitment to the sales agents' interests. However, there were a few executives who believed MetLife should be exploring new channels of distribution that would allow them greater control.

MetLife Interactive Commerce Development

From the web site's inception, MetLife decided marketing should drive its electronic commerce efforts (Exhibit 2). About this time, in 1995, there were a few individuals in the marketing department monitoring MetLife's experiments with new technologies like interactive television and kiosks. One of the most promising of these new technologies was the Internet. MetLife decided that a formal Internet experiment was required; IC was officially formed in 1995 as a division of the corporate marketing department with Richard at the helm. The Internet experiment was initiated without a stated goal in mind, but it was implied that IC should evaluate this new medium as a distribution channel.

Realizing that he did not have the capabilities to develop a user-friendly web site in-house and wanting to act quickly, he decided to seek help outside MetLife. Richard interviewed several traditional and new

EXHIBIT 2 MetLife Organizational Chart

May 1998

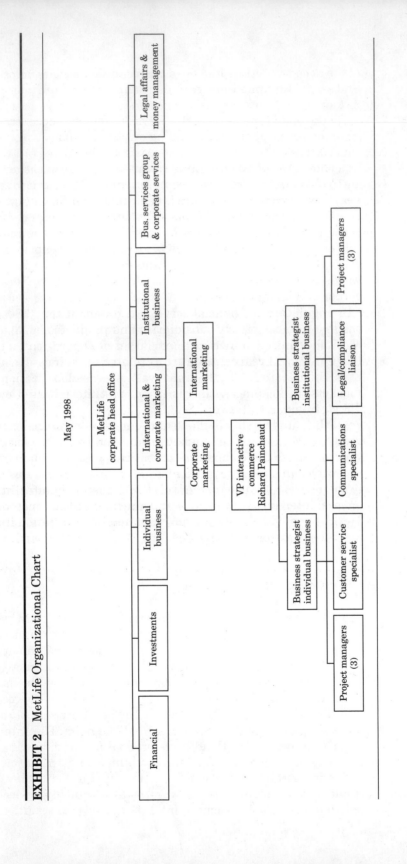

media agencies. Eventually, his search led him to Chan Suh and Kyle Shannon. Chan and Kyle were two entrepreneurs who had recently founded the online communications agency called Agency.com. After a series of introductory meetings, MetLife became Agency.com's first major client as they helped create MetLife's first web site, known as MetLife Online®. The site was launched on December 17, 1995, just one day before MetLife's primary competition, Prudential Insurance, launched theirs. The MetLife web venue focused on the Life Advice program that provided consumers with valuable information on everything from family matters (like *Caring for Your Aging Parents*), to money matters (like *Creating a Budget*). The site was a success from the beginning and won numerous awards and accolades for its design from both the media and company executives.

Much of IC's efforts in 1996 were focused on building credibility internally through extensive promotion of the web venue. The purpose of this internal promotion was to solicit projects from other divisions, increasing the demand for IC's services and allowing Richard to justify a larger budget request. Merchandise like posters, videos, and t-shirts was created while an informational booth was set up in the lobby of MetLife's downtown Manhattan office tower.

By 1997, web-site usage was growing exponentially; there were more site visitors in the first month of 1997 than during the entire year of 1996 (Exhibit 3). Under pressure to take advantage of site acceptance and to demonstrate returns through cost savings, Richard began to consider moving MetLife IC beyond simply providing information to delivering customer service. By allowing customers to service themselves through the web site, substantial cost savings could be realized. For example, it was more cost-effective and quicker to have consumers download forms from the site than to mail them. Part of this initiative was the creation of the business-to-business section of the site, which was

EXHIBIT 3   MetLife Web Venue Usage Statistics

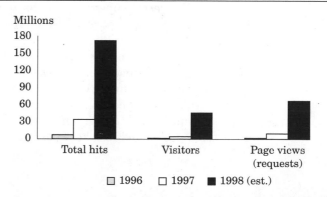

one of the main efforts of 1997. The business-to-business section was highly practical, allowing corporate clients to download forms (like claim forms) and submit changes through the Web to speed processing. These features had direct and measurable returns, and enabled MetLife IC to track the savings being created by the site.

The rate of growth had other effects. Richard had to rapidly add people to the IC staff to support its growing popularity and meet the increased demands for web projects from almost every department. MetLife IC was coordinating everything from major business-to-business projects requiring systems integration, to banner ad creation for supporting marketing promotions in other channels. By early 1998, MetLife IC was working on more projects than the group could handle given their staff and budget. In addition, each project had become significantly more complex, time-consuming, and expensive. There was little time left for an overall Internet strategy or for the planning required by large projects, development was becoming more like patchwork.

INSURANCE COMPETITION ON THE INTERNET

Competition in the insurance industry had been increasing rapidly due to deregulation, globalization, and shrinking demand in developed markets caused by an aging generation and introduction of non-insurance products. This increased competition started a trend towards consolidation and specialization worldwide. For many of the larger insurers, the Internet was an unwelcome addition to these competitive forces. More troubling, perhaps, was that the nature of competition on the Internet was very different and unfamiliar. However, with the online insurance industry expected to reach $4 billion by 2002 (Forrester Research), new entrants were flocking to the Internet and developing innovative solutions to serve the customers' needs for comparison and convenience.

The Internet was bringing together traditional, other financial, virtual, and indirect competitors in the insurance industry (Exhibit 4). Traditional competitors were being forced to compete in new ways and in greater scope. Large financial institutions, like banks and mutual fund companies, were leveraging the Internet to market insurance to existing and new customers. New entrants to the insurance marketplace like virtual insurers, e-brokers, and aggregators were quick to exploit new technologies on the Internet. Finally, there was increasing indirect competition from infomediaries who, though not selling insurance, were positioned to take a percentage of the sales margin.

EXHIBIT 4   Web Venues Examples

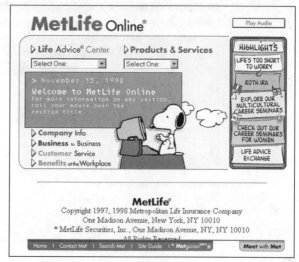

Source: www.Metlife.com, October 1998.

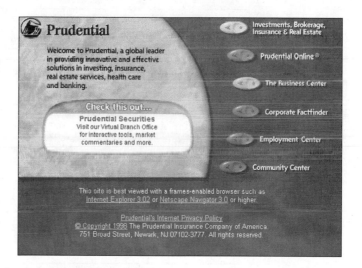

Source: www.prudential.com, October 1998.

EXHIBIT 4 (Continued)

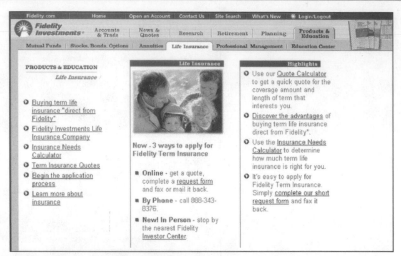

Source: www.fidelity.com, October 1998.

Source: www.BudgetLife.com, October 1998.

EXHIBIT 4   (Continued)

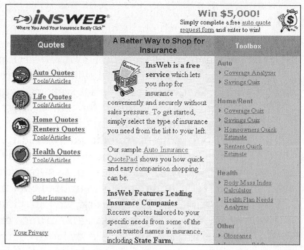

Source: www.insweb.com, October 1998.

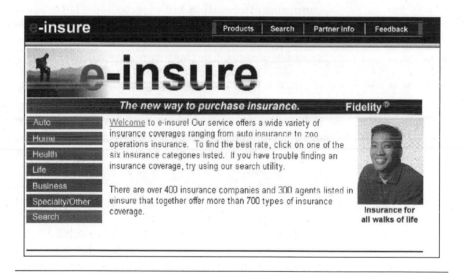

Source: www.e-insure.com, October 1998.

Traditional Competitors Online

Competition between the major insurers on the Internet in 1998 was weak, as each of the big players seemed to wait for the other to make a move before following. According to Booz•Allen, "just 1 per cent of current insurance web sites and fewer than 30 per cent of those planned for the year 2000 will allow users to purchase insurance policies."[2] Most of all, insurance companies were reluctant to embrace the Web as a legitimate sales channel for fear of aggravating their sales associates, who were at the time the main source of sales. If the agents felt they were being disintermediated by the Internet and thus losing sales commissions, there could be a mass exodus. Most insurers were using the Web to provide information, to support sales agents by providing qualified leads, and to perform limited customer service. Only one of the major insurers, John Hancock, was offering quotes online, and none of the major insurers was selling insurance directly online. The general attitude that top insurance executives possessed towards the Internet could be summed up by William F. Yelverton, CEO of the individual-insurance group at the Prudential Insurance, the country's largest life insurer, who said that computers may be fine for gathering and exchanging information but rejected the Internet as a vehicle for sales and, therefore, did not see it coming between Prudential and its 12,500 agents. "We see the agents as the preeminent way to distribute life insurance, now and in the future," he said.[3]

Banks.   Banks (especially conglomerates such as Citigroup) were expanding their efforts in the insurance industry quickly due to deregulation. The leading banks were far ahead of insurers online, and strong online competition between them was pushing innovation. They offered full account access, transactions, brokerage services and many new innovative web-only services—like life insurance quoting. The Internet was making it easier for banks to become one-stop financial centers because they could quickly expand their offering in the virtual market space.

Banks had a number of competitive advantages in the online financial services industry. The banks had been able to quickly embrace the Internet because their information systems were well prepared by systems work required to introduce the automatic teller machine standard. Banks were ahead of insurers in the use of advanced data mining

---

[2] "Booz•Allen & Hamilton Study Says Insurance Industry Building Internet Presence—but Not Realizing Full Cyberpotential," New York, February 24, 1997, http://www.bah.com/press/insurance.html.

[3] *The New York Times* "When the Agent of Change Is a Click of the Mouse," September 6, 1996, http://nytimes.com.

tools to finely target their marketing efforts. These data mining skills were being transferred to the Web environment, allowing banks to personalize their sites for customers. In addition, online customers typically visited their bank web venues on a regular basis for common transactions, which allowed the banks to learn more about customer habits and to market specific products (like insurance) to them with each visit.

Mutual Fund Companies.   Mutual fund companies were another new source of competition. They were merging insurance with other investment products to create all types of annuities that added new value to traditional insurance offerings. Mutual fund companies were beginning to successfully differentiate these insurance products by associating them with successful and recognized funds. Their web venues had become popular sites that customers repeatedly visited to learn about their investment performance. Mutual fund companies were also significantly ahead of insurers online since most allowed web account transactions.

Virtual Insurers.   New, totally virtual entrants to the insurance industry, like Budget Life, posed a major threat to the established players in the insurance industry. These new entrants had thin operating structures and were not constrained by commitments to other channels or by large investments in fixed assets. They could be compared to online brokerages, which at the time, were successfully capturing a substantial share of the retail stock and mutual fund trading business from established brokers by drastically cutting margins. If these online insurance brokers gained a critical mass, they could have the same effect on the insurance industry.

New technologies were even threatening insurer price positions. For example, "intelligent agents" could further increase price competition by allowing customers to send out searches for the best-priced insurance products that would meet their stated criteria.

Keeping E-Brokers.   What appeared to be the most formidable new competitors in the online financial services industry, however, were online brokers including companies like E*trade, Schwab, and Datek. A then recent study by Jupiter Communications predicted that online brokerages would control more than 50 per cent of personal finance activity online by 2002, taking significant market share away from banks. Online brokers were doing a superb job of rapidly implementing new technology, creating needs-based solutions, and marketing their products and brand online. Expansion into insurance and other financial products was a natural direction for these competitors. Recently, E*trade signed on one of InsWeb's insurance shopping services, making a major step towards the insurance market.

Christos M. Cotsakos, President and CEO of E*trade, once provided all new accounts with a free copy of the book, *Boot Your Broker,* with a new message: "boot your agent."

Aggregators and Infomediaries.   Aggregators and infomediaries, like InsWeb, Quicken, e-insure, Quote Smith and others were working to become insurance gateways or portals. These web venues presented a strong value proposition to customers by providing convenience, selection, and comparison at a single location. It was thought they had the potential to act like independent "mega-agents," marketing a huge selection of products from many different providers and taking profit margin on each contract sold. By gaining a significant bargaining position with insurance underwriters, they could also capture a larger share of the margin. Major insurers would have to participate in these sites, as they were becoming the first and only stop for many customers online. InsWeb had been forming partnerships with everyone and at the time had signed deals with both Yahoo and E*trade.[4] "Until the Internet, there has not been an easy way to shop for insurance," said Enan Hussein, chairman and CEO of InsWeb. "Our goal is to do end-to-end insurance sales (competing directly with the major insurers), but now we're focused on what consumers really want, and that's comparison shopping."

Independent Brokers.   A few small "Net savvy" independent brokers were creating well-designed web venues to support their operations and marketing and to attract new customers in the marketspace. Transferring current customers to the Web was easier for these agents, because the customers knew they could always visit the agency or agent in person. Their strengths had always been in cultivating loyal customer relationships, which, if transferred to their web venues, would provide them the same advantage online. The threats posed by independent brokers were much the same as aggregators but on a smaller scale. On the upside, these small independent brokers could become valuable online associates, using a strategic model similar to the Web bookseller, Amazon.com.

Richard was well aware of the drastic effects that fierce competition on the Web could have on other distribution channels. In the worst case scenario, the Web would lead to extreme price competition in all segments, customers would be encouraged to purchase on the Web, agents would begin to feel the crunch, the insurers would begin unsustainable cross-subsidization of their other channels, and slow their adoption. Richard knew he would have to be prepared for all scenarios, even the unlikely "guys down the street in their garage," who might be inventing a new method for risk management.

---

[4]C/Net News.com, "Yahoo Launches Insurance Center," April 6, 1998, http://www.news.com.

Emerging Internet Technology

Internet technology was evolving at such a frenzied pace that corporate web venues were often outdated by the time they were launched. Discerning those technologies that would create value for the consumer was a daunting task that required the full-time attention of someone who clearly understood the broader picture.

Dynamically generated content, personalization, data mining of site usage statistics, collaborative filtering, and automated response e-mail software were just a few of the new features that were required to be a player in the online game. Being able to determine relevant technologies and quickly implement them was in itself a competitive advantage. It was certain that more advanced systems, tools, and ideas would be required to continuously renew competitive advantages going forward.

Ubiquitous Internet video conferencing was an example of evolving technology that could change the nature of competition by enabling "face-to-face" Internet contact between sales representatives and customers. This could return a somewhat personal touch to insurance sales, but would require large investment in personnel and training. Large insurers might again be capable of differentiating themselves through this close interaction.

New technologies were even threatening insurer price positions. For example, "intelligent agents" could further increase price competition by allowing customers to send out searches for the best-priced insurance products that would meet their stated criteria.

Keeping up with new developments was becoming a crucial activity, but unfortunately one that was often the first to be squeezed off the priority list as it did not provide immediate returns. As part of his overall strategy, Richard felt IC needed a plan for monitoring these technological developments.

Internal Challenges

Whichever Internet strategy Richard pursued would have to be one that could also be successfully implemented internally. Richard felt there were many internal barriers that significantly reduced his options. First, and foremost, was the challenge of convincing senior management that the Internet should be viewed as an opportunity, not a threat. Secondly, IC had to deal with MetLife's legacy systems and the task of integrating them with the Web. Then there was the urgent Y2K problem, the growing complexity of the Internet projects, and internal challenges from IT and other divisions to IC's total control over MetLife's Internet presence.

The first and highest level challenge was convincing upper management that the Internet was a viable sales channel and that it would not necessarily have to disintermediate the sales agents. MetLife highly valued its sales agents and was nervous of how its actions in other channels would be perceived by its agents. Top management had not yet supported the concept of selling insurance directly on the Internet; instead, they had opted for the indirect lead generation approach. This approach was to invite those individuals interested in MetLife's insurance products to submit their contact information so that an agent could contact them. Harry P. Kamen, CEO of MetLife, had repeatedly told sales agents he did not believe the Internet was a viable channel for selling insurance and would thus not be pursued by MetLife. According to Mr. Kamen, "selling insurance requires face time."

Secondly, MetLife's information systems software was both complex and proprietary and many departments had incompatible software applications leading to poor information integration within the company. Most of these systems processed data in batches rather than in real time, which meant they were not ready for real time integration into the Web. Furthermore, the company's Internet server was not even connected to MetLife's systems. For example, each sales lead generated by the web venue had to be manually keyed into MetLife's information systems and sent electronically to a sales manager for printing and finally passed to a sales agent. Due to many incompatible systems and duplicated customer accounts, MetLife could not then offer consolidated account reporting for individuals. This feature, however, would be a minimum expectation of customers on the Web.

A third complication was the urgent Y2K problem, which was consuming the majority of IT resources. There was a lot of systems and web integration work required, but with Y2K on the horizon, IT would not be of any assistance in this process. Richard might have to outsource any systems integration work—which would be costly with the current demand in the marketplace, could rob his staff of valuable experience, and could diminish his control over the final product. It might also make him dependent on the outsourcer.

A fourth challenge surrounded the rapid increase in project complexity that required more extensive communication and coordination efforts with other departments and Agency.com. This issue was only likely to get worse since the next stage of development would require significantly more complex integration with many areas within the organization. Moving the web venue to a transactional stage would require participation and cooperation from all departments like marketing, product development, and customer service.

Finally, other departments were beginning to question IC's total control over the web venue and all Internet projects, especially as many projects were far behind schedule. Some departments were asking to work directly with outsourcing agencies of their choice. Richard would have to be wary of challenges to gain control of part or the whole of the web venue, or attempts to outsource projects that should be managed by IC. Losing the support of the many departments IC served would mean the end of IC. Without the concentrated and coordinated effort that IC provided, MetLife's goal of profitability from the web venue, Richard thought, would be seriously hindered.

THE DILEMMA

Richard believed all along that the Internet had the potential to "make money," but daily management had become so chaotic that there was little chance to think about a strategy for accomplishing this goal. Jim Valentino's questioning about Internet profitability, however, was an indication that top management was beginning to look for concrete results from the IC department. Moreover, popular literature increasingly trumpeted the potential for Internet business profits.

Richard was certain the Internet would become a key component of MetLife's future corporate strategy, and that the pressure for that component to create revenue would build. It was clear to him that the Internet was a lower cost delivery channel and would put pressure on margins in all channels. "The Internet could cut costs across the insurance value chain by more than 60 per cent,[5] with the most dramatic savings in distribution and customer service," according to Booz•Allen. These cost savings, combined with convenient and customized service, could encourage consumers to buy policies on the Web. Companies that offered online policies would undercut traditionally priced products and threaten insurers' profitability. Richard believed MetLife would be precluded from competing in an entire market segment if it did not wholly embrace the Internet as a legitimate sales channel. Richard understood the worst case scenario, but he also felt there were many best case scenarios where he could lead the organization.

The Main Options

Richard felt there were many strategies he could pursue to generate revenues from the MetLife web venue and establish it as a viable sales channel. They seemed to coalesce into three types: selling insurance directly to customers through the web venue, the indirect strategy of keeping sales people in the loop, and the strategy of selling through new intermediaries.

---

[5]"Booz•Allen & Hamilton Study Says Insurance Industry Building Internet Presence—but Not Realizing Full Cyberpotential," New York, February 24, 1997, http://www.bah.com/press/insurance.html.

The first strategy, selling directly through MetLife's web venue, had a number of benefits. MetLife could increase its margins and thus have more flexibility for competing on price. It could build relationships and interact directly with its customers, eventually transferring customer loyalty from the agents to the company. However, this move would likely be viewed negatively by the sales agents and could cause many MetLife agents to leave MetLife and independent agents to end distribution of MetLife products. Attracting customers to purchase products at the MetLife site could be difficult unless it matched the price and other comparison services that many aggregators currently offered.

The second strategy, which could avoid resistance by the sales agents, would be to involve them in the sales process either by allowing them to close deals arranged over the Internet (for smaller margins), or by creating web pages for them to utilize in selling directly to customers. The former transmediation strategy would transfer customers to agents once the limits of the Web were reached for a particular product. Thus, customers would be directed to agents only for complex or customized insurance needs that could not be provided via the web venue, while simple sales could be performed through self-service at the web venue. This would maximize utilization of both channels. The latter strategy would help to maintain sales agent relations in the short term, and build strong customer relations. And if done properly, MetLife could later strip out the sales agents from the process by moving to the first strategy.

The third strategy—selling through online intermediaries like associates or aggregators—also had some potential benefits. "If MetLife could build a powerful sales network online through associate programs, it could create a sustainable competitive advantage just as it has with its current sales network. It is really the same thing, but in the virtual world," said an Internet strategist at Agency.com. MetLife could enable any web site, whether an insurance broker or online community site, to set up a sales office for marketing its products. This could even allow some of MetLife's more technical agents to move their clients on to the Web. Any customers who chose to purchase through these online offices would be transferred to the main MetLife site to finalize their purchase. Many online organizations, including Amazon.com, U-Frame it! and many shopping sites, were using this strategy with huge success.

Aggregators offered many benefits, like selection and convenience, to the customer and could thus attract the majority of insurance buyers. Not all aggregators were the same; some were solely infomediaries offering comparison services, while others sold the products and took a commission. Regardless, all aggregators had the potential to pit insurers against each other in direct price competition, and in the process, increase their bargaining power and capture a growing share of the sales margin. Richard had considered purchasing one of these aggregators, but he felt that competitors would quickly end their participation, as MetLife would obviously have the motivation to promote its products first and foremost. Without participation from the majority of leading insurers, the site would not be able to attract customers looking for selection.

Other Opportunities

Richard also pondered a number of other Internet opportunities for MetLife. One interesting alternative was to set up a virtual sales office on the Web to target the European market where the company had no sales agents. This would get around the sales agent problem, and could lead to a significant increase in European sales. One problem would be that prices would be open to inspection from individuals in all other areas of the world, and sales could be made to individuals outside of Europe—quite easily cutting into other markets. In addition, the Internet was less developed in Europe, perhaps limiting the possibilities for experimenting with new web technologies.

Another interesting option was to partner, or even purchase, a successful online broker like E*trade. This could provide MetLife with a customer base, technological expertise, and a more complete web offering. However, this would not likely solve the major problem of integrating MetLife's current systems with the Web—and could still be perceived by the sales agents as a move into their territory.

Richard knew he had plenty of options. His challenge was to choose the best ones—those which would provide MetLife with a profitable return on the required investments, enthuse and maintain a forward-looking IC group, and generate sustainable competitive advantages for MetLife. "I am confident that with all the options we have, we can get the MetLife Web venue making money."

GLOSSARY OF TERMS

aggregator   Aggregator is the term for online operations that provide information and sometimes the sale of the majority of products/services in a given industry. Aggregators are an online equivalent of "category killers" like HomeDepot or PetsMart.

associate   Associate is the common term used to describe an online partner who promotes the products of a larger vendor at its site in return for a commission on sales or a "bounty." Associate programs can allow companies to organize large proprietary sales networks. These associate programs are being built in cooperation with many types of web venues including community sites (e.g., Association of Retired Persons), personal home pages, non-profit sites, and other business sites of all sizes.

collaborative filtering Collaborative filtering occurs when both a consumer and the database of that consumer's former interaction with the web venue collaborate to personalize the data or web venue for that consumer. This could involve knowledge learned from a consumer's interaction with the site and the specific requests of the consumer at that time.

disintermediation Disintermediation is the process of by-passing an agent or middleman, and occurs when a middleman is no longer adding sufficient value relative to the open market. Insurance agents could be disintermediated by the Internet where consumers can easily find the services that previously were delivered by the agent.

dynamically generated content Dynamically generated content is created in real-time in a process where a database is queried for relevant information and this information is then posted into a standard web page framework or template.

infomediary An infomediary provides information on products or services, but does not sell them. An example would be *Consumer Reports* which provides consumer product information, but does not endorse, advertise, or sell commercial products. One theory is that in the virtual world the information regarding a product is as valuable as the product itself.

marketspace Marketspace is a term for describing the virtual marketplace on the Internet.

personalization Personalization is the customizing of content and/or context to each individual's preferences. There are obviously many levels of personalization, but the tendency on the Web is towards further customized interactivity.

portal An Internet portal acts as a gateway to other sites. Portals vary from general gateways such as search engines, to gateways dedicated to a specific industry, product, or consumer interest. They do not contain information at the site, they only provide links to relevant sites.

server In general, a server is a computer that provides services to computer programs in the same or other computers. Specific to the Web, a web server is a computer that provides, or serves up, requested HTML pages or files. The web browser in a computer is a client that requests HTML files from web servers.

transactional Transactional refers to the commerce ability of a web venue. A web venue that is transactional allows the purchase of information, products, or services entirely over the Internet.

Y2K Y2K refers to the problem that many software applications will encounter due to the year being expressed in a two-digit format (e.g., 98 vs. 1998). In the year 2000, some software programs may incorrectly interpret the "00" or freeze some information systems.

Dominion Trust: Distribution Channel Development

By Professor James McKeen and Paula Bund

There had been a sense of urgency in the tone of the Internet strategy discussion paper (see Appendix 1) circulated six months ago by John Davidson, the webmaster at Dominion Trust. In it, John had forcefully argued that Dominion Trust should pursue a leadership strategy by developing the Internet as a full service medium.

> The emergence of the Internet represents a fundamentally important development that has the potential to impact Dominion Trust's core businesses, internal operations, and create new business expansion opportunities. Those who embrace the technology sooner, will have greater opportunity to understand the issues and react accordingly.

As a result of John's hard work, Dominion Trust was on the verge of being the first financial institution in Canada to launch a national full-service Internet banking web site. It was now April 1, 1996, and the launch of the full-service site was scheduled for June 1. Much of the ground work in terms of the look and feel of the site had been completed, but John had not yet come to a conclusion about how much, if anything, Dominion Trust should charge for this new distribution channel. In addition, he also had yet to decide whether Dominion Trust should pursue the option of developing a fully secure private net, DT Access, in partnership with a large, multi-national company.

Carl Shellon, Vice President, Distribution Development, had read with satisfaction John's strategy paper. He liked John's aggressive recommendations and innovative strategies. It was Carl's job, however, to integrate Internet banking with the number of new distribution channels that were rapidly being brought to market. In addition to Internet banking, the launch of DT Link, Dominion Trust's proprietary banking software was set for May 15, another first for Dominion Trust. In addition, Tim Daniels, New Media Consultant, had reported back to him just that morning that the meeting with third-party financial software developers had reached a critical stage and Carl must decide whether to go ahead or break off talks altogether. As well, Bell Canada had only yesterday informed him that the screenphone technology was doing very well in their recent introduction in London and Saint John's, and they should be launching the product in Toronto and Montreal in August, 1996. Finally, kiosk banking was in its final stages of development and should be launched sometime in the summer.

Source: This case was prepared by Paula Bund under the supervision of Professor James McKeen as a basis for class discussion. © 1997 Queen's School of Business, Kingston, Ontario.

Carl couldn't help but laugh softly to himself. The world of banking was rapidly changing. It was hard to know who the competitors really were—outside financial institutions or newly developed distribution channels within Dominion Trust itself! Dominion Trust had just spent $2 million on developing DT Link, but screenphone technology and strong brand name third-party software were already eroding market share even before the product was launched. In addition, Internet banking competed with all of these channels as it will likely be the lowest cost channel with the added bonus of being highly functional and easily accessible for a rapidly growing segment of the Canadian population. As Dominion Trust was pushing to be the first in the market in many of these channels, there were no benchmarks, and no way of knowing what the competitive reaction may be. Despite the high number of uncertainties, decisions had to be made.

As a matter of fact, in preparation for a meeting of the board scheduled for April 30, Bill Michaels, Senior Vice President Banking and Information Services, had asked Carl to report on several of the outstanding decisions that Distribution Development had been working on. In particular, Bill wanted to know:

1. What John will recommend in regard to the pricing and positioning of banking on the Internet, and whether Dominion Trust should develop a private net.
2. What Tim will recommend in regard to partnering with third-party software providers.

Carl looked over his already full calendar, pencilled in a time slot four days hence, and called a meeting with John and Tim. In the meeting both John and Tim were expected to present a brief report outlining their final recommendations.

HISTORY OF DOMINION TRUST

Dominion Trust had targeted the personal banking sector of the banking industry since the early 1970s and had built a steady reputation of innovativeness and personal service. Throughout the 1980s, while Canada's big six banks were preoccupied with loans to Third World countries, leveraged buyouts and real estate, Dominion Trust grew steadily. As the LBOs began to dry up and Third World countries began to default on their loans, the banks began to take greater notice of the domestic market. As a result, Dominion Trust's market share began to slip through the late 1980s and early 1990s.

However, Dominion Trust was not about to lose their hard earned gains, and again, through aggressive product offerings and innovative service, Dominion Trust started to regain marketshare in 1993 to hold 8 percent of the personal financial services market. In 1994 Dominion Trust gained another 11 basis points, and added another 15 basis points throughout 1995.

In the mutual funds market Dominion Trust added 10 percent to hold $3.5 billion in assets in 1994. In the same year Toronto Dominion Bank gained $7.5 billion to hold $5.46 billion and Royal Bank added .25 percent to hold $11.9 billion. All the other banks lost volume. However the toughest competition in mutual funds did not come from the banks but from the mutual fund companies: Investors Group Inc. gained 11.8 percent to hold $17.1 billion; Mackenzie gained 14.6 percent to hold $9.4 billion; Trimark added 36.8 percent to hold $6.8 billion, and; Fidelity added 11.5 percent to hold $5.2 billion of the mutual fund market.

Most recently, banks and other financial institutions had been trying to win marketshare through personal financial service, which had been Dominion Trust's traditional market niche. The threat they posed was substantial as the banks had strong brand names and strong ties with customers that go back generations. While Dominion Trust had the edge in product innovation, they now had to not only beat the banks on service (to offer better, more innovative products and services) but they also had to reduce costs sufficiently to compensate for margin pressure on their core products.

As Dominion Trust moved into 1996, their strategic focus remained on building those core banking accounts and dollar balances that are vital to revenue production both through net investment income and fee income. To do this Dominion Trust had targeted the development of innovative means of meeting the changing needs of their growing customer base. Increased accessibility was thought to be one of the key components to achieving crucial volume targets. Therefore the challenge was to deepen the customer relationship while at the same time maintaining consistent quality in whatever means or location the customer wished to interact with Dominion Trust.

DISTRIBUTION DEVELOPMENT

Why make the world more confusing than it already is?

Bill Michaels, Senior Vice President Banking and Information Services

The slogan *Go Wide, Go Deep* aptly captured Bill Michaels' philosophy and the mood of the Distribution Development team. Because Dominion Trust had a broad spectrum of customers with a range of desires for various channels of interaction with the bank, Bill Michaels and the

Distribution Development team had been endeavoring to develop and integrate the options presented by proprietary software, third-party software and the Internet. In the words of Bill Michaels:

> By taking advantage of all options, we hedge against being behind the learning curve in any one channel, and advance our drive to create a virtual banking experience for our customers. This will position Dominion Trust as innovative, potentially increase our market share, and allow us to reap benefits in terms of direct fee income and reduced distribution costs.

By 1996, Dominion Trust customers could interact with the company through the Quick Serve telephone banking and brokerage service, 300 full-service branch locations, 800 automated banking machines (which included 50 drive thrus), and the Internet. Each channel of distribution had its own cost structure and positioning strategy. While Bill Michaels was firm in his position that Dominion Trust would never force its customers to use one channel over the other, they would give people the benefit of using the more cost efficient channels. In other words, Bill was committed to bringing a broad spectrum of competitively priced channels to the market to allow their customers to choose the channels that best fit their needs.

As well, in terms of technology, Bill recognized that it was unlikely that a single device, software package, or communicating network would completely dominate the interactions between consumers and Dominion Trust. It was therefore important that Dominion Trust operate with an open platform policy to ensure Dominion Trust's ability to communicate with many devices and/or software, and to ensure that wherever possible Dominion Trust would be able to seek leadership where logical opportunities arose.

In terms of the effect on the structure of Dominion Trust of these newly created alternate distribution channels, Bill Michaels predicted that this would be minimal. Long considered a competitive disadvantage, Dominion Trust had fewer physical points of distribution. Therefore, as new electronic distribution channels gained acceptance, this historical disadvantage may become a competitive advantage as no major reorganizational impact would be needed. On the other hand, the introduction of telephone banking at a larger bank, would more than likely have a greater impact on their infrastructure in terms of redundancy and downsizing. By implementing these new forms of distribution channels, it was Bill's opinion that Dominion Trust would benefit in terms of: reduced staffing requirements in the push for growth: a reduced need for the expansion of physical distribution points; ability to participate in currently untapped markets (such as rural communities); enhanced customer retention capabilities; new revenue streams; and, brand image enhancement.

TELEPHONE BANKING

Quick Serve

Distribution Development has developed various channels over the years. The first and most successful initiative was the introduction of telephone banking in January 1993. Branded under the name Quick Serve, its initial objectives were threefold: to acquire new customers, to mitigate the disadvantage of a smaller branch presence across the country, and to take a leadership role in the industry vis-à-vis this new distribution channel. While other banks were using telephone banking as an add-on to existing branch interactions, Dominion Trust took the position that Quick Serve would allow customers to do anything they could do at a branch except that which was physically impossible. In effect, the customer would have a branch office at the touch of their fingertips.

Carl Shellon headed the introduction of Quick Serve. To launch the service successfully, Carl took lessons from the introduction of Dominion Trust's automatic bank machines (ABMs) in 1983. When the first ABMs were introduced they were simple to use, however, as customers became familiar with the technology and Dominion Trust added functionality, the ABMs gradually became more complicated. With Quick Serve, Carl took a similar position believing that Dominion Trust's customers had to become comfortable, in terms of safety and security, with long-distance banking over the telephone. Therefore, and in contrast to other financial institutions, Dominion Trust customers always had access to a live operator to lead them through step by step if they requested it.

However, the biggest challenge at the time was not whether customers would use the new service. Rather the challenge was to decide whether the business model for Quick Serve would disenfranchise the branches, or would the branches incorporate Quick Serve within their system. Ultimately it was decided that Quick Serve would be launched as a cost-center in support of the branch. In this way it was thought that branch staff would sell Quick Serve and not see it as competing with the branch for business. Therefore any business booked through Quick Serve (i.e., buying an RRSP or opening a chequing account) is allocated back to the branch of the customer's choosing. All fee revenue that is generated (i.e., paying a bill over Quick Serve) is booked with the distribution channel. This remains the business model of Dominion Trust today.

As a result of the above customer and branch policies, Dominion Trust has an interactive voice response (IVR) rate of 80–84 percent, as compared to an estimated 73–75 percent at other banks.

Pricing of Quick Serve

While customers were never pushed toward the new service, they were encouraged to try it. Quick Serve was initially offered at "no additional charge" with regular account charges being applied only for transactions, plus the pricing of bill payments over the phone or ABM has been positioned below those performed in branches. The intention was to overcome customer resistance to trying this new type of banking and to attract new customers.

Dominion Trust has experienced a tremendous amount of growth in the number of customers and the number of calls into the Quick Serve service. However, with their success, the cost of the service also grew, and with the current fee structure it was projected that Dominion Trust would lose over $5 million in 1996. This despite the fact that a projected 30 million calls would be placed to the Quick Serve service, of which approximately 6 million would be handled by operators and 24 million would be interactive voice response. Finally in February, 1996, Dominion Trust's management had to make the hard decision that the status quo was not sustainable. The company was losing too much revenue opportunity (see Appendix 2). Carl Shellon was charged with the task of pricing Quick Serve so as to recover as much of the shortfall between costs and revenue as possible but without destroying the competitiveness of the Quick Serve service.

It was Carl Shellon's philosophy that the pricing of Quick Serve must at least be partially determined by the actual expense of operating that channel. Therefore: in-branch service should be the most expensive; electronic service where Dominion Trust offered service (e. g., Quick Serve live operators) should be the second most expensive; electronic service where the customer self-serves should be the lowest cost, and; sales calls/interaction should be free.

However, Carl was also aware that banking traditions and competitive realities limited the extent to which Dominion Trust could appropriately price branch service, despite the fact that Quick Serve offered value in terms of low-cost convenience. The solution had to not only be fair and equitable for the 450,000 active Quick Serve customers, but it must also be consistent with current overall pricing strategies.

Carl proposed the following options:

Option 1   Maintain the status quo.

Option 2   Introduce a flat rate service charge of $1.95 per month per customer.

Option 3   Introduce a service charge of .25 per IVR call and $1.00 per live operator call.

Option 4   Introduce a modified per transaction service charge using incremental charges for use of operator where IVR is an option, and the introduction of fees for inquiries.

In the end, Carl recommended the conservative adoption of Option 4 because it was a modified version of the existing price structure with the introduction of several new transaction based fees, as opposed to the introduction of a new type of fee for access. In this way, Carl hoped to mitigate the tide of potential customer complaints or defections. It also had the advantage of being a user pay system, which was the direction that Dominion Trust wanted to start pushing its customers in. However, the solution did not recover the full revenue shortfall and in some instances the fees for in-branch services were still lower.

DOMINION TRUST'S PROPRIETARY SOFTWARE

DT Link

The idea of PC banking has been around since 1975, and in fact was introduced by some of the major banks in the U.S. in 1985. However the market at that time did not have a critical mass of PCs and a PC friendly population. Therefore the first effort to introduce PC banking was a massive flop and the banking industry had for the most part written it off. The advent of telephone banking, however, gave PC banking not only the necessary infrastructure in terms of bank processing but also the customer acceptance of doing banking from a distance.

As Bill Michaels commented:

> To imagine that a personal computer in 1985 would have been trustworthy enough to effect a banking transaction I think was hoping for a lot more than people were prepared to accept then. It is a big psychological step to push a button on a telephone to transfer money from point A to point B. You don't do that lightly! Therefore Dominion Trust took the position that the bank had to gradually ease its customers into using these emerging distribution channels. For example, a customer that is trying telephone banking for the first time may initially do a query on the balance of an account. When they find that it is safe and easy they are next encouraged to transfer some money from account A to account B and then check the account to make sure it all happened, and it did, and they feel safe. As people become comfortable with the new technology, Dominion Trust will lead them into the more robust functions that PC banking can offer.

The actual proprietary software, DT Link, was developed for $2 million from November 1994 to January 1996. It was designed to be a very simple, but function-rich Windows-based software that connects Dominion Trust and the retail or business banking customer in a very private, computer-to-computer, secure session. (See Appendix 3 for key features and benefits of DT Link.)

Based on the positive results of a PC banking pilot completed in August 1995, and the fact that by March 1996, Dominion Trust had nearly 15,000 people preregistered, Dominion Trust planned to launch DT Link, nationally on May 30, 1996. The software would be available at Dominion Trust branches, or could be requested through the telephone service and mailed. This launch date would position Dominion Trust as the first financial institution to offer a PC banking product nationally. Not surprisingly, other financial institutions, were also set to launch similar products.

Pricing and Marketing of DT Link

While this was a new service with very little competitive activity, research had indicated a willingness among customers to pay for DT Link. National Bank was offering a regionally limited PC Banking program and was charging $7.50 per month, which included access to telephone banking. After weighing the options, Carl Shellon's final recommendation was $7.95 per month, plus a one-time $10.00 start-up fee. This fee would include access to Quick Serve and regular account service charges would apply. Based on historical Quick Serve figures, on average, Dominion Trust customers would pay 3.2 bills and perform 1.2 transfers per month. Net average fee revenue was estimated at $0.41. The help desk was estimated to cost $8 per call and Carl assumed that 15 percent of new and 3 percent of existing DT Link customers would use this customer support service. Host processing, or CPU costs, were based on an average of 8 connects per customer per month at $.07 per connect.

DT Link would be marketed nationally with press releases and Internet support. The development of its packaging and user guides would be designed to reinforce Dominion Trust branding. The customers who had preregistered would be targeted first. However by September, Carl Shellon had planned to proactively market to non-primary Dominion Trust customers and potential Dominion Trust prospects by using Internet direct response, direct mail and statement inserts. Therefore by the end of 1996, Carl expected to have 26,000 customers using DT Link, with 30,000 new sign-ups by 1997, and finally 94,000 customers by the end of year 2000.

Future functions planned for personal PC banking included the ability to receive MasterCard statements electronically, and an enhanced payment facility. Business accounts could also be enhanced by establishing linkage to EDI, plus a payroll service package. In turn, Dominion Trust would benefit from new record keeping options that would suppress the issuance of statements or the requirements of passbooks.

Third-Party Software Opportunities

Software providers, such as Intuit and Microsoft, had developed technology that could deliver remote banking services to personal computers through personal financial software products. Instead of spending substantial time and effort on creating and updating their financial picture, customers would be able to download their account balance and transaction information from any bank that had partnered with a third-party software provider directly into their computer through a gateway owned by the software provider. The financial software packages were powerful, allowing customers to create meaningful views of their entire financial situation through state-of-the-art graphing, report creation, financial advice, budgeting and planning. Customers would pay the financial institution for the ability to connect to the software provider, and the software provider would act as a trusted party delivering the financial institution's information to them. In turn, the software provider would charge banks a small amount every time a customer passes through their gateway to their bank.

The market for PC banking through third-party software had proven to be lucrative and many corporations had set aggressive goals. Intuit, for example, envisioned the ability to deliver the benefits of their product, *Quicken,* on behalf of most financial institutions in North America. In fact, as of January 30, 1996, 37 banks in the United States were working with Intuit. According to Intuit's data this represented 7 of the top 10 banks, 14 of the top 20 banks, the first and second largest discount brokers, the United States' oldest investment bank, and the largest proprietary charge card issuer.

As part of the package, Intuit was also providing an Internet service. Intuit's security was based on state-of-the-art RSA data security encryption. A communications module within Quicken connected directly to customers' financial institutions via a private network. All transactions were therefore secured by end-to-end encryption. While access to the Quicken Financial Network web site would be free to the financial institution's customer, for a minimum monthly charge Intuit would also provide full Internet access. As of February 1996, Internet access cost Quicken users $1.95 for one hour per month. Frequent users had the option of buying 7 hours for $9.95 per month. All additional hours were $1.95 per month. As the telecommunications was provided by Concentric Network Corporation, Quicken users had access to Concentric's network which included over 200 points of presence, covering 90 percent of PC owning households in the US, and 71 percent of households in Canada.

The Risk and the Benefits

The biggest risk to Dominion Trust in developing a partnership with one of these third-party software providers was considered to be the loss of control of the customer interface. The financial institutions risked losing the ability to differentiate, to add new products, or to build brand identity. Bill also noted that many of the software providers were still targeted largely at the U.S. market. One of the important differences between the Canadian and American banking systems was that, in the U.S., bill payment was not considered a banking function.

On the other hand, Dominion Trust would benefit from an association with a strong brand name in personal financial software and the ability to meet the needs of many existing and potential customers—consumers and small businesses, Windows and Macintosh users, financial sophisticates and financial novices, and users of multiple software and online interfaces. For example, Quicken was Canada's premier personal financial software, holding approximately 75 per cent of the market (an estimated 700,000 Canadian households), while Microsoft Money held an additional 18 per cent. The other software companies split the remaining market. Further, 93 per cent of Quicken users rated it as excellent or above average. It was for these reasons that one Internet critic thought that banks developing their own software was folly:

> What proprietary edge these banks hope to gain by private-labelling a package that badly trails Quicken and Microsoft Money in the marketplace, and in the process limiting customer's choice of financial package, is hard to imagine. (http://www.idcresearch.com/96pred.htm)

The Deal

Dominion Trust had been negotiating with one large software provider for a short-term window of exclusivity in the marketplace and a longer-term partnership. The proposed deal was as follows:

- Dominion Trust would have an opportunity to be alone in the marketplace if launched by May 15, 1996.
- Dominion Trust could use the software provider's customer mailing list and develop a public relations win.

The Problem

Despite the apparent win-win opportunity, Bill Michaels was still doubtful. He wondered:

> Does the Canadian consumer want to bank with a financial software package? Or does that consumer want to bank with brand image that emphasizes security? Research has suggested that people are not worried about the capability of their PCs, but when it comes to banking consumers first think about security, reputation and trust, and with banking the rest is "glitz." People give money to banks to keep it safe. Banks and customers tend to forget that, but in the back of their minds, this attitude continues to reside.

Bill continued with an example:

> I have $100,000. If you think about it, would I give it to Quicken? I don't think so. Would I give it to a financial institution like the Royal Bank or Dominion Trust? Yup, I think so. I don't know if this attitude will last, but it is very powerful at the moment.

Bill Michaels also pointed out that the "disintermediation" of the software provider would, for the first time in banking history, drive a wedge between the context of banking and its content. The third-party software provider would control the context: they would make it easy for people as they provide the repairs, the software interface, the switch to go from point A to point B, etc. In this context, the financial institutions become the content, and in this position the institution could be viewed basically as a commodity. Most of the banks in Canada viewed this as a real threat, and it was Bill's sense that it would be highly unlikely that the financial institutions in Canada would let the commodification of banking happen.

The Options

The options are as follows:

- Announce a partnership and commit to a launch date of June 30, 1996, to coincide with the launch of DT Link.
- Announce a partnership but work towards a launch date in the fourth quarter of 1996 or later presuming a Canadian real time solution can be articulated.
- Hold off on an announcement of a partnership and work towards a launch date in the fourth quarter of 1996 or later.
- Break off partnership plans.

The Eleventh Hour Opportunity

Recently another software provider had come to the table with a different potential opportunity: they would build into a bank's proprietary software a switch that would allow the customer to download into their financial software package for a very low cost. Or they would give the Dominion Trust's customers a code that could write a conversion utility that would go between Dominion Trust's proprietary products and their financial software package. Therefore, if a customer had DT Link, she could also use the national brand name software package without any bother. In other words, this software provider would not stand between the bank and the customer, but would stand in support. This change in direction had only appeared in the last four months.

Distribution Development

Tim Daniels was confident that Dominion Trust could only gain by partnering with the third-party software providers. They offered a strong brand name in personal finances and high customer satisfaction. However, he had to ask himself whether the current risks outweighed the benefits and perhaps a wait-and-see approach would be more beneficial for Dominion Trust in the long term.

Tim also had to recognize the problem of cannibalization of the market for Dominion Trust's own DT Link by third-party software. In his opinion, however, there were different products for different types of people.

The Quicken and Money market, for example, is for people who want to have active control over their finances. They faithfully punch in their receipts and review their budgets and reports every week to keep track of their money. DT Link, on the other hand, is built for people who want passive control over their finances, or simply do not have the time to rigorously punch in the data but still want to review their budget and track finances. These are the Quicken and Money wannabees. We also have a third market of people who just want to know how much money is in their account so they can go out and have a beer. Dominion Trust is not willing to pick the product for the consumer. First, it is arrogant, and second it is wrong. Simply put, Dominion Trust is trying to cover as many bases as possible—without losing its shirt.

INTERNET BANKING

> *Just because people are signing up on the net like crazy, does it mean that they will want to do their banking there?*
>
> Carl Shellon, VP Distribution Development

Bill Michaels was of the opinion that, as of yet, only technically sophisticated Internet users would put up with the vagaries of the Internet and even those folks would worry about the safety of their money. Therefore Bill was reluctant to invest a lot of money in the Internet while the level of service, in terms of response time and consistency, was not there. However, this is not to say that Dominion Trust was going to ignore the Internet. In late 1995, Bill Michaels committed Dominion Trust to spending essentially $1.75 million for research and concept development to learn about the Internet and the role it could play within Dominion Trust. Michaels' strategy was to build on all the strengths of the Internet medium, being considerate of the issues of security. Over time Dominion Trust would build an entire array of online services for customers who chose to interact with Dominion Trust through this channel. In fact Dominion Trust had chosen to pursue a leadership strategy that would encompass not only strategic partnerships in order to capture the full-service vision, but also actively seek breakthrough opportunities.

Even though no Internet budget existed at the beginning of 1995, the first Dominion Trust sites were nevertheless launched by May of that year. In fact, Dominion Trust was the first financial institute to have a multi-site presence on the Internet.

In July 1995, Carl Shellon hired John Davidson to the position of webmaster. It was John's job to articulate and execute an Internet banking strategy for Dominion Trust. To allay any lingering doubts about the viability of the Internet as a source of revenue and market share growth, John quickly established that the Internet was not a passing fad, but was in fact a medium that Dominion Trust must quickly develop as a full-service channel. Since then he had been proved right as the number of people accessing the Internet had grown at a startling rate.

John also saw the Internet not only as a customer-focused service provider, but also as a great direct marketing tool. For example, customers could sign up to get mutual funds and interest rate information through an e-mail service. From the tracking of which sites the customer hits most often, Dominion Trust could develop a sophisticated customer profile. For Dominion Trust this was very important because for many people Dominion Trust was their second institution. The Internet offered an intelligent opportunity to strengthen customer relationships.

By November 1995, John had developed a site whereby customers could not only be informed of product and service areas, but they could also interact with their demand account details, and access other services such as investment recommendation tools. John had targeted June 30, 1996, as the launch date of Dominion Trust's full-service Internet banking, which would allow customers to become aware of products and services, become educated about costs/benefits, be able to select those products and services that met their needs, actually purchase the product, and finally manage that product post-purchase. The site's functionality would be extended by August 30 to include transactions and bill payments. By November 1995, 10,000 people had registered for the Internet banking service and John expected to have 35,000 people signed on by the end of 1996.

Competitive Environment

The Internet was emerging as an efficient delivery channel for financial services. In Canada, all of the Big Six banks had Internet sites. Each site had different features and took advantage of the variety of opportunities the Internet offered. For example, the Toronto Dominion Bank's web site allowed customers to conduct simple financial planning, and the Royal Bank had financial software tools that customers could download.

Also, small financial institutions, such as Toronto based Bayshore Trust, had been jumping online with innovative and strategic offerings. By December 1995, Bayshore Trust was offering loan approvals over the Internet. When web site customers applied for a loan, the information obtained from the loan applicant was transferred to a credit bureau via a secure electronic link and approved or rejected in less than two minutes. While waiting, the customer could also order investment vehicles and learn more about GICs, mutual funds and retirement savings plans.

The Internet was also emerging as the channel of preference for delivering brokerage services. Mutual fund providers, such as Scotia-McLeod, insurance companies and stock brokers were all rushing on to the Internet. Further, these companies were hoping to offer banking functions, just as banks have been interested in providing insurance and brokerage services. Therefore feasible strategies could arise for a player with a large customer list to target their customers for electronic banking. In addition, these players may partner with a U.S. firm such as Security First National Bank to bring these services to market quickly.

On a different front, the credit card companies and technology companies such as Intuit, Microsoft, IBM, Netscape, DigiCash and others had been scrambling to create new processes to mediate transactions between consumers and merchants, and cut out or limit the role of the financial institutions altogether.

Pricing and Positioning of Internet Banking

Although similar in many respects, Internet banking differs from PC banking. With PC banking, the application software program runs on the customer's PC. The customer dials into the bank with a modem, downloads data and runs the programs that are resident on their computer, perhaps sending back a batch of requests such as transfers between accounts. Upgrades are incorporated into new releases, and as more functionality is added, these programs can take up more and more space on the customer's computer. The Internet eliminates the need for special bank-issued software as the actual software resides on the financial institution's server in the form of their home page. As financial institutions continue to differentiate themselves by customizing the services and information they provide over the Internet, the software can be updated at any time and functionally expanded without becoming cumbersome for the customer to operate.

To Carl Shellon and John Davidson the spectre of cannibalization was readily apparent. After investing in a proprietary PC banking product, the Distribution Development team was at the same time building a service that not only would probably be required by the public to offer at a very low cost or to give away, but the service would also have basically the same functionality. Carl Shellon couldn't help but wonder whether PC banking was a concept that was worn out before Dominion Trust could get it to market:

> The faster I advance one solution, I am chipping away at the audience of other services, and at some point I may even be killing it. Further, Internet banking and PC banking, as well as a host of other banking services, are going to be launched at about the same time. At what point does the consumer get confused?

John Davidson was also concerned about tensions both within Dominion Trust and within the Canadian marketplace itself.

> The fundamental tension in pricing the Internet service arises from the extent to which Dominion Trust wants the channel to pay for itself, versus the extent to which Dominion Trust wants to shy away from creating barriers for customers to use the service. As well, there are tensions within the marketplace. Historically people expect to pay very little or nothing at all for service over the Internet. On the other hand by making the customer pay for the Internet service, the customer begins to understand that there are costs associated with the service and enable them to perceive value.

Therefore, the biggest decision that John was facing was how to price and position Internet banking in relation to the other channels. The hurdle set by Carl Shellon was that full-service Internet banking had to pay for its development and ongoing costs within 18 months. John had budgeted for the following fixed expenses for 1996:

Marketing—$225,000

Network—$125,000

Consulting—$90,000

Labour—$400,000

In addition, John had already purchased $225,000 in hardware and another $125,000 in software, and planned to spend approximately $75,000 and $50,000 respectively each year for the next four years. Given these expenses, what would be the most appropriate price point to offer Dominion Trust's first full service Internet banking channel?

PRIVATE NET

DT Access

In partnership with a large, international computer company, Dominion Trust had trialed the concept of a proprietary network that would guarantee Dominion Trust customers quality and security in their Internet banking. For $5, Dominion Trust customers could purchase an

Internet Access Kit which would include Netscape, Trumpet Winsock, Eudora, and a dial service for TCP/IP. This kit not only allowed the customer to access the Dominion Trust homepage, but also to gain access to the Internet. There were no monthly charges if the customer just wanted to perform banking interactions with Dominion Trust, however the bank would be charged $5.50 per hour for local access and $11.00 per hour for 1-800 access. It was estimated that 10 per cent of the calls would be on the 1-800 line and that the average user connect time per month would be 60 minutes. There was also a monthly charge of $2,000 for a dedicated T1 line. Approximately 15,000 customers would use the service.

While there were compelling reasons to go with this Internet package, both Carl Shellon and John Davidson had their doubts. Perhaps a better solution would be to lobby a service provider such as a telephone company or cable company and offer to bake their Internet package right on to the CD-ROM sent to the customers of PC banking. Once loaded, all of these customers could be invited to visit the Dominion Trust site at no charge, but once the customer steps through the door onto the Internet they will be the customer of the service provider. This could be compelling for the service provider, because instead of a potential customer trying to make a value decision about whether they want Internet access from no experience, they would have a reason to access the Internet via Dominion Trust.

OTHER OPPORTUNITIES

Kiosk Banking, Screenphone Technology

Kiosk Banking.   Dominion Trust was also developing Kiosk Banking, which was viewed as a new distribution tool capable of functioning as a self-service device, as a point of remote access to experts, as well as a method of interactive marketing. For example, a Self-Service Plus Kiosk would be part of an automated or partially manned branch where expertise was not located.

Carl Shellon gave the following illustration:

A customer interested in an RRSP is seated in a private kiosk. The customer may on her own interact with a program to determine which mutual funds are best for her, and then call upon the assistance of the RRSP expert by pressing a "LIVE HELP" button on the key board. At this point, a video agent will appear on the screen and provide assistance to the customer, and/or take over manipulating the software. When a decision is made to purchase a product or service, the agent would manipulate the "Sales Tech" applications to complete the sale while the customer looked on. Should there be a requirement for a document to be signed, the attached printer would print and deliver the documentation. The customer would then sign a copy and either hand it over to Dominion Trust staff, or place it in the depository.

Other applications would include wills and estates, financial planning, and even instant mortgage approval.

According to Tim Daniels, kiosk banking held the key to future applications:

> Today you can play a video off your CD-ROM. Why can't that be a picture of me, your banker, giving you some advice through your television? These public access devices are just a method of getting the learning into place so that eventually the bank can get into the home. This represents a tremendous opportunity which requires broad band technology to develop a little further. As a matter of fact, however, Rogers Cable is trialing this same concept in Newmarket at the moment.

Screenphones.   Dominion Trust first got involved with screenphone technology from a "test" perspective as an alternate method to deliver Quick Serve. Screenphones add a data screen similar to that of an ABM to a regular touch-tone phone. The data screens are supported by voice or audio recordings. It was thought that the addition of visuals would result in a higher number of calls being completely handled by automation by comparison to a regular telephone. However, the decision to invest in screenphone technology had always been linked with the decision to be prepared to distribute the devices.

Now the telcos have adopted the ADSI (Analog Display Service Interface) technology as an industry standard, and have developed a suite of applications that run on a Northern Telecom telephone. They have introduced the product in London and Saint John's and will be introducing the product to Toronto and Montreal in August 1996. Dominion Trust will be running a visually based Quick Serve service on the ADSI sets.

CONCLUSION

John Davidson and Tim Daniels all but collided with one another at the doorway to the printer. Both were busily preparing for their meeting with Carl. "You know, John," Tim said, "I have been doing some thinking. Traditionally banks have built strong reputations by dealing with people on a personal service level. Now they are developing those same ties through personal computers in homes. It really makes you wonder what banking is. Is banking going into the branch and performing deposits, withdrawals and bill payments, or is it using a software product to punch in your receipts. Most banks are appalled to discover that it is quickly becoming the later. Therefore the banks have to discover which are the right interfaces to interact with the needs of the customer. If Intuit is the preferred interface then the banks have to research that channel and find out how it can apply it without losing margins or control of the industry. The same is true for Internet banking and the host of other channels that are being developed."

John nodded in agreement. "The problem is," John continued, "how do you know what the future will bring?"

Appendix 1

INTERNET STRATEGY OVERVIEW FOR DOMINION TRUST

The potential of the Internet for Dominion Trust should not be understated. It is the lowest-cost channel available to serve our customers and, in spite of this low cost, the medium is rich with both marketing and distribution opportunities. In the years ahead, we will see the Internet become a medium widely available in homes, offices, and public spaces and used to provide information and services to broad consumer markets. The technologies underlying the Internet can also be exploited internally as low-cost, robust mediums for sharing information with the organization.

Dominion Trust must enter 1996 under the assumption that during the year the Internet will emerge as a viable commercial medium in which all financial institutions will be participating: either as leaders or scrambling to catch up. Over the past several years, the Internet has continued to surprise the industry, forcing giants such as Compuserv, AT&T, Bell, and Microsoft to reinvent their proprietary networks in favour of Internet-based solutions. This recognition by the major players removes any doubt that the Internet will continue its explosive growth—likely at a faster rate due to their support.

Security concerns are also expected to be resolved to the satisfaction of business and consumers during the year, fuelling the emergence of commerce on the Internet. Several banks in the U.S. are already online with secure solutions and some Dominion Trust competitors in Canada have already announced similar plans.

Dominion Trust's goal for 1996 must be to integrate the Internet with established Information Services and Marketing operations, establish a sound technological and business infrastructure upon which applications can be built, and continue to expand our Internet offerings with a steady stream of enhancements to our existing base.

Source: *Internet Strategy '96,* a discussion paper circulated by John Davidson, webmaster.

Appendix 2

COMPETITIVE POSITIONING OF QUICK SERVICE, FEBRUARY 1996

	Dominion Trust	Royal Bank*	Toronto Dominion	CIBC	Bank of Montreal
Part of flat fee	Yes	No	Yes	Yes	Yes
Free to seniors	Yes	No	Yes	Yes	Yes
Cost for IVR service	$.50 for bill payment; no charge for transfers, balance, or history inquiries	20 free balance inquiries, then $.50 each	$.50 for each bill payment and history inquiry, but no charge for transfer and balance inquiries	$.50 for each bill payment and 20 free inquiries	Only available as part of flat-fee package, which costs between $8.85 to $13.00 per month
Cost of operators	No additional charges for operators	No live operators	$1.30 for bill payments; $.75 for transfers; $.50 for balance inquiries; $1.10 for last five history transactions	No additional charges for operator	No live operators

*The Royal Bank also offers a $2.95 package for 20 free bill payments, transfers, balance and history inquiries, then $.50 each.

Source: Internal Dominion Trust document.

Appendix 3

KEY FEATURES AND BENEFITS OF DT LINK

Features	Benefits
Automatic set-up on first connection	Saves customers the hassle of setting up each of their accounts in the software. Makes getting started easier than other packages.
Online, real-time record keeping with categorization and report tool	Quick account updates with a few key strokes. Add own information and better understand your financial situation.
Online bill payment and transfers	Simplify finances make fewer calls to Quick Serve or trips to the branch.
Cheque service—issue, print and reconcile cheques from your PC	Saves time, helps better manage your chequing account activity.
E-mail access to Dominion Trust customer service officers	Easy to manage correspondence with Dominion Trust for service and purchases of additional products. No need to queue for service.
Export information to other popular applications (e.g., Quicken, MS Money)	Simplify customer use of other software, such as personal financial management, or spreadsheets.
Financial tools and information (e.g., mortgage, loan calculations, product rates)	Provides an opportunity to create "what if" scenarios for mortgages and loans, and stay on top of interest rates. Make better decisions.

Chapter 9

Electronic Commerce Marketing

Electronic commerce is where information systems and marketing converge. For many organizations, sales and marketing decisions, efficiencies, and impact provide the impetus for creation of an Internet presence. In fact, many of the specific contexts considered in previous chapters represent various forms of marketing using electronic channels. For example, the ISP business discussed in Chapter 4 essentially represents a new medium through which electronic commerce merchants and consumers can transact; Chapters 5 and 6, which covered electronic commerce products and services, discussed the creation of customer value using electronic commerce channels.

This chapter brings all of these perspectives together, integrates them, and presents cases that consider the following key electronic marketing decisions: product decisions, price decisions, channel decisions, and promotion decisions. Product decision questions include: What forms can electronic commerce products take? How are products best bundled and presented to consumers. How can consumer response be gauged? Price decision questions include: What pricing models (subscription, fee-for-service, etc.) exist, for what range of products, and under what circumstances? How can a company create and exploit value in an electronic commerce context? Channel decision questions include: What channels are best, for what products, and for what consumers? What are customer needs, and how can these best be met through electronic commerce? Finally, promotion decision questions include: What is the best way of advertising on the Web or advertising a presence on the Web? Is it more appropriate to use a push or pull strategy? How does one get noticed on the Web, and how much should be paid for advertising services? How can the effectiveness of advertising expenditures and messages be measured?

There are five objectives of this chapter. The first is to understand the benefits and limitations of the Internet from a marketing perspective. The second objective is to understand how to lead change by identifying areas in need of change, setting priorities, and selecting appropriate actions to achieve these changes. The third is to appreciate how to assess the value of investments in electronic commerce information technology by determining the costs and benefits of each option, in both monetary and strategic terms. The fourth is to learn how to develop new channels of distribution by integrating established practices into an electronic commerce environment. The fifth is to understand the actions necessary to educate and sell customers on the benefits of electronic commerce.

The first case in the chapter is "First Virtual (B)." "First Virtual (A)" in Chapter 7 outlined the efforts of First Virtual Holdings Incorporated to promote their Internet payments system. As time progressed, it became increasingly clear that the system was not gaining the widespread acceptance the company's management had hoped for. In order to stay afloat, the company switched its strategy to focus on interactive messaging solutions. The company had developed interactive banner ad product that functioned as its own mini–web page within a web page. The First Virtual banner ad allowed interested buyers to investigate, and even purchase, items without leaving the page on which the banner ad was found. The company intended to market this product to Internet retailers and direct marketing firms. The case addresses effectiveness issues of online marketing. It also broaches the issue of the acceptability of various marketing techniques by looking at the fine line between what is regarded as acceptable (banner ads) and what is not (spam).

The second case is about Medisys, a holding company for a consortium of corporate health care program providers. The case begins with the company's founder, president, and CEO bursting in to the VP of operations' office exclaiming that the company *needs* a web site. The VP in question is left to ponder exactly what this means. First and foremost, she must decide on the site's overall purpose. Is it to generate new business? Create awareness? Increase customer satisfaction? Where does the site fit into the company's overall marketing strategy? This case examines the suitability of the Internet as either an advertising or distribution channel. It is intended to illustrate the decision-making process a company goes through as it establishes a presence on the World Wide Web.

First Virtual Holdings Incorporated (B)

By Professor Sid L. Huff and Michael Wade

It was November 1997, and Keith Kendrick, the new president of First Virtual Holdings Inc. (FVHI, www.firstvirtual.com), was waiting to speak to Lee Stein, FVHI's co-founder and CEO. As he waited, he scanned photographs of Stein with Ronald Reagan, Bill Clinton, Rod Stewart, Gene Hackman, Barry Bonds and most recently a photograph of Stein accepting the *San Diego Union Tribune*'s award of Entrepreneur of the Year. Kendrick was as impressed now as he had been six months ago when, as a senior vice president at AT&T, he had accepted the position of vice president and then president of FVHI. Kendrick and Stein had been instrumental in moving FVHI from its first product, the First Virtual Internet Payment System (FVIPS) to the Interactive Messaging Platform (IMP).

FVHI's primary focus until recently had been the FVIPS, an innovative approach to Internet commerce designed to facilitate payments in cyberspace securely and simply. Retail commerce on the Internet, however, hadn't grown as quickly as expected. As for the retail commerce that was conducted online, most was done so far via credit cards, with no security or with security provided through SSL, the "secure sockets layer" technology available on the popular Internet browsers.

CFO John Stachowiak noted,

> It was a chicken and egg problem, how to get enough consumers on one side and merchants on the other for the FVIPS to reach critical mass. In the end, we had trouble attracting enough merchants to the system. They didn't like the loss of spontaneity associated with our system of e-mail confirmation.

THE INTERACTIVE MESSAGING PLATFORM

In late 1996, a transactional media technical team was formed at FVHI led by co-founder Marshal T. Rose. This team developed the VirtualTAG, which is a multilayered, interactive web advertising banner (see

www.virtualtag.com, www.virtualadz.com for examples of VirtualTAGs).
What sets the VirtualTAG apart from regular web advertising banners is
that it has more than one layer, like a small web site. The whole buying
process can be completed through the banner. So from the users' perspective, an entire buying transaction can be executed without ever leaving
the web page to which they were connected. Originally, the idea had been
to promote the FVIPS though use of the VirtualTAG. However, as time
went on, Stein and Kendrick began to see the full potential of the idea.

"We sat down and took a hard look at our core competencies," says
Kendrick, "and came up with one overriding thing: e-mail. Three of the
four founders are e-mail experts, while none have payments experience." Director of Development Winn Rindfleisch points out that during
the process of perfecting the FVIPS, the development team had to deal
with compatibility issues of hundreds of e-mail programs. "E-mail in
theory is simple, but in practice it can be extremely complicated.
Thanks to our work with the FVIPS, we now say that we can deal with
every known major e-mail system."

The idea Stein and Kendrick came up with was to use VirtualTAG
banners in e-mail messages. They dubbed the process "interactive messaging." When a VirtualTAG is embedded in HTML enabled e-mail, it
will behave just as it does on a web page. That is to say, those receiving
the e-mail will be able to interact with the VirtualTAG, purchase an
item, submit information and so on, all without having to switch over
to a browser to visit another web site. If the user is not capable of receiving HTML e-mail, the software senses this and, instead of placing
the VirtualTAG, First Virtual can embed a URL into the e-mail so the
user can click through to a web site with the VirtualTAG or other
graphically rich content. The nature of the technology makes it necessary for the user to be online while the VirtualTAG is being accessed.
One possible application would be for the airlines. Kendrick elaborated,

> Distressed inventory is a huge problem for airlines. If a plane takes off and
> there are empty seats, that's revenue that is lost forever. Last-minute seat
> sales are often not last minute enough. By the time advertisements are writ-
> ten, sent to newspapers and printed, it's too late. E-mail, however, is a per-
> fect medium for advertising last-minute flight deals. Our idea is to work with
> airlines to send VirtualTAGs on a regular basis to consenting travellers by e-
> mail, through which they could find and pay for the best flight deals around.

Other possible applications include cross selling between related businesses such as rental car agencies, hotels and restaurants. VirtualTAGs
can be designed to solicit donations to charities and other good causes.
Basically, whenever an e-mail is sent, a VirtualTAG can be included.

A recent article from *Web Track,* an online journal, described the VirtualTAG as follows.

> VirtualTAG uses cross-platform multimedia tools such as Java and Shock-
> wave to create impressive interactive advertisements inside a standard-

sized banner: graphics and animation can fly in and out; text fields and forms can unfold and retract; real-time voices and music can underscore the action. An interactive selling and transaction tool as well, VirtualTAG allows users to view product information in the banner, register to receive information via e-mail, enter contests, and even shop, browse and buy through VirtualTAG's VirtualPIN standard, all without leaving the banner or—more importantly from the publisher's perspective—the site on which the banner is residing.

Stein identified five potential primary markets for interactive messaging:

- financial services companies (credit card issuers, banks)
- direct marketing firms
- catalogue companies
- travel companies (airlines, car rental agencies)
- publishing companies

An open question was whether or not to support payment methods other than the FVIPS in VirtualTAG banners. Director of Strategic Business Initiatives, Chris Wand explained,

> In general, any encryption solution is going to be more awkward to fit into a small "engine" because it relies on computational algorithms to protect the sensitive information. SET is likely to be even more awkward than SSL because it is more than just encryption—SET uses digital certificates to perform functions beyond just encryption of information, such as performing user and merchant authentication. That said, it is difficult to say with certainty where things stand with SET since it isn't truly implemented yet and standards are still being decided. We are currently evaluating the feasibility of incorporating an SSL payment engine into the VirtualTAG, but it's a bit too early to tell conclusively if it will work. The FVIPS payment engine is just 1.5kb making it possible to keep the size of VirtualTAG banners down to approximately 10kb, today's accepted standard for many high traffic sites. In comparison, the SSL payment engine is orders of magnitude larger than the FVIPS payment engine, even when it's compressed. This makes incorporating SSL a difficult task.

SPAM AND INTERACTIVE MESSAGING

Stein and Kendrick were quick to point out the difference between their form of interactive messaging and *spam,* or junk e-mail. Kendrick observed,

> Interactive messaging will be both solicited and targeted. We don't want to get a reputation as a company that uses spam. For example, take the credit card industry. Upwards of 20 per cent of calls credit card issuers get to their hotlines are from credit card holders checking if their payments were posted before the due date. This represents a vast amount of resources. E-mail is a perfect vehicle

for this. Credit card companies could automatically send out verification messages when payment is posted to a cardholder's account. In addition, they could send monthly statements by e-mail rather than regular mail, saving them millions a year. We could include a VirtualTAG banner with each e-mail. Credit card companies have the databases to target their advertising, so the VirtualTAG would advertise something the cardholder would be likely to buy. Most importantly, VirtualTAGs and other interactive messages will only be sent to customers who have elected to participate in the service and have a pre-existing relationship with the company "sponsoring" the e-mail.

MARKETING

Promoting the IMP required a different approach than promoting the FVIPS. FVHI planned to target large companies and become a corporate brand name rather than a consumer brand name.

Regarding the response the company has had so far to the IMP proposal, Stein said,

> This is the easiest sell I've ever seen. It's very simple for our clients to see the potential to reduce costs and increase efficiency using interactive messaging. For many, it's just putting online what they already have in other forms. Our success with IMP is "big deal weighted." If we can attract three or four large clients, the rest will follow. It's quite a long sales cycle, but corporate customers understand that they need this capability.

Kendrick added, "In a sense, the IMP is an easier sell than the FVIPS since we are going after a few big players rather than thousands of smaller players. We can focus our resources much more effectively."

As far as FVHI was aware, there was no direct competition in interactive messaging. Director of Strategy Pierre Wolff said, "There are companies out there that deal in messaging, and there are companies that have payment systems, but there is no one out there but us who can do both. That's our competitive advantage. We can provide a full service solution to clients. Technically speaking, our development team estimates that we're years ahead of our competition."

Revenue for the IMP would be structured as follows.

- one time development/customization/installation fee
- a per account setup fee
- a monthly per account maintenance fee
- a per transaction fee

Although detailed revenue forecasts were not available, FVHI was confident that once the interactive messaging infrastructure was in place, significant revenue generation would follow.

FINANCIAL INFORMATION

FVHI lost $11,972,936 on revenues of $1,111,905 through the first nine months of 1997. Their balance sheet was bolstered at the beginning of October 1997, when the company negotiated a private placement of $5,000,000 with a New York investment syndicate. See Exhibits 1, 2 and 3 for recent financial information.

Stein summed up the current strategy:

> It's a testament to the culture around here that we've come so far. While employee turnover in the industry is high, especially in the technical areas, we have not lost any of the key original technical team. The Interactive Messaging Platform is a culmination of what we have worked so long to develop— the opportunity to provide our customers with interactive Internet capabilities that go far beyond our present payment application.

On October 14, 1997, FVHI announced its first IMP client: computer giant Gateway 2000.

EXHIBIT 1   First Virtual Holdings Incorporated Statements of Operations

	Nine Months Ended September 30, 1997	Year Ended December 31, 1996	Year Ended December 31, 1995
Revenues	$1,111,905	$695,866	$197,902
Cost of revenues	217,662	265,900	123,375
Gross margin	894,243	429,966	74,527
Operating expenses			
Marketing and sales	4,015,239	1,836,545	346,400
Research and development	4,876,311	4,652,582	543,074
General and administrative	3,536,161	4,237,637	1,280,576
Total operating expenses	12,427,711	10,726,764	2,169,990
Depreciation and amortization	821,901	524,125	106,628
Loss from operations	(12,355,369)	(10,820,923)	(2,202,091)
Interest income (expense), net	382,433	130,983	(67,890)
Net loss	(11,972,936)	(10,689,940)	(2,269,981)
Net loss per share	(1.36)	(1.25)	(0.30)
Shares used in per share computation	8,827,919	8,524,068	7,599,106

EXHIBIT 2   First Virtual Holdings Incorporated Condensed Balance Sheets

	Nine Months Ended September 30 1997	*Year Ended December 31, 1996*	*Year Ended December 31, 1995*
Assets			
Current assets			
Cash and cash equivalents	$5,315,133	$17,127,971	$2,091,651
Short-term investment, available-for-sale	—	200,000	—
Accounts receivable	319,517	88,278	—
Prepaid expenses and other	120,591	83,840	10,953
Total current assets	5,755,241	17,500,089	2,102,604
Furniture and equipment, net	1,793,298	1,964,635	304,320
Information technology, net	26,565	59,226	113,333
Organization and other costs, net	84,672	105,798	50,569
Deposits and other	158,433	62,809	4,000
Total assets	$7,818,209	$ 19,692,557	$2,574,826
Liabilities and stockholders' equity			
Current liabilities			
Accounts payable	$1,091,299	$ 1,626,198	$513,893
Accrued compensation and related liabilities	254,144	372,739	8,170
Accrued interest	265,903	196,340	100,340
Deferred revenue	670,917	64,683	—
Current portion, amount due to stockholder	1,600,000	400,000	—
Other accrued liabilities	588,439	576,077	—
Total current liabilities	4,470,702	3,236,037	622,403
Amount due to stockholder	200,000	312,500	—
Notes payable to stockholders	—	1,200,000	1,200,000
Total stockholders' equity	3,147,507	14,944,020	752,423
Total liabilities and stockholders' equity	$7,818,209	$19,692,557	$2,574,826

EXHIBIT 3 Share Price in US$ per Share

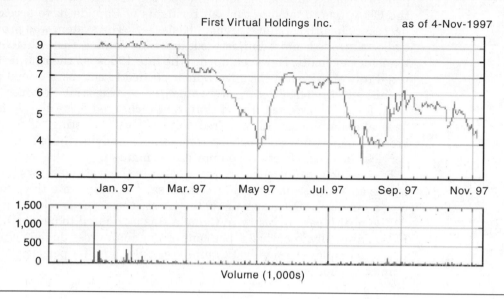

Source: Yahoo! http://quote.yahoo.com. © 1997 Yahoo! Inc.

Creating a Web Site for Medisys Health Group Inc.

By Professor Michael Parent and Stuart Elman

It was a sunny Monday morning in early July 1997, and France Mail-hot, Vice President of Operations at Medisys Health Group Inc., was settling into her office. Suddenly, Sheldon Elman, President and CEO, burst in and exclaimed, "France, we need a web site!"

THE HEALTH CARE INDUSTRY IN CANADA

The Canada Health Act (CHA), passed in 1984, affirmed "the federal government's commitment to a universal, accessible, comprehensive, portable and publicly administered health insurance system. . . ."[1] The goal of Health Canada, the federal department charged with fulfilling the CHA, was to "ensure that all residents of Canada have access to necessary health care on a prepaid basis. . . ."[2] The system was provincially controlled and administered, and was funded through federal transfer payments. However, during the late 1980s, as the country entered into a recession, the government needed to cut costs. Social programs, including health care, were among the hardest hit. Services that were formerly provided free of charge now charged fees ranging from several dollars to several hundred dollars. This "de-listing" of services created opportunities for private companies to provide these and other services in a cost effective, and profitable, manner.

Due to the growing concern over health in the workplace, with such issues as wellness and workers' compensation coming into the public's eye, a number of firms sprang up to address these needs.

The health care industry in Canada was estimated to be worth $72 billion annually,[3] nearly 9.7 per cent of Canada's gross domestic product, and employed roughly 1.2 million people[4], or 11.1 per cent of the employed population.

PRIVATE HEALTH CARE

The private health care sector consisted of a few major companies, and a multitude of smaller firms. Due to the broad range of services, a number of firms specialized in one area of corporate health care, but very few "total solution providers" covered a broad range of services. Some examples of these services included:

- Occupational Health
- Workers' Compensation (WCB/CSST)
- Industrial Hygiene
- Executive Health, wellness programs
- Insurance services, paramedical exams, etc.

These "corporate health care services" ranged anywhere from Repetitive Stress Injury (RSI) evaluations to wellness programs that sometimes included stress testing, nutrition analysis, and complete physical evaluations.

The lack of "total solution providers" in this industry led to a cleaving of the competition along the two main classes of services—Executive Health and Occupational Health, as well as segmentation on the

[1]Health Canada web site, URL http://www.hc-sc.gc.ca, May 1998.
[2]Health Canada web site, URL http://www.hc-sc.gc.ca, May 1998.
[3]Health Canada, National Health Expenditures in Canada, 1975–1994, 1994.
[4]Statistics Canada, Catalogue no. 72F0002.

basis of geographical area. This latter situation was mainly due to the fact that most providers were not national in scope, but rather limited to one province, or even to one city.

In terms of Executive Health, the main competitors in Ontario were Medcan (www.medcan.com) and Kings Health. The main competitors in Quebec were MDS (www.mdsintl.com) and Physimed. The rest of the competitors in these provinces were mostly smaller, regional players. Due to the fragmented nature of the industry, no single competitor had more than a 20 per cent market share, and most had about 5 per cent.

In terms of Occupational Health, the industry was again quite fragmented, with many smaller players often divided along geographical lines. Wilson Evans and Assured Health (www.assuredhealth.com) were the main competitors in Ontario, concentrated mainly in the Toronto area, and Physimed and Sanagex were the primary competitors in Quebec.

COMPANY BACKGROUND

Medcomp Health Systems was founded in 1981 by Dr. Sheldon Elman, in an effort to provide preventive health evaluations and programs for executives. Soon thereafter, numerous requests were received from corporate Human Resources departments for other health care services. On March 9, 1987, Medcomp merged with Secamed, a nursing placement and insurance paramedical evaluation company, Lesage, Dumont & Associes Inc. and Clinique de Medecine du Travail de Montreal Inc., firms specializing in workers' compensation management and industrial hygiene consulting. This new entity was named Medisys Health Group.

Shortly afterwards, Medisys entered into a joint venture with Eco-Research, a company specializing in management of hazardous materials and environmental concerns in the workplace. Other acquisitions between 1988 and 1990 included Evaluation Medex and Robert & Lizotte Clinic, both located in Montreal; the Price Waterhouse Quebec City health and safety consulting practice; and the Montreal General Hospital's executive health center.

In 1991, Medisys acquired Laurentian Health Services, a division of Imperial Life Assurance Company of Canada. This acquisition made Medisys the largest provider of corporate health programs in Canada, with offices in Quebec City, Montreal, Toronto, Calgary, Edmonton and Vancouver.

Over the next several years, Medisys consolidated its position as the pre-eminent provider of corporate health care services in Canada through strategic alliances with Corporate Health Services in British Columbia, and Groupe Cogesis in Quebec. In 1994, Medisys acquired SanTra Inc., a Montreal-based firm offering professional medical services to businesses. As a result, Medisys became the top-rated occupational clinic in North America, with over 40,000 exams performed yearly. Dr. Elman explained the rationale behind this series of acquisitions: "We wanted Medisys to become a medical information management company, and we undertook these acquisitions in order to broaden our product line, penetrate new markets, as well as achieve certain synergies and efficiencies." An organization chart for the company is shown in Exhibit 1.

The marketing strategy of Medisys was to emphasize preventive maintenance as a route to better health for corporate officers. Depending on the service, Medisys targeted different constituents within organizations. For Occupational Health, the primary consumer was the HR function in the organization. For Executive Health, the primary consumers were upper management (CEO-level).

Medisys continued to create new service offerings which were not covered by Medicare. For a partial list of these services, see Exhibit 2. However, the marketplace was evolving rapidly—new competitors were entering certain geographical areas and customer segments, and certain services were becoming commodity-like. One such service was Occupational Health. Margins in Occupational Health were eroding, and price was becoming increasingly important to winning contracts. Consequently, Medisys focused on differentiating its services through additional product offerings. The broad product line that Medisys offered included value-added software applications like Medgate (an occupational health and safety program which was used by case managers) and Purkinje (a smart medical record software package which was used by nurses and other medical staff), as well as national coverage. Other components of the marketing strategy were to build brand equity and increase recognition of the Medisys name. This was to be done through client education and segment development, increased marketing efforts, and better salesforce training.

Increasingly, companies were looking for ways to control costs. One method of doing this was to outsource the health function to firms such as Medisys. Consequently, Medisys' focus was to create strategic partnerships with clients, and become an integral component of their delivery of health services. Medisys' ability to be the "one-stop shop," and to provide full national coverage, placed it as the leading firm in this industry, with an estimated 25 per cent market share across all services.

A BRIEF HISTORY OF THE INTERNET

The Internet was created by the U.S. military as the ARPANET, a telecommunications system which would be able to withstand a nuclear war. However, after the end of the cold war, it was turned over to the National Science Foundation (NSF) to be used as a mechanism of

EXHIBIT 1 Organizational Chart

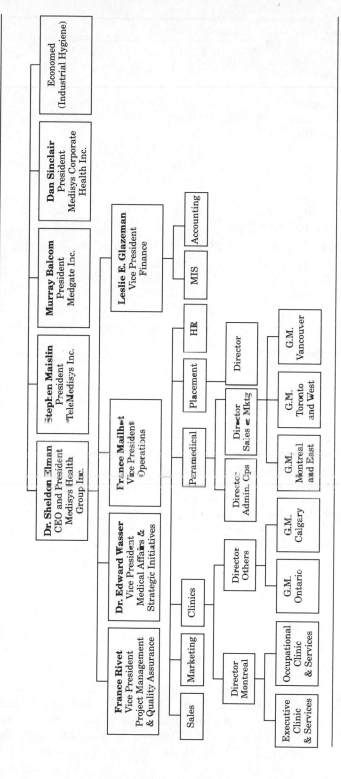

Source: Medisys Health Group Inc. documents.

EXHIBIT 2 Sample Medical Programs and Rates

Pre-employment medical exam	$45
Complete physical exam	$85
Orthopedic services	$380–490 per visit
Psychiatry and other specialties	$535 and up
Management of absenteeism	$70–$200 per hour
Drug and/or alcohol testing	$20–$57 per test
Radiology	$35–$120

Mini Profile $415
- Complete medical exam
- Complete blood analysis
- Complete urinalysis
- Stress electrocardiogram (treadmill)

Mini check-up (mini profile w/o stress test) $325

Executive protocols:
- Select $440
  Complete medical examination
  Hematology
  Biochemistry profile
  Urinalysis
  PSA (prostatic specific antigen)
  Hemoccult (blood in stools)
  Spirometry (pulmonary function)
  Vision test
  Tonometry (intra-occular pressure)
  Audiometry (hearing test)
  Resting electrocardiogram
  Feedback
- Select Plus (Select + stress electrocardiogram) $560
- Prestige (Select Plus + fitness assessment) $635
- Prestige Plus (Prestige + nutritional assessment) $750
- Elite (Prestige Plus + abdominal echography) $990

Source: Medisys Health Group Inc. documents.

communication among geographically dispersed universities. E-mail was the primary application (the so-called "Killer App"), and the main method of communication.

The Internet gained a new lease on life in the early 1990s with the advent of the World Wide Web (WWW). Developed by Tim Berners-Lee of CERN—the European Particle Physics Laboratory—the WWW was the first instance of displaying information on the Internet in a graphically appealing form. The WWW also offered something that no other medium to date had been able to accomplish—interactivity. What the user saw was solely dictated by what he or she chose to click on. As a result, the WWW became the fastest growing segment of the Internet, with thousands of pages added daily. It was estimated that by July 1997, there were 19.5 million host computers connected to the Internet. IDC Research estimated that there would be over 200 million people using the Internet by the end of 1999, with over 125 million people using the WWW. The economics of the Internet industry were equally staggering. Forrester Research estimated that the Internet/Intranet software market would explode from US$127.5 million in 1995 to US$8.5 billion in 1999.

The Motivation behind Corporate Web Sites

As the Internet began to gain commercial acceptance, companies began creating corporate web sites. However, the acceptance of buying and selling through the Internet was slow to catch on in Canada. A recent poll[5] revealed that only 29.2 per cent of Canadian firms currently had a web site, and only 18.9 per cent of firms bought or sold products and services through the Internet. The highest concentration of Internet-savvy firms were located in Ontario, with almost 43 per cent of firms having a web site.

Why would a company want to create a corporate web site? There were several different schools of thought. One explanation was that the Internet was just another form of media, and as such, it should simply be used as an extension of regular marketing efforts. In this camp were companies that took their printed marketing material, and just transferred it into HTML (Hypertext Markup Language—the format for web pages).

A second perspective saw the Internet as a form of media unlike any other, and as such, it warranted a completely different marketing approach. The strategy adopted by firms advocating this perspective aimed to take advantage of (a) the interactivity of the Web, and (b) the different audience that the Web had versus traditional media.

CREATING A WEB SITE FOR MEDISYS

France knew that a wide range of decisions needed to be made regarding Medisys' web site. The first question she felt needed to be addressed concerned the web site's objectives. Was it to generate new business? To increase awareness? To increase existing customer satisfaction through better communication? All of the above? How would a web site do this? Was this just another passing fad, or would it complement the existing marketing strategy?

---

[5]Report on *Business Magazine,* February 1998. Study conducted by Dun & Bradstreet Canada.

Another important decision had to do with content on the site. She was pleased with the current corporate brochure, but wondered whether or not new material should be created exclusively for the Internet in order to take advantage of the medium's interactivity. She wondered what the benefits were to this approach. More importantly, who would develop the content? The marketing staff currently had their hands full with promotions and requests for proposals. She estimated that hiring someone to complete this task might cost as little as $8,000, or as much as $50,000. Would this be a one-time cost, or would the content need to be updated regularly, she wondered? Since a search for "web design" on the Internet retrieved thousands of responses, finding a firm to outsource this task would not be difficult. However, selecting the right firm for the job, with some knowledge of Medisys' style and corporate identity, might prove more difficult.

Beyond that, who would translate the content into a format suitable for the Web? The Hypertext Markup Language (HTML)[6] had come a long way, and was now relatively easy to use, but who had time to sit and type in brackets? Were any commercial software programs available to make this process easier? Who had the time and expertise to do this?

Should Medisys invest the time and money to hire and train an in-house developer, or should it outsource the process entirely? What about the IS group? While she thought they had the talent to do this, did they have the time to spare? They were currently creating shared networks with some clients, and formatting new computers to Medisys standards. Would they have the time (or the budget) to devote to this project? The current IS budget was generous, but staff time was at a premium. On the other hand, the IS group knew the company culture and style well, and would probably be able to create a web site which reflected this better than could a commercial firm. France felt, though, that the IS group's skills were in the area of system integration and programming, not creating marketing literature.

Last, but certainly not least, France wondered how to attract people to the site. Would typical marketing approaches like including the address on all of Medisys' print materials, and advertising expenditures be enough of a draw? Or would following the approach of other companies—banner ads, meta-tags, and search engine listings—be the more prudent method? Banner ads involved placing a rectangular advertisement on another web site, and trying to induce visitors to that site to "clickthrough" and visit Medisys' site. Depending on the popularity of the referring site, and the number of "impressions," the cost of these ads

---

[6]The Hypertext Markup Language is the common language that all pages on the Internet are written in. It is a relatively simple formatting language made up of opening and closing tags—for example, to write something in bold, you would include the text to be bolded within <B> and </B>.

could range anywhere from \$40 to \$1,000 CPM.[7] Meta-tags were hidden HTML suffixes that allowed "spiders"—search engine software packages—to index the site, and locate sites based on keyword searches. In order to speed up search engine indexing processes, a web site could submit its site directly to the search engine (with, sometimes, a fee), and provide a description of the site.

Another matter which needed to be addressed was the registration of the Medisys domain name with the various search engines and directories on the Internet. Without this, a user lacking prior knowledge of the Medisys address would be unable to find the web site. Registering with all the different search engines (currently numbering over 300, and increasing daily) would take a lot of time. There were companies whose business was registering new web sites, and who generally charged between \$300–\$500 to do so.

The Ordering System

Another motivation for creating the Web site was the result of an idea by the paramedical division to differentiate itself from the competition. The paramedical division coordinators believed that insurance agents and brokers might appreciate the convenience of being able to order paramedical exams over the Internet. However, how far could they take this idea? Should they fully integrate the existing proprietary system with the new Internet-based system? The current proprietary system was written in BBX,[8] and was used on a Unix[9] operating system. In order to integrate the two systems, it would take a significant amount of time, energy and money. An outside consultant had submitted a proposal for this integration, estimating it would cost \$50,000 and take up to nine months.

The other alternative was a stand-alone system. A form could be created which could simply put the data into a readable format that could be printed out whenever an order was received. This would be approximately the same as receiving a fax from a client, but could be implemented easily over the Internet. A simple form and order processing script could be created in several hours, and would require a basic knowledge of HTML and PERL,[10] the language in which most CGI (Common Gateway Interface) scripts were written.

---

[7]Cost per 1,000 impressions.
[8]A basic programming language.
[9]An advanced operating system.
[10]Practical Extraction and Reporting Language.

OTHER DECISIONS

The more France thought about it, the larger this project seemed. This type and level of investment merited some sort of return on investment calculation, but exactly how to do this was a lingering question in her mind. On what basis could Medisys calculate this ROI? Increased customer service and satisfaction were nice ideas, but somewhat difficult to quantify. The most common method for web sites to calculate level of use was to count the number of "hits" or visitors to the site over some interval of time. A number of commercial and shareware programs and services[11] were available that counted the number of hits a site received, but once again, how could this information be linked into new business revenue?

Assuming that all these broader objectives could be satisfied, many smaller issues remained.

One was what to do regarding e-mail and administration of the site. Who would administer the site as a whole? Who would be responsible for troubleshooting problems with the ordering system, should they choose to pursue that option? Was site administration really necessary?

Typically, larger companies hired a full-time "webmaster" to administer the site, ensuring its smooth operation. The salary of a webmaster could range anywhere from $30,000 for smaller sites to $100,000 for major corporate undertakings. Additionally, most sites implemented an e-mail system, assigning an e-mail address to each and every employee for both internal and external communication. Each staff member already had an internal e-mail address over the company's internal network, which could not be accessed externally. France wondered whether each employee required an e-mail address, or should an e-mail address be created for each division? Typically, a service package for e-mail would cost $5/account/month, with a minimum cost of $50/month.

Alternatively, would an e-mail system be more of a headache than it was worth? Again, who would administer this service? Who would be responsible for ensuring that staff checked their e-mail?

Giving employees full-time access to the Internet posed other problems. For instance, one informal study of a U.S. corporation revealed that the most popular site visited during working hours was *playboy.com*. Some studies suggested that giving employees access to the Internet actually resulted in reduced productivity. Consequently, some corporations monitored which sites employees visited, and made it company policy to fire employees who visited "inappropriate" locations on the Web.

---

[11]Some of these commercial services and programs had fees ranging anywhere from several dollars per month to several thousand dollars for a site license.

Before anyone could view Medisys' site, it needed to be stored (hosted) on a computer that was permanently connected to the Internet. Medisys did not have this kind of computer. Also, Medisys would have to purchase a router, and other miscellaneous telecommunications equipment. The approximate costs of doing so ranged anywhere from $45 to $150 per month.

Other companies offered hosting services, but this meant giving up a certain measure of control and flexibility. Companies offering these services tended to charge $25/month, for contracts that typically ran two years. Reliability of service was also an issue. Entry and exit into this industry were easy, and companies had been known to open and close within one month. Conversely, having your own computer connected to the Internet might allow more control, but required spending more time and effort maintaining, troubleshooting, and controlling the potential security risk.

There was also concern over what to call the web site. All web sites on the Internet required a unique URL,[12] also known as a domain name, which needed to be registered with Internet governing bodies. Network Solutions Incorporated (NSI) controlled the registration of the most common domains on the Internet (.com, .edu, .gov, .org, .net). In order to register a domain name, it had to be unique. The typical contract with NSI was for a two-year term at a cost of US$100. After an initial two-year term, a firm had the right to renew its domain name, or to let the name become available to other firms. *Medisys.com* was currently taken by another firm, which had yet to develop its web site. Fortunately, there was an alternative. In Canada, an organization called CAnet governed the distribution of .ca domains, making *Medisys.ca* a possibility. They offered this service for free, but the processing of an application might take anywhere from one to six weeks.

France wondered if it would be worthwhile to negotiate with the firm who held the rights to *Medisys.com*. What value did a .com domain have over a .ca domain? More importantly, how much might this cost? Other companies, whose trademarked names were already registered by domain name speculators, had paid upwards of $50,000. MTV was rumored to have paid $100,000 for the rights to *MTV.com*, and McDonalds had made a donation of $3,500 in computer equipment to a Brooklyn primary school in order to get the rights to *McDonalds.com*.

---

[12]Universal Resource Locator—the system that the Internet uses to locate information.

WHAT NEXT?

Looking at the wide range of decisions that needed to be made, France knew that this was an issue which required some serious thought. There appeared to be more to developing a web site than just coding pages. Her major concerns were costs, and the time required to implement. The quicker, the better, but at what price? She wondered how much this project would cost, in total, and where the funds for it might come from—marketing, the paramedic division, or a little bit from every division? Clearly, there were some tough decisions ahead, and Dr. Elman would be expecting her recommendations soon.

Chapter 10

Business-to-Business Electronic Commerce and Virtual Organizations

Electronic commerce can be divided into two segments: business-to-consumer and business-to-business. While the former gains more "press," the business-to-business segment is considerably larger. Although estimates vary considerably, the business-to-business segment is thought to be between 4 and 13 times the size of the business-to-consumer segment. Business-to-business electronic commerce is estimated to exceed $US1 trillion annually by 2003 or 2005, depending on the survey.

Electronic commerce has transformed both goods and services. The effect on traditional manufacturing industries—while stunning in terms of value, volume, and scope—represents an evolutionary extrapolation of trends beginning with the emergence of electronic data interchange. Since then, enterprise systems such as SAP have supported the integration of firms' value chains and supporting functions. This has created information standards and architectures that facilitate electronic business-to-business transactions. That being said, most products today must be wrapped in *services* to differentiate them from the competition, and these services are often delivered electronically.

The service sector as a proportion of GNP surpassed goods some time ago. By their very nature, services are not held hostage by physical logistics, leading to the emergence of new services, new structures for delivering these services, and virtual corporations. Virtual organizations, in particular, are redefining business models. The physical location of facilities, employees, customers, and suppliers are becoming less and less important. Organizations whose primary product is knowledge have found that the flexibility and cost advantages of being virtual can be used as a competitive lever, without significantly eroding service levels.

This chapter contains three cases. The first is about the National Library of New Zealand. This case draws the reader's attention to the emergence of "digital libraries" and to the challenges real libraries face as they try to embrace the electronic future. The National Library of New Zealand has launched a large project to renew the computer systems it uses for interfacing with its customers. Because of the expense, it has partnered with the Australian National Library. The rationale underlying the NDIS (National Document Information Service) project is to provide electronic access to library holdings without being physically in the library. During the design phase of the project, the Web emerged as a universal interface, causing the NDIS designers to pause and to consider the Web's effect on the design. The NDIS project also reveals organizational and managerial issues within the library itself.

The second case is about the Euro-Arab Management School. This case concerns the benefits and challenges of operating and managing a virtual organization. It also discusses the future of education in the age of the Internet. The Euro-Arab Management School is an academic institution established in 1995 by the European Union and the Arab League. The school is a virtual organization in that it does not operate bricks-and-mortar classrooms. Instead, programs are offered in an innovative manner that combines web-based learning with local tutoring. There are many decisions to be made. These include how to manage a physically dispersed workforce, how to ensure academic quality, and how to market the system to attract qualified students.

The final case, entitled "Scantran," concerns an online translation agency. The company has no permanent staff except the founders, but they work daily with clients and translators through e-mail, phone, and fax. Even though the founders have developed close professional relationships with both clients and translators, they have met very few of them face-to-face. In this sense they represent a purely virtual company. Thus far, the company has only focused on translating between the languages of Scandinavia (and Finland) and English. There are a number of issues in the case. Should Scantran take on a more traditional structure in order to expand? Should it expand by covering additional languages? Should it offer more services to customers, such as desktop publishing and the like? What competitive threats does the company face, both now and in the future? Scantran nicely illustrates many of the advantages, as well as the disadvantages, that come with being a virtual organization.

The National Library of New Zealand, Te Puna Matauranga o Aotearoa, *A Library Without Walls: The NDIS Project*

By Professors Sid L. Huff and David Keane and Tracy Priest and Jane Farley

May 1995, Richard Hatfield, the NDIS project manager at the National Library of New Zealand, sat thinking about the day ahead. The meeting of the Management Group at 11 A.M. would be critical to the continued development of the National Document and Information Service (NDIS) project, a joint effort with the National Library of Australia (NLA). A variety of issues had recently been raised that needed to be addressed before the project could move ahead. Six years had passed since the concerns regarding the library's organizational structure and product focus had first been raised, and the library had come a long way towards its goal of achieving a flatter, more responsive structure, and a stronger customer focus. Much of the improvement to date had occurred as a result of the planning and strategizing that had gone into the NDIS project; hopes for further improvements depended heavily on the NDIS project's success. But now the library had to decide if the way it was proceeding was the correct one. There were major risks associated with committing the estimated NZ$13 million required to move NDIS from the definition phase to the build phase. Hatfield also knew that a decision would have to be made about whether to keep the NDIS project within the National Library, or to set up a separate company and transfer the development and implementation of the project to it.

The library had traditionally been risk adverse, and Hatfield could hear in his mind the questions that would be raised about all the changes being proposed:

- What exactly is the library's core business?
- Do we really want to commit ourselves to providing so much online service?
- Do we have the resources and skill base required to accomplish such a large project?
- Just how certain are we that it will pay for itself?

IVEY Tracey Priest, Jane Farley, Professor David Keane and Professor Sid L. Huff prepared this case solely to provide material for class discussion. The authors do not intend to illustrate either effective or ineffective handling of a managerial situation. The authors may have disguised certain names and other identifying information to protect confidentiality.

Because the project was a joint one with the NLA, the project timetable had to be respected. They couldn't wait. The concerns had to be addressed soon.

THE NATIONAL LIBRARY OF NEW ZEALAND—BACKGROUND

The National Library of New Zealand is a department of the New Zealand government, whose role is to "link the people of New Zealand with information." Its mandate is to "contribute to the building of a learning society and an enterprise economy within New Zealand by supporting the creation of an environment where information is readily available and widely used."

Before 1965, library services within New Zealand were fragmented into a number of different independent units serving a variety of different customers. The National Library Act of 1965 logically amalgamated these units to form the National Library of New Zealand. In 1987, most of the library staff, collections and other material were

---

EXHIBIT 1   National Library of New Zealand Building on Molesworth Street in Wellington

---

brought together physically into the National Library building on Molesworth Street, in downtown Wellington (see Exhibit 1).

Until 1988, the National Library had been administered by the Department of Education; in 1988, it became an autonomous government department, although the Minister for Education continued as the minister responsible to the government for the National Library. The National Film Library was added in 1990, resulting in the National Library becoming the largest holder of information in New Zealand. In 1989, the organizational structure of the National Library was hierarchical and departmentalized, as shown in Exhibit 2.

The library's customers could be roughly divided into six main groups:

- Businesses
- Schools
- Other libraries
- Individuals
- Researchers
- Government

The various business units of the library, formed to support particular products and services, regularly shared the same customers. The resources used to support functional tasks were often duplicated across the various business units. The Reference and Research unit of the Turnbull Library provides a good example of this. It regularly shared the same business customers as the online Kiwinet service. However, the photographic, pictorial and audio information held in the Turnbull Library and other library collections could not be disseminated via the Kiwinet online service offered by the library. Individual customers frequently had to deal with two or more separate departments to gain access to the library's information resources.

EXHIBIT 2   NLNZ Organizational Structure Circa 1989

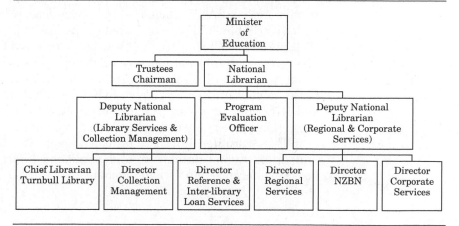

Until relatively recently, the large majority of the information re-source managed by the library had been in the form of printed materials. In recent years, advancement of computer-based technology had broadened the options of information access and delivery to include online services. The library provided two major online services: the New Zealand Bibliographic Network and Kiwinet.

The New Zealand Bibliographic Network (NZBN) was an online bibliographic database service that provided information relating to printed material existing throughout the world. Items in the database typically contained a number of attributes such as title, physical location and subject matter. This information was primarily used by other libraries and educational facilities throughout New Zealand. The NZBN acted as a link for public, university, government and other more specialized libraries to a central bibliographic database.

> The NZBN's prime function is to support libraries throughout New Zealand in their reference, cataloguing, interloan and acquisitions activities.[1]

Users of NZBN were assigned account numbers, and were charged a one-time joining fee, an installation fee, a monthly charge, as well as us-age fees that were charged per command issued. If they did not need permanent online access, user organizations could obtain dial-up access to NZBN by paying a monthly fee for the communication software, plus a usage fee.

Kiwinet was an online information network offering fast access to New Zealand information either through the client's personal computer or through a computer in a library. Thirty-one databases provided information on all aspects of New Zealand, including business, the social sciences, arts, commerce, the humanities and law. Kiwinet's clients included most libraries and educational institutes, government agencies, businesses, schools and individual researchers. Kiwinet service charges were based on connect time, so that users paid only for the time they were on the system.

In 1985, the library began offering a professional information search service called SATIS (Science and Technical Information Service), which until then had been operated by the public libraries in Auckland, Wellington and Christchurch. It was later renamed Infoserve. Infoserve was a one-stop information service, designed to meet the information needs of the New Zealand business community. Library customers could employ Infoserve professionals to conduct information searches on their behalf. For example, Infoserve could be used to conduct an information search on technical research, or to develop company, market or industry profiles. Infoserve provided access to 5,000 online national and international databases, and published information from many books, conference papers and journals.

---

[1] NLNZ Internet pages.

Skilled information consultants take the client's request, develop a brief for the work and provide an estimate of the time and cost involved. After that they will deliver the material to the client in the format required—within the time limit. Infoserve keeps their clients informed of progress and will inform the client of any delay in meeting the deadline.[2]

Each service was set up as a separate business unit, each with a different product focus. Both NZBN and Kiwinet online services had been developed using mainframe technology. The software of each was incompatible with the other. NZBN was based on a system called the Washington Library Network.[3] Kiwinet was based on a database system called BRS, a computer-based text search tool developed by Dataware Technologies of Cambridge, Massachusetts in the U.S. Worse, neither WLN nor BRS was being maintained or upgraded anymore.

Exhibit 3 provides recent National Library of New Zealand (NLNZ) data from the library's annual reports.

THE NEED TO CHANGE

By the end of the 1980s, there was growing recognition by management that the library was becoming unresponsive to the changing information needs of its customers. Raylee Marfell, the manager of the library's organizational development unit, explained:

> The library has had a product (collections) focus in the past. It was felt that these collections, and the information held in them, needed to be made available to people across N.Z.—not only those able to come to Wellington. The information age is here and people are expecting to see and get access to what we hold. The role of the librarian is changing, we are no longer gatekeepers but facilitators of access to information.

The inflexibility that had developed was due in part to the library's traditional product focus. The various business units had been designed originally to support specific information products. As well, the information technology and software being used to provide the library's online services was antiquated and required upgrading. It was limited to providing access to textual information; images or other non-textual information could not be accessed this way.

---

[2]How to Use Infoserve—NLNZ Internet pages.

[3]In the computer software and networking business since 1976, Washington Library Network (later renamed Western Library Network) was a non-profit corporation devoted to the provision of information products that included online bibliographic databases. WLN's main customers were libraries, government agencies and other information provision services.

EXHIBIT 3   Recent NLNZ Data from 1995 Annual Report

Introduction by the National Librarian

This year has seen the implementation of significant changes in the way the National Library conducts its business.

As we move ever closer to the year 2000, there is increasing emphasis on the Library as an electronic resource, rather than solely a holder of books. Electronic access to information is racing ahead, and in future, technology will complement the more traditional ways in which the Library provides its material. New technology is one of the ways the National Library is meeting its goal of increasing access to its rich and varied collections. Much effort is going into planning for the day when the Library will truly be a library without walls—its information available by computer to schools, libraries and home users.

As the Minister has already mentioned, good progress has been made towards achieving our goals as outlined in *Strategic Directions*. Supporting the Library as it works towards these strategic goals is the comprehensive Organizational Development Project, which is changing the way the library works as an organization so that it can become more client focused and mange its collections more efficiently and effectively.

As you will read in the body of the report, the 1994/95 year has seen us move closer to our goal of increasing New Zealanders' use of online services, as the first point of access to information, with developments in the National Document and Information Service.

The National Library's commitment to access has been further strengthened with the launch of the Alexander Turnbull Library's Image Services. The state of the art image scanning and copying facility has opened up access to the pictorial treasures of the Heritage Collections and will ultimately enhance the conservation of these documents.

Throughout the year, the Collections Policy Project laid the groundwork for the development of a policy to define how the Library's collections should be developed for the future.

School access to information continued to be strengthened through the work of the School Libraries 2000 Programme, which assists schools in the development of their libraries, develops tools to increase access to the National Library's material and provides curriculum related resources.

I am pleased to report that the Library's operations were carried out within budget for the year. The major change in the Library's financial statements was the transfer of the Heritage Collections to the Crown on 1, July 1994 at their book value of $522 million. The management of the collections remains the responsibility of the Library. As the following graph shows, third-party revenue was up by 5% on the previous year.

Third-Party Revenue

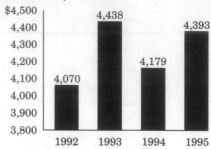

Revenue from the Crown dropped by over 50% due to the transfer of the Heritage Collections to the Crown.

Revenue—Crown

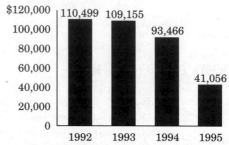

The National Library's operating expenses dropped from $97 million in 1994 to $45 million in 1995. This was due to the lower capital charge resulting from the transfer of the Heritage Collections to the Crown.

Operating Expenses

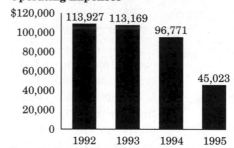

Overall, the year has been a demanding one for myself and the staff of the National Library. We have undertaken the twin tasks of managing our existing operation and carrying out a massive strategic change to prepare ourselves and our clients for the information world of tomorrow. It has been a challenging year and all credit is due to National Library staff for the professional way in which they have carried our their work.

P G Scott
P G Scott
National Librarian

Recognition of the need to change led the library to search for ways to shift to a stronger customer focus. It was felt that improving the delivery of online services, and changing the structure of the organization, would both ultimately lead to a greater customer focus.

The need to improve the library's online services was first raised by Isobel Mosley, the manager of the New Zealand Bibliographic Network (NZBN). She saw that the NZBN's current hardware platform and supporting software required updating. The technology being employed in 1989 was typical of the legacy mainframe environment, wherein various key applications were often incompatible with each other, and were no longer being supported by the developers. Mosley recognized that it would be very difficult for the library to provide major improvements in the functionality of its online services if it remained saddled with the old technology. Helen Meehan, the manager of the library's Infoserve service, also recognized a need to review the entire information technology (IT) architecture that supported the library's online services, not just NZBN, with the possibility of broadening the library's entire array of online information services.

Recognizing that their objectives were similar, Mosley and Meehan collaborated on a study to examine the advantages of changing the platform for all of the library's online services. The resulting study was presented to the management team in 1991. Agreement was secured that the library should begin to examine in detail how the needed changes to online services—both software and the supporting technology platform—could be achieved.

HANDS ACROSS THE TASMAN

The National Library of New Zealand had much in common with the National Library of Australia (NLA). For example, NLA operated online services similar to those of the NLNZ, namely, the Australian Bibliographic Network and Ozline; NLA also based their bibliographic network on the Washington Library Network system. In fact, the original development of the NZBN database was based on the online bibliographic system implemented by the NLA in 1985. Because of these commonalities and historical connections, Mosley was in the habit of conferring occasionally with her Australian counterpart.

The two libraries shared information at other levels as well. For example, each library had formed its own advisory committee, called a Network Advisory Service, to provide customer feedback and advice on the institution's online services. The Australian and New Zealand committees occasionally shared information with each other.

While researching possible approaches to upgrading the NLNZ's online systems, Mosley learned that the National Library of Australia had also identified the need to migrate their online services to a new platform. She recalled seeing a note from NLA, floating the idea of re-developing their bibliographic network:

> During the early 1980s, ABN's system support staff realized that the complete redevelopment of the system would eventually become unavoidable. This is a daunting prospect given the problems involved in just maintaining the current software with a high turnover of systems staff. As late as mid-1988, we were still thinking in terms of modular development of the system leaving the core of the software in place and rewriting, one module at a time, the parts which had the greatest enhancement requirements.[4]

In light of this, it was not surprising to discover that the NLA had been experiencing similar problems with their WLN bibliographic system and was also considering updating its online services.

In July of 1988, the National Library of New Zealand informally approached NLA to discuss the possibility of joint redevelopment to both libraries' online services. Slow progress was made during the following 18 months while the individual steering committees undertook separate organizational needs analysis, but it finally became apparent that both organizations had similar requirements. Recognizing that the case for redevelopment was a solid one, the two organizations formally came together in 1991 on a feasibility study to explore all possible approaches to new online services. In the NLNZ, Isobel Mosley was assigned responsibility for managing the New Zealand side of the effort. Mosley remained in that position until December 1994, when Jane Farley, then deputy project manager for NDIS, took over as project manager until the arrival of Richard Hatfield in early 1995.

THE FUTURE ACTION TEAM

At the same time that Mosley and Meehan were looking into how online services could be redeveloped, the National Library's executive management began investigating broader organizational issues that would need to be addressed in order to create an environment within the library that supported change. Emerging from this was a new strategic direction, that embraced the notion of changing the library from a product to a customer focus. Much background work was undertaken between 1989 and 1993, including an initial organizational restructuring in 1990.

In 1993, as a result of a government requirement, the National Library was faced with the need to develop a comprehensive business plan. In response to this need, the Future Action Team (FAT) was created. Made up of senior managers and other library staff, the FAT was charged with developing a new strategic direction for the institution.

---

[4]From the "History of the NLA Bibliographic Database," NLA Internet WWW page.

Library senior management believed that a greater focus on customer needs could only be achieved through better co-ordination between the library's various business units. With that in mind, the FAT began looking at the best way to structure the library's organization so that it would be able to best support the new strategic directives. At that early stage, only a loose connection had been made between the need to improve online services and the need to change the organization. It was anticipated by many that the organizational development effort would run parallel to any changes to the online services.

The FAT eventually recommended another organizational restructuring for the National Library. It also confirmed the appropriateness of improving and expanding the library's online services.

BIRTH OF NDIS

Even though the idea of a joint project was, on the surface, an acceptable direction in which to proceed, uncertainties still remained and much groundwork needed to be done. Following the consultation with the NLA, a joint steering committee was established in 1992. Between 1992 and 1994 the scope, structure, functional and technical specifications, and budget for the New Zealand arm of the project was fleshed out. In October 1993, the two libraries issued a joint request for tender, to seek bids for third-party systems integrators to undertake the development work. A joint project director was appointed, and a variety of other personnel were drafted in to assist with the planning and vendor negotiations. By the end of 1994, a systems integrator had been chosen to develop the software, and a proposed budget had been approved. One more thing was needed at this point: a project name. The joint New Zealand–Australia project was named the National Document and Information Service, or NDIS.

A LIBRARY WITHOUT WALLS

As the thinking about the National Library's system redevelopment matured, a new concept emerged: that of a "Library Without Walls." The idea was that, using computers and telecommunication technologies, a large proportion of the National Library's resources would be electronically accessible by all of their customers throughout New Zealand and beyond. Peter Scott, the national librarian, said,

> This system will open the way for making electronic services the first point of access for users into library systems, and the idea of a "library without walls" will replace the traditional vision of a library as a self-contained storehouse of knowledge.

One of the key factors enabling the new Library Without Walls vision was the growing comfort people in all walks of life were developing with using computers to access information. An important driver of this was the rapid emergence of the Internet, especially that component of the Internet called the World Wide Web (WWW). Peter Scott explained:

> Nobody had ever even heard of the World Wide Web when we started thinking about rebuilding our online systems. However, by the end of 1994, the Web had started to emerge, and it was clear to us that it changed everything. We quickly saw that the Web could provide a universal window on the National Library's electronic information resources. It just provided that much more validity to the Library Without Walls vision.

It was decided that a three-year phased development plan would be the best approach. Phase 0, the Definition Phase, of the project was begun. The Library Without Walls concept was indeed becoming a reality.

NDIS JOINT PROJECT MANAGEMENT

It was agreed that both libraries would share the cost and development of the joint project, while remaining separately responsible for managing the changes to the technology and business within their own organizations. A joint project team, consisting of staff from both NLNZ and NLA, was established to manage the system design and development in conjunction with a team from Computer Sciences Corporation (CSC), the chosen systems integration vendor. This joint project team would reside in Canberra, where the NLA was geographically located, and where much of the systems development work was to be undertaken. The National Library of New Zealand also created their own project team located in Wellington, and headed by Isobel Mosley. As well, the NLA established their own project team located in Canberra. The two libraries followed different paths in allocating their project staff. The NLA placed most of their project staff in the joint project team in Canberra, while only a few marketing staff were assigned to the NLA-specific project team. In contrast, the NLNZ assigned only a few staff to the joint project team, while its NLNZ-specific project team in Wellington included about 20 people from a number of areas within the NLNZ. Exhibit 4 depicts the overall organization of the NDIS project.

It was an exciting time, getting the joint NDIS project formalized and off the ground. A variety of skills were sought, and new positions created. Diane Wyber, manager of Policy Research & Executive Services (one of the seven new senior management positions) recalled:

EXHIBIT 4   NDIS Project Organizational Arrangement

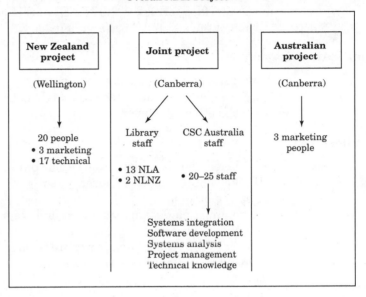

Not only is this one of the few national projects of this type in the world, but nowhere else in the world are two national libraries working together in this way. Instead of CER,[5] we have dubbed it CIR—Closer Information Relations.

COMPUTER SCIENCES CORPORATION AUSTRALIA

In December 1993, the two National Libraries received tenders from five systems integration companies. From those five, Computer Sciences Corporation Australia (CSC) was selected as the winner.

CSC was contracted to:

- Complete a detailed design for the hardware and software architecture
- Develop the software
- Install the hardware
- Train the trainers
- Provide base documentation

The technical architecture proposed by CSC was highly integrated, and consisted of three layers, as shown on the next page.

---

[5]A New Zealand–Australia government initiative to forge Closer Economic Relations (CER) between the two countries.

A Client Layer

This layer would consist of software on the user's microcomputer, or the user's local network, which would provide services such as a graphical user interface for using the NDIS; worksheets for creating data; validation of the created data; and help services.

An Application Layer

This layer would consist of software on the central NDIS computer, which would provide most of the NDIS services, and would interact with the other two layers.

A Database Layer

This layer would consist of the Oracle database software on the central NDIS computer. It would interact with the central data, which would be stored on disk.

The proposed design was an example of a client-server architecture. In a client-server arrangement, computers are connected in networks, and share activities. Client computers, used by the users of the system, primarily handle information formatting and presentation (user interface) tasks. Server computers handle the "back-end" jobs such as database access and searching. Because the computing work in a client-server arrangement is split, or distributed, between the client and the server computers, using the network, such systems are sometimes referred to as distributed computing. Further details of the NDIS architecture and technologies used are provided in Exhibit 5.

THREE-YEAR PHASED PLAN

To facilitate the development and introduction of NDIS, the project was divided up into three phases.

Phase One

NDIS would enable customers with IBM-compatible computers to search current National Library databases including existing Kiwinet databases as well as NZBN data. The user interface would be a windows-type graphical user interface, or GUI. At the end of Phase One, Kiwinet would, in its original form, cease to exist.

Phase Two

New databases would be added, giving access to Australian data. Gateways providing access to overseas databases would also be added. Electronic ordering and delivery of documents would be made available. Online cataloguing would be made available. An Apple Macintosh interface would be added.

EXHIBIT 5   Computerworld Story on NDIS

ONLINE LIBRARY SYSTEM BREAKS NEW GROUND

By Randal Jackson

The National Library has signed a contract for a new national document and information service (NDIS) that is the first step in implementation of a world leading library system.

Project manager Richard Hatfield says a library project which has been progressively developed in Canada over the past few years is the most similar and that the French national library is reputed to be "doing something but not telling anyone." There is nothing else as advanced as the joint project the National Library has undertaken with its Australian counterpart.

The goal at the end of the three-year project is for the library to host 20% of the data it will offer, with 80% being sourced online from institutions such as the Library of Congress, from other New Zealand sources, and from its Australian counterpart.

In the grand scheme of things, the National Library envisages, eventually, all school and universities having access, as well as offering a commercial service. "We have both a commercial and a social responsibility," Hatfield says.

To this end, an internal project team is focussing on developing the library's core business, essentially a business re-engineering exercise. The joint-libraries fixed-price contract was let to CSC, of Australia (formerly Computer Sciences). What was required was a custom application solution which could scale to handle very large numbers of users and thousands of simultaneous queries, flexibility in handling large interactive and batch workings, and simple architectures and ease of management. Phase one, which will take 18 months, is to completely revamp the Kiwinet databases to a different form, with more intelligent algorithms and the ability to search multiple databases. Currently the library runs an Amdahl mainframe, with an Adabas database and ERS search software. Hatfield says the mainframe will be progressively phased out over the life of the project.

The replacement platform is IBM's RS/6000 model SP2, which is based on the Power architecture and Power 2 microprocessor technologies. It provides high-speed switching and up to 512 nodes, according to IBM account manager Michael Liapis, who says it is the first SP2 sold in New Zealand.

"CSC put up several proposals," Hatfield says. "The SP2, as I see it, gives a very powerful option and a great upgrade path in incremental steps.

"Because it is a loosely coupled environment, it will more ideally cope with this type of workload, most of which is free text searching.

"We'll start with t2 nodes in New Zealand (Australia will have 181 but we may go to t0 times that if we put in multimedia." He conceded that it is not a matter of if but of when for a multimedia capability to be installed.

The system will run Oracle Parallel Server, with a 156Gb database.

"That was a CSC recommendation," Hatfield says. "We'll also be running Oracle Text Search—which puts text in a hierarchy and makes it easier to search—and Oracle Context."

Broadly, the philosophy is that the client is the end user, that researchers are not required as an intermediary. The user will access via a Windows-based PC or a terminal—later, Macintosh will be included—and connect via a LAN or WAN to an intermediate host on which most of the application will reside. That host may also be accessed via the Internet.

Continued

EXHIBIT 5   (Continued)

ONLINE LIBRARY SYSTEM BREAKS NEW GROUND (*Continued*)

It will be connected by a variety of means—Internet, direct line—to the SP2 search engine which will be divided into the application manager with functions such as Bibliographic control, data loading and Oracle Context; and the Oracle database. Tuxedo will run on both the SP2 and intermediate host as transaction processing base communications.

Hatfield says he expects the intermediate host will initially be a high-powered PC, such as a Pentium, essentially acting as a controller. "I expect this to become a PowerPC," he says.

The primary development tool for the front-end graphical user interface is C++, along with a package called Zinc, which eliminates work in repainting windows.

When multimedia joins the system, ATM will become part of the networking plans. Phase two of the project covers delivering value-added services for other libraries, which will use the same software but with extensions on.

"We hold the national union catalogue, which shows where all material is held in New Zealand," Hatfield says. "We will treat bibliographic software as another database."

Phase two, which is scheduled to take nine months, also includes the first step of implementing full access to international databases.

Phase three is the delivery of Maori language interfaces. The Australian National Library, in turn, is delivering Kanji and other Far Eastern language interfaces.

Throughout the project, full Internet access will be delivered.

There are issues yet to be resolved. The first is charging and billing for some usage. Hatfield thinks it likely that most will be by credit card. The National Library may enter into contracts with other libraries and it will be up to them what level of access they offer their users.

"Currently we're working through a market strategy, a process of sorting out project combinations and charging. We want to position things for market segments.

"The other major issue is likely to be copyright. But that's a policy issue to be decided at government level.

"All up, the project is expected to cost the National Library between $10 million and $13 million. That includes half of SA6.7 million for total software development, from CSC, and around $A3 million for the SF2 system.

"The joint partners have retained all the intellectual property rights. This is because they see the final system as being an eminently marketable product on the world market," Hatfield says.

Source: *New Zealand's Information Systems Management Weekly,* IAwI, 1995, No. 402.

Phase Three

Document delivery would be made available. A Maori language interface would also be implemented. Customers would also have transparent access to third-party sources, such as other library databases or information from electronic publishers. At the end of Phase Three, the NZBN service would be discontinued.

Users would be able to access the library's electronic information using direct communication lines as in the past. Also, full Internet access would be provided, via WWW browsers such as Netscape.

EXHIBIT 6   NDIS Project Time Line, 1991 to 1995

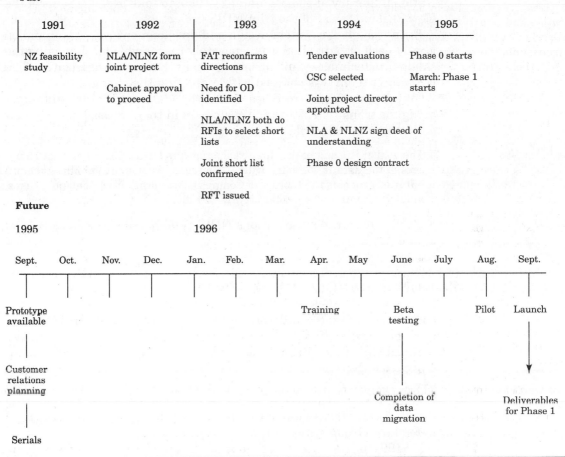

NDIS Project Time Line

Past

1991	1992	1993	1994	1995
NZ feasibility study	NLA/NLNZ form joint project	FAT reconfirms directions	Tender evaluations	Phase 0 starts
	Cabinet approval to proceed	Need for OD identified	CSC selected	March: Phase 1 starts
		NLA/NLNZ both do RFIs to select short lists	Joint project director appointed	
		Joint short list confirmed	NLA & NLNZ sign deed of understanding	
		RFT issued	Phase 0 design contract	

Future

1995				1996								
Sept.	Oct.	Nov.	Dec.	Jan.	Feb.	Mar.	Apr.	May	June	July	Aug.	Sept.
Prototype available							Training		Beta testing		Pilot	Launch
Customer relations planning									Completion of data migration			Deliverables for Phase 1
Serials												

Each phase was designed to take 12 months to complete. The target was to have the complete online library service become fully operational by the end of 1997 (see Exhibit 6).

The NDIS will replace the National Library's current online services. It will also extend and enhance them by providing services not covered at all by NZBN or Infoserve; for example: provision of direct full text access to New Zealand and Australian document collection, and provision of sophisticated interconnection services that will upload data and act as transparent search gateways.[6]

---

[6]1994 National Library press release.

RICHARD HATFIELD

The New Zealand–based project was Richard Hatfield's primary area of responsibility. Hatfield, a professional project manager, had joined the National Library at the beginning of 1995, to take over the reins of the New Zealand "arm" of the joint NDIS project.

Even though the system design and development would be handled jointly, each organization was separately responsible for managing the changes to technology and business within their own organization. The NZ project team was charged with managing the changes to the technology and business processes within the National Library, and managing the transition of existing customers in the proposed move to new online services. Hatfield stated:

> The goal at the end of the three-year project is for the library to host 20 per cent of the data it will offer, with 80 per cent being sourced online from institutions such as the Library of Congress, from other New Zealand sources, and from its Australian counterpart.

Exhibit 7 illustrates the various NDIS project responsibility areas as of mid-1995.

THE ORGANIZATIONAL DEVELOPMENT PROJECT

One of the mandates of the Future Action Team was to consider what type of organizational structure would best support the library's planned shift in strategic focus, and how the National Library might move from the current organization to the new one most effectively. A new structure had been proposed, but as yet nothing substantive had been done to change the old structure. This whole effort—restructuring the National Library into customer-focused business units—had been named the Organizational Development Project.

In 1994 it was decided that a seven-member management team should be created to oversee and run the Organizational Development (OD) Project. The purpose of the OD Project was to execute the transition of the library's products and services as the new customer-oriented business units were brought in and the old organizational arrangements phased out. It was anticipated that the hierarchical structure of the library would be flattened, the library would become more responsive to customer needs, and an overall team working environment would be introduced that would result in greater empowerment of library staff. Exhibit 8 provides an overview of the library's new organizational structure.

EXHIBIT 7   NDIS Project Responsibility Areas

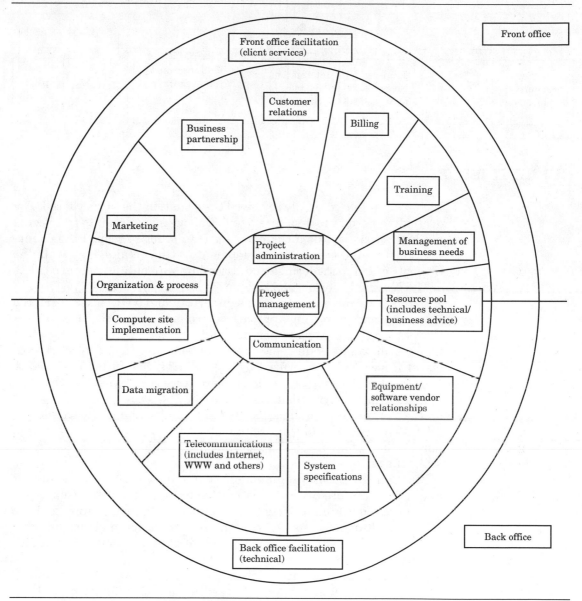

Front office

Front office facilitation
(client services)

Customer
relations

Business
partnership

Billing

Training

Marketing

Project
administration

Management of
business needs

Organization & process

Project
management

Resource pool
(includes technical/
business advice)

Computer site
implementation

Communication

Data migration

Equipment/
software vendor
relationships

Telecommunications
(includes Internet,
WWW and others)

System
specifications

Back office facilitation
(technical)

Back office

EXHIBIT 8 New (Planned) Organizational Structure

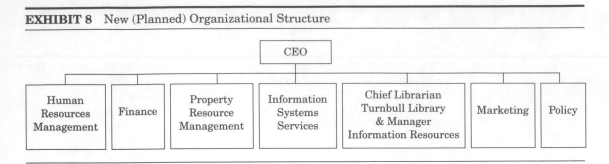

CURRENT ISSUES

Richard Hatfield mentally reviewed the situation the library faced. The overriding need to restructure itself, to move away from its traditional product focus towards a customer focus in order to respond to changing political and economic developments, still remained. As well, the library needed to modernize and extend its core online systems.

The National Library had begun to address both issues. The Organizational Development Project was underway, and NDIS was considered a realistic and promising approach to evolving online services to meet current and future customer demands. However, the Management Group still had its doubts, particularly about the NDIS project. A variety of issues had been raised by the steering committee assigned to monitor the NDIS project, which needed to be resolved before the project could move forward. First, concerns had been raised as to the amount of resources and skills needed to undertake a project such as NDIS. The National Library would have to bring on board a variety of new skills, and it was not certain that they would be able to obtain the skills they needed.

Future regulations were another source of concern. It was unclear and difficult to predict how the legal requirements of the Copyright, Commerce, and Finance acts would limit the implementation and use of the resulting systems and contents. Restrictions in access to material, usage of the system and development of market share would ultimately impact on future revenue streams.

A third area of concern involved cost. Like all government departments, the National Library received a funding allocation, and the money to pay for the NDIS project would come out of this funding. It was estimated that overall, their share of the joint project would cost the National Library between $10 and $13 million. The budget for the New Zealand arm of the project had been restricted to $6.8 million. So overall, the library was faced with putting approximately $18 million into the NDIS project. The Management Group was concerned about whether it was desirable to use up such a large proportion of the library's overall budget on one project. Peter Scott, the national librarian, put it this way:

> We would be betting the farm on this project, Australia would be also. We'll face some very tough financial challenges over the next couple of years as the new systems come on, in part because we'll be having to operate the old and new systems side by side. When the new system goes live we'll be starting to pay depreciation on the new system and still have to pay to operate the old system.

Although costs would be initially covered by the library's budget allocation, there was an expectation from the government that the new service would pay for itself within five years of completion. Customers would be expected to pay for the new services. Charging for services was not new, as NZBN and Infoserve had had charging frameworks in place since their inception. However, it was not at all certain whether a firm market existed for a new set of online services, or what form a new charging framework should take. It was clear that well-defined revenue and cost streams still needed to be established.

In addition, there were concerns as to the impact any changes would have on existing and potential customers. Management of customer expectations would be crucial. Misrepresentation of what the system could deliver, and in what time frame, could have a negative effect, resulting in a migration of customers away from the National Library, and an ultimate loss in revenues. Some customer frustration in the past stemmed from the fact that, while external customers paid to use resources such as NZBN and Kiwinet, there was no cross-charging (transfer charging) within the library itself. External customers, therefore, felt they were unfairly subsidizing internal library users of the online systems. By revamping the existing system and increasing the range of services available to their customers, would the National Library be adding to this perception? If the online services were offered through an independent business, internal users within the National Library would also have to pay, potentially establishing a more equitable system of charging and hopefully altering such negative customer perception.

Any major change would require extensive consultation throughout the organization, and perhaps within the government as well. As Peter Scott put it,

> How do you manage something like this, within a government department, which traditionally has not been very flexible, when you're dealing with a very rapidly changing technology? Getting people comfortable with the new technology is always a challenge, especially when it will be cutting across their traditional ways of doing things.

Concerns were raised as to whether consensus could ever be reached given the level of consultation involved. If not, would partial consensus be enough to successfully implement the required changes? Furthermore, the size and scope of the changes that were coming as a result of NDIS were likely to be massive—yet, no one really knew just how massive they would be. Should everyone be alerted as to the full extent of the potential coming changes up front, or should the library follow an incremental, step-by-step approach to change management?

The NDIS project would require not only change, but, rapid change. The National Library was an organization not accustomed to having to move quickly. But because NDIS had been set up as a joint project with the NLA, "we can't just slow it down to suit ourselves—it's going to roll on, and we have to keep up, otherwise we might not have our needs met in the end," said Scott. "We need to be able to make decisions quickly."

Yet another concern was the National Library's working relationship with its Australian counterpart. Peter Scott and his counterpart in the NLA enjoyed an excellent working relationship. Scott elaborated:

> Where it gets sticky is in making sure that decisions from the CEOs of both organizations get translated through the organization. They are not much larger than we are, but they have more money—mainly because we've been operating under a retrenched fiscal environment like everybody else in the public sector in New Zealand. That's not the case over there. Most of the differences we've had have been differences over our different organizational strategies. We have a somewhat different approach to our business, and different clients. We're very strong in the NZ business community, for example, more so than the NLA. Also, they do not have the extent of indigenous issues that we have here. Their federal-state structure makes a difference. Furthermore, we are much more market focused than they are.

NDIS would clearly require changes to be made to the way parts of the organization conducted business. There was some question as to whether these needed changes should be incorporated into the organizational development project, or handled independently of it. And who should be driving the NDIS-associated changes? Initially, NDIS had been very much driven by the library's business side. However as the project grew, there was a possibility of IT issues becoming dominant. However, generally speaking, Hatfield knew that IT staff have traditionally not been very effective at managing change associated with large IT projects.

THE "NEW BUSINESS" OPTION

One possibility raised within the NDIS project team was to "spin off" the NDIS project into a new business, to be operated at arm's length from the library itself. Under such an arrangement, NDIS would operate autonomously, independent of the National Library. The new business would develop and implement the NDIS project, and would maintain and manage the service. The use of, and contents of, the resulting online document information system would be sold back to the National Library, which would buy the services they required. Existing customers of the National Library would also purchase the services they required from the new business. With this approach, the National Library itself would be considered just another customer of the new business. It was anticipated that the existing customer base of National Library's online services would migrate to the new business; however, it was by no means guaranteed that customers would patronize the new service provider. The new business would have to try to draw in existing customers of the library, as well as proactively seek new customers, so as to achieve a satisfactory return on investment.

BUSINESS PROCESS RE-ENGINEERING

Another idea being discussed within the NDIS project team involved applying the methods popularly termed "business process re-engineering," or BPR. To some extent it was recognized that the Organizational Development project was in fact already performing re-engineering on certain processes within the library. However, this was occurring on more of an ad hoc basis. A proper BPR approach would entail a much more thorough examination of the library's overall business processes, and a formal redesign of those processes in light of the NDIS project. The kind of radical process redesign typically championed by BPR advocates included such things as:

- putting the customer first
- using teams
- empowering staff
- rewarding performance
- tearing down divisional walls.

As Richard Hatfield contemplated all that had happened in the last four years at the National Library, he realized that they had come a long way indeed. The external press was starting to pick up on the National Library's plans, and anticipation was heightening (see Exhibit 5). As the pressure increased, Hatfield had begun to see himself and his staff in the role of mountain climbers, who had just completed a tough climb only to find that they had just begun—the mountain seemed to go on forever. With that somewhat disheartening image in his mind, Hatfield packed his briefcase and headed off to the Management Group meeting.

Euro-Arab Management School

By Professor Sid L. Huff and Michael Wade

Tawfik Jelassi, dean of Academic Affaires of the Euro-Arab Management School (EAMS), stared past the Al-Hambra palace toward the distant snow-capped Sierra Nevada mountains on Spain's southern coast. The town of Granada, where he was located, was rich in cultural and political history. For centuries it had been regarded as a crucial bridge between the Arab and European worlds. Indeed, this was one of the main reasons that the European Union, along with the League of Arab States and the Spanish Government, had decided to locate the joint management school in this Andalusian center.

It was January 1999, and Jelassi pondered the year ahead. Even though EAMS had been operating for over three years, this would be the first year the school would take in students, through its partner institutions, for its Euro-Arab Management Diploma. He felt the school was ready for this step, although some lingering doubts did remain. Could a business school which counted only 14 full-time staff members on its payroll, from the janitor to the director, really compete with established academic institutions? Could a truly "virtual" multinational organization be managed effectively? Had management education really come to the point where students would accept the learning model proposed by EAMS?

THE EURO-ARAB MANAGEMENT SCHOOL

The Euro-Arab Management School (EAMS) was formed in 1995 by the European Union (EU). The idea for the school developed from a Euro-Arab dialogue as a way to further develop economic relations between Europe and the Arab World. The school was referred to in the Action Program of the EU's 1995 Barcelona Declaration in reference to its contribution to the development of human resources, especially in the fields of professional training and educational technologies. The venture was initially funded 100 per cent by the EU, but had the full support of the Arab League and the Spanish Government. In 1999, the Arab League and the Spanish Government also financially contributed to the School project. The EAMS mission was to prepare, through different educational, training and research activities, competent managers from the Arab world and Europe.

The EAMS was owned by the Euro-Arab Foundation, a trust consisting of representatives from the EU Commission, the European Parliament, the Arab League and the Spanish Government. The owners of the trust appointed a board of trustees to oversee the EAMS governance structure. The board appointed a governing council consisting of representatives of the EU Commission and the Spanish Government Ministry of Education and Ministry of Foreign Affairs. This body, in turn, appointed the Executive Committee of the school, the group which managed the school on a day-to-day basis. The Executive Committee consisted of the director and the dean of Academic Affairs. The committee shared much of the managerial responsibility for the school with two other bodies, the Council of Partner Institutions, which approved the delivery of EAMS programs in partner institutions, and the Academic Council, which granted the diplomas and degrees, set the admission and assessment policies and controlled the quality of the content and its delivery. For a schematic representation of EAMS's governing structure, refer to Exhibit 1.

EXHIBIT 1   Euro-Arab Management School's Governance Structure

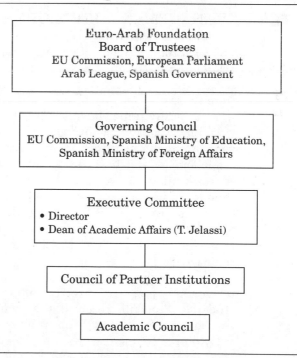

The school's mission statement stated that the goal of the EAMS was to "deliver managers/entrepreneurs capable of working within the Euro-Arab marketplace, equipped with the skills to function in a rapidly changing business environment" and to "extend the understanding of managerial, economic and social issues that confront Arab and European managers in dealing with each other." The school would offer a "train-the-trainers" program, a one-year management diploma, a one-year MBA program and various executive education seminars and customized programs to students and executives in the 15 countries of the EU and the 22 countries of the Arab League.

It was determined that, even though the management school would be located in Spain, educational programs would be offered throughout Europe and the Arab world. There was considerable debate early on as to the most efficient method of accomplishing this. It was considered impractical to establish a physical infrastructure in multiple locations. The cost of building and staffing multiple campuses was prohibitive. Other models were considered, including various self-directed learning options such as web-based education, correspondence courses and the like. However, it was felt that priority should be placed on some form of interaction between students and EAMS tutors and professors. After much consideration, a model was adopted that combined self-directed learning with local tutorship by EAMS-trained and certified trainers.

THE MASTER IN MANAGEMENT DEVELOPMENT PROGRAM

The Governing Council of EAMS decided to work in collaboration with academic institutions throughout Europe and the Arab world to oversee the local delivery of EAMS programs. EAMS would train tutors from these partner institutions at its Granada facility. The tutors, who were typically junior business professors or business Ph.D. students, would meet for five modules, each lasting three weeks during the one-year program. The tutors would learn skills in bi-cultural (Euro-Arab) management and be exposed to EAMS's pedagogical structure and course content. Between sessions in Granada, the tutors would have to complete various pedagogical projects and assignments. Upon passing the course, tutors would be awarded a Master in Management Development Program (MMDP) diploma. They would then return to their institutions to act as tutors to students taking EAMS courses locally in their native countries.

The role of the tutor was different from that of a teacher. Tutors didn't teach EAMS programs directly, but acted as "facilitators" or "helpers" to students. Students received the course material either by mail or through the World Wide Web (WWW). Students would work independently on the course material and meet with the tutor usually once per week for three hours or for a whole day every two weeks. The tutor would answer questions about the course material and provide advice on particular approaches or directions for projects and assignments. The tutors would also lead students in case analysis. Case-based learning was prioritized in the EAMS system.

Another key function of the tutors was to help students appreciate the "cultural dimensions" of the course material. An essential part of the program was to provide students with an appreciation of the similarities and differences between European and Arab cultures. Part of the tutor's responsibility was to facilitate this type of learning.

EAMS began taking in students for its MMDP (train-the-trainers program) in October 1995. Students came to Granada for five, three-week modules throughout the ten months of the academic year. Each module was organized around a particular theme, such as "bi-cultural learning" or "managing a pedagogical project." EAMS picked up all the expenses of the admitted MMDP participants. This included tuition fees, travel between Granada and their home institutions (typically five round-trip air tickets), accommodation and a small weekly per diem rate while studying in Granada.

Most of the faculty would also travel to Granada to conduct the sessions, often for a week or a few days at a time. This was necessary since EAMS staff was kept to a minimum (EAMS had 14 employees in December 1998). Instructors came from all over the world, although most worked for European academic institutions. The future tutors would typically receive instruction from 15 to 20 instructors during the year-long MMDP. All courses were conducted in English.

Three batches of tutors had graduated by the end of 1998. These three groups represented 55 tutors from 18 institutions in 13 countries throughout Europe and the Arab world. A fourth group of 18 tutors was set to graduate in late 1999. A fifth MMDP was set to begin in January 2000. By December 1999, EAMS would have graduated 73 tutors from 27 institutions in 16 countries, 8 of which were Arab and 8 of which were European. See Exhibit 2 for a list of these institutions and countries.

STUDENT PROGRAMS

Once the tutors were in place throughout Europe and the Arab world, student courses could begin. The first course for students, the Euro-Arab Management Diploma (EAMD), was scheduled to be launched in October 1999. The EAMD was a ten-month management training course, which included, among others, modules on: communications skills, managing people, conflict management, human resource management, planning techniques, organizational design, change management, operations, marketing, information systems, data analysis, accounting and budgeting. Special emphasis was placed on bi-cultural contextual learning. In addition to regular course work, students would

---

EXHIBIT 2   List of EAMS Partner Institutions

Algeria	Institute Supérieur de Gestion, Algiers
	Institute Supérieur de Gestion d'Annaba (ISGA), Annaba
Egypt	TEAM International, Cairo
Finland	Åbo Akademi University, Turku
France	Ecole Supérieure de Commerce (ESC), Toulouse
Germany	Hochschule Bremen
Italy	Scuola di Amministrazione Aziendale (SAA), University of Turin
Jordan	Applied Science University, Amman
	Institute of Public Administration, Amman
	Jerash University, Amman
Lebanon	TEAM International, Beirut
Morocco	Ecole Nationale de Commerce et de Gestion (ENCG), Settat
	Groupe Ecole Supérieure d'Informatique et de Gestion (ESIG), Casablanca
	Groupe des hautes Estudes Commerciales et Informatiques (HECI), Casablanca
	Institut des Hautes Estudes de Management (HEM), Casablanca
Palestine	Al-Azhar University of Gaza, Gaza
	Hebron University, Hebron
	Islamic University of Gaza, Gaza
Saudi Arabia	Arab Development Institute (ADI), Al-Khobar
	TEAM International, Ryadh
Spain	Escuela de Administratión de las Empresas (ESADE), Barcelona
Sweden	Uppsala University, Uppsala
Tunisia	Ecole Supérieure de Commerce (ESC), Tunis
	Institut des hautes Etudes Commerciales (IHEC), Cathage
	Institut Supérieur de Gestion (ISG), Tunis
U.K.	School of Business, University of Bradford, Bradford

---

complete various projects and case analyses. Students would meet with tutors in their native countries often during the program. The EAMD was estimated to require 450 hours of self-study time and 110 hours of study time with a tutor (three hours a week for nine months). In addition to course work, there was a major project component, which was estimated to add an additional 250 hours to the time required to complete the course, making a total of 810 hours to receive a EAMD.

In order to complete the EAMD, students had to attend at least 90 per cent of classroom sessions with the tutor. Assessment of the student would be made by the tutor monthly on a five-point scale (strong pass, pass, bare pass, bare fail, fail). The tutor also assessed project work. An EAMS-designed final exam would be administered by the tutor at the end of the course. Students must pass this exam in order to pass the course. Students who passed the final exam and completed their projects with a passing grade, and regularly attended tutor sessions would be referred to the Academic Council, which made the final decision on whether or not to award the EAMD to the student.

For admission into the EAMD program, candidates had to hold an undergraduate university degree, have two years of work experience, be proficient in English and pass the EAMD admission test. Candidates who failed to fulfill any of these requirements might still be admitted in exceptional circumstances with special permission from the EAMS Executive Committee and the Academic Council. The EAMD targeted managers and entrepreneurs working or intending to work in a Euro-Arab context. Students who successfully completed the EAMD, or managers with substantial and related work experience could apply to the Euro-Arab Masters in Business Administration program (EAMBA). The EAMBA was a one-year course designed around a "business process" approach to learning in contrast to the "functional area" approach adopted by most business schools. The functional area approach, which was characterized by learning from distinct perspectives such as marketing, finance, information systems, organizational behavior and so on, was not considered fully representative of actual business practices. The business process approach analyzed a process, such as a new product launch or an expansion option, from a variety of perspectives. The consequences of business decisions on all functional areas were to be studied concurrently. Case-based learning lent itself particularly well to this style of learning. It would be taught partly in Granada and partly in the student's native country utilizing the same methodology as the EAMD program, namely tutor-facilitated self-study. The first EAMBA program was scheduled to be launched in September 2000.

Tuition fees for students taking the EAMD program would be collected by partner institutions. For example, students taking an EAMS course in Finland would pay tuition fees to the EAMS partner institution in that country. That institution, in turn, would transfer a "franchising fee" back to EAMS, typically 20 per cent of the gross tuition amount. EAMS recommended tuition fees for the EAMD program to be between 3,000 and 4,000 Euros (about US$3,500 to $4,600), although a certain amount of variability in this rate was expected to reflect local market conditions. While rates for the EAMBA program had yet to be finalized, the tuition was expected to be around US$16,000.

In addition to the flagship EAMD and EAMBA programs, the EAMS offered public, as well as company-specific, executive education seminars that focused on bi-cultural management (Euro-Arab). EAMS also conducted research activities primarily from its Granada headquarters. Research in 1998 focused on two areas, banking and finance and information technology and telecommunications. See Exhibit 3 for a schematic diagram of the EAMS learning model.

EXHIBIT 3 The Euro-Arab Management School Education Delivery Process

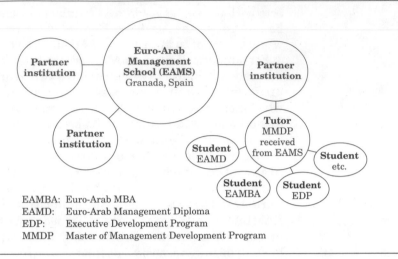

EAMBA: Euro-Arab MBA
EAMD: Euro-Arab Management Diploma
EDP: Executive Development Program
MMDP Master of Management Development Program

ACADEMIC QUALITY

A concern with any virtual learning model is to ensure consistent quality of education. In an attempt to ensure the quality of its programs, EAMS set up an Academic Council consisting of internationally recognized management education experts from Arab and European countries. This body examined the EAMS academic plan, pedagogical standards, admission policies, assessment guidelines, granting of degrees, and so on. Furthermore, the Academic Council decided that it would individually audit partner institutions and tutors on an ongoing basis to enforce and ensure a homogeneous quality throughout the EAMS network of partner institutions. More specifically, the Academic Council evaluated, by means of an EAMD validation sub-committee, the local delivery of the diploma, the provision of services and student performance. The sub-committee validated the EAMD on a regular basis and consisted of the dean of Academic Affairs and two members of the Academic Council provided that they were not from the local partner institution or its home country. The validation sub-committee reported back in writing to the EAMS Academic Council, placing particular emphasis on adherence to the due process and on the quality and extent of tutoring. It would thus visit the different partner institutions, attend tutorial sessions, and talk to tutors and students, thereby ensuring the quality of the tutoring at the partner institution.

COMPETITION

The EAMS was not the only institution offering business education programs on a "virtual" basis. A number of universities had begun to offer various forms of distance learning options for students who wished to study remotely. The most established option offered by many institutions was distance learning through correspondence courses. These programs typically followed a self-learning model where students would receive learning material and assignments from an institution, often by mail, which they would complete and send back to the institution for marking. Correspondence courses usually involved minimal direct contact between students and faculty. Time periods for completion of these courses were often flexible.

The U.S.-based research organization, The Gartner Group, estimated that demand for online training would increase 10 per cent per year between 1998 and 2000, to $12 billion. Another research organization, Quality Dynamics, also based in the U.S., predicted that half of all corporate training would be delivered via technology by 2000.

Recently, many institutions had modified the traditional correspondence course learning model to take advantage of the speed, interactivity and ubiquity of the World Wide Web (WWW). Learning material was being posted on web sites rather than being mailed, and students were given the option of returning assignments by e-mail, and even corresponding with faculty through interactive means such as "chat" programs or video-conferencing. Other institutions had begun to offer full video-conferencing MBA programs, where students would gather in small groups in remote locations and conduct classes with students from other remote locations and faculty, through the use of cameras, microphones and TV monitors.

The trend toward the "virtual MBA" was being led by business schools in North America; yet by the end of 1998 some European universities had also begun to offer distance learning options. A number of schools in the U.K., such as the Open University, Brunel University, Henley Management College, the University of Warwick and Leicester University, had established accredited MBA programs which were administered remotely, mostly using some form of web-based learning. Some continental schools were also offering MBA programs on a "virtual" basis. This list included the Virtual University of Hagen in Germany and the Open University of the Netherlands. In addition to schools offering accredited programs, there were many academic and quasi-academic institutions that offered MBA programs and other management degrees and diplomas over the WWW.

Tawfik Jelassi was comforted by the fact that the mix of self-study, IT-based distance education and tutored learning, as adopted by EAMS, was unique in Europe. Also, EAMS was the only business school tailored to an Euro-Arab audience. Clearly, there were many students, of both Arab and European descent, who were interested in a bi-cultural (Euro-Arab) management education. Now that tutors were in place throughout Europe and the Arab world, these students would be able to study in their native countries through the EAMS systems. But how would they adapt to EAMS's distance learning model? And how would EAMS adapt to the inevitable changes and developments which would occur as new courses and new students entered the system?

Scantran

By Professor Sid L. Huff and Michael Wade

"This is a purely virtual company," said James Warren, vice president of Scantran. "We are completely dependent on the Internet; it is our business lifeline. We never see or speak with our clients, we never meet with or talk to our translators. All the work is done out of our apartment, most of it by my wife Heidi, and all of it is passed back and forth electronically over the Internet, or sometimes by fax. Our web page *is* our marketing and advertising. Our growth rate is phenomenal, to the point where we are having to turn away more business than we can accept. While we started out doing the translation work itself, Heidi does very little actual translation any more; she just manages others, remotely. And the business is doing *very* well financially, thank you, far better than we ever imagined when we started. Our biggest problem right now is, how should we manage growth? We'd like to stay the size we are, but can we? If we decide to get bigger, we'll need to move to a new business model, and we're not exactly sure what that should be."

BACKGROUND

James Warren was born in England, and moved to Canada when he was 14. After earning an undergraduate business degree at the University of Western Ontario in 1991, he moved to Japan and took a job teaching English there. On the side, he started a small business, translating documents for Japanese companies. Since his circle of friends and acquaintances in Japan included people from a number of different countries, he was easily able to locate people who could translate text from English to other languages. He would hire one of his Japanese friends to translate a Japanese document into English. He would then edit the English version, then pass it to other friends to translate it to German, Italian, or whatever the Japanese client wanted. Since the age of the Internet had not yet dawned, he did most of the work using his fax machine. The biggest frustration, he found, was constantly having to type and re-type text, in English as well as other languages, since fax was essentially a paper-based (not electronic) medium.

He left Japan in early 1994 and spent six months in Costa Rica, mainly studying Spanish and learning about the country. A short time later he accepted a job with a consulting firm in Norway, where he spent much of his time helping Norwegian businesses better understand North American and Japanese business practices. At a Christmas party in 1994, he met Heidi Bjerkan.

Heidi Bjerkan was born in Copenhagen, Denmark. Her mother was Danish, her father Norwegian. She spent her early years in Denmark, three years in Greece, then moved to Norway when she was 14. She had to master Norwegian in order to complete high school there. She completed a year of university in Norway, and three more years at U.B.C. in Vancouver. After completing her degree she returned to Norway to work. On the side she did some freelance translation work, in which her fluency in three languages—English, Norwegian and Danish—was an obvious advantage.

Towards the end of 1995, James accepted a job with a Canadian company that manufactured mining equipment. Because the firm did substantial business with companies in Latin America, it had decided to establish a presence in Costa Rica. James was the "point man" whose job it was to move there, find a suitable location, and generally pave the way for the firm's establishment of its Costa Rican–based operations. Consequently, James moved to Escazú, near San José, the capital of Costa Rica, and began the scouting work for his employer. Heidi joined him in January 1996, for what was originally to be just a few weeks. However, they soon decided to get married, which they did on April 1 of that year, in Costa Rica.

James was very busy with his work, and Heidi soon became bored working on her garden and her tan. She also discovered that, as a blonde woman, blending into the local social fabric was next to impossible. Both James and Heidi were quite familiar with the Internet, and hit on the idea of Heidi picking up freelance translation work via the Net. Heidi added her name to a few of the translator name and address lists that existed on the World Wide Web (WWW) and waited for the work to come in. Eventually, she was contacted by e-mail from a

Japanese company wishing to have some material translated from English into Norwegian. The company e-mailed the material to Heidi, who translated it and e-mailed it back. A few weeks later, to Heidi's delight, a cheque arrived in the mail for the work done.

LEVERAGING THE INTERNET

James, who had dabbled with web page design and HTML programming in his spare time, decided to create a web page advertising Heidi's translation services. They realized that since Heidi could already translate between Norwegian, Danish and English, they only needed someone who could translate between English and Swedish to cover all the Scandinavian languages.[1] A quick look on the Web indicated that there were no other companies focused exclusively on the Scandinavian tongues, so they felt they had found a nice niche market. They decided to call their venture Scandinavia Translations, or Scantran for short. James hoped that they might make an extra US$500 a month; however, Heidi was more optimistic, and thought the figure would be closer to US$1,000.

James and Heidi obtained access to the Internet through a service provided by the Costa Rican telecommunications monopoly. However, the quality of the service left something to be desired. They were limited to a single telephone line into their home (getting a second telephone line in Costa Rica was essentially impossible for ordinary people, even when bribes were offered). Even the one telephone line they had was unreliable, and often stopped working during the frequent Costa Rican rainstorms.

While they used a local Internet service provider (ISP) for Internet connection services, they contracted with a site in California to host their web page. James explained:

> The main reason we used the California server was cost. Because once you're on the Internet it doesn't really matter where you store your web page files, your web host can be totally separate from your access point. Our California host charges us one dollar a month to store our web files. Typically, web hosts charge $25 or more, and in fact Sympatico, the Canadian ISP we currently use, charges over $200 a month!

The company's home page is shown in Exhibit 1.

After setting up their home page on the server in California, James set to work making sure that the Scantran home page came up in the top 10 results of the most popular search engines when key criteria

---

[1]While many people would naturally assume Finnish to be a Scandinavian language, in fact it is not. Finnish has its roots in Mongolian, as do the languages of Estonia and Hungary.

EXHIBIT 1   Scantran's Home Page—Norwegian Version

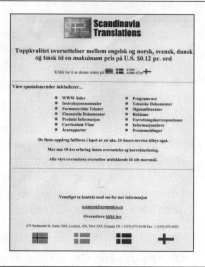

such as "Norwegian," "translation" and "language" were used.[2] Driven solely by advertising provided by their home page, and by Heidi's listing of her name in translation lists on the Web, by the end of 1996 she had more work than she could handle. Through the Internet she managed to find other translators who could take some of the load, but found that she was becoming more and more constrained by the level of Internet service available in Costa Rica.

For example, it was not uncommon to have to dial repeatedly, for over an hour, to get connected. Sometimes, inexplicably, the connection wouldn't work at all. Other times, especially when it rained, there would be no phone service whatsoever. The fact that they were limited to a single telephone line made juggling the telephone, fax machine and modem a challenge. When the connection did work, it was often painfully slow. Large files from clients might take an hour and a half to download, and then the same again to upload, if the material had to be sent to another translator. Heidi recalled:

> I remember one time, playing backgammon all day, waiting for a set of large files from one key client to download. Often a file would make it 80 to 90 percent of the way through, then "die," and we would have to start it all over again.

---

[2]There are ways of "seeding" search engines, such as including the appropriate key words frequently in the web page's front-end text, or using "meta tags" in the document, or submitting information to directory search engines such as Yahoo. Some of these change over time as search engines change their indexing strategies.

Despite these restrictions, during the first months of 1997, Scantran was making in excess of US$5,000 a month in revenue, and almost all of that was profit.

James's project was scheduled to finish in the summer of 1997. Although they were tempted to remain in Costa Rica to enjoy the tropical climate and low living costs, they eventually decided to move back to Canada. James enrolled in the MBA program of the University of Western Ontario. They decided that Heidi would work full-time for Scantran while James concentrated on his studies. James would provide part-time marketing help and provide support functions on an as-needed basis.

Upon arrival in Canada they rented a roomy apartment with a large area they could use as an office, and filled it with the necessary computer and communications equipment. They arranged for multiple phone lines to be installed, and obtained a high-speed connection to the Internet. Once everything was set up, Scantran resumed operations.

SCANDINAVIA TRANSLATIONS' BUSINESS DYNAMIC

A typical translation project cycle began when a large corporation needed a document, say a user manual, translated into all major world languages. They normally contracted with a large translation agency such as Harvard Translations of Boston, Team International in Germany, or Omega International in Monterey, California, to do the entire job for them. The large agency executed some portion of the translation work in-house (most large agencies covered the major European and Asian languages in-house), and looked for subcontractors to do the rest. Scandinavia Translations' business usually came from such large agencies, with the request to translate the document into all the Scandinavian languages.

The proposal to Scantran would have included the size of the project in number of words, the source and target languages, per-word rate, completion deadline, and perhaps some other special requests specific to that project. Scantran then either agreed to take on the contract, or declined. If Scantran accepted the project, the large agency sent the document to Scantran by e-mail attachment. Scantran then located individual translators for the project, typically one translator for each of the four Scandinavian languages. Once a translator was found, Scantran sent the project to him or her, usually in the form of a text document attached to an e-mail message. The translator completed the translation, then sent the translated file back to Scantran by e-mail attachment. Scantran (Heidi) then checked the work to make sure the format was as requested by the client, skimmed the translated text for obvious errors, and forwarded the complete translation back to the client. Payment was received from the contracting agency, and made to the individual translators, by mailed cheque. Exhibit 2 summarizes the process.

EXIIIBIT 2   Diagram of the Process Flow for a Typical Translation Job

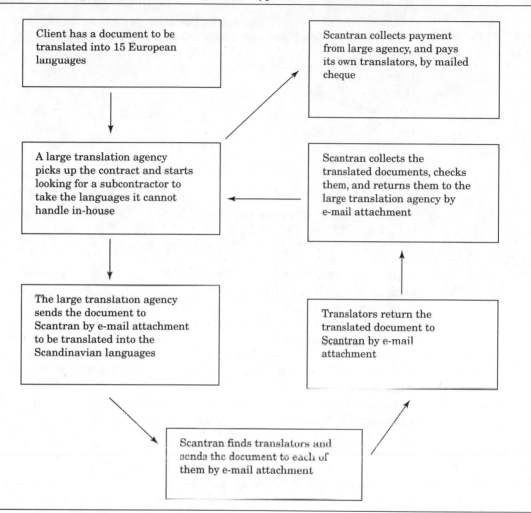

PRICES AND REVENUES

Scantran had a simple pricing system. It charged its clients US$0.10 per English word for translation, and paid its translators US$0.05 per English word for the same work. Both these rates were well below the industry average. Typical industry practice was to charge on a sliding scale depending on the total number of words in the project, subject matter complexity and deadline. Rates for the Scandinavian languages were generally somewhat higher than for other European languages. Typical rates for medium-sized jobs (5,000 to 10,000 words) were US$0.15 to US$0.25 per word. Typical rates paid to the individual

EXHIBIT 3   Recent Scantran Income Statement

Scandinavia Translations
Income Statement for the Nine-Month Period from
June 1, 1997 to March 1, 1998

Total revenue	$163,070
Payments to translators	58,245
Gross profit	$104,825
Expenses	
Start-up expenses	$5,121
General overhead	$8,514
Total expenses	$13,635
Net profit	$91,190

Notes: All figures in U.S. dollars. "Payments to translators" does not include payment to the co-owner, Heidi, for translation work, calculated at $23,290.

translators were US$ 0.07 to US$0.15. Precise competitor rates were somewhat hard to determine, since very few companies followed Scantran's practice of posting its rates on its web pages.

Scantran's only variable costs were the fees paid to the translators. Fixed costs included office rent, Internet connection costs, and general overhead. The combination of low fixed costs, healthy margins and a high volume of business meant that the business had a solid positive cash flow. The business had no bank debt.

An income statement for the time period June 1, 1997, through February 28, 1998, is shown in Exhibit 3. Monthly gross revenues for the same time period are shown in Exhibit 4.

SCANTRAN'S STRENGTHS AND WEAKNESSES

What did it take to be successful as a translation agency? James commented:

> Translation is an unusual business in that the quality of the work done is very hard for most customers to determine. Typically, translation services are seen by clients as a "cost of doing business." Translation is often somewhat of an afterthought that usually comes at the end of a large project such as a new software product development, and companies do not generally give it a lot of attention. Plus, there are almost always tight deadlines involved. The factors that matter most to our clients include customer service, speed and price.

> Most clients underestimated the time required to translate a document. Translation companies were constantly working under tight deadlines, and those agencies that worked well under this kind of pressure

EXHIBIT 4   Chart Showing Scantran's Recent Revenue Growth

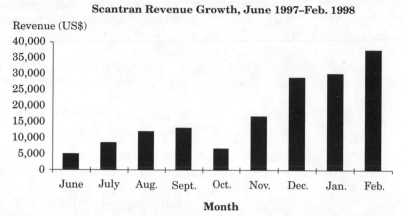

Scantran Revenue Growth, June 1997–Feb. 1998

Note: During the same time period, Scantran completed 417 translation jobs for 39 clients using 25 translators. They managed the translation of approximately 1.6 million words, or approximately 4,000 pages of text.

were popular with clients. Customer service, too, was a very important part of the translation business. Those agencies that provided prompt and courteous service invariably attracted repeat business.

Prices for translation varied widely throughout the industry. Most clients did not shop around, but if they did, they would have found that translation rates varied considerably from agency to agency. Prices tended to depend on project size, complexity, language, client profile and deadline. The market for translation services was very elastic. If a client seemed desperate, the prices went up dramatically; if a project was being "shopped around," the prices dropped.

Scantran tried to address the market using a number of tactics. It focused heavily on service. Among other things, Scantran had never missed a deadline, a common occurrence in the translation business. The company was always civil and courteous in its communications with clients, and had a policy of replying to e-mail messages within one hour. Scantran's geographical location in southwestern Ontario facilitated the company's ability to respond quickly to requests. As Heidi noted,

> Our clients are all over the world, and they all expect a response from us in 30 minutes. They forget about time zones and things like that. So we have to be able to conduct business 24 hours a day. Living here we are just 3 to 4 time zones away from the west coast, and 5–6 time zones for most of Europe and Scandinavia. If we lived in Vancouver, we probably couldn't run this business at all. Bermuda would be perfect!

Also, Scantran was the only translation agency on the Internet exclusively dealing with the Scandinavian languages. Other agencies generally offered one language, or all languages. For big translation agencies, it was a huge bonus that Scantran could take care of all their subcontracted Scandinavian work.

Thanks to low operating costs, Scantran was able to profitably charge less than its competition for comparable translation work. Also, their pricing policy was transparent. There was no need for clients to request a quote.

Scantran was not perfect. Some of the weaknesses the Warrens were well aware of included:

Quality: the quality of Scantran's translation work was very good for most types of work. Translation of highly technical material—e.g., medical or pharmaceutical documents containing a preponderance of technical terminology—was the most challenging, and Scantran sometimes turned down requests for such work for that reason. James commented, wryly, "if you're translating a document describing a new type of heart treatment, it's got to be right!"

Range of services: Scantran was a "translation factory" with limited capability to take on added value work such as desk top publishing, audio work and the like.

Size: due to its small size and lack of access to constantly available full-time staff, Scantran could not easily take on great numbers of large projects concurrently without reaching operational bottlenecks. The biggest bottleneck was usually the availability of translators. The company was currently attempting to increase its number of on-call qualified translators.

COMPETITION

On the Internet, the search directory Yahoo listed hundreds of translation agencies, varying in size from a single translator to large publicly traded multinationals. However, as far as James and Heidi were aware, there were no other companies exclusively covering the Scandinavian languages.

Scantran's main *direct* competition was independent translators. These translators, a fragmented group, usually covered one or two languages and, like Scantran, advertised on the WWW. Also like Scantran, they were usually contacted by larger translation agencies for specific translation projects.

Scantran's main *indirect* competition was the translation companies based in Scandinavia. However, these agencies tended not to advertise or represent themselves on the WWW. On a research trip to Scandinavia, the Warrens visited a few translation agencies, and concluded that they were rather "fat and happy." They got the impression that these companies were doing a brisk and profitable business translating from Scandinavian languages into English, mainly on behalf of Scandinavian multinationals. Rates for such translation averaged about US$0.70 per word, and ranged from US$0.50 to US$0.90 per word, with all kinds of complicated extras such as deadline premiums, minimum order costs, complexity surcharges and the like.

Both James and Heidi felt that there was excellent potential to steal business away from these companies, but they were unsure how to do so without an office in the region. They felt that companies in Scandinavia were less "Internet-friendly" than were companies in North America, less accepting of the Internet as a business tool. Consequently, they were wary of trying to sell these firms on the concept of the Internet in addition to translation services.

WHERE TO FROM HERE?

James and Heidi felt they had been quite fortunate to have succeeded as well as they had to date. They both thought that their current business "model" was working very well for them, but they weren't sure about where to try to take things in the months and years ahead.

Stay the Same

The Warrens were fairly confident that Scantran could simply continue forever at its current size and scale of operations. As long as the company continued to pay its translators piece rates, then fixed costs could be maintained at their present levels. The question in James's mind was whether anything might happen that would disrupt the business were they to try to keep it just as it was at present.

Also, the Warrens wondered whether they were "leaving money on the table." In other words, could they be doing more business, and making more money, using the same or a similar business model? Or had they reached the maximum of the opportunities available through the present business model?

At the current level of operation, there seemed to be little problem obtaining clients. Marketing was done over the Web to target clients, i.e., large translation agencies. In October 1997, James decided to try using the Internet to market Scantran in a more proactive way. He simply went through the Yahoo listings of translation agencies and sent an introductory e-mail to all the companies that seemed at first glance to be large. On a trial basis, he targeted only those companies between A and F. The response was immediate, and overwhelming. Business poured in so quickly that he suspended all further marketing efforts.

Clearly, there was still plenty of untapped opportunity (at a minimum, companies G through Z) out there. Expanded marketing through the Internet, coupled with continuous searches for new translators, could be one way to grow the business while maintaining the same operating model. However, Heidi had been working "flat out" in recent weeks, and had little, if any, excess capacity.

Expansion Options and Issues

Full-Time Staff Versus Contractors.   If Scantran really wanted to expand its size, one option was to hire on-site, full-time translators. This represented a major change from their current policy of maintaining a simple home office and only hiring piece-work contractors.

The overriding advantage of using piece-work contractors to do the translating was that fixed costs were kept to a minimum. It also meant that the company didn't need to obtain and pay for expensive office premises. Nor did it require the company to deal with the contractual obligations of an employer-employee relationship, including the payment of payroll taxes. It allowed James and Heidi to operate the business literally from the den in their apartment. Another advantage was flexibility. Contractors could be added and removed quickly and cheaply, depending on the level of business. Furthermore, Heidi could handle the company's day-to-day operations from practically anywhere in the world. This allowed her the opportunity to spend some time in her native Norway each year, while taking the company's work with her. This was more than just a chance to visit her family; as well, it allowed her to keep her language skills sharp.

But there were disadvantages to this mode of business as well. Contracting with translators was somewhat inefficient. Since many had other jobs, part-time translators were often unable to take on assignments, especially on short notice, which was the usual modus operandi of the business. The process of sending and coordinating large e-mail attachments, or arrangements to courier or fax documents, could become quite cumbersome. In addition, since translators were not full-time employees, they sometimes did not feel a very strong sense of loyalty to the company. This was especially true of Scantran, since the translators were invariably located in a different country. In fact, James and Heidi had used 15 translators over the past six months, some practically full-time, and had never met any of them face-to-face. In most cases they had never even spoken to them on the telephone.

Another disadvantage was inconsistent quality. Although Scantran received few complaints from clients, there was a concern that since the translators they used were not full-time translators, nor were most of them officially qualified as translators, quality problems might crop up. In fact, Scantran had occasionally turned down lucrative, highly technical translation work due to concerns over quality.

Role of the Internet. One consideration for Scantran was to reduce its reliance on the Internet for the generation of business. Scantran had the option of locating and working with Canadian and U.S. firms directly, rather than through the Internet. One reason for considering this was the issue of payment. Even though bad debts to this point had been negligible, there was a considerable amount of trust and good faith required when running a business through the Internet. Since it was easy to hide behind e-mail and a web page, it was often difficult to determine the size and legitimacy of business partners. Getting paid was always a concern, especially with new clients. Scantran had found that a "communal trust" existed on the Internet—as if among pioneers—but how long was this likely to continue? Collection of bad debts and/or legal action across borders or through the Internet was an unappealing proposition.

Another reason for abandoning the Internet involved working with individual translators who were not knowledgeable about the Net. The Warrens knew from experience that there was nothing more frustrating than trying to walk a contractor through the process of zipping a file, then attaching it to an e-mail message, when the person knew little more about using a PC than how to operate the word processor. Multiple versions of Internet software such as e-mail programs, or capabilities provided by different Internet service providers (ISPs), further complicated things. For example, James pointed out that users of America Online, one of the largest ISPs in the world, were not able to handle messages with multiple file attachments, while other e-mail systems could handle such things easily.

Contractor or Subcontractor. Another choice facing Scantran was whether to continue its role as mainly a subcontractor for other translation agencies, or try to become a prime contractor by actively seeking contracts directly from end-user clients. An important advantage of being a subcontractor was that it was easy for Scantran to remain a niche player dealing exclusively with Scandinavian language translation. If it were to deal directly with end clients it would likely have to expand, in three specific areas.

The first concerned the range of languages it handled. It would either have to offer other language options itself, or make strategic alliances with firms to take the non-Scandinavian language work. The Internet

might facilitate such an alliance: the members of the alliance could create a "web ring" by cross-linking each other's web pages, referring work to each other over the Net, and so forth. A concern with this was that quality would become harder to monitor. Shortly after its inception in Costa Rica, Scantran started to offer Spanish, French and Portuguese translation services. Heidi and James found, however, that there was no easy way to check the quality of the work which was done by the translators. Scantran dropped all non-Scandinavian work when it moved to Canada (and added Finnish, which, though not considered part of Scandinavia, was frequently requested by clients).

The second area concerned the range of services it would have to offer. Usually a customer not only wanted a project translated, but also wanted the finished product to be delivered in a very specific format. Because of this, most translation agencies had desktop publishing staff and facilities on site to fulfil the often complex document formatting and layout requirements of the client. Scantran currently had very limited skills and equipment for handling anything but the most simple desktop publishing work.

The third area in which Scantran would have to change involved its sales and marketing presence. If it were to deal with end clients, especially large ones, it would likely have to shed its "back office translation factory" image. It would likely need to establish a proper office, hire a receptionist and perhaps full-time sales staff, take clients to lunch, and so forth.

The main advantage of dealing directly with end clients and being a contractor rather than a subcontractor was financial. Scantran would be in a position to charge client fees (e.g., US$0.20 a word) to such customers, as opposed to subcontractor fees (US$0.10 per word).

Agents in Scandinavia.   While Scantran's clients were scattered around the globe, 90 percent of its business consisted of translating documents from English *into* Scandinavian languages. James and Heidi believed that their failure to get much business *from* Scandinavia mainly stemmed from the fact that the company had no physical presence there. Scandinavian companies were much more hesitant to use the Internet as a vehicle for business, and relied on an "on-the-ground" presence when they went searching for translation firms.

Recently, one of Scantran's best Swedish translators, Erik Zettervall, raised the possibility of coming to Canada and working for the company full-time. Erik had been one of the first people to contact the Warrens about translation work after Scantran had put its web page on the Internet. In fact, he had pointed out errors, and helped them correct the text on the Swedish version of their web page (which the Warrens had developed without the benefit of personal fluency in Swedish).

However, James and Heidi were concerned that, once they committed to taking on a permanent employee, they were starting down a "slippery slope" of changing their current business model, perhaps into something that would work less well for them. Consequently, they discouraged Erik, much preferring to keep him as a contract translator, in Sweden.

The risk they saw in doing this was that they might lose him as a contractor by turning down his request to become a full-time employee of theirs. He clearly was looking for a larger role, a bigger "piece of the action," than simple piece-work translation jobs. James and Heidi were worried that if they refused him a larger role in the company, he might turn away from them entirely, and take some of their business with him as well.

One possible way of keeping Erik working for them (and generating a portion of their profit) was to create an agency agreement, where Erik would represent Scantran in Sweden (use Scantran's letterhead, business cards and such); he would be paid commissions on business brought in to Scantran, but would not receive a salary from the company. Erik could continue to do English-to-Swedish translation, but more importantly, he could become an on-the-ground presence that might help generate Swedish-to-English translation work as well. However, it was unclear to the Warrens how they should structure such an arrangement. How should they arrange the cost and profit-sharing with Erik? And how should they monitor his efforts to make sure he wasn't "cheating" them by using the Scantran name but locating and doing translation work by himself, without telling James or Heidi Warren about it?

Sitting in their comfortable apartment watching their young son Christopher play, with the computers that constituted their company's existence humming away in the adjoining room, James and Heidi Warren thought about how far their "purely virtual" business had come in such a short time. Since James had decided to enter a Ph.D. program in the fall, they knew they would continue to be dependent on Scantran for much of their income for the next few years. The decisions they faced were critical to their future.

Chapter 11

Critical Success Factors for Electronic Commerce

Since it first took flight five years ago, Internet commerce—buying and selling goods and services over the Internet—has come a long way. A recent estimate by Forrester Research put business-to-business electronic commerce at US$43 billion last year; they expect this amount to double every year for the foreseeable future. For a large majority of firms today, creating and maintaining an effective presence on the Internet's World Wide Web is no longer an option, it's a necessity.

It's tempting to cede the whole business to outsiders: just bring in a few high school kids and tell them to create a web site for you. That would be a serious mistake. The Internet can enhance a number of business strategies, including improving corporate image, providing customer service and processing transactions, just to name a few. Good corporate web sites, however, don't come cheap. Forrester Research estimates that average annual operating costs are US$206,000 for large promotional sites, US$893,000 for content sites, and US$2.8 million for transactional sites. The very fact that the Web has become a critical—and increasingly expensive—channel for your firm implies that senior management cannot escape the responsibility for identifying, thinking through, and making the key decisions about your company's presence on the Web.

Over the past two years we have studied and written cases about numerous companies attempting to cope with Internet commerce, many of which are contained in this book. Some common threads have begun to emerge from our research. We have summarized these into a set of critical success factors (CSFs) we believe every senior executive

Source: This chapter was written by Sid L. Huff and Michael Wade.

involved with his or her company's web presence should consider when planning the firm's web strategy. Each of the CSFs discussed below are illustrated with examples drawn from our cases or from other well-known electronic commerce ventures.

CSF 1: Add Value

Fundamentally, creating a successful *online* business is no different than creating a successful *offline* business. In order to succeed, firms operating online businesses need to add value to their products or services. This, of course, is easier said than done. In the online world, there are often hundreds or even thousands of competitors chasing similar markets. New business models are communicated and copied quickly. *Creating* a competitive advantage in the hypercompetitive online world is often a necessary condition for success, but not a sufficient one. The challenge is to *sustain* that competitive advantage. To accomplish this requires constant reevaluation of strategy. What works today, might not work six months down the road.

The first step is to create added value to your online offering. There are at least six ways in which firms can do this online: convenience, information value, disintermediation, reintermediation, price, and choice.

Convenience.   Companies like Peapod, the online grocer, have built their online business around convenience, not price. In general, groceries purchased through Peapod are no less expensive than groceries purchased at a local supermarket. With shipping costs thrown in, the groceries are often marginally more expensive. Peapod's target customer is the busy executive who does not have the time to shop. Groceries are delivered by courier to the customer's front door, seven days a week, at the time specified. Peapod's customers are willing to pay a little more for greater convenience.

Home banking is another example of using a convenience strategy. All of Canada's banks are ramping up their online banking facilities, which serve the dual purpose of reducing branch transaction costs and providing a more convenient interface through which consumers can do their banking—from home. What started off as merely monitoring account balances has now expanded into bill payments, stock trading, and money transfers.

The importance of providing convenience to online users has not been lost on the so-called Internet portals. These sites have been doing battle to become the Internet's launching pad. In order to do this, they have been consistently adding options and services to their web sites. Yahoo, for example, now offers e-mail, stock quotes, news, and horoscopes in addition to its flagship Internet directory.

Information Value.   Homegrocer, an online grocery store and competitor to Peapod, has tried to attract customers to its service by providing them with value-adding content. Buyers can order groceries by selecting individual items, much as they would in a grocery store. But they can also access a large collection of popular recipes maintained on the site. One click on a recipe loads *everything* needed to make the meal into the user's virtual shopping cart. Furthermore, site users can store their own favorite recipes as well. Amazon.com has had great success with its book review and referral program. Users are encouraged to write reviews for books they purchase through the site, which are then posted for prospective buyers to see. Also, they use sophisticated software to analyze purchases and suggest compatible selections. This information value, or "intelligent leverage" as it has been called, is generally not available at the local supermarket or book store.

Aon, a large Chicago insurer makes potentially useful information available for clients on its web site. This information, which might include the status of new government legislation or recent judicial decisions that may potentially affect client operations, can be used by the clients to plan their insurance needs as well as other aspects of their business. For Aon, the cost of collecting the information is outweighed by the benefit the company receives from client goodwill and higher sales penetration per client.

Disintermediation.   Disintermediation refers to the removal of elements in the supply chain. This can often result in reduced cost for the customer. Companies such as MegaDepot.com, an online office supplies reseller, have found that selling direct to the customer can save warehousing, consolidating, and retailing markups. However, there are other benefits to disintermediation. Dell Computer has used disintermediation to give consumers immediate access to the newest technologies, usually much sooner than they appear in local stores. Dell now sells a whopping US$14 million of goods through its web sites every day. MicroAge, a large computer distributor, reacted to the threat of being "disintermediated" out of existence by direct-to-consumer sales, then it reinvented itself as a service organization, focusing on installation, training, and service contracts.

By shipping direct from the nursery, virtual flowers can get flowers into the hands of customers two to three days earlier than if the flowers were bought at a local florist. That means they last longer. Online brokerage services, such as E*trade and eSchwab have made money by cutting out brokers and pushing the ordering and tracking work down to the consumers.

Reintermediation.   While the Internet's power to promote disintermediation has received a lot of attention, there is another effect that appears to run in the opposite direction: the creation of new forms of intermediaries, or reintermediation. Most examples of this occur in the content and information provision areas. The Internet contains so much information that to find what you are looking for is like looking for a needle in the mother of all haystacks. Search engines, directories, and other *infomediaries* have stepped in to help organize this vast repository of information. Revenue for infomediaries—often coming purely from advertising—is predicted to grow from US$290 million in 1998 to about US$20 billion by 2002, according to a *Business Week* study. Keenan Vision, a market research firm, estimates that infomediaries will handle 29 percent of all Internet commerce by 2002.

Some firms have found profitable infomediary niches. Stock Research Group (SRG) of Vancouver, for example, started by offering a one-stop shop for information on small-cap mining firms. The company took information from all over the Internet and placed it on one site. Now, in addition to information gathering, SRG is designing and hosting web pages for mining companies, and what's more, it has been profitable from the start. Similarly, a host of electronic "news clippers" are appearing to gather, organize, and present specific information of interest to customers who are increasingly willing to pay for it.

Price. Perhaps surprisingly, competing on price has so far been comparatively rare in the online world. Primarily due to transportation costs and complicated local sales taxes and import duties, prices for products online are little different from prices offline. If anything they may be higher. Despite Amazon.com's 10–25 percent discount off cover prices, the price of a book shipped to the door is often slightly more than it would cost at a local bookstore. A recent survey of web strategies showed that low-cost/low-price strategies were much less prominent than focus or differentiation strategies. However, this may change as the Internet develops.

Buy.com has been trying to lure customers to its web site by selling products at impossibly low prices, in effect, treating every item as a "price leader." It hopes to gain customer loyalty and repeat business in the process. Ad revenues make up some of the shortfall, but the company is still far from profitability. And numerous Internet service providers are luring new customers by bundling their services with a very cheap, or even free, new computer.

Choice. A final value-adding strategy, one of the first and most successful, has been to offer a choice of products online that no offline merchant can possibly match. Megadepot.com, an online supply store, offers a massive selection of office supplies, software, and hardware and delivers for free anywhere in North America. Amazon.com offers more than three million books for sale, while the average neighborhood Chapters store can stock only about 250,000. Art.com, based in Illinois, sells over 100,000 prints, more than a hundred times that of large art stores.

CSF 2: Focus on a Niche . . . then Expand

Being able to provide the variety of an Amazon.com is not always possible, or even desirable. However, in most cases it is not enough to offer an average product line and hope to compete successfully with the multitude of others doing exactly the same thing. Barriers to entry for most Internet-based businesses are low. Jobnet, a Canadian Internet-based job-matching business, was one of the first such firms to focus exclusively on the Internet. However, the market was soon saturated with hundreds of other firms offering similar services, often for free. Jobnet, offering no particular specialty or focus, found it very difficult to build its business.

In contrast, Scandinavia Translations, a London, Ontario–based translation agency, only translates between English and the languages of Scandinavia. The reach and range of the Internet compensate for the narrow focus, in volume of business. The company's profit margin is strong, in part because of its focus. Other, more common languages such as French, German, and Spanish are more competitive, with lower margins and more demanding service levels.

Often, a niche can be regarded as a starting point for growth. Bid.com, an online auction based in Mississauga, Ontario, built a niche by focusing on Dutch auctions rather than traditional high-bid auctions. In a Dutch auction, prices go down in set increments as the clock marks off the seconds. The first bidder stops the clock and pays the corresponding price. The longer the bidders wait, the lower the price goes. The auction has proven popular as it creates excitement in the bidding process. Bid.com's stock price has risen tenfold in the past year, and the company has expanded its service to include top-bid auctions. SpringStreet, based in San Francisco, started by listing vacant apartments and expanded into providing quotes for moving vans, furniture, and home loans. Intuit's web site began as a promotion and support outlet for its financial software, then morphed into a financial services site offering investment advice and mortgages, making traditional banks very nervous in the process.

CSF 3: Maintain Flexibility

The Internet changes constantly, and so should an Internet strategy. Firms frequently need to make radical shifts in strategy in order to be successful. This often means jumping on new ideas, and throwing out old ones, overnight. This process has been termed *e-engineering*. First Virtual Holdings Inc., a San Diego–based Internet payments company, devised an intriguing method of paying for products and services over the Internet securely using a credit card. The idea, however, did not catch on, and the company failed to switch strategies quickly enough, even though it had another promising technology in the wings. The company ran out of money before the new strategy could take hold.

Waterloo, Ontario–based Open Text Corporation, on the other hand, realized early enough that its original strategy was going nowhere and switched before it was too late. The onetime search engine company, whose stock traded at $4 in late 1996, is now a leading producer of Intranet application software, with a share price of more than $50.

Being able to balance focus with flexibility requires managers to walk a strategic tightrope. On the one hand, firms need to be focused in order to differentiate themselves from the competition. On the other hand, they need to keep their eyes and ears open for signs that their strategy is not catching on, or that other, better opportunities are available. They then need to be able to switch from the old niche to a new one. This is not for the faint of heart. Most of the successful Internet firms we have studied have had to make at least one radical shift in their Internet strategy somewhere along the line.

CSF 4: Segment Geographically

In cyberspace it is tempting to think of the whole world as your marketplace. While this may be true in theory, it is extremely complicated in practice. Promotional material needs to be adapted to local conditions. This includes taking into consideration language and local cultural norms. Local, regional, and national taxes and duties must be factored into prices. Shipping costs, too, need to be figured in—even though they can vary greatly depending on distance and borders. Acceptable payment mechanisms may vary by region. Credit card sales are still rare in many parts of Europe and Asia. Time zones should also be considered for providing customer service. For example, most of continental Europe is nine hours ahead of the North American west coast.

Dell Computer maintains 38 separate sites for different nations and regions. Each site must be maintained separately, not a small task. However, Dell has had great success internationally, partly due to its localization policies. Dell's sales have risen 38 percent in the past year, more than double the industry average, with much of the growth coming from outside the United States. Gateway, on the other hand, has had less success outside its core U.S. market. It doesn't even have a dedicated Canadian order number. All Canadian sales go through its U.S. sales offices, and charges are made in U.S. dollars. Canadian sales are correspondingly dismal.

Homegrocer, the online grocery store, decided that even though its site can be accessed from anywhere in the world, its service area would consist of just 50 kilometers around its Bellevue, Washington warehouse. This policy has enjoyed some degree of success since, unlike Peapod, which ships to many locations, Homegrocer is profitable.

CSF 5: Get the Technology Right

There are three distinct operational levels of commercial web presence: basic, interactional, and transactional. At the basic level, your company provides simple static information—in effect, an electronic version of a paper brochure (for that reason, basic-level content is sometimes disdainfully referred to as "brochureware"). At the interactional level, content is no longer static, but is updated, and a degree of interaction between your web site and your customers—such as the opportunity for customers to e-mail company officials—is incorporated. At the highest, transactional level, full online commerce—buying and selling—is also provided.

The technical challenges in moving up this e-commerce food chain are considerable. It is roughly 10 times more difficult to operate an interactional site than a basic site, and 10 times again more challenging to move to a full transactional site. The message for management is to be careful not to underestimate the rapid escalation of cost and technical resources needed as the company climbs the ladder. Some of the issues to be faced include:

Rent versus Own.   Renting the necessary equipment and contracting staff is fine for getting started, but as you move up the chain, the risk associated with not controlling your own e-commerce destiny grows rapidly. Many firms—for example, Bid.com—start out renting, then later on decide to "in-house" their IT staff and equipment.

Security Management.   The amount of security you need to provide depends on where you wish to position yourself on the chain. Basic sites require no extra security considerations; interactional sites sometimes require a modest degree of security; and transactional sites normally require good, customer-visible security mechanisms. Many potential customers still today cite concerns about security as the most important issue stopping them from engaging in more electronic commerce. However, incorporating good security into your firm's web site adds yet another layer of technical complexity.

Scalability.   As the popularity of e-commerce grows, your customers rapidly become more and more demanding. Underpowered, sluggish web sites result in lost customers. Furthermore, the traffic on your web site may escalate with remarkable speed. It is critical that the system used to host the site can be scaled up quickly, as demand grows. When the ChaptersGlobe bookselling site first went live in Canada, it was clear to anyone using it that it was badly underpowered. Being a direct competitor to the Amazon.com site—one of the best designed and operated web sites anywhere—simply made the poor performance at ChaptersGlobe that much more obvious. However, ChaptersGlobe was able to scale up and improve its facilities quickly, and the initially pathetic performance improved correspondingly.

CSF 6: Manage Critical Perceptions

Perceptions matter a great deal when business is conducted face-to-face, but when doing business over the Internet, they matter even more. Three types of perceptions are especially critical: presence, brand, and trust.

Presence is the perception that a web-based company actually exists in physical form "somewhere"—that the company is not just virtual, but real. Customers interacting with a web site rather than a real person will feel a higher degree of comfort when they develop a perception of the company's presence—whether it is a two-man firm or a company employing hundreds of people. Operating through the Internet as a virtual company provides some major advantages in flexibility. When Scantran shifted its operations from Costa Rica to Ontario, the move went almost totally unnoticed by its customers or its translators. However, the downside of being virtual is the ephemeral nature of such firms. One recent study of retailers compared firms that sold only through the Web with those that sold through the Web and also through conventional physical outlets. While the virtual-only outlets enjoyed a higher rate of orders, they were lower than the virtual channels of the multichannel retailers in three other measures of success: revenues, numbers of unique visitors, and loyalty. Some of the difference can be explained by the greater degree of presence the multichannel retailers were perceived to have. A number of techniques can help develop a perception of physical presence. Homegrocer, for example, features pictures and a short text description of each of their staff, including truck drivers and stock pickers. Real people, a real company.

Brand is the perception of the firm's character, or appeal. Many successful companies spend millions each year developing their brands; well-known examples include Nike, Coca-Cola, The Gap, and Body Shop. They conscientiously try to develop an association with a particular image in the minds of consumers. Developing brand image on the Web is equally, if not more important. Few Internet companies have actually built successful brands yet, because they are so new. But firms such as Yahoo!, Amazon.com, and America Online are making good progress. Real-world companies that also operate through the Internet benefit from whatever existing brand strength they have previously developed in the physical world, another reason the multichannel retailers did better than the virtual-only retailers in the study mentioned above.

Trust is, arguably, the most important perception of all for most Internet firms. Internet companies are automatically at a disadvantage because of their virtual nature. Questions such as How do I know they will actually ship the product to me? or How do I know my credit card number is safe? or What information about me will they give to others? occur to most people when they consider transacting with an Internet company. An Internet firm that can successfully generate a perception of trustworthiness automatically has an advantage over others. How do the best Internet firms generate trust? Some of the most effective ways are also the most obvious.

- Making it very easy for customers to make personal contact: 1-800 telephone numbers (with minimal wait time), and callbacks when appropriate.
- Effective use of e-mail and the Web to keep customers informed of their order's status.
- Use of secure server technology to enhance the customer's sense of security.
- Prominent and useful FAQ (frequently asked questions) pages.
- A prominent and unambiguous policy regarding information privacy (a recent MIT study showed that 58 percent of the people surveyed were more likely to provide information to a web site that posts its privacy policies).
- Clear information on returned goods policies.
- No surprises, such as failing to mention anything about border duties or extra shipping charges.

CSF 7: Provide Exceptional Customer Service

The keys to customer service in the world of Internet business are responsiveness and "high touch." If everything else works perfectly, the need for customer service, in principle, should be minimal. But that's a very big if. One common scenario where fast response is necessary involves entering a credit card number. First-time online shoppers often want extra assurances that they won't lose their life savings when they click the "purchase" button. Having a clearly displayed 1-800 number they can call for reassurance, right at that point on the screen, can go a long way toward calming such fears. But if they do call and are made to wait 20 minutes, that may be worse than no number at all.

A growing proportion of "customer care" these days is being handled online, by everything from simple web-based information pages to sophisticated automated systems. Large online firms such as Dell Computer have found that a high proportion of customer queries center on a small number of common situations. They have developed software to intelligently walk customers through their problems online, often leading to a solution without the customer ever having to pick up the phone. Even simple techniques such as easily located and well laid out FAQ pages can go a long way to helping customers solve their own problems quickly.

But when online systems don't solve the problem, or when a customer simply wants to talk with a "real person," it's critically important that an Internet company be accessible in other ways, especially via the telephone. This need for high touch in customer service is arguably even more important for online businesses than it is for others. When customers are online, it's awfully easy for them to switch to another provider. With the growing popularity of comparison shopping facilities online, alternative suppliers are just a couple of mouse clicks away. Plus, customer service is key to building strong perceptions of trust and physical presence, discussed earlier. Jeff Bezos, CEO of well-known Amazon.com, has pointed out that in the offline world 30 percent of a company's resources are spent providing good customer service and 70 percent for marketing. In the online world, he argues, that should be reversed: 70 percent should go to creating a great customer experience, and 30 percent to "shouting about it."

CSF 8: Create Effective Connectedness

Imagine a shopping mall that stretches from here to the moon. That's the Internet. How can you make yourself stand out in such a huge crowd? The answer is to be in as many places at once as possible.

Online search engines such as AltaVista or Yahoo! remain the most common devices web users employ to locate sites of interest. Therefore, the first order of business is to ensure that your company web site is properly and effectively registered at all the major search engines. Many search engines allow you to submit your pages for automatic registration. Others use a manual process: in effect, *they* decide to register *you*. In either event, there are some creative things you can do to your web pages to try to improve the chance of your page being returned near the top of the list when someone executes a page search relevant to your business. Bob Brown, the proprietor of Goodnight Ben, a small retailer of high-end children's furniture, is his own webmaster: He created the web pages for his store and in fact has developed web pages for other small companies as well. Brown discovered that using obvious keywords (or *metatags,* as they are called) in his web pages, such as "children's furniture," was not very helpful. Someone using a search engine and searching on "children's furniture" would receive thousands of hits, and sure enough, Brown's company would be somewhere in the list—but much too far down to be helpful. Brown then tried indexing his pages using the names of his key suppliers. It turns out that many people looking for high-end children's furniture search using supplier names, but few children's furniture stores have thought of indexing their pages this way; now his web pages turn up at, or near, the top of the list.

Users of the Internet often find sites by following links from other sites. So it also pays to be interconnected as much as possible. One way is to be part of a web wheel: a grouping of similar web sites that agree to cross-reference each other for the greater good of the virtual community. Bob Brown actually created such a web wheel, by convincing other children's furniture stores outside his geographical area to interconnect their sites with his and others. There are other ways of achieving interconnection also, such as participating in virtual malls.

Then there is advertising. Advertising your firm's web page on the Internet is normally done by buying "banner ads" on other, popular sites, for example, portal sites such as Yahoo! or Canoe.ca. The problem with banner advertising is that it is not particularly effective. Most people browsing the Web tend to ignore them; the "click-through" rate is quite low. Therefore, you should not stop at Internet advertising. Simple techniques such as prominently placing your web address on your business card and on any and all paper advertisements you place in other media can have significant impact also. The key point is that you cannot put up a web page then wait for the world to beat a path to your door: You also have to cut the path through the Internet jungle, and then spend time and money keeping the vines from growing back over it.

CSF 9: Understand Internet Culture

Over the years, certain norms of behavior for users of the Internet have evolved. While the advent of commerce on the Web has attenuated the strength of Internet culture somewhat, nonetheless clear vestiges remain. It pays to be aware of Internet cultural norms and to observe them on your firm's web site and its other uses of the Net. Things that tend to irritate and turn off users include:

- The use of spam—voluminous unwanted e-mail—to communicate or advertise your site or your company's products.
- Requiring visitors to your site to register before they can browse the site. While forced registration may seem like a good way to gather data on visitors, in fact, the registration form is just like a large sign on your storefront saying "go away!"
- Extensive use of graphics. The recent trends in web page design tend toward minimalism. Cluttered, graphics-intensive sites take longer to download and are more difficult to look at and comprehend. They are like grafitti on subway walls.
- Secondary browser windows. Some sites forcibly open a second copy of the user's web browser on his computer, something that is unnecessary and that many people find irritating.
- Lack of an FAQ page. FAQ pages are an Internet staple. Not offering one on your firm's web site is like having a clerk in your store refuse to answer a customer's simple question.

There are plenty of other ways of violating basic Internet culture. One common problem relates to implicit trust that Internet users place in the sites they visit. Open Text created one of the early search engines used on the Web. Its search engine site was rapidly gaining popularity until Open Text management decided to offer "preferred listings"—allowing other firms to pay to ensure that their sites appeared at or near the top of the return list when a particular keyword was entered. This move violated a basic Internet cultural norm: that search engines should be "fair" in how they handle their searches. Subsequently, Open Text's fortunes declined rapidly, and its search engine was eventually withdrawn. Today the firm has revived quite strongly, but it is no longer in the search engine business. More recently, it became known that Amazon.com was providing a preferred treatment, in return for a fee, for certain books listed and reviewed on its site. The chorus of criticism was massive and instantaneous. Amazon.com quickly apologized and adjusted its policy.

Doing business successfully on the Internet calls for a mix of good old business smarts together with a very open mind—it is necessary to accept that many aspects of Internet business are *not* just an extension of traditional business. For those who can effectively blend the old and the new, the opportunities provided by online business appear to be endless.

Index